A Critical Companion to Stanley Kubrick

Critical Companions to Contemporary Directors

Series Editors:
Adam Barkman and Antonio Sanna

Critical Companions to Contemporary Directors covers many directors who have not been studied previously in academic publications and whose works nonetheless are highly renowned nowadays. The intent of the series is to offer interesting and illuminating interpretations of the various directors' films that will be accessible to both scholars of the academic community and critically-minded fans of the directors' works. Each volume combines discussions of a director's oeuvre from a broad range of disciplines and methodologies, thus offering the reader a variegated and compelling picture of the directors' works. In this sense, the volumes will be of interest (and will be instructive) for students and scholars engaged in subjects as different as film studies, literature, philoso-phy, popular culture studies, religion, and others. We welcome proposals for both monographs and edited collections that offer interdisciplinary analyses, focusing on the complete oeuvre of one contemporary director per volume.

Recent titles in the series:

A Critical Companion to Stanley Kubrick, edited by Elsa Colombani
A Critical Companion to Terrence Malick, edited by Joshua Sikora
A Critical Companion to Steven Spielberg, edited by Adam Barkman and Antonio Sanna

A Critical Companion to Stanley Kubrick

Edited by Elsa Colombani

LEXINGTON BOOKS
Lanham • Boulder • New York • London

Published by Lexington Books
An imprint of The Rowman & Littlefield Publishing Group, Inc.
4501 Forbes Boulevard, Suite 200, Lanham, Maryland 20706
www.rowman.com

6 Tinworth Street, London SE11 5AL, United Kingdom

Copyright © 2020 by The Rowman & Littlefield Publishing Group, Inc.

All rights reserved. No part of this book may be reproduced in any form or by any electronic or mechanical means, including information storage and retrieval systems, without written permission from the publisher, except by a reviewer who may quote passages in a review.

British Library Cataloguing in Publication Information Available

Library of Congress Control Number: 2020943930

ISBN: 978-1-7936-1376-9 (cloth)
ISBN: 978-1-7936-1378-3 (pbk)
ISBN: 978-1-7936-1377-6 (electronic)

To my parents

Contents

Acknowledgments — ix

Introduction — 1
   Elsa Colombani

Part I: Bending Genres — 21

1. Mental Landscapes and Subdued Bodies in *Killer's Kiss* — 23
   Vincent Jaunas
2. Burning Down the House in Kubrick's *The Shining* — 37
   Anne-Marie Paquet-Deyris
3. Kubrick's Gangster Artistry: Contradiction and Hybridity in *The Killing* — 51
   Carol Donelan
4. Adapting *Lolita*: Hybridizing and Subverting Genre Conventions — 65
   Gilles Menegaldo
5. History by Candlelight: How Stanley Kubrick Revolutionized Depictions of the Past on Film — 79
   Sean O'Reilly
6. Intertextuality, Distortion, and Echoes of World War II in Stanley Kubrick's War Films — 93
   Guillaume Mouleux

Part II: Master of Chaos and Transgression — 109

7. The Philosophy of War in *Dr. Strangelove* — 111
   Jerold J. Abrams

8 Stanley Kubrick and the Cinema of Chaos: The Theater of War 123
William Gombash

9 Joker's Ideological Becoming: The Limits of Irony in *Full Metal Jacket* 137
James R. Britton

10 "Violence Is a Very Horrible Thing": Brechtian Alienation Effect in Kubrick's *A Clockwork Orange* 151
Madison Mae Williams

11 Reading Reality in *A Clockwork Orange*: Film Censorship, Metalepsis, and "Media Effects" 165
Rachel Cole

12 Through a Glass, Darkly: The Slow Rise of Women in *Barry Lyndon*, *The Shining*, and *Eyes Wide Shut* 179
Elsa Colombani

Part III: The Visionary Auteur — 193

13 Kirk Douglas and Stanley Kubrick: Reconsidering a Creative and Business Partnership 195
James Fenwick

14 Auteur versus Author: Kubrick's Relationship with Literary Writers 207
Annie Nissen

15 "May I Have the Password?": Heterotopic Space in *Eyes Wide Shut* 221
Carl Sweeney

16 The Spectacle of Time, (Slow) Motion, and Stillness in the Films of Stanley Kubrick 235
Paul Johnson

17 *2001: A Space Odyssey*: Kubrick's Allegory of Melancholia 249
Maurizia Natali

18 The Everlasting Moment: Enchantment and Myth in *A.I.* and *2001: A Space Odyssey* 263
Joshua Sikora

Index 277

About the Contributors 281

Acknowledgments

I am deeply grateful to Adam Barkman and Antonio Sanna for giving me this opportunity and providing me with their helpful guidance.

I wish to thank Florence Colombani, Eurydice Da Silva, Marianne Gokalp, and Laura Singeot for their thoughtful insights and moral support.

Introduction

Elsa Colombani

"What kind of movies do you want to create?" asked the interviewer. The reply was brief and to the point: "Only one kind. . . . Good movies."[1] There have been many legends in Hollywood, but none of them have had quite the same enduring mystique as Stanley Kubrick's. Labeled a recluse, a provocateur with a "bleak vision,"[2] a ruthless perfectionist who would require hundreds of takes from his actors, Kubrick is today considered one of the greatest visionaries of filmmaking; a man who revolutionized film genres—from science fiction to horror—filmic narrative pacing and structure, depictions of war and violence, as well as the use of music on screen. Often misunderstood and undervalued at the time of their release, his films have since exerted a power so flagrant over upcoming and well-established filmmakers that Kubrick's position as an unequaled master of cinema can today hardly be disputed. More than twenty years have passed since Stanley Kubrick's untimely death in 1999, and yet the director's influence on contemporary cinema shines now more than ever. From his first feature film, *Fear and Desire* (1953) to his last, *Eyes Wide Shut* (1999), Kubrick directed thirteen feature films, all in different genres, from the epic (*Spartacus*, 1960) to the war film (*Paths of Glory*, 1957; *Full Metal Jacket*, 1987), while also taking on science fiction (*2001: A Space Odyssey*, 1968) and the horror genre (*The Shining*, 1980). And yet, however separate and distinct Kubrick's films can seem—both in scale and aesthetics—their themes, obsessions, and mise en scène interweave, establishing a self-reflective and thought-provoking thread throughout his entire filmography.

Martin Scorsese expresses best the awe induced by his work: "To watch a Kubrick film is like watching the top of a mountain from a valley. One wonders how anyone could have climbed so high up. There are scenes in his films, images and spaces charged with an emotion that has an inexplicable power, a magnetic force which slowly and mysteriously sucks you in."[3] In the twentieth century, Kubrick challenged and reinvented the rules of filmmaking. In the twenty-first, his legacy continues to define them. No war film can now unfold without a reference to the technical marvels of *Paths of Glory* (*Dunkirk* [Christopher Nolan, 2017]) or the clinical rawness of *Full Metal Jacket* (*Jarhead* [Sam Mendes, 2005]). No science fiction film can break from the indelible shadow of *2001: A Space Odyssey*'s dancing spaceships and existential melancholia (*Gravity* [Alfonso Cuarón, 2013], *First Man* [Damien Chazelle, 2018], *Ad Astra* [James Gray, 2019]). Throughout the years, the references made to Kubrick's films have grown increasingly obvious as more and more filmmakers yearn to be considered his heir. In 2018, Kubrick's friend Steven Spielberg paid an extensive tribute to *The Shining* in *Ready Player One* while Mike Flanagan's 2019 adaptation of Stephen King's *Doctor Sleep* (a follow-up to King's own *The Shining*) carefully replicated Kubrick's legendary rendition of the Overlook Hotel. In fact, Kubrick's *The Shining* truly seems to haunt American culture, from Jordan Peele's multiple references to the film in *Us* (2019) to the MTN Dew 2020 Super Bowl commercial featuring Bryan Cranston's reenactment of the famous "Here's Johnny" sequence. Meanwhile, Greek filmmaker Yorgos Lanthimos drew inspiration from *Eyes Wide Shut* for *The Killing of a Sacred Deer* (2017), giving to actress Nicole Kidman a look similar to the one she had in Kubrick's film. He later used candlelight—in a *Barry Lyndon*–like fashion—to light some scenes in *The Favourite* (2018).

The fascination exerted by Kubrick's films has been equally persistent among scholars. Since the 1970s, numerous books have been published, from biographies (John Baxter's, Vincent LoBrutto's) to analytical books and collection of essays, some spanning his entire oeuvre, others focusing on one specific production. Among the existing bibliography on the director, some works appear out of date in respect to contemporary critical and film theory while others remain essential in their approach to his films. Michel Ciment's *Kubrick* (Calmann-Levy, last edition 2011) is consistently regarded as a seminal book. Compiling his interviews with the notoriously reclusive filmmaker, Ciment also gathers testimonies from Kubrick's close collaborators and delivers several interpretative leads before analyzing each film. In the following books, those studying Kubrick's work continued weaving the thread, each providing enriching new thoughts and ideas regarding a cinematic universe that still mystifies. With *Kubrick: Inside a Film Artist's Maze* (Indiana University Press, 2000), Thomas Allen Nelson delivers a major contribution, offering his chronological interpretation of the director's films. Other insightful works include Mario Falsetto's *Stanley Kubrick: A Narrative and Stylistic Analysis* (Praeger, 2001), a detailed study around the "dualities of meaning"[4] in his oeuvre that however reduces its analytical corpus by excluding the director's first two defining films *Fear and Desire* and *Killer's*

Kiss (1955), as well as his career-turning point, *Spartacus*. The British Film Institute's *On Kubrick* (BFI Publishing, 2007), written by James Naremore, is particularly compelling, providing isolated analyses of the films along with information on each production, and highlighting the films' emotional power over the more traditional intellectual components. In 2005, Taschen published *The Stanley Kubrick Archives*, edited by Alison Castle, which presents additional unknown and previously unseen material from the director's archives, soon to be followed by *Stanley Kubrick's "Napoleon": The Greatest Movie Never Made* (ed. Alison Castle, Taschen, 2009), reuniting Kubrick's final script as well as his entire research for the unrealized film. Sam Azulys's 2011 essay *Stanley Kubrick, une odyssée philosophique* (Editions de la Transparence), confronts Kubrick's themes and aesthetics to the philosophical ideas of Nietzsche, Spengler, and Heidegger to demonstrate the modernity of his directing. All of these interesting studies offer an essential if global view on Kubrick's films by considering his films separately. Other books prove more informational than analytical, such as David Hughes's *The Complete Kubrick* (Virgin Books, 2001), Norman Kagan's *The Cinema of Stanley Kubrick* (3rd edition, Bloomsbury, 2000, first published in 1989), and Paul Duncan's *Stanley Kubrick* (Pocket Essentials, 1999).

Collections of essays offer some cross-analyses and comparisons. Jerold J. Abrams's *The Philosophy of Stanley Kubrick* (University Press of Kentucky, 2007) approaches his oeuvre as a coherent whole that "takes all the differentiated sides of reality and unifies them into one rich, complex philosophical vision that happens to be very close to existentialism."[5] *Stanley Kubrick, Film, and the Uses of History* (ed. Geoffrey Cocks, J. Diedrick, and G. Perusek, Wisconsin Film Studies, 2006) focuses on historical context and historiographical implications. In *Stanley Kubrick: Essays on his Films and Legacy* (McFarland and Company, 2007), Gary D. Rhodes reunites engaging essays, organized chronologically and dealing with an array of essential Kubrickian themes such as the use of music, the representation of politics, the Carnivalesque, and the Grotesque. Mick Broderick's recent *The Legacy of Stanley Kubrick* (Routledge, 2019) proves equally appealing, focusing on the traveling TIFF "Stanley Kubrick" exhibition, but choosing a narrow corpus.

In the last few years, studies have multiplied and offer a counterpoint to the mainly all-encompassing analyses of the 1990s and 2000s by putting one film or one aspect of Kubrick's universe under the spotlight. Among the many thematic studies are numerous books on Kubrick and music, such as Christine Lee Gengaro's *Listening to Stanley Kubrick: The Music in His Films* (Scarecrow Press, 2013), and Kate McQuiston's *"We'll Meet Again": Musical Design in the Films of Stanley Kubrick* (Oxford University Press, 2013). In *Stanley Kubrick: Adapting the Sublime* (University Press of Mississippi, 2013), Elisa Pezzotta analyzes his oeuvre from an adaptation studies standpoint, using both narratological and intertextual approaches.

Publications on *2001: A Space Odyssey* have surged starting with Robert Kolker's collection of essays, *Stanley Kubrick's 2001: A Space Odyssey* (Oxford University Press, 2006). Kolker had previously devoted a chapter to Kubrick in *A Cinema of Loneliness: Penn, Stone, Kubrick, Scorsese, Spielberg, Altman* (Oxford University Press, 3rd edition, 2000). Joe R. Frinzi's *Kubrick's Monolith: The Art and Mystery of* 2001: A Space Odyssey (McFarland & Company, 2017) offers interpretations of the film and focuses on special effects and the iconic use of music. The study of *2001* culminates with Michael Benson's masterful account of the film's preproduction, production, and release in *Space Odyssey: Stanley Kubrick, Arthur C. Clarke, and the Making of a Masterpiece* (Simon & Schuster, 2018). Among other studies on specific films, the most notable are Maria Pramaggiore's *Making Time in Stanley Kubrick's* Barry Lyndon (Bloomsbury Academic, 2015), Mick Broderick's *Reconstructing Strangelove: Inside Stanley Kubrick's "Nightmare Comedy"* (Wallflower Press, 2017), and Robert Kolker and Nathan Abrams's Eyes Wide Shut: *Stanley Kubrick and the Making of his Final Film* (Oxford University Press, 2019).

However compelling, the research concerning Kubrick still does not seem to measure up to the magnitude of the object. Proof of this is the growing demand for more analysis on Kubrick's films. From the success of Rodney Asher's documentary *Room 237* (2012) exploring various interpretations of *The Shining* to the acclaimed *Stanley Kubrick: The Exhibition* at the Design Museum in London with a BFI retrospective in 2019, Stanley Kubrick is, twenty years after his death, more relevant than ever.

Before his legend began, Stanley Kubrick was a boy from the Bronx with a passion for jazz, baseball, and chess. Born on July 26, 1928 in an American Jewish family with Austro-Hungarian roots, he was the son of Jacques, a doctor, and Gertrude, a housewife, and had a little sister Barbara. As a child, he skipped school to catch movies at the theater but dreamed of becoming a baseball player, a writer, or a jazz musician. On his thirteenth birthday, a decisive turn occurred when his father gifted him with a camera, unveiling the shape of another career: that of photographer. Considered an academic failure and bored by his classes, Kubrick devoted himself entirely to photography and started publishing pictures in the high school newspaper. At sixteen, he sold his first photograph to *Look* magazine, where he was hired the very next year. The picture in question depicted a desolate newsstand vendor sitting in his stall, surrounded by headlines announcing President Roosevelt's death. Inspired by photojournalist Weegee, Kubrick closely studied his style while also quenching his thirst for movies, as he discovered the Museum of Modern Art's entire film collection. Inspired by a photo sequence *Look* had assigned him to do on Walter Cartier in 1949, Kubrick finally decided to take the plunge and launch himself into a filmmaking career by documenting one of the boxer's fights. The result is the sixteen-minute-long *Day of the Fight* (1950), which Kubrick produced without any professional help and financed with his own savings. Selling the short film to RKO Pathé, Kubrick then quit his job at *Look* to direct another short, *Flying Padre* (1951), at RKO's request. *The Seafarers* followed in 1953, at the demand of the Seafarers International Union.

Fear and Desire, Kubrick's first foray into feature films, tells the story of four soldiers trapped behind enemy lines after surviving a plane crash in an unspecified country. Kubrick felt unhappy with the film, telling Jeremy Bernstein, "I didn't know anything about directing *any* actors. I totally failed to realize what I didn't know."[6] However flawed, the film already contains many of what would become Kubrick's favorite themes, among them man's violent and sexual impulses, the issue of moral compass during wartime, as well as the premises of his interest in fairy tale tropes. Released in a few arthouse theaters, *Fear and Desire* remained confidential but earned a few good reviews, prompting the director to persevere. Two years later, *Killer's Kiss*—a film noir centered on a boxer embroiled in a love affair with a gangster's girlfriend—was released. Using the characteristics of film noir, the film reveals Kubrick's growing interest in style and aesthetics, which are prioritized over character development. The scene of the fight in the ring between the main character Davey (Jamie Smith) and boxer Kid Rodriguez particularly stands out, its authentic and raw feel increased by Kubrick's use of a hand-held camera, while the surrealist imagery of the final confrontation between Davey and Vincent Rapallo (Frank Silvera) in a mannequin factory is often referred to as the most striking of the film. As in *Fear and Desire*, many of Kubrick's later obsessions are here introduced, most notably that of the double—symbolized by the extensive use of mirrors—and voyeurism,[7] as well as the director's growing interest in Freudian analysis, which the dream sequence illustrates.

Then came the friendship and partnership with James B. Harris, whom Kubrick met through his childhood friend Alexander Singer. After creating their own company, the Harris-Kubrick Pictures Corporation, the duo set out to produce *The Killing* (1956), with a United Artists distribution. The film is an adaptation of Lionel White's novel *Clean Break* (1955) and tells the story of a racetrack robbery gone wrong. In this second film noir endeavor, Kubrick's admiration for Max Ophüls can be felt. Many scholars as well as the director himself considered the film to be his first real entry as a professional director. His talent and dexterity behind the camera are evidently displayed throughout the film's ambitious non-chronological structure, its unreliable narrator, as well as the grim vision of life that would, from then on, become a regular tune in critical reviews. Among its numerous qualities, James Naremore remarks the dynamism of the mise en scène[8] while Michel Chion compliments the "exceptional" use of the wide-angle lens.[9] The film also benefits from its prestigious cast, Kubrick working for the first time with professional actors, Sterling Hayden among others. However, tension arose behind the scenes as Kubrick clashed with cinematographer Lucien Ballard, whose job he had previously handled himself. After the film's release, screenwriter and novelist Jim Thompson objected to his received credit, which specified he had only written the dialogs. As a means of compensation, Kubrick hired him to write Harris-Kubrick Pictures' following project, the adaptation of Humphrey Cobb's *Paths of Glory*.

Having first discovered the 1935 novel—inspired by the true story of French soldiers who were executed by a firing squad on false charges of cowardice during World War I—in his father's office as a teenager, Kubrick suggested adapting it, after a brief and sterile work at MGM went haywire.[10] Finding a studio to support them proved difficult, but Kubrick and Harris got their break when Kirk Douglas became interested in the project, thus securing United Artists' approval. The star being unsatisfied with the fleeting presence of his character, Colonel Dax, in Thompson's script, Kubrick worked on another draft with Calder Willingham, retaining only some of Thompson's dialog. With both of Douglas's requests fulfilled—expanding his role as well as giving his own Bryna Productions a production credit—filming started in Munich in 1957. Another major change induced by Douglas was his firm refusal for a happy ending, which Kubrick had been tempted to give to make the film more commercial. As a result, Kubrick came up with the idea of the now iconic scene in which the heartbreaking song of a German girl prisoner overwhelms a crowd of French soldiers. The film earned positive reviews in the United States but suffered disruption in Europe, especially in France, where the film was censored until 1974. Though the film was based on historical facts, the French government judged slanderous its portrayal of army generals. Overall, *Paths of Glory* was a major landmark for Kubrick, from directing major stars to his distinct clear-cut sense of style. Crucial to the film is how Kubrick spatially symbolizes the antinomy between soldiers on the front and higher commanders by opposing the muddy and narrow trenches—by way of suffocating tracking shots—where the soldiers struggle to survive, to the extravagant castle that harbors the generals. As many other critics, Bill Krohn notes how the geometrical conception of space, underlined by Kubrick's camera movements, strongly echoes the symmetry of a chess board.[11]

On a personal level, *Paths of Glory* also led to Kubrick's encounter with the woman who would become his third and final wife, Christiane Harlan, the German girl who sang her heart out and gave a hopeful conclusion to the desperate war film. "He saw me on television in Munich," recounted Christiane Kubrick to Peter Bogdanovitch. "He called my agent and hired me. I met him at a studio, and then he went to an enormous masked ball where I was performing. He was the only one without a costume. He was quite baffled."[12] A typical Kubrick scene if there ever was one, the image oddly recalls that of an unmasked Bill Harford (Tom Cruise) surrounded by a strange and unrecognizable crowd in *Eyes Wide Shut*, the director's last film. Before meeting Christiane, Kubrick had already been married twice: to his high school sweetheart Toba Etta Metz from 1948 to 1951; then to Ruth Sobotka whom he met in 1952—who appears in *Killer's Kiss* and worked on *The Killing* as an art director—from 1955 to 1957. Christiane and Stanley remained happily married for forty-one years until the director's unexpected death. The couple raised three daughters, Katharina (Christiane's daughter from a previous relationship), Anya, and Vivian.

On a professional level, the aftermath of *Paths of Glory* was somewhat disappointing for Harris-Kubrick Productions. Kubrick wrote a couple of scripts that never saw the light of day and worked a full six months on Marlon Brando's *One-Eyed Jacks* (1961), which the actor ended up directing himself. It had been two years since Kubrick had directed last when Kirk Douglas came asking for him to take the reins on the slave-rebellion epic *Spartacus*. After shooting for only one week (resulting in the first sequence of the film), director Anthony Mann had left as his dissent with Douglas, the star and executive producer of the film, felt insurmountable. Kubrick's lack of input and final say on *Spartacus* turned out to be a major issue for the director, one that would lead him to disown the film and say: "It had everything but a good story."[13] Kubrick was mostly critical of the lack of historical accuracy in Dalton Trumbo's script.[14] The shooting was also strained by Kubrick's tense relations with Douglas and other famous members of the cast who "treated him, because he was so young, with a certain arrogance."[15] But Kubrick, Tony Curtis recalls, "would never capitulate. . . . He refused to allow anybody to tell him how to do the picture,"[16] especially cinematographer Russell Metty, who made no effort to hide his contempt and often jeered at the director.[17]

Sometime during the 167 days he spent shooting *Spartacus*, Kubrick bought with Harris the rights to *Lolita*, which would turn out to be the pair's last project together. Written in English by Russian novelist Vladimir Nabokov, the novel kept being refused by publishers because of its scandalous subject until Olympia Press agreed to publish it in Paris, in 1955. The book was then published in the United States in 1958 and quickly became a best seller. And so Kubrick came to earn his reputation as a provocateur. "How did they ever make a film of Lolita?" read the poster for the film, playing with the novel's sulfurous reputation. A first-person narrative, *Lolita* tells the story of Humbert Humbert, a university professor, obsessed with his widowed landlady's twelve-year-old daughter. After having asked Nabokov to adapt his own work into a screenplay, Kubrick ended up rewriting it entirely (although he did not receive credit), preserving a handful of Nabokov's 400-page draft. The financing being secured with Seven Arts, production started in 1961 in England, where Harris and Kubrick could manage to keep a low budget. Surrounded by a cast of experienced actors, such as James Mason, Peter Sellers, and Shelley Winters, fourteen year-old Sue Lyon was hired for the title role. This choice, which changed the nymphet's original age, brought criticism and accusations that the film alleviated Humbert's pedophile desires.[18] Admirers of the novel also chastised the film, arguing that it had been emptied of most of the sexual content. But Kubrick had censorship to deal with, which prevented him from portraying Lolita and Humbert's relationship explicitly and "forced [him] to embrace an erotic discourse via more subtle methods."[19] Patrick Webster lists some of the film's numerous innuendoes, Humbert feeling "as limp as a noodle"[20] being a telling example. In fact, what makes *Lolita* such a daring film rests precisely on Kubrick's inventive choices to deceive the censors. The most eloquent scene on this matter is probably when Humbert (Mason) intensely stares at a picture of Lolita for stimulus while about to have sex with her mother (Winters). In an interview with Terry Southern, Kubrick stated his belief that "the erotic viewpoint of a story is best used as a sort of energizing force of a scene, a motivational factor, rather than being explicitly portrayed."[21] Gene Youngblood remarks:

> Most critics today agree: *Lolita* is Kubrick's most misunderstood and underrated film. Stylistically it's a transitional work, marking the turning point from a naturalistic cinema (*Paths of Glory*, *Spartacus*) to the surrealism of the later films. Reality and fantasy coexist for the first time in a Kubrick film in the bizarre figure of Quilty's "Dr. Zaempf." Sitting in a darkened room in a pose that prefigures the sinister, chair-bound Dr. Strangelove, this scene anticipates the atmosphere of Kubrick's next film.[22]

In *Dr. Strangelove or: How I Learned to Stop Worrying and Love the Bomb* (1964), a madman general named Jack D. Ripper (Sterling Hayden) launches a nuclear attack on Russia behind the president's (Peter Sellers) back. In the Pentagon War Room, officials reunite to try and stop the attack. Having bought the rights to Peter George's novel *Red Alert* (1958)[23] from which *Dr. Strangelove* is adapted, Kubrick and Harris parted ways after a nine-year-long collaboration, as the latter decided to direct his own films. While his wife searched for a permanent home to settle in England with their children, Kubrick started working on the script in New York with George and comic novelist Terry Southern. The trio transformed the serious and well-documented thriller into a darkly audacious absurd comedy:[24] "one of the most biting satires of the nuclear destruction of the world, and of the perverted mechanisms of the Cold War and US society."[25] Once again casting Sterling Hayden, Kubrick (at the request of Columbia Pictures) entrusted improvisation genius Peter Sellers—already the ironic voice of *Lolita*—with three different roles, including that of the nuclear scientist, former Nazi turned

U.S. advisor, Dr. Strangelove. When released in 1964, the film was met with theatrical success but mitigated reviews. At the time labeled unbelievable, and even accused of promoting the Soviet doctrine, *Dr. Strangelove* has since been reevaluated as "a far more accurate description of the dangers inherent in nuclear command-and-control systems than the ones that the American people got from the White House, the Pentagon, and the mainstream media."[26] Roger Ebert, reviewing the film in 1999, praised the legendary performances of the actors, especially George C. Scott's "facial gymnastics"[27] as General "Buck" Turgidson. As Michel Chion argues, the film also implemented "the systemization in Kubrick's films of an alternation between underplayed films, smoothly restrained, and films largely overplayed by actors with contorted and convulsed faces."[28]

In Kubrick's following film, the face of a man would become emblematic: filmed in close-up, astronaut Dave Bowman (Keir Dullea) is staring into space as flashes of color stream past him, his eyes wide open, overwhelmed by the hypnotic vision. Evocative of psychedelic visions, the famous "Star Gate" sequence of *2001: A Space Odyssey* would lead the studio MGM to advertise the science fiction film as "The Ultimate Trip." In fact, the viewer of *2001* much resembles Bowman, immersed in a visual spectacle. An incredible and revolutionary work of art that appeals to the senses, the film is more of an experience than what was expected of a traditional film at the time. The reactions to Kubrick's epic on human evolution—from the "Dawn of Man" to the birth of the "Star Child"—were contradictory to say the least. After disastrous previews that led the director to make new cuts and shorten the film's length from 161 minutes to 142, the audience's response turned out massively positive, with many viewers coming back to see the film again and again. Reviews, on the other hand, were mixed, some critics finding the film pretentious, overlong, and dull, such as Pauline Kael, who infamously qualified it as "monumentally unimaginative."[29] "In retrospect," argues Michael Benson, "these initial waves of hostility and incomprehension can be understood as a result of the film's radical innovations in technique and structure."[30] Born out of the collaborative imagination of science fiction novelist and pioneer Arthur C. Clarke and Kubrick, *2001* has left an indelible mark on film history on more than one account. It first gave a new standing to a genre that used to be considered minor entertainment and, as Chion remarks, reunited the polarized popular picture with the intellectual art film.[31] It also broke new ground on a technical level, and was meticulous in its verisimilitude, with a number of prominent scientists being interviewed before production began. With barely forty minutes of dialogue, characterization was relegated to second place, the primary focus being placed on aesthetics: "the mood hitting you is the visual imagery,"[32] Kubrick would say. Equally inventive was the way the director used classical music, with Richard Strauss's *Also Sprach Zarathustra* (1896) and Johann Strauss's *The Blue Danube*

(1866): "I wanted to regard some sequences as I would a musical; only, instead of having people singing and dancing, there is a beautiful piece of music and evolving spaceships."[33]

The years following *2001* were frustrating for the director. In 1969, Kubrick finished writing the script for an ambitious account of the life of French emperor Napoleon, one of his lifelong obsessions. However, the script's complexity and prospective cost scared MGM, and the project was dropped despite Kubrick's impressive preparatory work.[34] Signing a deal with Warner Brothers, the filmmaker then undertook to adapt *A Clockwork Orange* (1971),[35] a British dystopia written by Anthony Burgess in 1962, which depicts the horrifying criminal acts of the droogs, a youth gang led by the magnetic Alex DeLarge. With its pop art aesthetics and surreal images, its satirical depiction of government, as well as a shocking portrayal of white masculinity (embodied by Malcolm McDowell's Alex), *A Clockwork Orange* "is the third part of a futurist trilogy"[36] after *Dr. Strangelove* and *2001*. The film was released in 1972 and, as previous Kubrick films, earned mixed reviews. What some deemed as exploitative and a glorification of violence, others hailed a "tour de force."[37] However, it was the British response to the film that aggravated the controversy. The British Board of Censors imposed a limited run in theaters, and when news came in the press of murders supposedly inspired by the film's droogs, Kubrick, who had started receiving death threats in his own home, decided to stop all showings of the film in England. Meanwhile, in the United States, the director cut some sexual footage so the film could be classified R instead of X. In spite (or because) of the fiery debate, *A Clockwork Orange* grossed a total of forty million dollars, guaranteeing Kubrick absolute control over his next projects, all of which would from then on be produced by Warner Bros.

The director then set his sights on adapting William Makepeace Thackeray's novel *Vanity Fair* (1847–1848). However, finding it difficult to condense Becky Sharp's rise and fall in British society into a reasonable film length, he turned his attention to another of Thackeray's tales of ascension and downfall: *The Luck of Barry Lyndon: A Romance of the Last Century* (1844). Casting Ryan O'Neal and Marisa Berenson in the roles of Barry and Lady Lyndon, Kubrick directed his actors into passive and silent performances, relying on their faces and muted expressions to convey their inner emotions. As Elisa Pezzotta remarks, Barry's "passivity is stressed by the director's choice of changing the homodiegetic narrator of the adapted novel into a heterodiegetic voice-over."[38] Pezzotta goes on to show how Kubrick's frequent use of the zooming technique, as well as the third-person narration, creates a sense of doom "leaving [the character] no chance to free himself from his destiny."[39] A known perfectionist, Kubrick's striving to achieve the utmost realism led him once again to break new ground. Production lasted for eight and a half months and was shot on location in Ireland, England, and

Germany, following the character's journeys through Europe during the Seven Years' War. Costumes were copied from eighteenth-century paintings, and lighting on set was achieved through window light by day and candlelight by night, made possible by the use of an f. 0.7 Zeiss lens, which had been designed by NASA for the moon landing. The film's gorgeous photography and painterly aesthetic have greatly contributed to its legacy, as well as Kubrick's use of classical music (Bach, Mozart, Handel), partly reorchestrated by Leonard Roseman.

After the commercial failure of *Barry Lyndon*, it took a few years before Kubrick became interested in another project. He remained cooped up in his Hertfordshire estate until 1977 when Warner asked him to direct Stephen King's *The Shining*. Kubrick, though having previously refused to direct *The Exorcist* (William Friedkin, 1973), had become interested in the possibilities offered by the horror genre and saw potential in King's story of the Torrance family's unraveling in the haunted Overlook Hotel. Discarding King's own screenplay, Kubrick hired novelist Diane Johnson, author of *The Shadow Knows* (1974) which Kubrick had briefly considered adapting, to help him write a new script. Kubrick and Johnson's work, as told by the latter, focused on how to "provoke fear."[40] Many changes were made from the novel: the main focus shifted from six-year old Danny Torrance to his father Jack; the supernatural, if present, was downplayed in favor of psychology;[41] King's famous animated topiaries were eliminated to put the spotlight on the labyrinth; and the ending was modified. After envisioning him as his Napoleon, Kubrick finally found the occasion to work with Jack Nicholson, fresh from his Oscar-winning performance in *One Flew Over the Cuckoo's Nest* (Milos Forman, 1975). For the role of Jack Torrance's wife Wendy, the director chose Shelley Duvall, whom he had admired in Robert Altman's films. Out of the five thousand boys who were interviewed for the challenging part of Danny Torrance, Kubrick found what he needed in five-year-old Danny Lloyd. The shooting went on for fourteen months, testing the endurance of both cast and crew. If Kubrick was particularly protective of little Danny, ensuring that the boy would not see anything that might scare him, his attitude toward other actors, especially Scatman Crothers and Duvall, was more controversial. At the time, Duvall qualified the experience as "almost unbearable."[42] *The Shining* is full of technical marvels, from the extensive and powerful use of Garrett Brown's Steadicam to the extravagant sets built at the EMI-Elstree Studios in England. Though the film had already been released in the United States, Kubrick kept making new cuts, reducing the original 146 minutes feature to 119 minutes. As is fitting for a film dealing with doubles, two versions of *The Shining* exist today: the longer "American" one, and the shorter "European" other. The mixed reviews trend continued, but the film turned out to be the highest grossing film of the director's career.

Seven years after *The Shining*, *Full Metal Jacket* was released. Structured in two parts, the film first follows Joker (Matthew Modine)'s harsh and dehumanizing training alongside other recruits, and then shifts to the brutality of the war in Vietnam. Once again, the film is the adaptation of a novel, Gustav Hasford's *The Short-Timers* (1979). To write the script, Kubrick called on Michael Herr, a war correspondent who had published *Dispatches*, a memoir of his experiences in Vietnam, in 1977. Herr had previously participated to the script of Francis Ford Coppola's *Apocalypse Now* (1979). Gathering a cast of young and promising actors—Matthew Modine, Vincent d'Onofrio, Adam Baldwin—and hiring Lee Ermey, an actual Vietnam veteran, for the part of the sadistic Sergeant Hartman, the ambitious production started in England. To re-create the bombed city of Hue, Kubrick and production designer Anton Furst used a gasworks in Beckton, while Bassingbourn Air Base was used for the Parris Island sets as well as the Da Nang base. The first planned eighteen weeks of shooting ended up lasting thirty-nine, partly because of a car accident that injured Ermey, forcing production to shut down for five months. Vivian Kubrick, who had previously directed a documentary on the shooting of *The Shining*, took over a more prominent role by supervising and composing the film's score. As always, reviews were contrasted but *Full Metal Jacket* proved another commercial success for the director, figuring among the top twenty grossing films of 1987. The film's legacy, on the other hand, turned out more ambiguous, as some worshipped the dehumanizing scenes at Parris Island as a model of macho masculinity. Georg Seesslen remarks: "Kubrick's film has moved and disturbed people, but at the same time it has reached a cult status for those people, who euphorically or tragically view themselves as 'soldierly.' . . . The history of the reception of *Full Metal Jacket* remains polyvalent."[43]

Twelve years would pass before audiences would discover another Kubrick film, one that would be his last, as *Eyes Wide Shut* was released posthumously on July 13, 1999. Before production began on the Nicole Kidman and Tom Cruise–starrer, the director, far from being idle, had worked on two other projects. The first one, *A.I. Artificial Intelligence*, was inspired by a 1969 Brian Aldiss short story entitled "Super-Toys Last All Summer Long." Interested in adapting the story, Kubrick spent about two decades working intermittently on the project—first with the help of Aldiss himself, later on with other writers. But unsatisfied with the existing technology to materialize the android boy story, Kubrick postponed the project, not without having first unsuccessfully tried to convince Spielberg to direct the film with a child actor. Spielberg would ultimately bring *A.I.* to the screen in 2001, using Kubrick's eighty-four-page treatment for guidance and hiring Chris Baker—who had produced designs for the project at Kubrick's request—as a conceptual artist. From 1991 to 1993, as the *A.I.* project was put on hold, Kubrick became interested in adapting *Wartime Lies* (1991), a novel by Louis Begley set in Poland during the Second World War. However, even though locations had been scouted and the casting of the two leads settled, what would have been *Aryan Papers* was put to a halt when news came that Spielberg had started filming *Schindler's List* (1993). With *A.I.* also deferred, Kubrick settled on an even more ancient idea: Arthur Schnitzler's *Traumnovelle* (1926), to which he had bought the rights in the 1960s. With a script co-written with Frederic Raphael, *Eyes Wide Shut* was officially confirmed as the director's next project in 1995.

"In a way, *Eyes Wide Shut* appears as a complement to *The Shining*," writes Michel Ciment. "Twenty years after showing us the threats withheld by all kinds of isolation, madness, and dereliction which lookout for any man cut out from the outside world, Kubrick offers us a cautionary tale on the dangers of going out in the world, on the deadly temptations harbored by a voyage into the unknown."[44] Filming the marriage story of Bill and Alice Harford—shaken to its core after the wife's confession of extramarital sexual fantasies—was achieved in about fifty-two weeks. Tom Cruise and Nicole Kidman, at the time a real-life married couple, settled in England for the occasion. The length of the shooting, the director's reputation, as well as the leading actors' star status, heightened the mystery and the high expectations surrounding the project, all of which intensified on March 7, 1999, when Stanley Kubrick died a few days after presenting his final cut to Warner. The film opened on the date wished by Kubrick and was met with commercial success in the United States and Europe.[45] Though a few critics' responses to the film were immediately positive,[46] the film remained largely misunderstood for a number of years, only to become reevaluated in time, as all of Kubrick's films before it. In 2019, for the twentieth anniversary of its release, a number of articles revisiting *Eyes Wide Shut* and its making were published in the press. "What critics saw as dated, I saw as timeless,"[47] writes Lila Shapiro in her analysis of the film's depiction of marriage, and more largely of male and female relations: "Kubrick, the most controlling and precise of directors, knew exactly what he was doing. He didn't make a naïve film—he made a film about naïveté, and the toll it takes on the world."[48] A filmmaker ahead of his time, Kubrick's visionary films constantly demand reconsideration, every passing moment opening new doors for interpretation and revealing new hidden meanings. The timelessness of his oeuvre, its universal nature, continue to prove that Kubrick still remains today "a great philosopher of the human condition."[49]

A Critical Companion to Stanley Kubrick delves into the complexities of the director's filmography and examines the wide range of topics and multiple interpretations that his films inspire: the historical, philosophical, theoretical, artistic, and cinematic dimensions. The eighteen chapters of this volume are academic in their approach to the subject as well as in their methodologies.

Built on rigorous research, each offers an enriching view of Kubrick's films that expands on the existing analytical books dedicated to the filmmaker and provides the reader with diverse angles and innovative readings that will surely spark new discussions.

The first section focuses on the variety of film genres in Kubrick's filmography and his ability to bend codified structures. In the first chapter, Vincent Jaunas analyzes *Killer's Kiss* through the prism of one of Kubrick's main thematic concerns: the depiction of a diegetic world seen through the subjective filter of the film's main protagonists, thus revealing the inner states of individuals whose highly rational mind wishes to impose its will upon the physical world and on taming the human body. In her chapter on *The Shining*, Anne-Marie Paquet-Deyris studies how Kubrick materializes on screen the notion of "crack-up" that contaminates every human being and type of space at the Overlook Hotel. Paquet-Deyris focuses on the filmmaker's choice to chronicle the inscription of abnormality and violence through his use of various narrative, aesthetic, and formal strategies, which departed from the conventions of the horror film at the time. In the third chapter, Carol Donelan delivers an in-depth analysis of *The Killing*, and how Kubrick's third feature film sets the stage for understanding his entire oeuvre—structurally, stylistically, and thematically. In his chapter dedicated to *Lolita*, Gilles Menegaldo analyzes the way in which the director plays with various genre conventions, at times subverting them through irony, parody, and pastiche, also echoing to some extent Nabokov's own strategies of hybridization in the novel. In the following chapter, Sean O'Reilly charts Kubrick's evolving understanding of history as a concept, and the unique "historiophotic" signature he brought to his depictions of the past, most notably in *Spartacus* and *Barry Lyndon*. In the last chapter of the section, Guillaume Mouleux argues that the very structures, tropes, and visual worlds of Kubrick's many war films are often reminiscent of the 1940s wartime imagery, in spite of the absence of World War II in his filmography.

The second section of the volume delves into Kubrick's chaotic and transgressive worlds. Jerold J. Abrams focuses on the satirical black comedy *Dr. Strangelove,* and how the cyclicality of war in Kubrick's film is drawn from Heraclitus's philosophy of war. In his chapter, William Gombash argues that Kubrick's war films' protagonists, who venture to rule by their own sense of order, inevitably fail because unforeseen circumstances create a state of disorder and chaos. In the third chapter of this section, James R. Britton addresses the limits of irony in *Full Metal Jacket* and explores how the film depicts an ideologically saturated American masculinity that forces not just conformity but also consent, through an analysis of the narrative structure as well as the main character's transformation. Madison Mae Williams's chapter examines the use of Brecht's alienation effect in *A Clockwork Orange* and how Kubrick forces the audience to think critically about their roles as passive observers of ubiquitous violence in contemporary society. In the following chapter, Rachel Cole considers another aspect of Kubrick's most polemical film, namely how the reception of *A Clockwork Orange* played a key role in developing different institutional processes of governance and debates about violence on film, and how the ability to identify reflexive violence from the burgeoning exploitation genres would become significant to the authority of modern processes of censorship. The section concludes with Elsa Colombani's study of the evolution of female characters in *Barry Lyndon*, *The Shining*, and *Eyes Wide Shut* and how, though shown through the lens of the male protagonists, they emerge from silence to claim the right to speak their minds.

The last section of the volume highlights the visionary aspect of Kubrick's oeuvre. James Fenwick addresses Kubrick's collaboration with film star and producer Kirk Douglas and considers how the relationship proved seminal and prolific for both artists, using neglected and overlooked archival sources. Annie Nissen's chapter examines the role of adaptation in the director's films—most notably his relationship with King and Nabokov—and explores the dynamics and conflicts between literary author and film auteur. In the third chapter of this section, Carl Sweeney draws on Michel Foucault's theory of heterotopic space to analyze how the spatialities Kubrick presents in *Eyes Wide Shut* can be understood as significant sites of meaning in relation to contemporary society. Paul Johnson's chapter investigates how Kubrick uses editing and adjustments to imagery to produce a temporal arena, using time to create dramatic conflict for his characters. In the following chapter, Maurizia Natali argues that *2001: A Space Odyssey* is an allegory of transhumanist melancholia that belongs to the tradition of Wunderkammern, and compares the film to an emblem of Humanism, Albrecht Dürer's *Melancholia I* (1514). The final chapter of the volume, written by Joshua Sikora, addresses the kinship between *2001: A Space Odyssey* and Kubrick's work on *A.I. Artificial Intelligence*, a project that the director spent two decades developing before his death. Sikora explores why Kubrick believed it was essential that *A.I.* (like *2001* before it) should be infused with elements of myth, magic, and fantasy in order to touch a deeper, mysterious part of our being—the human soul.

The diversity and range of the chapters compiled in this collection reflect the editor's belief that a study of the full complexity of Kubrick's films as well as the reassessment of their critical interpretations require both an interdisciplinary perspective and the drawing together of different intellectual approaches. The chapters demonstrate a collective awareness of Kubrick as one of cinema's great visionaries, a revolutionary filmmaker who left an indelible mark on contemporary culture. Contrary to the majority of the volumes on the subject currently on the market, this book explores new trends of research in film studies, includes the analysis of new archival sources, and also comprises a series of unique and novel perspectives on Kubrick's films that focus on specific aspects never sufficiently examined before.

NOTES

1. Jay Varela, "Conversation with Stanley Kubrick," in *The Stanley Kubrick Archives*, ed. Alison Castle, 312–13 (London: Taschen, 2005), 312.
2. Stephen Holden, "Stanley Kubrick, Film Director with a Bleak Vision, Dies at 70," *New York Times*, March 8, 1999, https://www.nytimes.com/1999/03/08/movies/stanley-kubrick-film-director-with-a-bleak-vision-dies-at-70.html (accessed February 20, 2020).
3. Martin Scorsese, "Preface," in *Kubrick*, Michel Ciment, 3 (Paris: Calmann-lévy, 2011), 3. My translation.
4. Mario Falsetto, *Stanley Kubrick: A Narrative and Stylistic Analysis* (Westport, CT: Praeger, 2001), p. xxii.
5. Jerold J. Abrams, *The Philosophy of Stanley Kubrick* (Lexington, KY: University Press of Kentucky, 2007), 1.
6. Stanley Kubrick quoted in Jeremy Bernstein, "Profile: Stanley Kubrick," in *Stanley Kubrick: Interviews*, edited by Gene D. Phillips, 21–46 (Jackson, MS: University Press of Mississippi, 2001), 25.
7. Paul Duncan, *Stanley Kubrick*, revised edition (Harpenden, UK: Pocket Essentials, 1999), 21–22.
8. James Naremore, *On Kubrick* (London: British Film Institute, 2007), 71.
9. Michel Chion, *Stanley Kubrick: l'humain, ni plus ni moins* (Paris: Cahiers du cinéma, 2005), 58.
10. Hired by MGM's head of production Dore Shary, Kubrick and Harris set out to work on an adaptation of Stefan Zweig's *The Burning Secret* (1945), but the project fell through when Shary was fired. Both Kubrick and Harris were dismissed shortly after. MGM would then distribute Kubrick's *Lolita* and *2001: A Space Odyssey* and finance the director's preparatory work on *Napoleon* before the studio finally turned it down.
11. Bill Krohn, *Masters of Cinema: Stanley Kubrick* (Paris: Cahiers du cinéma, 2007), 26–29.
12. Peter Bogdanovich, "What They Say about Stanley Kubrick," *New York Times*, July 4, 1999, https://www.nytimes.com/1999/07/04/magazine/what-they-say-about-stanley-kubrick.html (accessed February 20, 2020).
13. Stanley Kubrick quoted in Joseph Gelmis, "The Film Director as Superstar: Stanley Kubrick," in *Stanley Kubrick: Interviews*, 80–104, 102.
14. Ciment, *Kubrick*, 152.
15. Christiane Kubrick in "What They Say about Stanley Kubrick."
16. Tony Curtis in "What They Say about Stanley Kubrick."
17. Gene D. Phillips, "Spartacus," in *The Stanley Kubrick Archives*, 316–23, 318.
18. Gene D. Phillips, "Lolita," in *The Stanley Kubrick Archives*, 328–37, 330.
19. Patrick Webster, *Love and Death in Kubrick: A Critical Study of the Films from* Lolita *through* Eyes Wide Shut (Jefferson, NC: McFarland, 2011), 17.
20. Ibid., 17.
21. Stanley Kubrick in Terry Southern, "An Interview with Stanley Kubrick," in *The Stanley Kubrick Archives*, 340–43, 341.
22. Gene Youngblood, "Lolita," *Criterion.com*, September 24, 1992, https://www.criterion.com/current/posts/836-lolita (accessed February 20, 2020).
23. Penned under the name Peter Bryant, George's novel was first published in the UK under the title *Two Hours of Doom*.
24. The change of tone was decided to avoid similarities with Sidney Lumet's *Fail-Safe* (1964), which was also distributed by Columbia Pictures.

25. Boris Hars-Tschachotin, "Superpower Paranoia Expressed in Space: The War Room as the Key Visual in *Dr. Strangelove or: How I Learned to Stop Worrying and Love the Bomb*," in *Stanley Kubrick*, 2nd Edition, *Kinematograph* nr. 20, 75–87 (Frankfurt: Deutsches Filmmuseum, 2007), 75.
26. Eric Schlosser, "Almost Everything in 'Dr. Strangelove' was true," *The New Yorker*, January 17, 2014, https://www.newyorker.com/news/news-desk/almost-everything-in-dr-strangelove-was-true (accessed February 20, 2020).
27. Roger Ebert, "Dr. Strangelove," July 11, 1999, https://www.rogerebert.com/reviews/great-movie-dr-strangelove-1964 (accessed February 20, 2020).
28. Chion, *Stanley Kubrick: l'humain, ni plus ni moins*, 154.
29. Pauline Kael, "Trash, Art, and the Movies," *Harper's*, February 1969, https://harpers.org/archive/1969/02/trash-art-and-the-movies/ (accessed February 27, 2020).
30. Michael Benson, *Space Odyssey: Stanley Kubrick, Arthur C. Clarke, and the Making of a Masterpiece* (New York: Simon & Schuster, 2018), 33.
31. Chion, *Stanley Kubrick: l'humain, ni plus ni moins*, 168.
32. Kubrick in Maurice Rapf, "A Talk with Stanley Kubrick about *2001*," in *Stanley Kubrick: Interviews*, 75–79, 78.
33. Kubrick in Renaud Walter, "Entretien avec Stanley Kubrick," in *L'Odyssée de 2001*, edited by Michel Ciment, 110–24 (Paris: Institut Lumière/Actes Sud, 2018), 121.
34. Alison Castle, ed., *Stanley Kubrick's "Napoleon": The Greatest Movie Never Made* (London: Taschen, 2009).
35. *A Clockwork Orange* was Kubrick's first solo script.
36. Michel Ciment, "A Clockwork Orange," in *The Stanley Kubrick Archives*, 410–17, 415.
37. Vincent Canby, "'A Clockwork Orange' Dazzles the Senses and Mind," *New York Times*, December 20, 1971, https://www.nytimes.com/1971/12/20/archives/a-clockwork-orange-dazzles-the-senses-and-mind.html (accessed February 21, 2020).
38. Elisa Pezzotta, *Stanley Kubrick: Adapting the Sublime* (Jackson, MS: University Press of Mississippi, 2013), 100.
39. Ibid.
40. Diane Johnson quoted in Nicolas Saada, *Questions de cinéma: Entretiens et Conversations (1989–2001)* (Paris: Carlotta Films, 2019), 139. My translation.
41. Johnson recalls how Kubrick and herself were inspired by Freud's writings, Victorian Gothic novels, the sublime, as well as Bruno Bettelheim's *The Uses of Enchantment* for the writing of the script, in Saada, *Questions de cinéma*, 139, and John Baxter, *Stanley Kubrick: A Biography* (London: HarperCollins Publishers, 1997), 310.
42. Shelley Duvall quoted in Roger Ebert, "Interview with Shelley Duvall," *RogerEbert.com*, December 14, 1980, https://www.rogerebert.com/interviews/interview-with-shelley-duvall (accessed February 21, 2020).
43. Georg Seesslen, "Shoot Me. Shoot Me: On the Essence of War—*Full Metal Jacket*," in *Stanley Kubrick*, 2nd Edition. *Kinematograph* nr. 20, 208–23, 210.
44. Ciment, *Kubrick*, 257.
45. Rodney Hill, "Eyes Wide Shut," in *The Stanley Kubrick Archives*, 482–93, 491.
46. Ibid.
47. Lila Shapiro, "What I Learned After Watching Eyes Wide Shut 100 Times," *Vulture*, July 1, 2019, https://www.vulture.com/2019/07/what-i-learned-after-watching-eyes-wide-shut-100-times.html (accessed February 21, 2020).
48. Ibid.
49. Nicole Kidman quoted in Merle Ginsberg, "Nicole Kidman on Life with Tom Cruise through Stanley Kubrick's Lens," *Hollywood Reporter*, October 24, 2012, https://www.hollywoodreporter.com/news/nicole-kidman-stanley-kubricks-lens-382186 (accessed February 21, 2020).

REFERENCES

Abrams, Jerold J. *The Philosophy of Stanley Kubrick*. Lexington, KY: University Press of Kentucky, 2007.
Azulys, Sam. *Stanley Kubrick, une odyssée philosophique*. Paris: Editions de la Transparence, 2011.
Baxter, John. *Stanley Kubrick: A Biography*. London: HarperCollinsPublishers, 1997.
Benson, Michael. *Space Odyssey: Stanley Kubrick, Arthur C. Clarke, and the Making of a Masterpiece*. New York: Simon & Schuster, 2018.
Bernstein, Jeremy. "Profile: Stanley Kubrick." In *Stanley Kubrick: Interviews*, edited by Gene D. Phillips, 21–46. Jackson, MS: University Press of Mississippi, 2001.
Bogdanovich, Peter. "What They Say About Stanley Kubrick." *New York Times*, July 4, 1999. https://www.nytimes.com/1999/07/04/magazine/what-they-say-about-stanley-kubrick.html.
Broderick, Mick. *Reconstructing Strangelove: Inside Stanley Kubrick's "Nightmare Comedy."* New York: Wallflower Press, 2017.
———. *The Legacy of Stanley Kubrick*. London: Routledge, 2019.
Canby, Vincent. "'A Clockwork Orange' Dazzles the Senses and Mind." *New York Times*, December 20, 1971. https://www.nytimes.com/1971/12/20/archives/a-clockwork-orange-dazzles-the-senses-and-mind.html.
Castle, Alison, ed. *The Stanley Kubrick Archives*. London: Taschen, 2005.
———. *Stanley Kubrick's "Napoleon": The Greatest Movie Never Made*. London: Taschen, 2009.
Chion, Michel. *Stanley Kubrick: l'humain, ni plus ni moins*. Paris: Cahiers du cinéma, 2005.
Ciment, Michel. *Kubrick*. Paris: Calmann-lévy, 2011.
———. "A Clockwork Orange." In *The Stanley Kubrick Archives*, edited by Alison Castle, 410–17. London: Taschen, 2005.
Cocks, Geoffrey, James Diedrick, and Glenn Perusek. *Stanley Kubrick, Film, and the Uses of History*. Madison, WI: Wisconsin Film Studies, 2006.
Duncan, Paul. *Stanley Kubrick*, revised edition. Harpenden, UK: Pocket Essentials, 1999.
Ebert, Roger. "Dr. Strangelove." *RogerEbert.com*, July 11, 1999, https://www.rogerebert.com/reviews/great-movie-dr-strangelove-1964.
———. "Interview with Shelley Duvall." *RogerEbert.com*, December 14, 1980. https://www.rogerebert.com/interviews/interview-with-shelley-duvall.
Falsetto, Mario. *Stanley Kubrick: A Narrative and Stylistic Analysis*. Westport, CT: Praeger, 2001.
Frinzi, Joe R. *Kubrick's Monolith: The Art and Mystery of 2001: A Space Odyssey*. Jefferson, NC: McFarland & Company, 2017.
Gelmis, Joseph. "The Film Director as Superstar: Stanley Kubrick." In *Stanley Kubrick: Interviews*, edited by Gene D. Phillips, 80–104. Jackson, MS: University Press of Mississippi, 2001.
Gengaro, Christine Lee. *Listening to Stanley Kubrick: The Music in His Films*. Lanham, MD: Scarecrow Press, 2013.
Ginsberg, Merle. "Nicole Kidman on Life with Tom Cruise through Stanley Kubrick's Lens." *Hollywood Reporter*, October 24, 2012. https://www.hollywoodreporter.com/news/nicole-kidman-stanley-kubricks-lens-382186.
Hars-Tschachotin, Boris. "Superpower Paranoia Expressed in Space: The War Room as the Key Visual in *Dr. Strangelove or: How I Learned to Stop Worrying and Love the Bomb*." In *Stanley Kubrick* (second edition), *Kinematograph* nr. 20, 75–87. Frankfurt: Deutsches Filmmuseum, 2007.
Hill, Rodney. "Eyes Wide Shut." In *The Stanley Kubrick Archives*, edited by Alison Castle, 482–93. London: Taschen, 2005.
Holden, Stephen. "Stanley Kubrick, Film Director with a Bleak Vision, Dies at 70." *New York Times*, March 8, 1999. https://www.nytimes.com/1999/03/08/movies/stanley-kubrick-film-director-with-a-bleak-vision-dies-at-70.html.
Hughes, David. *The Complete Kubrick*. London: Virgin Books, 2001.
Kagan, Norman. *The Cinema of Stanley Kubrick*, 3rd edition. New York: Bloomsbury, 2000.

Kolker, Robert. *A Cinema of Loneliness: Penn, Stone, Kubrick, Scorsese, Spielberg, Altman*, 3rd edition. Oxford: Oxford University Press, 2000.
———. *Stanley Kubrick's 2001: A Space Odyssey*. Oxford: Oxford University Press, 2006.
Kolker, Robert, and Nathan Abrams. *Eyes Wide Shut: Stanley Kubrick and the Making of His Final Film*. Oxford: Oxford University Press, 2019.
Krohn, Bill. *Masters of Cinema: Stanley Kubrick*. Paris: Cahiers du cinéma, 2007.
LoBrutto, Vincent. *Stanley Kubrick: A Biography*. New York: Da Capo Press, 1997.
McQuiston, Kate. *"We'll Meet Again": Musical Design in the Films of Stanley Kubrick*. Oxford: Oxford University Press, 2013.
Naremore, James. *On Kubrick*. London: British Film Institute, 2007.
Nelson, Thomas Allen. *Kubrick: Inside a Film Artist's Maze*. Bloomington, IN: Indiana University Press, 2000.
Pezzotta, Elisa. *Stanley Kubrick: Adapting the Sublime*. Jackson, MS: University Press of Mississippi, 2013.
Phillips, Gene D. "Early Work." In *The Stanley Kubrick Archives*, edited by Alison Castle, 268–77. London: Taschen, 2005
———. "Spartacus." In *The Stanley Kubrick Archives*, edited by Alison Castle, 316–23. London: Taschen, 2005.
———. "Lolita." In *The Stanley Kubrick Archives*, edited by Alison Castle, 328–37. London: Taschen, 2005.
Pramaggiore, Maria. *Making Time in Stanley Kubrick's Barry Lyndon*. New York: Bloomsbury Academic, 2015.
Rapf, Maurice. "A Talk with Stanley Kubrick about *2001*." In *Stanley Kubrick: Interviews*, edited by Gene D. Phillips, 75–79. Jackson, MS: University Press of Mississippi, 2001.
Rhodes, Gary D., ed. *Stanley Kubrick: Essays on his Films and Legacy*. Jefferson, NC: McFarland and Company, 2007.
Saada, Nicolas. *Questions de cinéma: Entretiens et Conversations (1989–2001)*. Paris: Carlotta Films, 2019.
Schlosser, Eric. "Almost Everything in 'Dr. Strangelove' was true." *The New Yorker*, January 17, 2014. https://www.newyorker.com/news/news-desk/almost-everything-in-dr-strangelove-was-true.
Seesslen, Georg. "Shoot Me. Shoot Me: On the Essence of War—*Full Metal Jacket*." In *Stanley Kubrick*, 2nd edition. *Kinematograph* nr. 20, 208–23. Frankfurt: Deutsches Filmmuseum, 2007.
Shapiro, Lila. "What I Learned after Watching Eyes Wide Shut 100 Times." *Vulture*, July 1, 2019. https://www.vulture.com/2019/07/what-i-learned-after-watching-eyes-wide-shut-100-times.html.
Southern, Terry. "An Interview with Stanley Kubrick." In *The Stanley Kubrick Archives*, edited by Alison Castle, 340–43. London: Taschen, 2005.
Varela, Jay. "Conversation with Stanley Kubrick." In *The Stanley Kubrick Archives*, edited by Alison Castle, 312–13. London: Taschen, 2005.
Walter, Renaud. "Entretien avec Stanley Kubrick." In *L'Odyssée de 2001*, edited by Michel Ciment, 110–24. Paris: Institut Lumière/Actes Sud, 2018.
Webster, Patrick. *Love and Death in Kubrick: A Critical Study of the Films from* Lolita *through* Eyes Wide Shut. Jefferson, NC: McFarland, 2011.
Youngblood, Gene. "Lolita." *Criterion.com*, September 24, 1992. https://www.criterion.com/current/posts/836-lolita.

Part I

Bending Genres

Chapter One

Mental Landscapes and Subdued Bodies in *Killer's Kiss*

Vincent Jaunas

In her 1958 article, Joanne Stang eloquently summarizes what was to become the dominant view of Stanley Kubrick's first two feature films, *Fear and Desire* (1953) and *Killer's Kiss* (1955), by calling them "two post-adolescent flings at learning the trade"[1] —an opinion corroborated by Kubrick himself on various occasions. This chapter will suggest that even though *Killer's Kiss* may contain some aesthetic inconsistencies that could be attributed to Kubrick's youth, the film also offers a fascinating insight into the director's cinematographic style in the making. More specifically, it will highlight how the main mise-en-scène strategies of *Killer's Kiss* reveal this style to stem from the filmmaker's ambition to explore the ideological and philosophical framework that determines the worldview of humankind—with a particular focus on the worldview of white men. In order to do so, it will explore the way the film both develops a complex structure of subjective filming and constructs a reflexive criticism of the diegetic narrator, so as to depict the worldview of a man characterized by an excessive belief in the power of the rational mind to shape the self and the world around him, a belief entailing a nefarious subjection of one's body and one's affects that is shown as doomed to crumble.

Such a depiction of characters driven by a highly mental conception of the self that strives for utter rational control, along with the formal strategies enabling the director to depict it, may indeed be considered a central Kubrickian characteristic, one studied at length by various scholars. Mario Falsetto notably analyzes the way *A Clockwork Orange* (1971), *The Shining* (1980) and *Eyes Wide Shut* (1999) all develop an aesthetics enabling the viewer to perceive the diegetic world as seen through the eyes of a protagonist, so that the diegesis becomes a mirror of the focalizer's subjectivity.[2] Gilles Deleuze famously considers that Kubrick explores human subjectivity in his entire body of work, not just in films that focus on one single character's viewpoint. Kubrick's, he argues, is a "cinema of the brain": his films display a correlation between the diegetic world and the human organ, so that "the exploration of the world is also an exploration of the brain."[3] Eventually, these worlds tend to go haywire, for "the brain is not a reasonable system and the world is not a rational system."[4]

In a recent article, Sam Azulys analyzes how Kubrick's depiction of sick brains goes hand in hand with their submission to a "becoming-machine,"[5] while James Naremore had previously stated that Kubrick's portrayal of "grotesque bodies" lies at the core of the director's aesthetics, thus reflecting an anxious characterization of the body in tune with the characters' desire to turn into machines that Azulys underlines.[6] Such analyses tend to focus on the second part of Kubrick's oeuvre, and mention neither the films for which Kubrick did not enjoy full artistic control—from *The Killing* (1956) to *Spartacus* (1960)—nor his first two films, although Kubrick did have considerable control over their production. Yet in spite of obvious aesthetic differences, *Killer's Kiss* already contains the seeds of the artistic vision that would shape the aesthetics of Kubrick's major films.

At first sight, *Killer's Kiss* may seem a far cry from the aesthetic preoccupations mentioned above, as these require the diegetic world to represent a mental landscape, whereas the film's depiction of New York seems extremely realistic: one only has to compare the gritty city of *Killer's Kiss* with the surreal New York of *Eyes Wide Shut* to note how realistic the former appears. Such realism may be attributed to the film's low budget, as Kubrick could not afford to build his own sets and therefore contrived to film on location. However, the work does betray an unquestionable interest for the aesthetics of realism, unique in the director's oeuvre. Philip Mather argues that Kubrick's experience as a photojournalist for *Look* magazine caused the young artist to take an interest in realism: "it should no longer be possible to think of Kubrick's films without acknowledging that their impact owes something to the journalistic codes of realism he acquired at *Look* magazine."[7] In *Killer's Kiss*, this interest may be found through the influence of photographer Weegee, who "had been something of a teen idol for teenage Kubrick."[8] Weegee's dark, uncompromising realism—exemplified by his many photographs of New York murder victims taken on site—is reflected in *Killer's Kiss* through the film's emphasis on spatial realism—several shots reveal the names of the street or of the subway station the characters are in—associated with a realistic soundtrack and a stark black-and-white photography that underline the oppressive, even threatening reality of 1950s New York for the lower middle class. James Naremore writes that "Sequences like [the street scenes in Times Square, in which bystanders did not know they were being filmed] prompted Gavin Lambert, writing a review of *Killer's Kiss* in *Sight and Sound*, to praise Kubrick for taking 'a kind of neo-realist approach to human behavior, a feeling for the place and moment.'"[9]

Yet, even though Kubrick's interest in recording slices of life in *Killer's Kiss* is undeniable and sets the work apart from the director's subsequent aesthetic preoccupations, the film's realism conflicts with various constructed shots and with a complex overarching narrative structure that denote an interest in subjective representation foreshadowing the director's later films. One might add that such conflicting interests in both realism and a more subjective distortion of reality was already to be found in Kubrick's photography for *Look* magazine, as various pictures reveal the artist's desire to depict a mental landscape rather than a realistic setting. Let us think of the series depicting Walter Cartier, a professional boxer whose coach happened to be his identical twin brother, Vincent. In several instances, Kubrick shows the two men together—playing chess or training for instance—so that these pictures create a slightly surreal atmosphere due to the exploration of the theme of the double: Walter appears to be coaching himself or to be playing against himself.

In *Killer's Kiss*, it is first and foremost the narrative structure that indicates a departure from an objective representation of reality. The film opens as the hero, Davey (Jamie Smith), is waiting at the train station. The character quickly imposes himself as the film's narrator, as he starts telling his story in voiceover: a boxer, Davey got himself "in a mess" (as the viewer quickly comes to understand, Davey, after losing a fight, fell in love with a woman, which triggered a series of misadventures). A blurry dissolve then indicates a flashback, whose temporal marker is given by the narrator ("just before my fight with Rodriguez, three days ago"). In fact, the entire narrative takes place within the flashback, which only stops in the last few minutes, as the plot catches up with the initial situation—Davey waiting in the train station. As a result, the whole film is to be understood as a subjective narration, so that the audiovisual appears to stem from the hero's subjectivity.

Throughout the film, various elements remind the spectators that in spite of the overall realistic atmosphere, what we see is indeed a subjective perception of the diegetic world as filtered by Davey's point of view. Firstly, the voiceover narration recurs sporadically throughout the film. Secondly, one particular scene depicting Davey's nightmare stresses the fact that the viewer has entered the character's mental world. As the viewer is given access to mental images depicting the protagonist's inner life, Davey's role as the focalizer through which the world is subjectively perceived is strengthened. In addition, several shots equate Davey's viewpoint with the spectator's, as the camera explicitly adopts his perceptual point of view under extreme circumstances, most notably during his defeat in a boxing match. As Rodriguez punches Davey, the camera films the event from the latter's standpoint, so that it seems to be knocked out instead of the boxer: it falls on the floor, while the referee looks straight at it as he counts to ten. By appropriating the character's point of view in such a visually striking manner, the camera seems to fully embody the protagonist. A similar extreme point of view technique would later be used in *A Clockwork Orange*, when the main protagonist, Alex (Malcolm McDowell), attempts to commit suicide: instead of showing the character fall from the house's top floor, the camera itself is thrown to the ground, so that the audience feels it is falling alongside Alex. In both cases, the focalizer's position as the subjective source of the audiovisuals is strengthened, as such highly subjective elements encourage the viewers to consider all the other shots of the film may act as what Edward Branigan calls "projection shots": even when the camera does not adopt the character's point of view, "we understand that we are shown what the character sees, thinks or experiences through 'metaphors.'"[10]

In *Killer's Kiss*, therefore, the threatening quality of New York may evoke Davey's subjective perception of the city, and reflect the character's state of mind rather than an objective reality. In this context, the quasi-documentary representation of New York City may be seen as an aesthetic inconsistency in a film otherwise focused on depicting a subjective perception. Various scenes do depart from the aesthetic codes of neorealism and construct a more stylized diegetic world, which can thus be more easily perceived as Davey's subjective worldview. For instance, in the first scene within the flashback, Davey is seen walking around his apartment. A panning shot reveals another apartment through the window, in which a woman is clearly visible. At this instant, the viewer does not know her to be the female lead, Gloria (Irene Kane). However, the mise en scène stresses this woman's narrative importance, as the depth of field enables her to be clearly seen, while the two windows act as frames within the frames underlining her presence, so that one may easily assume her to be the cause of the troubles Davey had mentioned in his voiceover introduction. The complex panning shot, associated with the intricate set design, departs from the tradition of realism as it underlines the constructed, discursive quality of the filming. Significantly, Davey does not see the woman through the window, so that her presence is only visible for the viewers. The dramatic irony prevailing in this shot—the viewer feels the narrative importance of a character that the hero has yet to notice—underlines the subjective quality of the audiovisual as a representation of events subsequently reconstructed by the narrator. Gloria's haunting presence in the background underlines the fact that the diegesis objectifies Davey's poetic rendering of the events, as reconstructed from an ulterior viewpoint. Various such highly constructed shots remind the viewers they are watching a subjective representation of events—one narrated *a posteriori*—rather than an objective slice of life.

Another example occurs the morning after Davey manages to chase away Vince (Frank Silvera), a gangster dating Gloria, whom he has seen mistreating his girlfriend through the window of his apartment. After making sure of Gloria's well-being and putting her to bed, Davey comes back to check on her in the morning, and stays for breakfast. At this point, Davey's voiceover narration takes over the soundtrack. The narrator summarizes the topics discussed by the couple during the meal. As the voiceover recounts a discussion the viewer is seeing unfolding, a hesitation occurs as to the status of the audio. When the narrator stops his voiceover narration ("what his boss Rapallo was so sorry for"), Davey's onscreen voice takes over ("Anyway, let's talk about you") without any interruption or modification in the quality of the soundtrack. As a result, Davey's voice seems to simultaneously occupy the role of overarching voiceover narration and onscreen direct dialogue, the viewer being temporarily unable to tell one from the other. Such confusion is enhanced by the fact that at this precise moment, Davey breaks the fourth wall and looks straight at the camera (he is in fact looking at the pictures in Gloria's apartment, as the counter-shot subsequently reveals), so that Davey temporarily blurs the boundary between narrator and character, thus reminding the audience we are watching a subjective projection of past events.

This example reveals how the soundtrack fosters the subjective dimension of the film. Naremore explains that Kubrick initially sought to shoot the movie with direct sound, but had to resort to a post-synchronized soundtrack for financial reasons.[11] Such a change may be the result of exterior constraints, but the less realistic quality of the soundtrack—the dialogues are slightly out of tune with the characters' moving lips—reinforces the film's subjective quality, whereas direct sound has come to be associated with neorealism. Likewise, Kubrick's acting direction may have been impaired by the director's financial inability to hire the best actors of his time—Kubrick implied so when he declared that the first time he "could afford good actors" was during *The Killing*[12]—but it results in each character being performed in a mechanical, underplayed fashion, thus creating a distancing effect that underlines the discursive nature of the audiovisual. Such a performance style would later become a Kubrickian trademark, even after the director started working with accomplished professionals: let us think of Keir Dullea's performance in *2001: A Space Odyssey* (1968), or Tom Cruise's in *Eyes Wide Shut*.

If various unintentional factors may have contributed to enhancing the film's subjective quality, several choices add a layer of narrative complexity and encourage the viewers to question the source of the audiovisual. Indeed, a number of scenes focalize on a secondary character and take place in Davey's absence, even though they are technically integrated in the character's flashback. If the filmic events do represent Davey's subjective perception, how could he have known what was going on in his absence? Various clues suggest these scenes are indeed meant to be understood as Davey's reconstructions of what may have been happening behind his back. The obviously biased quality of these reconstructions enables the viewers to question the narrator's reliability. One such scene occurs at the very beginning of Davey's overall flashback. Right after the scene where Gloria has been introduced through his apartment—unseen by him—a shot reveals the perspective from within the woman's flat, and shows her intensely staring at the hero. The shot may thus easily be understood as a self-gratifying representation of reality on the part of Davey: it suggests Gloria was initially attracted to him, and not the other way round. After this scene, both characters are seen getting ready to leave their apartments through parallel editing. Once again, the shots focusing on Gloria—unseen and still unknown to Davey—nevertheless serve the narrator's self-characterization, as the parallel editing, by stressing the timing of the events, suggests the inevitability of both characters' encounter in the courtyard. All the events that stem from this love affair—including Davey murdering Vince—thus seem to have been determined by the inevitability of fate.

Likewise, Vince appears in several scenes in which Davey is absent. Significantly, all of them portray the character as a worthless creature, a stock villain (Vince is the head of a gang) as well as a despicable old pervert, crazy about a young woman (Vince is in love with his dancer, Gloria, whom he frequently gropes in rape-like scenes; he eventually abducts her). The stereotypical character of Vince, a black mustachioed arch-villain who opposes the positive white hero Davey—thus evoking the archetypal binary opposition between blond heroes and dark-haired villains in classical Westerns[13]—reinforces the subjective biases of the audiovisual, as the narrative may be understood as a way for Davey to glorify himself through a subjective depiction of the events that led him to commit a murder.

A similar intent explains the problematic addition of two flashbacks within Davey's overall flashback. Indeed, Davey's narrative is interrupted twice as Gloria depicts her own past in a diegetic monologue that triggers a filmic representation of the events. Since these scenes are inscribed within Davey's flashback, the hero's point of view must still determine the way the events are depicted, thus shaping the viewers' perception even though the scenes portray someone else's memories. The first flashback takes place after Davey manages to chase Vince away from Gloria's home. Gloria then tells Davey about the events that took place before he intervened, while these events are simultaneously pictured onscreen. Such a flashback may easily be integrated within Davey's overall narrative ambition as it portrays Gloria as very hostile toward Vince (thus legitimizing her love for Davey) and Vince as a desperate man, ready to lose all dignity and beg Gloria to keep him before resorting to violence. Its discursive usefulness for Davey's narrative thus questions the very status of the images as a flashback. Rather, they may indeed translate a subjective interpretation from the main protagonist.

In the second flashback, Gloria tells Davey about the reasons that led her to become a dancer in Vince's club. She did so in order to symbolically get closer to her older sister, a successful ballet dancer who committed suicide after giving up her career to take care of her dying father while Gloria was still a child. In this case, the visuals explicitly contrast with Gloria's words, as throughout the entire monologue the viewer only sees a ballet dancer on stage (played by Ruth Sobotka, Kubrick's then wife), whom one assumes to represent Gloria's sister. The discrepancy between the visuals and Gloria's story emphasize the problematic subjectivity behind the visuals, which may thus easily be interpreted as Davey's poetic rendition of Gloria's sister. As he never encountered her, Davey, as a narrator, would be unable to represent the events depicted in Gloria's story. However, he is previously seen looking at a photograph of the sister, in which she is wearing the exact same makeup as in the dancing scene, so that the viewer is encouraged to interpret the latter as a mental image of Davey's, not Gloria's: the abstract image of Gloria's sister dancing may represent the images that formed in Davey's mind when Gloria was telling her story. Furthermore, this scene once again develops a subplot that fits Davey's overall narrative goal, as it enables him to portray Gloria not as a cheap low-life, but as a tragic figure who got involved with Vince because she bore the weight of a deep-seated trauma.

These two problematic flashbacks may thus be considered as part of Davey's overall subjective version of the events, as they support the main subjective biases of the film's overall flashback, whose entire discursive intent may be to shine a positive light on Davey's attraction for Gloria. Indeed, we have established that Davey's narration tends to depict Vince's feelings for Gloria as both dangerous and despicable, while the hero's attraction toward her is presented as the pure (Davey is not a voyeur looking at her through his window—instead, Gloria is the one watching him), transcendent (their meeting is marked by the inevitability of fate) and socially acceptable (after chasing Vince away, he has breakfast with her in a scene evoking marital bliss) attraction for a virtuous woman. This representational bias impregnates the entire flashback and is clearly shown as stemming from Davey's subjectivity, as it contrasts with the horizon of expectation established in the film's opening scene, in which Davey, anxiously waiting in a train station, suggests in voiceover that he may have been the victim of a dreadful chain of events that he is not able to "think about with any sense." Given this initial stress on the character's dire situation, generic expectations encourage the viewers to expect Davey to have fallen for a femme fatale. In the pure tradition of film noir, Davey may be a "sap," a man who let himself be seduced by a sexually aggressive woman who nearly led him to his downfall. The whole flashback may thus be an attempt by Davey to rationalize the events into an acceptable narrative, an honorable love story that portrays the character as a hero rather than a sap.

Nevertheless, several elements do suggest Davey's attraction to Gloria to be of a threateningly sexual nature. Naremore remarks how "Davey's curiosity about Gloria seems perverse,"[14] as the way he kisses her is reminiscent of the way Vince kisses her, thus suggesting the two characters to be doubles, instead of the exact opposites the narrative suggests them to be. Michel Chion suggests that Kubrick originally meant to stress Davey's sexual attraction with a violent sex scene which would have strengthened Davey's characterization as the film noir sap who fell for a femme fatale[15] and, in the process, would have shown him to be driven by his sexuality rather than by his rational mind. Despite the absence of such a scene, the film nevertheless encourages viewers to distance themselves from the biased depiction of its narrator, as a second interpretative layer suggests these events, far from depicting a romantic love story, reveal how Davey is trapped within a flawed worldview that crumbles due to both his boxing failures and his encounter with Gloria.

From the onset, Davey's world is characterized as prison-like. The film opens with the character in a station, a place of openness and freedom of movement, yet Davey seems trapped within the frame as he walks to and fro, while many bystanders freely walk through the frame and disappear offscreen. A close-up then isolates the character as his voiceover narration begins, so that while he explains his situation to be dire, Davey occupies the entire frame. Thus, his entrapment contrasts with the openness of his surroundings, and suggests Davey's to be a mental prison. As the flashback brings the viewer into his subjective point of view, this feeling is confirmed by the many allusions to entrapment: a triple panning shot of his studio apartment depicts it as an enclosed space, whose only escape is, significantly, the window opening onto Gloria's home.

This scene opens with the first of many mirror shots in the film. The boxer is seen intently examining his face on the eve of his match. The camera angle enables both Davey and his reflection to appear simultaneously on screen, thus depicting Davey as a double figure. This duality becomes synonymous with a split between mind and body, the character being driven by a strict mental discipline entailing a submission of the body through sheer will. As the character touches his own face, a dissociation occurs between the intense gaze of the real Davey (whose face and hand the viewer cannot see in this angle) and his reified body as it appears in the reflection, highlighting the way the character's boxing ambitions result from an ideal of control of the mind over the body. The character's face indeed seems to be felt, studied, and examined by an exterior, critical, and a-corporal gaze.

As Davey prepares for the fight, a rapid montage of New York street life takes on a symbolic dimension, as it seems to further suggest the character's dualistic worldview, revealing Davey's ideal of subjection of the body—the body being reduced to a mechanical automaton—while foreshadowing its limits: an uncanny shot focuses on a Santa Claus automaton seen through a shop window raising its mechanical arms so as to pretend to eat candy. This shot is followed by two close-ups on street food (hot dogs and ice cream), themselves followed by a shot showing a photography shop window—the shop neon occupies the foreground whereas various portraits are seen in the background, so that the photographed bodies appear imprisoned behind neon bars. Finally, an even more uncanny shot depicts a mechanical doll swimming around a small water basin. The boundary between organic and mechanical bodies is thus once again blurred through the symbolism of the doll,[16] which seems entrapped within a circular prison as a high angle shot associates the basin with a cell from which there is no escape. The montage then ends with several shots of signs for a club picturing female dancers.

The strangeness of this montage highlights its symbolic function, as none of these shots aim at evoking the reality of New York in any way. As such, they may be divided into two categories: some suggest the satisfaction of bodily needs (through food and evocations of male sexual gratification), while others inversely depict mechanized, entrapped bodies. As it occurs right before Davey's fight, the uncanny mechanized bodies seem to evoke the boxers' own, the product of intense training and rigorous discipline. The uncanny dimension of the character's ideal of mental discipline is therefore stressed. However, its opposite—the satisfaction of bodily needs—is also evoked in a disturbing manner through close-ups and rapid editing. Given the way this montage appears to symbolize Davey's subjective worldview, these shots suggest that Davey's rigorous mental discipline entails a rejection of the body, seen as the grotesque locus of physical needs and sexual drives. Such an interpretation is encouraged by the scenes taking place in Vince's club immediately afterward: while Davey fights, Vince is seen grotesquely groping Gloria. Vince's sexual excitement seems to increase as he watches Davey lose his fight. As a result, Vince appears as a projection of everything Davey stands against: the lewd, body-driven character symbolizes a grotesque reversal of Davey's ideal self-representation of mental discipline. Davey's pretention to bodily mastery through the power of the mind finds its exact opposite in the grotesque body-driven lewdness of Vince (an emphasis on bodily needs and drives is a fundamental characteristic of the grotesque, as Mikhail Bakhtin famously analyzed in his study of François Rabelais[17]). Vince, then, comes to symbolize the grotesque mastery of the body over the mind that Davey's worldview seems built against. Such a character pairing would become a central characteristic of Kubrick's work, foreshadowing the Humbert/Quilty duality in *Lolita* (1962), for instance.

However, this clear-cut antagonism is questioned when Davey loses his match. Through various shots of the boxing ring as seen from the outside, the match is closely associated with Davey's entrapment within a rigorous worldview of bodily subjection, as the ring itself becomes a prison (the cords look like prison bars in the foreground). Presented as a boxer "plagued by a weak chin and the unlucky knack of being at his worst for the big ones," the character's ideal seems to crumble following his defeat. After the match, Davey appears to be given a way out of his mental entrapment and excessive bodily subjection, as he reads a letter sent by his uncle asking him to join him in his ranch near Seattle. The—somewhat awkwardly portrayed—promise of bucolic escape represented by the uncle's ranch (as evoked by the stereotypical accent of the uncle, whose voiceover is rhythmed by a lyrical musical background) contrasts with the cityscape, which has come to symbolize the oppressiveness of Davey's worldview.

However, the character is denied his escape, as his move to the countryside is prevented by his involvement in Gloria's affairs. Whereas Davey's narrative desire to portray his love for Gloria as pure may suggest this escape to be simply delayed by the character's need to save a damsel in distress, the suggestions as to the purely sexual nature of his attraction for Gloria imply otherwise. After having been entrapped within an ideology of mental control over the body that crumbled with his defeat, Davey's attraction for Gloria may reveal the character is now entrapped within its grotesque opposite: The character's body, previously repressed, controlled and mastered by his will, may now dictate his every move. Davey's mental entrapment within a prison-like diegetic world could now result from his body having taken over, Davey now being driven by his sex drive. In addition to the parallelism between his attraction to Gloria and Vince's, various elements indeed suggest Davey is now controlled by imperious corporal drives, even though the film's own narrator would like the story to suggest otherwise.

As he anxiously awaits Gloria in front of Vince's club, Davey is accosted by two street performers, who tease him and end up stealing his scarf. These two men radically contrast with Davey. His straight posture and self-composed attitude is opposed to the performers' clownish dancing and singing, so that their grotesque bodily expressions mirror the bodily drives that also threaten to enslave Davey. These performers turn out to occupy a central role, as by stealing Davey's scarf, they force the hero to leave his post and pursue them, thus making him miss his appointment with his manager, who was supposed to give him the money necessary to leave New York. As a result, Vince's men, who were ordered to kill the boxer, mistake the manager for Davey. The manager ends up killed instead, which leads both to Davey being suspected for the murder and to him actually killing Vince. The narrative disruption caused by these grotesque characters thus suggests that even though Davey refuses to depict himself as driven by his body, he may nonetheless be. The thieves might represent the way Davey's corporeal drives are perceived as an exterior force imposed upon the character. Simultaneously, the presence of characters symbolizing a part of Davey's own self highlights his reluctance to consider his drives to be an inherent part of his subjectivity, to the point that as a narrator, he can only depict them by projecting them onto someone else.

The famous fight scene opposing Davey and Vince in a mannequin store exacerbates this subtext. As Davey kills Vince in a store full of uncanny body-like objects, the character seems to be fighting with his mirror image, as both of them look equally grotesque while hitting one another with the mannequins' torn body parts. This climax opens up three contradictory interpretations of the ending. On the one hand, Davey's triumph over his grotesque double may suggest the character has managed to overcome the grotesque side of his own self, thus leading to the happy ending in which he manages to escape with Gloria to the bucolic countryside. Given how the countryside came to represent a potential escape from Davey's mental entrapment, this ending may entail Davey has managed to overcome his flawed worldview, thus paving the way for an ideal love affair with Gloria, one that would neither suffer from Vince's former ideal of total self-control, nor from the tyranny of unbridled corporeal drives that he overcame through Vince's death.

On the other hand, the fight with Vince may also exacerbate the way Davey is now fully driven by his body. By killing his double and his rival, Davey reveals himself to be Vince's equal, as killing for a woman suggests one is indeed driven by one's urges, the sex drive intermingling with the death drive.[18] Such an interpretation can be encouraged by the film's title, if one eventually chooses to consider it as an ironic pun: Davey now being a killer, his kissing Gloria in the last scene may indeed be a diegetic killer's kiss. No matter how happy the ending might seem, the fact that it could only occur through murder might ultimately imply Davey has become, like Vince, a man led by his corporal drives, be it the death drive (the murder) or the sex drive (the kiss).

Finally, Davey's very ambition to rationalize the events through a filmic narration that strives to downplay the role of the hero's bodily urges and to displace grotesque corporeal drives onto other characters may on the contrary suggest that Davey eventually remains stuck in his initial worldview. Indeed, as the filmic narration can only take place after the events depicted on screen, one may assume that Davey's escape with Gloria did not enable him to grow past the rational ideal of self-control that is originally displayed as a form of entrapment. Rémi Astruc notes how the grotesque has always been seen as a force that defies Reason, to the point that it may be considered to be what "the Other rationality is founded against."[19] Davey's attempt to deny the grotesque corporeality that had taken over his subjectivity through the course of his adventures may indeed be seen as a way for him to depict himself as a rational, self-possessed being. These last two interpretations—Davey did become a grotesque figure akin to Vince or went back to an excessively rational ideal of mental control—thus question the apparent narrative closure of the film and implicitly depict a protagonist characterized by a fundamental lack of balance that his own narrative efforts failed to hide.

To conclude, *Killer's Kiss* thus illustrates the filmmaker's aesthetics in the making, as some of the main formal and thematic characteristics of Kubrick's films may be found alongside other aesthetic paths, such as realism, that the director chose not to explore further throughout his career. Indeed, the film develops a highly subjective narrative, while simultaneously suggesting the viewer may be misguided by the narrator's biases, thus constructing a reflexive criticism of the latter's worldview that multiplies the film's potential interpretations. Thus, the events may depict the character's ideology of control of the mind over the body failing to the point that he is now driven by his urges, a fact denied by various subjective mise-en-scène choices stressing how Davey himself would rather construct the events as a self-gratifying romantic love story. Distancing the viewer from a diegetic narrator's point of view, in order to question the ideological worldview determining his subjective perception of reality, would indeed become a key characteristic of Kubrick's cinema.

NOTES

1. Joanne Stang, "Film Fan to Film-Maker," *The New York Times Magazine*, December 12, 1958, http://www.archiviokubrick.it/english/words/interviews/1958filmfan.html (accessed November 14, 2019).
2. Mario Falsetto, *Stanley Kubrick: A Narrative and Stylistic Analysis* (Westport, CT: Praeger, 2001), 105–48.
3. Gilles Deleuze, *Cinéma 2: L'image-Temps* (Paris: Editions de Minuit, 1985), 267. My translation.
4. Ibid.
5. Sam Azulys, "Stanley Kubrick: le corps et l'esprit. Volonté de puissance et *Mètis* dans l'œuvre du cinéaste," in *Stanley Kubrick: Nouveaux Horizons*, ed. Jean-François Baillon and Vincent Jaunas, 19–42 (Bordeaux : Essais, hors série no. 4, 2018).
6. James Naremore, *On Kubrick* (London: British Film Institute, 2007), 247.
7. Philippe D. Mather, "A Portrait of the Artist as a Young Man: The Influence of *Look* Magazine on Stanley Kubrick's Career as a Filmmaker," in *Stanley Kubrick: New Perspectives*, ed. Tatjana Ljujic et al., 20–47 (London: Black Dog Publishing, 2017), 46.
8. Ibid., 25.
9. Naremore, *On Kubrick*, 53.
10. Edward Branigan, *Point of View in the Cinema: A Theory of Narration and Subjectivity in Classical Film* (Berlin: Walter De Gruyter, 1984), 82.
11. Naremore, *On Kubrick*, 53.
12. Stanley Kubrick, "The Film Director as Superstar," interview with Joseph Gelmis, 1969. http://www.visual-memory.co.uk/amk/doc/0069.html (accessed November 14, 2019).
13. Daniel Worden shows how this trope influenced the Western genre from its onset, as this dichotomy was already established in the Western literature of the late nineteenth and early twentieth centuries. Daniel Worden, "The Popular Western," in *A History of Western American Literature*, ed. Susan Kollin, 111–26 (Cambridge: Cambridge University Press, 2015). George

Stevens's *Shane* (1953) exemplifies how, by the 1950s, films could self-consciously play with this dichotomy.

14. Naremore, *On Kubrick*, 63.
15. Michel Chion, *Stanley Kubrick: L'humain ni plus ni moins* (Paris: Cahiers du cinéma, 2005), 39.
16. Sigmund Freud, whose influence on Kubrick is well known, views the blurring between animate and inanimate occurring with dolls and automata as one of the main sources of the uncanny. Sigmund Freud, *The Uncanny* (New York: Penguin Books, 2003), 135.
17. Mikhaïl Bakhtin, *L'œuvre de François Rabelais et la culture populaire au Moyen-âge et sous la Renaissance* (Paris: Gallimard, 1996).
18. In his foundational study, Michel Ciment views the intermingling of the sex drive and of the death drive, or Eros and Thanatos, as a central thematic characteristic of Kubrick's work. Michel Ciment, *Kubrick* (Paris: Calmann-Lévy, 2004).
19. Rémi Astruc, *Le Renouveau du grotesque dans le roman du XXe siècle* (Paris: Classiques Garnier, 2010), 9. My translation.

REFERENCES

Astruc, Rémi. *Le Renouveau du grotesque dans le roman du XXe siècle.* Paris: Classiques Garnier, 2010.
Azulys, Sam. "Stanley Kubrick: le corps et l'esprit. Volonté de puissance et Mètis dans l'oeuvre du cinéaste." In *Stanley Kubrick: Nouveaux Horizons*, edited by Jean-François Baillon and Vincent Jaunas, 19–42. Bordeaux: Essais, hors-série no. 04, 2018.
Bakhtin, Mikhaïl. *L'oeuvre de François Rabelais et la culture populaire au Moyen-âge et sous la Renaissance.* Paris: Gallimard, 1996.
Branigan, Edward. *Point of View in the Cinema: A Theory of Narration and Subjectivity in Classical Film.* Berlin: Walter De Gruyter, 1984.
Chion, Michel. *Stanley Kubrick: l'humain ni plus ni moins.* Paris: Cahiers du cinéma, 2005.
Ciment, Michel. *Kubrick.* Paris: Calmann-Lévy, 2004.
Deleuze, Gilles. *Cinéma 2: L'image-Temps.* Paris: Editions de Minuit, 1985.
Falsetto, Mario. *Stanley Kubrick: A Narrative and Stylistic Analysis.* Westport, CT: Praeger, 2001.
Freud, Sigmund. *The Uncanny.* New York: Penguin Books, 2003.
Kubrick, Stanley. "The Film Director as Superstar." Interview by Joseph Gelmis, 1969. http://www.visual-memory.co.uk/amk/doc/0069.html.
Mather, Philippe D. "A Portrait of the Artist as a Young Man: The Influence of *Look* Magazine on Stanley Kubrick's Career as a Filmmaker." In *Stanley Kubrick: New Perspectives*, edited by Tatjana Ljujic et al., 20–47. London: Black Dog Publishing, 2017.
Naremore, James. *On Kubrick.* London: British Film Institute, 2007.
Stang, Joanne. "Film Fan to Film-Maker." *The New York Times Magazine*, December 12, 1958. http://www.archiviokubrick.it/english/words/interviews/1958filmfan.html.
Worden, Daniel. "The Popular Western." In *A History of Western American Literature*, edited by Susan Kollin, 111–26. Cambridge: Cambridge University Press, 2015.

Chapter Two

Burning Down the House in Kubrick's *The Shining*

Anne-Marie Paquet-Deyris

In the viewer's mind, much of the visual persistence of Stanley Kubrick's *The Shining* (1980)[1] has to do with the eerie framing of abnormality. Jack (Jack Nicholson), as a prime vector, is often staged poised between comedy and horror and Nicholson's visceral acting style inscribes on screen the increasingly apparent cracks plaguing him and his relatives. From the opening sequence onward, his smug face is materialized as a mask onto which real or fake emotions and reactions are being projected. The eerie correspondences between Jack's mindscape and the outside world the director and his screenwriter Diane Johnson choose to chronicle redefine a new map of violence, deviations from the socio-psychological norm, and eventually from a style of "horror" itself deviating from conventional *horror film clichés* and confounding the viewer's expectations while seemingly fulfilling them. The haunting effect seems to function very differently in Stephen King's novel and Kubrick's film, where the general breaking-down process is incarnated by Jack Nicholson. As his persona starts cracking up, he takes in the haunted space of the Overlook, visibly reshaping the hotel's historical texture and turning it palpable in a never-ending cycle of violence.

The ponderous and distorted notes of Wendy Carlos and Rachel Elkind's opening main title theme "Dies Irae" accentuate the looming sense of abnormality and doom as Jack's small Volkswagen winds its way up some increasingly deserted Rocky Mountains wilderness. Dysfunction is inscribed on screen the moment Jack starts telling Danny (Danny Lloyd) about the Donner party, oddly associating the words cannibalism and television when addressing Wendy: "it's OK. He saw it on television." His sarcastic remark already hints at the onset of his mental meltdown. In 1936, Scott Fitzgerald started his essay *The Crack-Up* with the following sentence: "[o]f course all life is a process of breaking down"[2] and charted the course of such a downward spiral. Jack's bleak reference to the Donner party is already proleptic of a similar journey toward disintegration. This chapter will explore the way in which mental and geographical displacements take over the frame and mark the explicit beginning of the whole process. It will first discuss the modes of inscription of what Stephen King calls "[A]reas of unease"[3] in his seminal book on horror, *Danse Macabre* (1981), then try to uncover what lies beneath[4] this perverse play of hide-and-seek the maze becomes iconic of, and finally, it will turn to the inscription of Jack's arrested development while analyzing the forms of still lives in the film's end sequence. This chapter will consequently seek to examine the relevance of the dissolution of the self as a critical tool to study how Kubrick reworks the conventions of the horror genre, toying with a breed of eeriness that would spring out of ordinariness and "some submerged capacity for unease"[5] but remains equivocal about the existence of the supernatural to the end.

From the start, the wide-angle, atmospheric aerial shots of Jack's small car swooping though the Rocky Mountains impose the first major variation on the maze pattern. Already, the troubling parallel between the exterior landscape and the inner one is ushered in when Danny's early monstrous visions of the elevator disgorging blood and the freakish and mute sisters in blue register on screen thanks to parallel editing. The first signs of distortion and parasitic activity are born of this quasi-simultaneous inscription of different spaces and seemingly unrelated images in the frame. As Jack keeps progressing, Danny's visions at the Denver apartment fill up the screen, *de facto* uncovering some kind of disturbing connection with the hotel's interior. The latter belong to a long tradition of representing the uncanny and the destabilizing doubling factor, which goes all the way back to the Middle Ages and its rehabilitation of the medieval grotesque as later theorized by Mikhail Bakhtin.

American photographer Diane Arbus built up an entire career framing just this variety of the uncanny in ordinary people's lives. One of her photographs, 1967's "Identical Twins, Roselle, New Jersey," used to mesmerize Kubrick. Just like Arbus, he always struggled with the inscription of identity on film. From his early film *Fear and Desire* (1953) where he has Lieutenant Cordy say, "I think we've all traveled too far from our own private boundaries . . . to come back to ourselves"[6] to *A Clockwork Orange* (1975) and *Eyes Wide Shut* (1999), he always questioned the permanence and unicity of human identity. His own quasi "still" photography of the look-alike sisters has a lingering creepy effect on the viewer and initiates a grisly solve-the-mystery game for both characters and spectators. In their first appearance as in the following ones, the girls stare straight at the camera with an enigmatic half-smile that enacts an immediate visual connection between everyday life and the uncanny, the living and the dead. It also generates what King calls endless "areas of unease" in his 1981 analysis of the anatomy of horror, *Danse Macabre*: "These 'areas of unease'—the political-socio-cultural and those of the more mythic, fairy-tale variety—have a tendency to overlap, of course; a good horror picture will put the pressure on at as many points as it can."[7]

These pressure points seem first to be emerging from some unknown and inexplicable source. They inscribe themselves uninvited as early as the title credits/prologue and the "Interview" section and quickly tie in with real social, economic, and historical tragedies. In the first section of the film, Stuart Ullman (Barry Nelson), the Overlook manager, is quick to mention the "complete mental breakdown" of Charles Grady, the previous caretaker who killed his entire family during a bout of winter "cabin fever," and that the hotel was built on an ancient Indian burial ground. The close-up of Jack's expressionless face when he learns about the murders provides the first hint of some blank page about to be filled in. The apparent disconnection between the crosscut scenes foreshadows the gradual but complete isolation Jack will fall into. Nicholson constantly accentuates the blank mask effect to render all the more palpable the physical and psychological alterations affecting his persona.

The official reason underlined by Ullman is "cabin fever," which heralds the later exchange about the Donner party during Jack's second ascent to the hotel with his wife and son. As they evoke the party members' lapse into cannibalism when crossing the Sierra Madre in the winter of 1846–1847, Jack eventually remarks on the fact that it was necessary "in order to survive." The reference already functions like a silent virus, summoning up visions of dead, deformed, and decomposed bodies subjected to the ultimate taboo of human consumption. It also ties in with the grotesque mode of representation. Jack Nicholson is at this very moment poised between genres and tones, comedy and tragedy, the real history and the ghostly world of the hotel. His predatory smile, highly mobile, alternately utterly passive and broadly expressive features are very much akin to some canvas Kubrick can infuse with increasingly grotesque effects. In his seminal analysis of the aesthetics of the grotesque in Kubrick's movies, James Naremore insists that: "In the cinema, the grotesque can be created with masks, makeup, wide-angle close-ups, or simply with the casting of actors who seem grossly fat, emaciated, or ugly in ways that make their faces potentially both comic and frightening."[8] Nicholson's masterful art of composition keenly resembles the type of "carnival freak show"[9] that so fascinated Kubrick in the work of photographers like Arbus but also Weegee. Interestingly, the latter had been chronicling the lives of New Yorkers as well as crime and accident scenes in the city for decades when he was hired as a still photographer and "technical consultant" by Kubrick on the set of *Dr. Strangelove* in 1964.[10] The impact of these close shots, at once enigmatic and gruesome, already paves the way for a complex inscription of the unknown and the unsettling.

When first told about the Grady murders Jack reacts with a slight time lag that becomes visually conspicuous and on which the viewer can project his own interpretations. His slightly open mouth when digesting the historical reality of the killing is actually one of the characteristics Naremore highlights in Rabelais's own brand of grotesque. The moment also materializes on screen the first visible impact of the grotesque effects on the main protagonist. The emotional reaction is delayed and immediately replaced by Jack's denial that such mental distress will ever affect him since he has a book to write. The displacement of the emotional response with the intellectual one is one of the processes Naremore identifies as characterizing Kubrick's representational strategy:

> one of the keys of [Kubrick's] style lies in his anxious fascination with the human body and his ability, which he shares with all black humorists and artists of the grotesque, to yoke together conflicting emotions, so that he confuses both our intellectual and emotional responses. . . . Again and again he uses grotesque effects to unsettle social norms, whether liberal or conservative, thereby inducing a sort of moral and emotional disequilibrium.[11]

Such confusion between the two types of responses foreshadows the actual representation of Jack's profound imbalance. His oddly inappropriate answer in the manager's office is the first signal of some deep disjunction, some widening gap between what his reaction should be like and what actually registers on screen. The scene somehow points at some invisible mental scape whose operative notion is that of "disequilibrium" and whose unfolding matches the opening of the various material and immaterial spaces harbored by the Overlook. The eerie correspondence between inner and outer space is indicative not only of the protagonist's increasing disorientation but also of the viewer's. On numerous occasions in the movie, Kubrick deliberately confuses the spectator by framing the voyeur's face or some metonymic object and toying with the relativity of scales. Jack is first captured merely referring to various time frames before getting literally lost between these periods. Just as the notion of time becomes relative, the scale of realistic space is also systematically remodeled to operate in synch with his increasingly unhinged perspective. What was originally discretely inscribed on Jack's questioning face in Ullman's office starts to literally take on substance. His often grotesque wolfish grin and increasingly unfocused gaze operate like some grisly mask opening onto some other parallel dimension. As the visions take flesh, Jack Torrance's progressive disengagement from family life and reality at large parallels the hotel's increasing encroachment and derealizing impact. In an odd process of circulation, the source of Jack's sense of disorientation seems to be both himself and the hotel premises. That the maze's perfectly geometric lines and orderly pattern should be proportional to his mental disorder ironically demonstrates his growing restlessness and the birth of his sporting and hunting mentality.

Its first chilling inscription consists in the fascinating and much commented-upon maze sequence, which in itself is a master class in mental and visual manipulation. As Jack is looking at the hotel maze model in the lobby, the camera seamlessly transitions to the actual maze outside where Wendy (Shelley Duvall) and Danny literally become fair game in a mind-dizzying tilt-down. The variations in scale are breathtaking as the diminutive symmetry of the model explodes first into the large-scale bird's eye-view of the actual geometric maze where toy-sized Wendy and Danny are imprisoned before returning to full size. Beyond the obvious entrapment symbolism, the sudden changes of scale render hauntingly manifest the protagonist's descent into madness. It is virtually the same process as in the titles sequence with the notable exception that the malevolent eye is now clearly identified as being—also Jack's. But the sequence's paroxysmal effect lies in the actual reduction of Wendy and Danny's sizes the minute Jack starts poring over the model. In a succession of close shots, the camera frames him scrutinizing their miniature animated figures in hunting mode. Their sizes only go back to normal once Jack has disappeared offscreen. Such a variation on scales highlights the idea that the protagonists are mere pawns to be manipulated at will in the Overlook universe.

The other key sequence displaying Jack's disturbing perspectival changes is that of Wendy's horrified discovery of her husband's real manuscript. Because the typewriter and eventually the pages themselves turn into obvious metonymies of Jack's persona, the scale variations are even more chilling. As the camera zooms in on the manuscript, then on the bundle of pages, it finally goes down to the level of one page filling up the entire screen, which is literally taken over and possessed. The close-up paradoxically imprints on the page Jack's ever-expanding mindscape. The borders of this new type of expanse become as unascribable as the nature of the expanse itself as announced by Wendy's earlier remark about the hedge maze, ominously proleptic of the magnitude of Jack's mental disturbance: "I didn't think it was gonna be this big." The endless litany of words contains slight variations on the sentence "All work and no play makes Jack a dull boy," which optimize their horrific effectiveness. In this nonsensical *infra* universe, the written sign reveals the subversion of genre conventions. The planned novel turns into a sick form of autobiography literally in the making, which in turn adds horror genre motifs to the overall family drama. Evil here is in the details: the minute displacement of and the disjunction in the words' spelling and disposition on the page further emphasize Jack's dysfunctional grasp of a complex reality and expose a sense of identity fast becoming "out of joint." The sign fully works as an in-depth replica of the shattered inner world of an individual with a disintegrating personality. Both sequences are twisted variations on the maze motif. In Greek mythology, the labyrinth represents a journey to one's center before being able to go back out into the world enlightened in one way or another. Jack's own trajectory tends, on the contrary, toward some ever-darkening center point allowing neither interface with the outside world nor any sense of higher consciousness. His itinerary partly resembles Theseus's journey into the Minotaur's Labyrinth, which somehow turns him into a heroic villain as he abandons his helper Ariadne but also indirectly causes his father's death upon returning from Crete.

In this perverse play of hide-and-seek, the maze becomes an ironic icon of what lies beneath and beyond the classic systems of boundaries, redoubling but also challenging them. As Thomas Allen Nelson underlines in *Kubrick: Inside a Film Artist's Maze*:

> Mazes are highly artificial human contrivances whose orderly and complex sense of purpose involves a twofold conceptual game in which the player must not only search for the center but *remember* how to get out. . . .Within the mazelike designs of *The Shining*, Kubrick develops a series of doubling/mirroring effects that go far beyond anything found in King's novel. And because the film so completely integrates these doublings into a narrative and visual labyrinth, the viewer-turned-critic needs a descriptive map before daring to chart any interpretative course.[12]

For Jack, finding his way in the hotel's space-time continuum is precisely what's at stake. With Jack seemingly lost in the real-life dimension, John Alcott's camera tracks him trying to reconnect with a new environment profoundly disconnected from what he used to know. His hesitant journey in between the two types of environment is closely monitored by the newly invented Steadicam (1975). Alcott's hand-held camera allows for the authentic immediacy that best captures the central tension between the matching closed circuits of the hotel and the maze and the paradoxical boundlessness of the new space Jack inhabits and his exhilarated sense of false freedom and alarm at proving incapable of escaping the Overlook. The conflict between the sense of constriction and the feeling of limitlessness becomes increasingly apparent as the pace of the filmic narrative accelerates. In the section entitled "Tuesday" and after having followed Danny pedaling by room 237, the camera takes in the majestic beauty of the golden Colorado Room and glides toward Jack typing away at his small desk. As Wendy comes in to check on him, the logistics of the "camera chase" starts reflecting his own erratic itinerary. When Wendy invades his creator's den, he raises his voice to her and is increasingly framed as a blood-crazed predator in shots that encase him. For him, time and space no longer seem to exist independently of the mind and movement becomes unpredictable, eerily mirroring his own mental circumvolutions. The hotel somehow heightens the sense of loss of bearings by impacting the characters' bodies and reinserting them in some larger, unidentified entity. Once Wendy is ousted, Jack starts typing on the keys of his typewriter harder and harder. The absence of music and the sound of the typewriter materialize on screen the crushing weight of the Overlook's influence. As in late-nineteenth- and early-twentieth-centuries Naturalist novels,[13] the environment operates like some deleterious and irresistible force. By tightening the frame from a wide shot of the vast golden lobby to Jack's desk, the camera foregrounds not only what it does to the protagonists, but also what they do to each other. They end up somehow losing themselves in some larger-than-life scheme that destroys any possibility of safe place and any form of coherent mindscape rooting them in the realistic world. The fast-deteriorating nature of their relationships, from those of a tightly knit family circle to a predator-prey relationship are enhanced by the use of the Steadicam originally meant for running and chase scenes as in *Marathon Man* and *Rocky* (1976).

Alexander Walker, Ulrich Ruchti, and Sybil Taylor underline how the lithe tracking shots of the camera, which is often at ground level but also the numerous close shots of the characters, accentuate the sense of oppressiveness: "The contrast between open and closed spaces is an important example of the duality on which the film elaborates. The variety of spaces and how they are shown are one way the film articulates its conception of metaphor and mental landscape."[14] The change of scale in the characters' inscription on screen develops into a full-fledged scale game, which is programmatic of their variously impeded courses. While Danny is tracked at ground level trying to dodge the various obstacles and threats he discerns, Jack's predatory bird-eye view of the model maze paradoxically foreshadows his own stasis to come, as if he were already stuck in some fatally arrested development. Conversely in the source novel, Stephen King has mainly chosen to materialize the thinly disguised sense of threat by featuring hedge animals closing in on the protagonists in front of the hotel. The agonizing sense of being hemmed in is much more prominent and unequivocal, something Kubrick has vigorously resisted. The horror writer has always been very vocal about his distaste of the film adaptation. In response, he scripted in 1997 Mick Garris's miniseries that he vengefully titled *Stephen King's The Shining* and had the manager Ullman tell Jack, "[i]n the winter, the Overlook is full of edges." In the three mediums then, the broken lines motif takes center stage and diversely materializes what Ullman calls the necessity "[t]o be constantly alert to any and every contingency"[15] in the novel. Just like in the book, with the material design of the labyrinth, the viewer is given a foretaste of the hindered progress of characters trapped in some troubling loops and "edges." But by toying both literally and metaphorically with the endless connotations of the words "edges" and "broken," Stanley Kubrick and his screenwriter Diane Johnson reshape their meanings into arresting visual icons. Actively resisting any form of "faithful" adaptation of the classically terrifying and supernatural source novel, they translate King's dark edges into peculiar mazes that quickly lose their traditional symbolism of gates to some higher form of consciousness. The now world-famous obsessively symmetrical geometric shapes in the carpet, rug patterns, and tortuous circuits in the hotel's kitchen or corridors seem to be inhabited with a life of their own that mimics Jack's increasingly split personality and the film's entire organic structure.

The six tightly controlled sections starting with "A Month Later" and ending with "4pm" not only materialize Jack's descent into madness but also constrict the filmic space and increasingly restrict the characters' movements until the final stasis. The key image is one of inversely proportional loss of control. Space then becomes a representational device that registers the modalities of distortion and eerie expansion of the Overlook inhabitants' lives. It manufactures chaos and the emergence of some parallel universe causes the protagonists' existences to no longer make sense, preventing any form of closure. Such manipulation of space turns their lives into what Wilfred Bion calls "non-existence[s]." Quoting the British psychiatrist on the way Evil colonizes a patient's mind, Anna Migliozzi remarks that:

> As Meltzer (1982, 1992) points out, the evil state of mind destroys the apparatus for thinking—the place for the creation of meaning—a generative sense of emotional life disappears and is replaced "by excitement shadowed by nameless dread" (Meltzer, 1992, p. 152). What remains is an ego-destructive superego (Bion, 1959, 1962), which asserts its superiority, fosters manic grandiosity and creates a silent terror. Ultimately, this object "is cruel, denuded of all the (human) characteristics . . . [and] has the characteristics of "non-existence" (Bion, 1970, p. 20).[16]

The numerous close shots of Nicholson's often strained and deformed face materialize how the seduction of evil and progressive corruption of emotional meaning drive Jack to complete confusion and suffocation. The disturbing ambiguity of his smiles, especially in the scene with the caretaker Delbert Grady (Philip Stone) in the red restroom testifies to the deliberate strategy of disorientation governing the shaping of the filmic narrative. Kubrick and his cinematographer Alcott toy with the bright artificial lighting, the past and present dimensions, and Grady's duality—Charles, the winter manager suffering from cabin fever Ullman first refers to, and Delbert, the English-style butler Jack meets in the bathroom who tells him that "[he 's] always been the caretaker." They design a sign and linguistic system that contributes to inducing a hypnotic, immersive state neither Jack nor the viewer can fully emerge from. Stripped of its connection with reality, the environment spawns a being no longer ruled by the laws of basic social interaction and logic.

Nelson also discusses Jack's "hypnotic, slack-jawed trance[s],"[17] which foreshadows his descent into madness in his chapter on "Remembrance of

Things Forgotten." Expression here functions like a mask covering up what brutally resurfaces in an array of ambiguous incarnations. Moments of realistic human pain and pure fright register on the characters' faces—as when Wendy is assaulted by Jack in the staircase of the lobby for instance—and alternate with the conventional trappings of horror fiction in which perception and focalizer are critical. The systematic inscription of the intense fear of a woman being preyed upon, her helplessness, and close ups of her terrified face are interspersed with that of the characters reacting to shots of blood gushing out, or facing the sudden inexplicable appearance of ominous-looking ghosts like the lady in the bathtub with a decomposing body in room 237. Hence the very nature of horror is rendered problematic by its generic hybridity. The maze-like kitchen Wendy remarks on upon arrival becomes the actual *locus horribilis* of the only truly supernatural event in the whole movie: the door to the walk-in freezer magically opens to free the murderous Jack from confinement. The primary consciousness and agency at work in the scene cannot be ascribed to anyone in particular and neither Wendy nor the viewer can come up with any logical explanation. The void left by the absence of normality is concomitant with the rise of a very specific breed of monstrosity. Seizing upon King's epigraph in the novel, Goya's 1797 print "The Sleep of Reason Produces Monsters," Kubrick inscribes on screen a resurgence of the monstrous vastly different from the elusive and forever resurfacing monsters of the horror genre.

Garrett Brown's mobile camera captures the protagonists at these crucial moments of profound interpretative crisis, which impact the spectators as well. He shows Danny for instance cycling by and then stopping in front of room 237 and proving unable to understand its powerful attraction. Lost in a forest of cryptic signs emblematized by the contorted rug pattern, the child—just like the viewer—cannot crack the mystery of the Overlook's sign system. At the end of the first thirty minutes, the image of the sisters in blue enacts this repeated breach of narrative logic and once again contaminates the frame for a split second. Based on excess, the system suddenly becomes undecipherable, forever unassignable, neither totally grounded in some realistic dysfunction nor completely exempt from the imprint of the supernatural. Recurring shots and scenes (the blood pouring out of the elevator) and the doubling pattern (the virtual twins, the two incarnations of Grady . . .) are characteristic of the film's structure. The latter in turn mirrors a diegesis which seems to be reenacting the same story over and over again. The resurfacing of the murdered Grady sisters or of the hotel room's ghostly lodger so radically alter the realistic frame of reference that it eventually breaks down and tangibly represents the notion of breakdown itself. Danny, for example, is repeatedly framed holding conjointly in his mind two images, which causes him to momentarily lose the ability to function. The tension created by the confrontation of the two competing storylines generates what Nelson aptly calls "crevices of unreason."[18] His yellow ball, which seems to appear out of nowhere—or, at least, out of no realistic space-time continuum—is emblematic of such fault lines and sudden holes in the texture of everyday life.

In a universe ruled by the principle of *non sequitur*, the shots of doors opening on their own mark a form of resurgence of the monstrous and arrested development that also reflects the breaches in the generic logic of the filmic narrative. They inscribe in the frame untenable and instable viewpoints and express the enigmatic precisely because these cannot be ascribed to any clear form of individual agency. Danny sees them and so does Jack but the very nature of these images remains so elusive and unreliable that they cannot capture subjectivity or convey any accurate sense of the objective.

These fragments of unmoored images contaminate the protagonists' experiences of reality to such an extent that they all seem to reach a form of arrested development. The final photograms materialize in the frame the variations on the different stages of stasis. As the camera captures Danny's desperate journey through the hedge maze to escape his father's murderous hunt, it frames him retracing his own steps in the snow to leave the frozen world behind. The only way out of this still life composition is to backtrack and his carefully documented movement is pitted against Jack's, who keeps advancing to the center of the labyrinth until he can no longer move. Structurally, this horrific image of Jack's body frozen in midstride both echoes the living corpse trapped in the bathtub of room 237 and foreshadows the revelers' perfect imitation of life in the enigmatic Fourth of July, 1921 pictures on the Gold Room's wall. What Kubrick seems to focus on in these literal *danses macabres* is the uncertain ontology of the antihero, poised between the sorrows and decrepitude inherent to the human condition and the spectacular palingenesis of the final section of the film. In the final scene, photography as a work of art captures the essence of the failed artist willing himself to become a transcendent work of art. In this sense, the indeterminacy of what he is and what he has achieved becomes the focal point for Kubrick and such ontological indeterminacy is enhanced by the movie's own generic uncertainty. For King in the source novel as well as Garris in his serial adaptation, the endeavor rather consists in inscribing the troubling incarnated reality of ghosts along a more conventional treatment of the horror genre's codes and conventions.

The film deliberately cultivates ambiguity and paradoxically validates Jack's own mental images by matching them with some of the other characters' mental projections. Because the latter also saw the revelers, the last photographs provide a troubling but still unreliable insight into the hotel's past. More precisely, they open up onto a past intersecting with and reverberating through the present and more particularly Jack's now eternal present. They incorporate him "forever and ever and ever" as the little girls in blue would say into some parallel storyline, always already there like some palimpsestic script. In this sense also, the notion of crack-up comes to the fore as the protagonist's other type of decomposition under the strain of reality is eventually erased by the eternal dimension of the photographic medium.

The question of some potential paranormal activity is therefore left purposely unresolved as the camera zeroes in on Jack in the exact center of the photograph, leaving open the possibility that it might be some uncanny doppelganger. The focalizer is once again constructed as some mysterious entity as the Steadicam zooms in and eventually singles out "Jack" to trap him in the timeless dimension of a parallel spatiotemporal framework, some discrete point in time that redoubles the previous image of the frozen Jack. He becomes the very essence of the photographic object, both long since past and ever-present, exhibiting the distinctive paradoxical attribute of the photograph Roland Barthes identifies in *Camera Lucida: Reflections on Photography* (1980) as a simultaneously immortalized and gone-for-ever dimension, containing the "having-been-there" quality of the original. And in *Art beyond Representation: The Performative Power of the Image* (2004), Barbara Bolt asks a fundamental question as she remembers Oscar Wilde's *The Portrait of Dorian Gray* (1890): "If a painting comes to perform rather than merely represent some other *thing* what is happening? . . . Does the visual image, like the speech act, have the power to bring into being that which it figures? Can the image transcend its structure as representation and be performative rather than representational?"[19]

In this perplexing end sequence, the image is not a painting but a photograph whose transcendent quality seems to bring into being some otherworldly reality and hence to function as a visual proof, palpable trace of Jack's phantasmatic life. The photo montage creates a major narrative disruption in the main plotline as it lets loose a narrative surplus, possibly what Jack has so frantically been searching for in his manuscript. It eventually takes over the filmic narrative in an ultimately destabilizing and extreme displacement that resists representation and disrupts but also exceeds the overall narrative to such an extent that it defies closure. It ironically actualizes one of Jack's greatest wishes, to be the artist in residence. In this sense, the narrative excess of the montage also enacts another meaning of *crack-up*, which is to split apart from the main narrative and become another creative force behind a parallel construction.

In his 1944 essay "The Ontology of the Photographic Image," André Bazin suggests that:

> photography is a feeble technique in the sense that its instantaneity compels it to capture time only piecemeal. The cinema makes a molding of the object as it exists in time and, furthermore, makes an imprint of the duration of the object. . . .

> The photographic image is the object itself, the object freed from the conditions of time and space that govern it. No matter how fuzzy, distorted, or discolored, no matter how lacking, in documentary value the image may be, it shares, by virtue of the very process of its becoming, the being of the model of which it is the reproduction: it is the model.[20]

Kubrick carries the presence/absence paradox to extremes as the smiling reveler in the end sequence is both a doppelgänger endlessly reenacting the horrors of the past and a mimetic reconstruction of the man Jack might have been, testifying to some ineradicable possibility of being. A manifestation of the real-life Jack, he is also another creative treatment of the filmic character thus combining photography's seminal instant and film's persistence over time. This two-fold inscription and the blurring of the boundaries between original and reproduction materialize on screen the performative dimension of the image to which Bolt refers. The effect of the final zoom-in on the picture within the frame is then to reshape the limits and reframe the master narrative so that photos and close-up eventually open onto new interpretative walks. Technically, the ultimate zoom-in on Jack's face materializes his ultimate break-up from the main narrative. He becomes the central detail in a collective and evolving whole with an internal logic of its own radically differing from the prevalent logic so far. His face is the poignant "punctum" that forever redefines Jack's existence and life story. It inscribes on screen his protean temporality and revisionist capabilities and taunts the viewer with its own fabricated and enigmatic dimension. As a fragment that broke away from the larger whole, it transcends the limits of the frame, leaving things unclosed. Operating as a synecdoche of the elusive figure in the picture and its emotional fractures, it refuses to open itself up to easy analysis and ends up being the most extreme figuration of Jack's own alienation and intractable otherness.

Like the demarcations of Jack's persona, the narrative is left forever incomplete and the film proves impossible to categorize. It may very well be this irreducible dimension that resulted in *The Shining* being selected for preservation in the U.S. National Film Registry by the Library of Congress in 2018. Forever open to interpretation and lost in its own surplus meaning, it was added to a list of twenty-four other "culturally, historically, or aesthetically significant" movies. Ironically, the question of absence of narrative closure took a literal turn when Mike Flanagan's sequel *Doctor Sleep* was released in November 2019.[21] Overstepping the limits of the final picture frame and of Kubrick's original movie in general, this new filmic narrative further actualizes the workings of the phantasmic and of what one of screenwriter Diane Johnson's characters calls "the terror of the real beneath the form."[22] It continues to create ways of engaging and misleading protagonists and viewers in a maze of remembering and reenacting storylines. As Flanagan provides identical replicas of some scenes and sets of Kubrick's Overlook Hotel from the scary sisters in identical blue dresses or the word REDЯUM appearing to the older Danny (Ewan McGregor) to the blood-filled elevator, he revisits the most iconic moments from *The Shining*. He also inscribes on screen another process of breaking down such iconicity to a new limit where the remembrance of things past becomes literalized and imposes itself on the middle-aged character and the viewer alike with a vengeance and the same terrifying visual persistence.

NOTES

1. This chapter analyzes the European version of *The Shining*.
2. Scott Fitzgerald, *The Crack-Up* (New York: New Directions Publishing, 1945). http://www.pbs.org/wnet/americanmasters/f-scott-fitzgerald-essay-the-crack-up/1028/ (accessed July 2, 2019).
3. Stephen King, *Danse Macabre* (New York: Berkley Books, 1983), 133.
4. After the title of Robert Zemeckis's eponymous film released in 2000.
5. Kyle Smith, "A Brief History of *The Shining*," *National Review*, last modified November 9, 2019, https://www.nationalreview.com/2019/11/the-shining-stanley-kubrick-great-horror-film-made-to-be-re-watched/ (accessed June 12, 2019).
6. Kubrick, *Fear and Desire*.
7. King, *Danse Macabre*, 133.
8. James Naremore, "Stanley Kubrick and the Aesthetics of the Grotesque," *Film Quarterly*, Vol. 60, No. 1 (Fall 2006): 7.
9. Naremore, "Stanley Kubrick and the Aesthetics of the Grotesque," 8.
10. Ibid.
11. Ibid., 10.
12. Thomas Allen Nelson, *Kubrick: Inside a Film Artist's Maze* (Bloomington, IN: Indiana University Press, 2000), 204–5.
13. Frank Norris's *Mc Teague: A Story of San Francisco* (1899) or Theodore Dreiser's *An American Tragedy* (1920, 1925) for instance.
14. Mario Falsetto, *Stanley Kubrick: A Narrative and Stylistic Analysis* (Westport, CT: Praeger, 1994), 80.
15. Part One. Prefatory Matters, Chapter 1, "Job Interview": https://novels77.com/the-shining/part-one-prefatory-matters-chapter-1-job-interview-996250.html.
16. Anna Migliozzi, "The Attraction of Evil and the Destruction of Meaning," *The International Journal of Psychoanalysis*, Vol. 97 (2016): 1022.
17. Nelson, *Kubrick: Inside a Film Artist's Maze*, 219.
18. Ibid., 205.
19. Barbara Bolt, *Art Beyond Representation: The Performative Power of the Image* (London and New York: I. B. Tauris, 2004), 3–4.
20. André Bazin and Hugh Gray, "The Ontology of the Photographic Image," *Film Quarterly*, Vol. 13, No. 4 (Summer, 1960): 4–9. http://faculty.georgetown.edu/irvinem/theory/Bazin-Ontology-Photographic-Image.pdf (accessed April 28, 2019).
21. Adapted from Stephen King's own belated sequel of the same name published in 2013.
22. Diane Johnson, "Talking about 'The Shining' with Diane Johnson," *Chicago Review*, Vol. 33, No. 1 (Summer 1981), https://www.jstor.org/stable/25305098, 76, accessed April 29, 2019.

REFERENCES

Allen, Graham. "The Unempty Wasp's Nest: Kubrick's *The Shining*, Adaptation, Chance, Interpretation." *Adaptation*, Vol. 8, No. 3: 361–71.
Barry, Robert. "*The Shining*'s Hauntological Score." *Electric Sheep*, December 14, 2010. http://www.electricsheepmagazine.co.uk/2010/12/14/the-shining%E2%%80%99s-hauntological-score/.
Barthes, Roland. *Camera Lucida: Reflections on Photography*. New York: Hill and Wang, 1999.
Bolt, Barbara. *Art beyond Representation: The Performative Power of the Image*. New York: I.B. Tauris, 2004. https://www.academia.edu/939327/Art_beyond_representation_the_performative_power_of_the_image.
Falsetto, Mario. *Stanley Kubrick: A Narrative and Stylistic Analysis*. Westport, CT: Praeger, 1994.
Fear and Desire. Directed by Stanley Kubrick, 1953. Films sans frontières, 2012, DVD.
Gengaro, Christine Lee. *Listening to Stanley Kubrick: The Music in His Films*. Lanham, MD: The Scarecrow Press, 2013.
Holland-Toll, Linda J. "Bakhtin's Carnival Reversed: King's *The Shining* as Dark Carnival." *Journal of Popular Culture* Vol. 33, No. 2 (Fall 1999): 131–45.
Jaunas, Vincent, and Jean-François Baillon. *Stanley Kubrick. Nouveaux Horizons. Essais. Revue interdisciplinaire d'Humanités*. Pessac: Ecole Doctorale Montaigne-Humanités / Université Bordeaux Montaigne, Hors série 2017.
Johnson, Diane. "Talking about 'The Shining' with Diane Johnson." *Chicago Review*, Vol. 33, No. 1 (Summer 1981): 75–79. https://www.jstor.org/stable/25305098.
Kagan, Norman. *The Cinema of Stanley Kubrick*, 3rd edition. New York: Continuum, 2000.
Kilker, Robert. "All Roads Lead to the Abject: The Monstrous Feminine and Gender Boundaries in Stanley Kubrick's *The Shining*," *Literature-Film Quarterly*, Vol. 34, No. 1 (January 2006): 54–62.
King, Stephen. *Danse Macabre*. New York: Berkley Books, 1983.
———. *Doctor Sleep*. London: Hodder & Stoughton, 2013.
———. *The Shining*. New York: Doubleday, 1977.
Luckhurst, Roger. *The Shining*. London: BFI Film Classics, 2013. https://www.salon.com/2018/07/08/the-6-stages-of-madness-in-the-shining/.
McAvoy, Catriona. "The Uncanny, the Gothic and the Loner: Intertextuality in the Adaptation Process of *The Shining*." *Adaptation*, Vol. 8, No. 3 (2015): 345–60.
McCaffery, Larry, and Diane Johnson. "Talking about 'The Shining' with Diane Johnson." *Chicago Review*, Vol. 33, No. 1 (Summer 1981): 75–79.
Migliozzi, Anna. "The Attraction of Evil and the Destruction of Meaning." *The International Journal of Psychoanalysis*, Vol. 97 (2016): 1019–34.
Naremore, James. "Stanley Kubrick and the Aesthetics of the Grotesque." *Film Quarterly*, Vol. 60, No. 1 (Fall 2006): 4–14.
Nelson, Thomas Allen. *Kubrick: Inside a Film Artist's Maze*. Bloomington, IN: Indiana University Press, 2000.
Rasmussen, Randy. *Stanley Kubrick: Seven Films Analyzed*. Jefferson, NC: McFarland, 2001.
The Shining. Directed by Stanley Kubrick, 1980. Benelux: Warner Home Video, 2001, DVD.
Smith, Kyle. "A Brief History of *The Shining*." *National Review*, last modified November 9, 2019. https://www.nationalreview.com/2019/11/the-shining-stanley-kubrick-great-horror-film-made-to-be-re-watched/.
Walker, Alexander, and al. *Stanley Kubrick, Director: A Visual Analysis*. New York: Norton, 1999.
Wang, Ya-huei. "Archetypal Anxieties in Stanley Kubrick's *The Shining*." *K@ta: A Biannual Publication on the Study of Language and Literature*, Vol. 13, No. 1 (1 Jan. 2011): 112–22.

Chapter Three

Kubrick's Gangster Artistry

Contradiction and Hybridity in The Killing

Carol Donelan

Stanley Kubrick drew inspiration as a filmmaker from one of his lifelong passions, chess. Prevalent in his films are references to chess and other forms of game play, chessboard visual patterns, the blocking of actors in space as if on a chessboard, and heightened attention to the timing of decisions and actions familiar to chess players. A half hour into *The Killing* (1956), Kubrick's third feature, considered his first mature work, gangster Johnny Clay (Sterling Hayden) walks into the Academy of Chess and Checkers, a mock-up of a Times Square establishment frequented by Kubrick as a teenager, in search of someone with whom to play. Johnny, in search of friend Maurice Oboukhoff (Kola Kwariani), intends to hire Maurice to play a role in a racetrack heist. He finds Maurice, a master chess player, coaching a patzer, an inept player, after a strategy blunder involving the failure to think ahead. "Stop talkin.' I can't think with all this noise!" exclaims the befuddled patzer, hesitating to make his next move.

Kubrick's characters are often confronted with the difficulty of thinking objectively within the constraints of time, environment, and resources, a theme self-reflexive of Kubrick's own experience as a director on set. In interviews, Kubrick explicitly posits an analogy between chess and the practice of directing, in that both demand "patience and discipline in choosing between alternatives at a time when an impulsive decision seems very attractive."[1] He credits chess with "sharpening his awareness of the time factor"[2] and teaching him to "think objectively rather than shoot from the hip in the noisy, confusing, high-pressure atmosphere of a film set."[3] However, Kubrick acknowledges that objective thought has limits: "Even the greatest International Grandmasters, however deeply they analyze a position, can seldom see to the end of the game. So their decision about each move is partly based on intuition."[4] Analogously, for Kubrick, the relation of analysis and intuition is a factor in directing:

> The reality of the final moment, just before shooting, is so powerful that all previous analysis must yield before the impressions you receive under those circumstances, and unless you use this feedback to your positive advantage, unless you adjust to it, adapt to it and accept the sometimes terrifying weaknesses it can expose, you can never realize the most out of your film.[5]

Ultimately Kubrick's directorial strategy is holistic, premised in thought and feeling, science and art. He masters his subject matter objectively through research and planning while exercising subjective "taste and imagination" on set.[6]

Maurice greets Johnny warmly and commiserates sympathetically, given that Johnny has just been released from prison. "It was very difficult, no?" Maurice inquires. "Yes, very difficult," Johnny responds. Thinking objectively, Maurice anticipates that Johnny is oblivious to a possibility: that despite his release, Johnny's difficulty persists, in that he remains existentially caged, having failed to acknowledge or accept that he is predetermined from without by a fate beyond his rational control, a fate premised in the irrationality of "love and death."[7] Intuiting that Johnny is a patzer, Maurice the master proceeds to coach him on accepting his limitations as a human being, which are the limitations of rational thought. Unfortunately, Maurice's heavily accented words fall on tone-deaf ears. "Yeah, like the man said, life is like a glass of tea," Johnny responds, not getting it, despite the irrationality of his mixed metaphor.[8]

Maurice's words of advice to Johnny not only address Johnny's fate, premised in the irrationality of love and death, but also that of Johnny's double, Kubrick the director, who in attempting to synthesize his art cinema–oriented expressive individuality with the conventions of classical Hollywood style and genre, risks undermining the expectations of professional collaborators and putting an end to his budding career in Hollywood. "You have not yet learned that in this life you have to be like everyone else. The perfect mediocrity," Maurice counsels. "Individuality is a monster, and it must be strangled in its cradle to make our friends feel comfortable." The self-reflexive doubling of Johnny the gangster and Kubrick the director is underscored when Maurice remarks that the "gangster and the artist are the same in the eyes of the masses, admired and hero-worshipped." And yet, there is always an unconscious desire "to see them destroyed at the peak of their growth." Is it the fate of Kubrick the gangster artist to be destroyed at the peak of his growth by collaborators dissatisfied with his choices and decisions? "There was an air of resentment all around us," recalls producer James B. Harris, who teamed with Kubrick on three films. "Stanley had his own ideas how things were to go, and people resented his encroaching on their contributions."⁹ To borrow a quote from Sartre, "Hell is other people."¹⁰

Among the collaborators with whom the twenty-eight-year-old director tangled was veteran Hollywood cinematographer Lucien Ballard. At one point, Kubrick instructed Ballard to use a 25mm wide lens and shoot up close, producing distortion in the image, in keeping with his taste for expressive stylization, taking inspiration from the films of Orson Welles. Ballard instead chose a 50mm normal lens and set up the camera at a distance from the action, seeking to eradicate the distortion, in keeping with classical style. Feeling bullied, Kubrick quietly told Ballard to do what he asked or leave the set. Ballard complied and there was no more trouble. Another collaborator, hardboiled writer Jim Thompson, credited with contributing dialogue, complained to the Writers Guild that he was not properly credited as coauthor of the screenplay, attributed solely to Kubrick. Although Kubrick made up for it by hiring Thompson to coauthor the screenplay on his next film, *Paths of Glory* (1956), he developed a reputation for not respecting writers. At a sneak preview of *The Killing* during postproduction, Sterling Hayden's agent Bill Schifrin complained that the fragmented structure of the plot hurt his client's performance. Under pressure, Kubrick and Harris recut the picture in chronological order, but concluded that "it stunk." The fragmented, looping, non-chronological plot is what inspired them to adapt Lionel White's 1955 pulp novel *Clean Break* in the first place. They reassembled the film the way they had it and delivered it to United Artists, where it was screened by executive Max Youngstein, who also expressed concerns about the complicated plot structure. Pressing Youngstein to rank them as a producer-director team, Youngstein replied, "not far from the bottom."¹¹

Youthful doubles Johnny-Kubrick have much to learn, but each is capable of thinking objectively, as evidenced in the highly rationalized plan-plot of *The Killing*, which interweaves the actions of multiple characters on an imaginary chessboard toward convergence at the start of the seventh race, the one mile $100,000-added Lansdowne Stakes. Johnny enlists older friend and father figure Marvin Unger (Jay C. Flippen), a racetrack bookkeeper, to finance the heist set-up by skimming from the proceeds at the track. Marv is guaranteed a return off the top in addition to an equal share of the stolen loot. No further involvement is expected of Marv—nor of United Artists, the studio putting up $200,000 to produce the $320,000 film, necessitating that Harris-Kubrick Pictures Corporation come up with $120,000-added. "Keep away from the track. Go to a movie or something," Johnny-Kubrick instructs. Collaborators Nikki Arano (Timothy Carey) and Maurice, hoods with specialized talents, are hired for flat fees to create diversions during the seventh race—Nikki by shooting a horse (cinematographer Lucien Ballard, "a man with your eye would hardly need a sight") and Maurice by initiating a bar fight (writer Jim Thompson, who loves Kubrick despite his taste for mixed metaphors), while other members of the (film) crew, track cashier George Peatty (Elisha Cook Jr.) and track bartender Mike O'Reilly (Joe Sawyer), work behind the scenes to ensure Johnny's access to the backroom office containing the safe. Johnny is to bag the dough and toss it out the window to crooked cop Randy Kennan (Ted de Corsia). Randy is to deposit the bag in Johnny's motel room, relying on the no-questions-asked complicity of motel manager Joe Piano (Tito Vuolo). Johnny is to deliver the cash to a designated location for distribution to members of the gang. Each member of the gang-film crew constitutes a "thread" in the "unfinished fabric" of the plot, each having "as much effect on the final outcome as a single piece of a jumbo jigsaw puzzle has to its predetermined final design," according to the voice-over narration (Art Gilmore). This commentary aligns with Kubrick's belief that the plot of a feature film need only supply six to eight autonomous "non-submersible units," each unit self-contained, of interest in itself, apart from its relation to the other units.[12] A screenwriter or director need not worry about the connections between the units. Rather, it is up to viewers to make the connections and construct the meaning of the story, thereby "revealing whether the picture [is] as he guessed it would be," according to the voice-over narration.

Inasmuch as each member of the gang constitutes an autonomous plot unit, ironically, no one exists within his unit autonomously. Each gang member is motivated or predetermined from without, by his responsibility to someone else. Therein is the story. Randy is responsible to his loan shark Leo (Jay Adler); Mike, to his sick wife Ruthie (Dorothy Adams); George, to his bored wife Sherry (Marie Windsor), and by complicating extension, her boyfriend Val Cannon (Vince Edwards). "None of these men are criminals in the usual sense," Johnny explains to Fay. "They all live seemingly normal, decent lives, but they got their problems." Paraphrasing Sartre, problems are other people. Johnny is himself responsible to Fay, and by complicating extension, Marv. Despite evidencing a capacity for objective thought, Johnny is denied subjective intuition about the story-complicating extensions of plot premised in fate, in the irrationality of love and death, as represented by Marv and Sherry. He does not know that Marv is a closeted homosexual and is interested in him. He does not know that Sherry is pumping George for information and reporting everything back to her boyfriend Val, who along with sidekick Tiny (Joe Turkel), plans to follow George to the meet-up location and steal the money. Johnny is limited to authoring the plot without knowing the story, in keeping with fate.

Everything works up to a point, in accordance with Johnny's-Kubrick's rationalized plan-plot, despite eruptions of irrationality rooted in their failure to understand or account for the whole of human identity with respect to love and death, not to mention differences of sexuality, gender, and race. Therein is the story. Marv shows up at the track drunk after "breaking up" with Johnny on the morning of the heist—but inadvertently helps Johnny avoid arrest by stumbling in front of a track cop. Randy is momentarily delayed by a woman in a bathrobe seeking the help of a patrol officer during a domestic dispute—but arrives at his assigned position at the track on time. Nikki is shot and killed by a track police officer shortly after racially disparaging a Black parking lot attendant (James Edwards)—but succeeds in his assigned task of shooting Red Lightning. Despite these unplanned occurrences, none impede the success of the rationalized plan-plot. All members of the gang—Marv, Randy, Mike, and George—convene at the designated meeting place as expected to await Johnny's arrival at 7:00 p.m. At 7:15, with no sign of Johnny, George expresses concern: "Everything runs on a timetable till it comes to payin' our shares. Then the timetable breaks down." A knock at the door raises expectations but it is Val and Tiny rather than Johnny who burst through the door. Impulsively, in a split-second decision premised in the constraints of time, environment, and resources, George "the jerk" shoots from the hip, killing Val and setting off a chain reaction. The resulting gunplay leaves everyone "on set" dead except George, who stumbles out onto the street just as Johnny arrives at 7:29, "still fifteen minutes late," according to the voiceover narration, which adopts the pretense of authoritative objectivity conventional of 1940s documentary and newsreel voice of God narration, but which is unreliable, as Johnny is now close to a half-hour late for the 7:00 p.m. rendezvous, having been delayed for fifteen minutes due to traffic around the track and for another fifteen minutes for which there is no accounting, and which "does not bear much looking into" if we are to abide by Maurice's admonition, lest we "go blind" staring at the screen "like the Siberian goat-herder who tried to discover the true nature of the sun." A temporal error on the part of the unreliable narrator also started the day, with Johnny breaking up with Marv "at 7:00 that morning" and arriving at the airport to purchase tickets in preparation for his escape with Fay at "exactly 7:00 a.m." that same morning, which is not possible. The upshot: from 7:00 a.m. on the morning of the heist to the scheduled meet-up at 7:00 p.m. that evening, the reliability of the voiceover narration is undermined by the story of fate, by the irrationality of love and death, putting Johnny-Kubrick out of sync with his rationalized plan-plot—out of sync with himself, with all that he is—from beginning to end.[13]

All Johnny-Kubrick can do is proceed to a contingency plan, which involves no more foresight than saving himself and the money. In contrast, Maurice the master strategist thinks ahead and does what he can, given the constraints of time, environment, and resources, to consider possibilities beyond his control and intention.[14] Anticipating one such possibility, the outcome of his role in the heist, Maurice leaves contact information for his lawyer with Fischer, the manager at the Academy of Chess and Checkers.

The assumption is that after a brief stint in jail for disorderly conduct, Maurice will be set free literally and existentially, released from jail and already accepting of his fate as a human being, which are the limits of rationality. In contrast, Johnny is to remain caged, locked up in prison and unwilling or unable to accept the workings of irrational fate in himself or in his "foolproof plan." Once the rationalized plan-plot breaks down, like George the jerk, all Johnny the gangster (and Kubrick the gangster artist) can do is shoot from the hip in response to irrational events befalling him from without, over which he has no control. The suitcase Johnny buys at a pawn shop and stuffs with stolen cash has a faulty lock and is too big to carry on the flight that will take him and Fay to freedom. Seemingly without choice, he checks it. In a chance occurrence, a poodle named Sebastian breaks free from her doting owner on the tarmac and runs in front of the baggage truck, which swerves. The suitcase falls off the truck and breaks open. All the money is scattered by the wind from the jet engines. "What's the difference," Johnny exclaims in existential resignation, just before he is captured and escorted back to prison. Failing to recognize the difference between choosing and not choosing his fate, between accepting and not accepting all that he is, which is limited to authoring the plot without knowing the story, Johnny-Kubrick the patzer remains existentially caged, the fool in the foolproof plan, lying to himself about himself to the bitter end.

Kubrick's epistemology of directing, which entails synthesizing objective thought and subjective taste and imagination, informs the style of his films, which are grounded in realism but skew toward authorial expressionism, toward foregrounded artifice and exaggeration.[15] In interviews, asked to address the relation of content and style in filmmaking, Kubrick repeatedly cites Chaplin and Eisenstein, with Chaplin representing realism, "all content, no style," "just get the image on the screen," and Eisenstein representing expressionism, "all style, no content," producing beautiful films that have "silly, moronic" stories. "Obviously, if you can combine content and style," Kubrick concludes, "you have the best of all possible films."[16]

Generically a heist film, *The Killing* is modally a film noir.[17] Among the conventions of film noir is the contradiction of styles, realism and expressionism.[18] Influenced by Italian neorealism and documentary newsreels, film noir shifted attention from high-class people and the artifice of studio settings to ordinary people in real-life location settings, making use of a newsreel-style voiceover narration. An influx of talent from Europe to Hollywood in the 1920s and 1930s also had a stylistic impact on film noir, importing techniques associated with German expressionism, including chiaroscuro lighting and subjective camerawork. James Naremore and András Bálint Kovács both position film noir as a transition step between the melodramatic realism of the classical Hollywood cinema and the modernism of the European art cinema.[19] As a film noir, *The Killing* is a hybrid, stylistically; a classical Hollywood modern art film. As such, it evidences the transformation of old Hollywood as it absorbs the influence of the art cinema and makes way for the emergence of the New Hollywood of the late 1960s to early 1980s, within which many of Kubrick's subsequent films are positioned, including *2001: A Space Odyssey* (1968), *A Clockwork Orange* (1971), *Barry Lyndon* (1975), and *The Shining* (1980).

Conventional of the art cinema, according to David Bordwell, is a loosening of narrative causality.[20] In the classical cinema, things happen for a reason, effects have causes, the narrative is motivated; in the art cinema, things happen for no apparent reason, effects lack obvious causes, the narrative is under-motivated. To fill gaps in narrative motivation, viewers of art cinema must look beyond the narrative, to style. Bordwell proposes that art cinema narratives are motivated by two things: realism and authorial expressivity. Realism, which encompasses a range of stylistic possibilities, justifies narrative gaps created by chance occurrences or characters who lack defined goals as realistic, as in keeping with real life. Authorial expressivity contrasts with the classical cinema's transparent or invisible style in that the art cinema's stylistic flourishes call attention to the medium and can be read as authorial commentary. Gaps in narrative motivation, disconnects between plot structure and story meaning, are typically justified in authorial commentary as in keeping with *la condition humaine*. And yet, these two means of motivating the art cinema narrative—realism and authorial expressivity—are contradictory, as that which purports to be realistic is not explicitly authored. The art cinema's solution to the problem of stylistic contradiction is ambiguity. Viewers confronted with gaps in narrative motivation first seek realistic motivation and, failing that, authorial motivation. The art cinema hesitates to resolve the contradiction, thereby maximizing ambiguity for viewers.

The Killing manifests the stylistic contradiction of realism and authorial expressivity conventional of the art cinema as described by Bordwell. Kubrick's path to realism includes long takes and composition in depth, techniques often associated with the art cinema–oriented "reborn realism" of the 1940s prized by French critic André Bazin, who famously valorized Hollywood directors Orson Welles and William Wyler and Italian directors Roberto Rossellini and Vittorio de Sica for "giving back to the cinema a sense of the ambiguity of reality" undermined by the rise of classical cinemas in Hollywood and France in the 1930s, which favored motivated narratives premised in tight cause-and-effect logic.[21] Central to Bazinian reborn realism is temporal duration, wherein the "duration of actions" on screen is aligned with "real time, in which things exist"—wherein reel time equals real time.[22] Temporal duration invites viewers to perceive film as analogous to reality itself, which has an ambiguous plot, is not automatically meaningful, and puts the burden of responsibility on us to supply the story meaning. In *The Killing*, Kubrick uses long takes primarily to preserve the integrity of actors' performances in real time. Long takes are especially notable in the scenes featuring Sherry the femme fatale interacting with her husband George and, alternately, boyfriend Val. However, Kubrick maintains a temporal flow in all dialogue scenes, punctuating these interactions with classical shot-reverse shot dialogue cutting and camera reframing motivated by figure movement. He also uses a wide lens to create more depth of field in the image than is typical of classical style, in this way generating "ambiguity of reality" in not only temporal but also spatial terms.

In addition to organizing time and space in *The Killing* to maintain the ambiguity of reality central to an art cinema–oriented Bazinian reborn realism, Kubrick uses expressive style to comment authorially on that reality, equating it with the game of chess. Among the techniques he uses to rationalize the flow of time expressively, countering the realism of long takes, is voiceover narration, which foregrounds the chunking and non-chronological reorganization of time, skipping with the rhythm of a chess timer from "3:45 on Saturday afternoon in the last week of September" with Marv at the track, to "about an hour earlier that same Saturday afternoon in another part of the city" with Randy attending to business with loan shark Leo, to "7:00 p.m. that same day" with Johnny romancing Fay in Marv's apartment, to "a half an hour earlier, at approximately 6:30" with Mike arriving home to Ruthie, to "7:15 that same night" with George arriving home to Sherry. Each gang member in not only positioned in time by the voiceover narration; he is also positioned in space by lateral tracking shots of varying lengths moving left to right—in the opposite direction of the tracking shots of the horserace depicted in the opening credit sequence, in which a horse named Stanley K is competing. The lateral tracking shots, which go through walls, position gang members as if they are chess pieces occupying squares on a game board, their moves predetermined by their identities as pawns, rooks, and knights. Rectilinear lines and grids—the horizontal results board at the track, the vertical bars of George's ticket window, the striped décor in the bar where Randy meets Leo, the grid of shadows cast from the windows in Marv's apartment, the checkered shirt worn by Mike—evoke the grid of the chessboard.[23] Elements in the spatialized deep-focus mise en scène contribute to our understanding of the characters. Maurice the chess master's rectilinear mise en scène, featuring an oversized chessboard window frame, contrasts with Nikki the crook's crooked one, featuring a ramshackle house, convertible sports car, and pockmarked gun target. Whereas Maurice is inclined to think objectively, to plan his moves, his double Nikki relies on subjective taste and imagination, shooting from the hip.

The set-up of the game board concludes with Sherry's visit to Val, which is untimed, significantly, given that it occurs outside of Johnny's plan, and the converging of all members of the gang in time and space at 8:00 p.m., 504 W Olive St, Apt 4B, to coordinate the heist. Having outmaneuvered diminutive pawn George and tricky knight Val as they mobilized around her in long takes, Sherry the queen interrupts the gang's meeting and checkmates Johnny the king. Their interaction, which takes place on a bed, is viewed through the vertical iron bars of the footboard, expressing Johnny's entrapment, like the caged bird in Sherry's apartment. This set-up is reversed, viewed through the bars of the headboard, when Johnny breaks up with Marv on the same bed. Johnny is imprisoned by fate, by the irrationality of love and death, as is every human being, man and woman, head to toe.[24]

Inasmuch as Kubrick uses style expressively, rationalizing reality in accordance with objective thought, like a chess master, contradictorily, he also uses style to comment on the impossibility of rationalizing and controlling reality, given the irrationality of fate premised in love and death. In the contradictory worldview of Kubrick the gangster artist, the classically motivated plot of reality will always be undermined by the art-cinema story of fate. This leads to what James Naremore aptly pinpoints as the aesthetics of the grotesque, "blackly humorous" visions, prevalent throughout Kubrick's oeuvre, designed to "provoke emotions such as shock, disgust, horror, obscene amusement and perhaps even sadistic pleasure."[25] In *The Killing*, Kubrick engages the aesthetics of the grotesque to comment on the limits of human rationality, to goad thinking viewers into feeling, especially in relation to that which human beings are most defended against, the irrationality of love and death.

The closer to death in *The Killing*, the more grotesque the imagery. It starts when Johnny hires sharpshooter Nikki. Whereas Johnny's hiring of Maurice at the end of act one is "strictly a muscle job, no gunplay," his hiring of Maurice's double Nikki at the beginning of act two involves "bumping off a horse." That horse, Red Lightning, "the best three-year old to come along in years," "a winner who won't pay even money 'cuz half the people will be down on him," doubles Stanley K, the horse introduced in the opening credit sequence. However, neither bumping off a horse nor taking out the director of a film is a crime. "In fact, I don't know what it is," Johnny remarks to Nikki. Johnny's hiring of Nikki introduces not only the motif of gunplay, but also that of the clown who holds, transports, and/or uses a gun to bring about death. The clown motif is advanced in act two through close-ups of Nikki, George, and Marv. Each actor distorts his face grotesquely while gesturing toward, touching, or covering his face with his hand, signifying that his character is in the position of choosing between love and death. Nikki loves his dog; George loves Sherry; Marv loves Johnny. The clowns all choose death. Kubrick forgoes the use of close-ups in favor of medium shots in the representation of Mike's clown identity. Mike dons a falsely cheerful demeanor on the morning of the heist, covering his face not with his own hand but Ruthie's when he bends to kiss it. Johnny hides a gun in a box of long-stemmed flowers, conventionally delivered to loved ones, and delivers it to a bus station locker. Mike picks up the box and delivers it to the track, stashing it in his locker. A medium long shot of Mike standing in the inky darkness of the track locker room, lit by a single diegetic ceiling lamp, staring directly at the camera, underscores the significance of his choice: flowers for Ruthie or gun for Johnny. Mike the clown chooses death. Meanwhile, Randy's relation to guns requires no elaboration; a crooked cop who carries a gun is by definition a clown.

The clown with a gun motif leads to spectacles of the grotesque, visions of irrational fate premised in love and death, enacted upon the body, distorting it. Nikki shoots Red Lightning, horse and jockey tumbling in a grotesque pile-up of animal and human flesh. Nikki is killed by a track cop, flopping over the side of his convertible like a dead fish, a horseshoe given to him by the Black parking lot attendant piercing his whitewall tires like a fish hook. Grotesque spectacles of death alternate with grotesque spectacles of love. Marv, who loves Johnny, shows up at the track stumbling drunk, making a spectacle of himself, in grotesque violation of Johnny's rationalized plan. Maurice, who loves Johnny despite his taste for mixed metaphors, initiates a bar fight, a grotesque fleshly spectacle. It takes half a dozen track cops to take out shirtless hairy bear Maurice, although it is strictly a muscle job, no gunplay. Standing in the inky darkness of the track locker room, lit by a single diegetic ceiling lamp, it is Johnny's turn to choose: flowers for love or gun for death. Johnny chooses death, displacing the flowers and donning the clown mask like the metaphor-mixing patzer that he is. Holding up the track office, he mugs for the camera in a grotesquely distorted close-up. He escapes death, but not his crew, who are held up by Val and Tiny, two more clowns bearing arms, to which George impulsively responds in kind, killing Val and setting off a chain reaction of gunplay that results in a grotesque pile-up of bodies, all crooked flesh and all dead except George. A mobilized subjective camera takes over, operated by Kubrick but attributed to George's point of view, as he surveys the scene, his masterpiece, the apotheosis of the grotesque spectacle. The feeling of the scene is enhanced by George-Kubrick's heavy breathing and a jazz score dominated by bleating trumpets, composed by Kubrick's high school friend Gerald Fried. Sound style in this scene is no less contradictory than the visual style in *The Killing*, oscillating from the realism of the voiceover narration, aligned with objective thought, to the authorial expressionism of subjectively embodied, non-linguistic sounds such as breathing and music, aligned with the irrationality of fate and its grotesque consequences.

His clown face pockmarked with buckshot, George stumbles home to find Sherry packing her bags for her planned escape with Val, doubling Johnny's planned escape with Fay. Declaring his love, George shoots Sherry, death substituting for love, Sherry's pain in the stomach substituting for the "hole in the head" she previously attributed to George. "It's not fair," Sherry declares, collapsing dramatically, with grotesque style. "I never had anybody but you. Not a real husband. Not even a man. Just a bad joke without a punchline." Like Johnny, Sherry is limited to authoring the joke (plot) that is her life, without knowing the punchline (story). She fails to accept her fate and take responsibility for herself, for all that she is, which is limited. Instead, she blames George. Holding tightly to the bird cage stand for support, George the squawker pitches forward grotesquely, clown face first, and dies, the downed parrot parroting Sherry's belief that life "ain't fair."

Structurally a third term, the grotesque spectacle visualizes a deep-seated original problem premised in the myth of Oedipus.[26] The problem has to do with a contradiction in understanding regarding the origins and identity of human beings in the transition from nature to culture, from animal to human being, from four-legged to two-legged existence. The contradiction is ultimately irresolvable, resulting in a hybrid figuration: the grotesque half-animal, half-human Sphinx. *The Killing* is a modern story-complicating plot-extension of the ancient myth of Oedipus, functioning on the level of myth to negotiate the contradiction of our enculturated human versus natural animal selves, as evidenced in the prevalence of animal imagery—a caged bird represents fated human beings, beloved pet dogs are treated like human beings, racehorses stand in for Johnny and gang members, director, and film crew. The outcome of the inability to resolve the irresolvable contradiction of our enculturated human versus natural animal selves is a hybrid figuration, the clown with a gun. Nikki, George, Marv, Randy, and Johnny are hybrid identities, clowns with guns, unable or unwilling to accept or take responsibility for all that they are, human and animal, thinking and sensing, rational and irrational. If only Johnny the clown with a gun (hybridity) had understood and embraced the irrationality of the mixed metaphor (hybridity) he offers to hairy bear Maurice the chess master (hybridity) rather than lying to himself about himself from beginning to bitter end: in the contradictory worldview of Kubrick the gangster artist (hybridity), like the man said, life is indeed like a glass of tea (hybridity). The structure of irresolvable contradiction and proliferating hybridity in content and style is the key to understanding the identity of the classical Hollywood modern art film (hybridity) that is *The Killing*.

NOTES

1. Alexander Walker, *Stanley Kubrick, Director: A Visual Analysis* (New York: W. W. Norton, 1999), 11.
2. Ibid.
3. Michel Ciment, *Kubrick: The Definitive Edition*, trans. Gilbert Adair (New York: Faber and Faber, 1982), 196.
4. Ibid.

5. Philip Strick and Penelope Houston, "Modern Times, an Interview with Stanley Kubrick," in *Stanley Kubrick: Interviews*, ed. Gene D. Phillips, 126–39 (Jackson, MS: University of Mississippi, 2001), 133.

6. Ibid., 131 and 134.

7. Leaving for the racetrack, Maurice remarks to Fischer, the manager at the Academy of Chess and Checkers, that "there are some things that do not bear much looking into" because they are irrational, "including love and death, and my business for today."

8. "Life is *like* a glass of tea" is actually a simile. "Life *is* a glass of a tea" is a metaphor. However, in popular discourse, the phrase "mixed metaphor" has a familiar ring, whereas "mixed simile" does not.

9. Gene D. Phillips, "The Killing," in *The Stanley Kubrick Archives*, ed. Alison Castle, 290–97 (Köln: Taschen, 2005), 296. James B. Harris produced three films for Kubrick under the banner of Harris-Kubrick Pictures Corporation, including *The Killing* (1956), *Paths of Glory* (1957), and *Lolita* (1962).

10. "Hell is other people," a well-known quote by French existential philosopher Jean-Paul Sartre, is from his play *No Exit* (1943). The quote expresses the idea that we are locked into a particular kind of being and deprived of our freedom by the presence and gaze of others.

11. The anecdotes about Kubrick's interactions with collaborators Lucien Ballard, Jim Thompson, Bill Schifrin, and Max Youngstein are from Phillips, "The Killing," 297.

12. British science-fiction writer Brian Aldiss, who wrote the short story upon which the Kubrick-produced Steven Spielberg film *A.I.* (2001) is based, refers to Kubrick's interest in "non-submersible units" of plot in the documentary *Stanley Kubrick: A Life in Pictures* (2001), directed by Jan Harlan.

13. Mario Falsetto speculates about the temporal errors in *The Killing* in *Stanley Kubrick: A Narrative and Stylistic Analysis* (Westport, CT: Praeger, 1994), 12. James Naremore somewhat misses the point about the temporal errors in the film when he suggests that the shootout between George and Val shortly after 7:15 p.m. is anomalous in relation to the following sequence depicting Johnny's arrival at Joe Piano's motel "forty minutes before, at 6:25." A flashback is not the same thing as a temporal error in the plot. See James Naremore, *On Kubrick* (London: BFI, 2007), 73.

14. Maurice and Johnny are story-complicating plot extensions of the ancient Greek myth of Prometheus and Epimetheus, twin brothers who personify the relation of logos and mythos, reason and the senses. Maurice is like Prometheus, the god of foresight, the clever one who thinks ahead, whereas Johnny is like Epimetheus, the god of hindsight, the foolish one who forgets to think ahead.

15. Thomas Allen Nelson refers to the relation of epistemology and aesthetics in Kubrick's oeuvre in *Kubrick: Inside a Film Artist's Maze* (Bloomington, IL: Indiana University Press, 2000), 18.

16. Maurice Rapf, "A Talk with Stanley Kubrick about *2001*," in *Stanley Kubrick: Interviews*, 75–79, 79; Strick and Houston, "Modern Times," 135.

17. Daryl Lee outlines the history of the heist film as genre and discusses *The Killing* and two other heist films from the 1950s, *Rififi* (Jules Dassin, 1955) and *Bob le Flambeur* (Jean-Pierre Melville, 1955), as allegories of collaborative creative activity.

18. Paul Schrader, "Notes of Film Noir," in *Film Noir Reader*, ed. Alain Silver and James Ursini, 53–63 (New York: Limelight Editions, 1998), 55; Foster Hirsch, *Film Noir: The Dark Side of the American Dream* (New York: DaCapo, 1981), 53.

19. James Naremore, *More than Night: Film Noir in its Contexts* (Berkeley, CA: University of California Press, 1998), 48; András Bálint Kovács, *Screening Modernism: European Art Cinema, 1950–1980* (Chicago, IL: University of Chicago Press, 2007), 246.

20. David Bordwell, "Art Cinema as Mode of Film Practice," in *Film Theory and Criticism: Introductory Readings*, eighth edition, ed. Leo Braudy and Marshall Cohen, 580–88 (New York: Oxford University Press, 2016), 582.

21. André Bazin, "The Evolution of the Language of Cinema," in *What is Cinema? Volume One*, ed. Hugh Gray, 23–40 (Berkeley, CA: University of California Press, 2005), 37.

22. Ibid., 39.

23. The lateral tracking shots that go through walls and the prevalence of horizontal and vertical lines in the mise-en-scène of *The Killing* were inspired in part by *Le Plaisir* (Max Ophüls, 1952). Kubrick was a fan of Ophüls's trademark moving camera and expressive mise-en-scène.

24. That Johnny is caged like the bird in Sherry's apartment is subsequently underscored when he stockpiles gear in one of the wooden motel "birdhouses" managed by Joe Piano.

25. Naremore, *On Kubrick*, 25. Naremore counters Thomas Allen Nelson's interpretation of *The Killing* as an existential parable with the argument that the most immediate effect of the film is emotional rather than philosophical-intellectual. Naremore's statement is valid in the context of his argument about the aesthetics of the grotesque in Kubrick's oeuvre. However, I propose that the effect of *The Killing* is ultimately not either-or but rather both-and, both philosophical-intellectual and emotional, given the proliferation of contradictions on both levels, (intellectual) content as well as (emotional) style. See Naremore, *On Kubrick*, 33 and 79.

26. Claude Lévi-Strauss, "The Structural Study of Myth," *The Journal of American Folklore*, Vol. 68, No. 270 (October–December 1955): 434 and 440.

REFERENCES

Bazin, André. "The Evolution of the Language of Cinema." In *What is Cinema? Volume One*, edited by Hugh Gray, 23–40. Berkeley, CA: University of California Press, 2005.
Bordwell, David. "The Art Cinema as a Mode of Film Practice." In *Film Theory and Criticism: Introductory Readings*, 8th edition, edited by Leo Braudy and Marshall Cohen, 580–88. New York: Oxford University Press, 2016.
Ciment, Michel. *Kubrick: The Definitive Edition*. Translated by Gilbert Adair. New York: Faber and Faber, 1982.
Falsetto, Mario. *Stanley Kubrick: A Narrative and Stylistic Analysis*. Westport, CT: Praeger, 1994.
Hirsch, Foster. *Film Noir: The Dark Side of the American Dream*. New York: DaCapo, 1981.
Kovács, András Bálint. *Screening Modernism: European Art Cinema, 1950–1980*. Chicago, IL: University of Chicago Press, 2007.
Lee, Daryl. *The Heist Film: Stealing with Style*. London: Wallflower Press, 2014.
Lévi-Strauss, Claude. "The Structural Study of Myth." *The Journal of American Folklore*, Vol. 68, No. 270 (October–December 1955): 428–44.
Naremore, James. *More than Night: Film Noir in its Contexts*. Berkeley, CA: University of California Press, 1998.
———. *On Kubrick*. London: BFI, 2007.
Nelson, Thomas Allen. *Kubrick: Inside a Film Artist's Maze*. Bloomington, IL: Indiana University Press, 2000.
Phillips, Gene D. "The Killing." In *The Stanley Kubrick Archives*, edited by Alison Castle, 290–97. Köln: Taschen, 2005.
Rapf, Maurice. "A Talk with Stanley Kubrick about 2001." In *Stanley Kubrick: Interviews*, edited by Gene D. Phillips, 75–79. Jackson, MS: University of Mississippi, 2001.
Schrader, Paul. "Notes of Film Noir." In *Film Noir Reader*, edited by Alain Silver and James Ursini, 53–63. New York: Limelight Editions, 1998.
Stanley Kubrick: A Life in Pictures. Directed by Jan Harlan. Burbank, CA: Warner Bros, 2001, DVD.
Strick, Philip, and Penelope Houston. "Modern Times: An Interview with Stanley Kubrick." In *Stanley Kubrick: Interviews*, edited by Gene D. Phillips, 126–39. Jackson, MS: University of Mississippi, 2001.
Walker, Alexander, with Sybil Taylor and Ulrich Ruchti. *Stanley Kubrick, Director: A Visual Analysis*. New York: W. W. Norton, 1999.

Chapter Four

Adapting *Lolita*

Hybridizing and Subverting Genre Conventions

Gilles Menegaldo

Vladimir Nabokov and Stanley Kubrick share, apart from their passion for chess and music, an interest in genre. The novel *Lolita* plays with fictional autobiography, crime fiction, fairy tale, travelogue, comedy, melodrama, etc. Before adapting it in 1962, Kubrick had already dealt with film noir (*Killer's Kiss*, 1955; *The Killing*, 1956), war film (*Fear and Desire*, 1953; *Paths of Glory*, 1957) and peplum (*Spartacus,* 1960). He was to go on experimenting with these or other genres (science fiction, horror, period piece). It is thus not surprising to find in his *Lolita* an experimentation with filmic genres present in the novel, but also traces of other generic formulas, narrative patterns, metaphors, formal devices, and visual and sound motifs.

This hybridizing process is already marked in Nabokov's novel. The full title, *Lolita or the Confession of a White Widowed Male* conjures up several genres, a variety of narratives and writing modes. The word "confession" harks back to the tradition of introspection and subjectivity, autobiography, real or fictitious, but also the analysis of a sense of guilt and atonement. The term "white widowed male" suggests "sexual confessions," as found in eighteenth-century pornographic novels such as *Memoirs of a Woman of Pleasure* (John Cleland, 1748) or recent ones like *The Sexual Life of Robinson Crusoe* (Humphrey Richardson, 1962), even if Nabokov suggests that his novel has little to do with that tradition. The presence of a foreword written by John Ray, a fictional psychiatrist, evokes medical case studies and confers a documentary value upon the testimony. The "story of a life," presented as authentic, is close to the Bildungsroman, with a picaresque bent because of the tribulations of the protagonist who narrates his experience. The novel adopts a structure of criminal investigation and plays upon the conventions of crime fiction and enigma narrative in which Nabokov introduces a variation. Since we know the identity of the murderer who is in jail, the traditional "whodunit" pattern is replaced by a "what dun he?" However, the reader does not know who the victim is even though Nabokov gives us clues that we identify only on second reading. The intertextual network evokes other genres such as melodrama, tragedy, fairy tales, theater, satire, and poetry. Nabokov disseminates allusions and references,[1] either implicit or explicit, to cinema, both as art, cultural product, or industry. He invokes devices (projection), but also stereotypes (the Hollywood kiss). Lolita herself is partly defined in relation to cinema, as starlet or femme fatale, eventually as a potential actress in "art" films as suggested by Quilty.

A study of *Lolita*'s opening scene will show how Kubrick mixes the codes of film noir, Western, gothic, and burlesque, setting the tone for the mingling of genres and moods that characterizes the film. We will then focus on the way in which Kubrick plays with genre conventions, mainly film noir, melodrama, and satire, often subverting or undermining them through irony, parody, and pastiche, echoing Nabokov's strategies of hybridization.

Kubrick starts throwing red herrings, answering spectators' expectations in order to better frustrate them. In the credit sequence, the combination of the title "Lolita" (whose erotic connotations have been enhanced by paratexts and artifacts, especially film posters with the nymphet's heart-shaped glasses and lollipops) and the sensual, intimate images, suggests a love relationship based on worship,[2] with a touch of fetishism. On a blurry backdrop of satin curtain, a naked female foot descends into the frame in close shot from the top right of the screen and is caught in the palm of a male left hand, entering from the bottom left. The right hand delicately inserts a tuft of cotton between the first and second toe and applies nail polish on the big toenail, then proceeds with the other toes while the credits unroll. The name Kubrick appears as paint is applied to the little toenail. The musical score, with string instruments and piano, conveys a romantic mood, playing the Lolita theme. The spectator is asked to participate in this intimate ritual suggesting submissiveness on the part of the male character, who remains offscreen like the female one, thus triggering curiosity as to their identity.

The opening scene conveys a different mood. After a fade to black, the sequence opens on a long shot of a grey, foggy landscape. The camera tracks forward upon a solitary car, keeping a distance, as if someone were following the car. A dissolve leads to a closer shot as an unidentified man drives toward a large mansion. With the third shot and another dissolve, the camera is set inside the huge hall of the mansion while the driver at the back of the frame (Humbert, James Mason) pushes the unlocked door open. These shots are evocative of a crime film while the musical score, with its eerie, almost dissonant sounds and its mysterious harpsichord melody conveys a dreamlike, uncanny atmosphere. The arrival in front of this mansion—whose owner is Quilty (Peter Sellers) as we soon discover—a baroque replica of a medieval castle, with its crenellated turrets, evokes the opening of *Citizen Kane* (Orson Welles, 1941), with the same misty atmosphere, tracking shots and dissolves leading us inside the house. This opening may remind of the fairy tale or gothic motif of the innocent visitor of an unfamiliar place, emblematized by Renfield's arrival at castle Dracula in Tod Browning's film (1931).

The interior arrangement of the house provides another shock, with its heterogeneous furniture and decorative patterns, its profusion of artistic artifacts from various periods and cultural realms, a true shambles akin to what is found in Kane's Xanadu castle or the decaying villa of Gloria Swanson in *Sunset Boulevard* (Billy Wilder, 1950). Apart from the mass of accumulated objects (such as paintings, statues of women, sculptures, vases, mirrors, rugs, stuffed animals, musical instruments, a harp, a piano) belonging to different styles and periods, what strikes the eye is the incredible disorder that prevails, betraying the owner's lifestyle. Empty bottles scattered on the floor, dirty glasses and dishes, ashtrays full to the brim with cigarette butts. All this contrasts with the presence of spectral sofa covers suggesting that the house is empty, which is belied by the abundant traces of previous meals and drinking binges. One last uncanny trait is the incongruous presence of some objects like the ping-pong table and the boxing gloves, a few traces of modernity in a place that looks more like a desacralized museum, full of fake artifacts close to authentic works of art, thus connoting the upstart status of the owner, a scriptwriter for television (not a playwright). The spectator is slightly lost, confronted with contradictory signs. Humbert's arrival and his shouting "Quilty" twice suggests a quest pattern. When Humbert draws a gun, he introduces the murder motif induced by the desire for retribution. At this moment, we come close to film noir, which often starts (*Mildred Pierce*, Michael Curtiz, 1945) or ends (*The Killers*, Robert Siodmak, 1946; *The Lady from Shanghai*, Orson Welles, 1948) with a murder scene motivated by revenge or rivalry in love, which brings us back to the credit sequence and the yet unknown couple. After a series of confrontations and a half comic, half grotesque chase, the sequence closes on Quilty's murder presented elliptically, partly to humor the censors.

The novel stresses the physical contact between the two antagonists and uses gore effects (the bloody bubble forming on the lips of the victim) in a scene both burlesque and grotesque where Quilty seems indestructible. Kubrick euphemizes the violence of the scene by having Quilty crawl on the floor and hide behind a large painting, in the style of Gainsborough, representing a young smiling woman. Humbert shoots and kills Quilty through the canvas, leaving several holes on the body and face of the model. Thus the spectator does not see the corpse and no blood is visible, Quilty gripping the frame before he collapses. In retrospect, this young woman may evoke the "love triangle" with Lolita (Sue Lyon), standing between Humbert and Quilty as the portrait stands between the murderer and his victim. The way the painting is punctured by bullets may also represent Lolita's body abused by Humbert. At the end of the film, Kubrick replicates the first shots with significant variations. There is one bottle left instead of two on Quilty's armchair. The scene is cut short even before Quilty's emergence from behind the armchair cover while Humbert shouts out "Quilty!" The film closes, however, on a close-up of the punctured portrait reminding us of the murder while a caption announces Humbert's death in prison. As Lara Delage-Toriel states: "The painting also directs our attention towards the triangular relationship between Lolita, Quilty and Humbert. The intimate connection between Quilty and Lolita is suggested by the fact that when the first bullet hits the girl's dress, it is Quilty who moans with pain, as though this were his crowning histrionic act, a case of ventriloquism."[3]

Here, Kubrick verbally and visually conjures up various genres, some of which he already experimented with. When drunken Quilty states he is Spartacus, it is a wink to Kubrick's *Spartacus*. Quilty drapes himself in a sheet, toga-like, and mentions "civilized senators," referring to "Roman ping-pong" instead of gladiators' fight and a ping-pong table as a circus arena. Crime fiction is conjured up: the man with a gun, the gloved hands to mask fingerprints, the avenger's stance, the chase throughout the room, the series of bullet shots. The Western is invoked with Quilty's imitation of an old-timer reminiscent of characters played by Walter Brennan in Howard Hawks's Westerns. The boxing gloves are an allusion to *Killer's Kiss*, but they refer more widely to a subgenre of the crime movie (*The Champion*, Mark Robson, 1949; *Body and Soul*, Robert Rossen, 1947). Quilty's proposal of rewriting a love song (incongruously based on Chopin's *Great Polonaise*, 1834), conjures up musical comedy and its lyrics: "The moon was blue and so are you, and I to-night, she's mine, yours . . . she's yours to-night." These words evoke romantic clichés and crisscross lovers' adventures while the posture of the pianist is a cliché of the Western. Quilty also mentions the theater, boasting of his fifty-two plays. The scene is burlesque, relying on a number or verbal and physical gags and visual props. The end is dramatic, though violence is euphemized, Quilty reminding us he is aware of genre distinctive features: "I know all about this sort of tragedy and . . . comedy and fantasy and everything." This prologue sets the tone for the mingling of genres and moods, reflected in the critical reception following the release of the film defined as tragi-comedy or "black slapstick."[4]

Kubrick uses the strategies of film noir[5] (retrospection, confessional narrative, voiceover), devices such as the use of *chiaroscuro* and projected shadows, and also some dramatic springs (the fleeing couple, manipulation and treachery, pursuit and revenge, insanity) and specific character types (the "femme fatale"). However, *Lolita* clearly departs from the film noir for reasons we shall outline. Kubrick also plays with the conventions of melodrama, often associated in classic Hollywood cinema with film noir. Both noir genre and melodrama are subverted by borrowings from other genre conventions, in particular those of burlesque and screwball comedy. The musical score is partly modeled upon generic codes, as illustration or exacerbation of these codes, as element of characterization linked to a specific genre or as ironic counterpoint.

The reference to crime fiction is explicit in the novel, which plays upon a strategy of suspense despite the revelation of the criminal's identity. Nabokov's script and Kubrick's film, by placing the murder scene at the outset, disclose the identity of the victim, thus foregrounding the character of Quilty, making him easily identifiable by the spectator. Both script and film leave aside the motivations of the murderer, hence the necessity of retrospection. Nabokov's novel quotes Poe's Auguste Dupin and Conan Doyle's Sherlock Holmes, and crime movies like *Brute Force* (1947), Jules Dassin's prison film or Curtis Bernhardt's *Possessed* (1947). Other films are identified through their labeling "underworld movies" or descriptive passages such as the final chase of the criminal through the sewer network of the city in *He Walked by Night* (Alfred Werker/Anthony Mann, 1948).

Kubrick exploits two main devices of the film noir, retrospective narration and voiceover, as he did in *Killer's Kiss* and *The Killing*. These devices are used either for a narrative of investigation (*The Killers*; *Murder My Sweet*, Edward Dmytryk, 1944) or a confession narrative (*Double Indemnity*, Billy Wilder, 1944), or a combination of both (*Out of the Past*, Jacques Tourneur, 1947). If *Lolita*'s retrospective narrative, composed of a single flashback fragmented by many fades to black, rather conforms to the norm, the murder scene is staged objectively and not mediated by Humbert. The flashback is not introduced through the medium of the narrator's consciousness by means of a camera movement or a tracking shot or a zoom on the face suggesting a plunge into the character's consciousness (as in Edgar Ulmer's *Detour*, 1945), or the use of a dissolve or fade to black—but by means of an informative caption: "Four years earlier." Humbert's voiceover assumes a different status.

In film noir, the protagonist is shown in the frame and the source of the voice is identified. In *Double Indemnity*, Walter Neff (Fred MacMurray) faces us while he records his statement. Sometimes, the film proposes a delayed identification as in *The Postman Always Rings Twice* (Tay Garnett, 1946). We know the identity of the narrator who at times addresses us in voiceover but it is only at the end of the film that the time and place of utterance are revealed, the prison where Chambers (John Garfield) awaits his execution. In Kubrick's *Lolita*, the only reference to Humbert's present situation is given by a caption announcing his death while in the novel the reader knows that Humbert tells his story from his prison cell. Moreover, Humbert's narrative voice is far from confessional and its status changes at each of the six occurrences. We are very far from the subjectivity of the film noir which at times even gives us access to the character's unconscious through the medium of his dreams (*Murder My Sweet*) or hallucinations (*Possessed*).

Lolita borrows narrative devices such as the crime motif also expressed in Charlotte's (Shelley Winters) fantasized murder, the flight motif, the narrative of a couple on the run, trying to escape from the police or a criminal gang. This motif, inspired by the biography of gangsters like Bonnie Parker and Clyde Barrow, is staged in *They Live By Night* (Nicholas Ray, 1949), *The Asphalt Jungle* (John Huston, 1950) and its pastoral and tragic end, or *Gun Crazy* (Joseph Lewis, 1949). Kubrick stages the flight of the Humbert/Lolita couple, pursued by a mysterious character (Humbert never identifies him while the spectator is given clues), but this chase triggers another flight, that of Lolita and Quilty, who run away, taking advantage of her stay at a hospital. This pattern structures both the textual and filmic narrative, harking back to a previous model, the gothic novel, often built upon the flight and pursuit motif leading to a dramatic end. Nabokov's novel multiplies the allusions to the Pole and Mary Shelley's *Frankenstein* (1818), structured like *Lolita* on a double flight and chase pattern. Quilty chases Humbert, who chases him in turn and hunts him down. Kubrick reminds us of this, in the drive-in sequence, by means of a quotation from a scene of Terence Fisher's *The Curse of Frankenstein* (1957), conjuring up another genre, the horror film.

Kubrick also takes up the narrative pattern of manipulation/betrayal so pregnant in film noir, for instance in *The Killers* where the Swede (Burt Lancaster) is betrayed by Kitty (Ava Gardner) and Colfax (Albert Dekker), Kitty's lover. In *Lolita*, Humbert manipulates Charlotte and Lolita at first, then is fooled by the nymphet with the help of Quilty, who impersonates various characters in order to destabilize Humbert. The disappearance of the heroine, another narrative device that in the novel induces Humbert's quest retracing Quilty's peregrinations, is not exploited, Kubrick only preserving the denouement. However, Kubrick invokes another important feature of *noir*, the rivalry between women, especially between mother and daughter, which feeds the plot of *Double Indemnity* and *Mildred Pierce*. In *Lolita*, this rivalry is staged at various moments, in particular in the drive-in scene with the hand motif, but it is also perceptible through Charlotte's aggressive behavior toward her daughter.

Kubrick exploits decorative aspects of the film noir. He uses the *topos* of the big mansion serving as a backdrop for murderous confrontations. Quilty's imitation castle is similar to Mildred Pierce (Joan Crawford)'s old mansion bought from Mexican aristocrat Monte Beragon (Zachary Scott), who becomes her lover and is shot by her jealous daughter. The last shootout in *The Killers* is staged in a similar mansion, the staircase motif reinforcing the intertextual link. Quilty is shot on top of a staircase like Colfax while Kitty

Collins implores the dying man, trying in vain to exonerate herself. Apart from the imposing character of the setting, which dwarfs human beings (as in *Citizen Kane*), Kubrick plays with a claustrophobic use of space, presented as a prison or a trap. In his use of light effects, he comes close to noir aesthetics by using low-key lighting while the global tonality of the film is high-key, a realistic flat kind of light, with "glossy"[6] effects where lighting is distributed evenly on the settings and the characters.

Conversely, the low-key sequences take place in restricted spaces like the bedroom at the Enchanted Hunters' hotel or the room where Quilty, masquerading as Dr. Zemph, the school psychiatrist, awaits Humbert in almost complete darkness (only his hands are visible) so as to startle him and make him feel guilt and fear in order to persuade him to allow Lolita to participate in his play. The same kind of lighting is used for the motel bedroom where feverish Humbert receives Quilty's nightly phone call. The shadows of the venetian blinds are projected upon the furniture of the room and the characters as in *Double Indemnity*. Kubrick plays upon bodily and facial fragmentation, suggesting behavioral ambivalence and the ambiguity of feelings. When Humbert attempts to slide into Lolita's bed, his face is partly lit, partly hidden in darkness, which underscores the duplicity motif typical of film noir, but usually associated with the femme fatale. Here Humbert acts as the duplicitous male on several occasions, in particular with Charlotte. However, Kubrick makes little use of the mirror motif, usually seen in film noir as a sign of narcissism, ambivalence, and identity trouble, while Nabokov underlines in his script the presence of the mirror in his bedroom scene: "There's a double bed, a mirror, a double bed in the mirror, a closet door with mirror, a bathroom ditto, a blue-dark window, a reflected bed there."[7] The hospital scene introduces the trope of psychological disturbance, verging upon insanity. Kubrick plays upon two kinds of light. On the one hand, when a hysterical Humbert is maintained on the ground by a doctor and two nurses, contrasted lighting enables an expressionistic play upon lengthened, distorted shadows that express the threat of the medical institution and Humbert's paranoid anxiety and panic when he realizes the loss of Lolita, taken away by a so-called "uncle." The other mode of lighting erases the contrasts, privileging a cold, clinical white light, conforming with the nature and function of the place. The feeling of unease is emphasized by the great depth of field that endows the hospital space with a labyrinth-like dimension.

Lolita and film noir both foreground the female object of desire. Lolita is constructed, to some extent, as an equivalent of the femme fatale insofar as her physical appearance triggers immediate desire. In film noir, the first vision of the seductive woman is either preceded by a shot of the male watching offscreen, which makes the spectator eager to get the reverse shot on what fascinates him, or followed by a shot on his desiring look, to which the spectator adheres because he already saw the object of the look. Another important device is the fragmentation and delayed revelation of the body. In *Double Indemnity*, Phyllis Dietrichson (Barbara Stanwyck) is first discovered in long shot, her body only covered with a large towel, but hidden behind the staircase. A medium close-up on the male character Walter Neff suggests this was a subjective shot. The scene then alternates high angle shots of him and low angle shots of her until she walks away to get dressed. In *The Postman Always Rings Twice* while Frank is waiting, a slight noise attracts his attention, that of a lipstick rolling on the floor. Following the direction of his look, the camera glides upon the floor patterned with a network of shadows and focuses on a woman's bare legs. The camera then moves up slowly, revealing Cora, white-clad with shorts and turbaned hat, her perfect body inscribed within the door frame, in full light, like an angelical vision. Garnett uses another artifact, a powder compact containing a mirror in which Cora checks her make-up, ostensibly refusing to look at Frank, but conscious of being watched by him.

Apart from the credits foregrounding the nymphet's foot, Kubrick offers two main moments of contemplation of Lolita's body, associated with the diegetic male gaze: her first appearance in the garden and the hula-hoop sequence. Lolita is first filmed in broad daylight, her whole body filling the frame. No obstacle prevents contemplation. Kubrick also chooses to show her as if she were focalized by Humbert, then reveals through editing that Humbert, who is just about to go out, discovers the nymphet after the spectator. Kubrick thus aims at dissociating Humbert's point of view from that of the spectator, giving some advantage to the latter in terms of information and knowledge as he often does, particularly in scenes featuring Quilty. Contrary to what happens in most noir films, Lolita is not only an object of the male gaze, but also a subject of the gaze. Filmed in close shot, she removes her sunglasses, observing Humbert at length with a malicious smile, her eyes turned toward the offscreen and the camera. This reversibility of the look can be found in film noir, but rarely staged so ostentatiously. In the hula-hoop sequence, Lolita is foregrounded as a performer in a spectacle offered to Humbert who pretends to be reading while he peeps at her. However, the situation is not dramatized, contrary to some moments of theatrical, choreographic, or musical performance in noir films. For instance, in *The Killers*, Kitty Collins sings a love song, under the fascinated look of Ole Anderson. In *Gilda* (Charles Vidor, 1946), Rita Hayworth performs the famous striptease with her long gloves in front of a largely male audience. In those scenes, the narrative stops, time is suspended to allow contemplation and seductive magic to operate. In Kubrick's film, this suspension is reduced to a minimum and the charm is broken by Charlotte's sudden unwanted intrusion, using her flash to take a snapshot of "relaxed" Humbert.

The reference to *noir* is prolonged in another filmic genre, the road-movie[8] that is not yet constituted at the time of the film's release. However, some tropes are already present as they are in some gangster or noir films (Edgar Ulmer's *Detour*), with the murderous or suicidal escapade motif. In *Lolita*, this aspect is not as foregrounded as it is in Nabokov's novel, yet the car motif is important and Humbert and Lolita undertake two different trips, driving through wide landscapes, staying at motels, being chased by a mysterious car, etc. Kubrick inserts shots that were filmed in the United States, using rear-projection, while most settings are filmed in England.

While Kubrick tends to subvert the film noir mood by means of burlesque elements and/or an exaggerated grotesque treatment of characters, he also undermines the conventions of melodrama, often associated with crime fiction in Hollywood, by reverting to parody and reversing certain roles and motifs. Like the novel, the film contains some melodramatic elements, staging a story of transgressive passion leading to a dramatic end while it also provides a parodic version of that romantic passion with Charlotte's infatuation with Humbert, who is obviously not attracted. Kubrick multiplies the references to the main features of the genre: Charlotte's jealousy, dealt with in a comic way when she asks her husband about his previous female conquests or Humbert's more morbid jealousy when he forbids Lolita to go out with boys. Kubrick stages various crises within the two couples, also displaying a range of emotions: fascination, anger, tears, pathos. He exploits the conflicting relationship between mother and daughter, an important *topos* of the genre, feeding upon the Hollywood heritage. It may be a relation of protection as in King Vidor's *Stella Dallas* (1937) where Stella (Barbara Stanwyck), the proletarian mother, clothed in gaudy, vulgar garments, pretends to discard her daughter and sacrifices herself in order to ensure her future within the privileged bourgeois milieu of her father and her new stepmother. More often, the conflict is motivated by a love rivalry as in *Mildred Pierce* or *Possessed*, two films that associate melodrama and noir. Those films like *Lolita* stage a love triangle in which a man seduces the mother, then the daughter, or seduces the mother only to possess the daughter.

The plot of *Possessed* is even closer to *Lolita*'s since the heroine of the film is, like Humbert, blinded by her passion and seeks (or pretends to) the vanished object of her desire. At the outset of the film, the female protagonist is in a state of mental disorder, wandering through the streets in quest of her former lover. The retrospective narrative will tell the spectator that she already killed her lover and that her insanity triggers her hallucinations. Quilty's murder also expresses criminal madness, though it is not dealt with in a melodramatic way. It is rather the last meeting between Humbert and Lolita that brings us closer to the genre.

The film contains other tropes of the genre that are mostly dealt with by means of parody or irony. Charlotte's death, which could have constituted a melodramatic moment, is elided. The accident takes place offscreen and we are only given a fleeting vision (one subjective shot) of the corpse shrouded in a cloth. Humbert learns about his wife's death through a phone call while he tries to humor her, thinking she is sulking upstairs in her bedroom, and fixing a strong drink for them both. Before being bumped off, Charlotte sheds bitter tears, eyes half-closed, clutching the urn containing the ashes of her former husband, but these tears are rather perceived as ludicrous and pathetic. Moreover, this unexpected death, far from being traumatic, is a relief for Humbert. Lolita is absent and will later express her grief at the beginning of their first road trip. The only traces of melodrama following the accident are found in the reactions of the Farlow couple feeling sorry for Humbert and fearing he may commit suicide (melodrama motif) as a gun filmed in close-up lies beside him. However, that fear is ridiculed as Humbert is perfectly at ease, in a kind of drunken elation, enjoying his hot bath, with a glass of whisky on his hairy chest. He clearly has no suicidal impulse. The gun, ostensibly exhibited and which almost served as a criminal weapon, is a mere decoy for unwanted inquisitive visitors. Like Nabokov, Kubrick dispenses with a wedding scene, using Nabokov's phrase: "The wedding was a quiet affair"[9] as well as with the mourning ceremony that is often dramatized in melodramas (Douglas Sirk's lavish scene in *Imitation of Life*, 1959). However, he keeps the melodramatic tribute to Harold Haze's memory (Charlotte's pathetic discourse and relative fidelity oaths), but with an ironic bent when Charlotte lays the blame on her husband ("Why did you die on me?") or on a burlesque mode with the visual gag of the funerary urn on which Humbert rests his hand, then swiftly withdraws it with a grimace, when he becomes aware of the true nature of the object. James Naremore states: "Her bedroom conversations with Humbert represent some of the novel's ability to shift suddenly from comedy into pain . . . in the cleverly written scene in which Charlotte soliloquizes to the ashes of her late husband Harold . . . she manages to elicit a degree of compassion alongside the satire."[10]

Lastly Kubrick conjures up an essential melodramatic motif, that of the letter, a narrative drive that often takes the form of a confession read in voiceover by its author as in Max Ophüls' *Letter to an Unknown Woman* (1948). According to Jean-Loup Bourget, melodrama implies a belief in the power of the letter: "In melodrama, the letter is an intuition of the spirit and the primary unity of the letter and the spirit is restored."[11] This belief is both confirmed and denied in *Lolita*. It is first denied and even ridiculed regarding Charlotte's love letter to Humbert. In the novel, that letter is reconstructed by Humbert's selective memory, condensed, commented, even altered by a change of lexis (Humbert uses the word "vortex" which Charlotte would not use). Humbert thus exposes Charlotte's maudlin sentimentality and pitiful naïveté. In the film, the letter is an object whose contents is read aloud by Humbert, who does not alter its meaning. An ironical distance is established by Mason's reactions and acting style, his little chuckles, his laughing out loud. The convention implying that the letter should be taken seriously is made fun of as well as Charlotte's outpour of bitter reproaches and threats after having discovered the true feelings of Humbert when reading his diary. Conversely, Lolita's final letter, more factual, sober, and laconic, is taken seriously by Humbert and by Kubrick, who stages it ostensibly. The white page fills the frame and the whole typing process is recorded by the camera (in one single static shot, no music, no camera movement), which adopts Lolita's point of view, even if Kubrick deprives the spectator of the sound of her voice. Lolita's plight is melodramatic. She is a poor young orphan, victimized by a sexually abusive stepfather, seduced and abandoned by another pervert. She is also married and pregnant, calling for help by sending a terse but moving letter to the same stepfather who is her lover, protector, and jailer (Humbert assuming all these roles), in order to get financial support.

The last meeting[12] is closest to melodrama. There is a gap between Lolita's relative indifference and Humbert's strong emotional involvement. Humbert seems unable at first to confront reality. Still convinced that Lolita cares for him, he refuses to take into account the mere facts, even after she confesses her love of Quilty, and offers her to start afresh with him: "I want you to live with me and die with and everything with me." When she refuses for obvious reasons (she is pregnant, does not want to betray her husband), Humbert eventually gives up, devastated. He expresses his grief by covering his face with his hands and starts crying, giving her the money he had brought for her while the Lolita theme is heard, increasing the pathos. Seated on a sofa, Lolita and Humbert are filmed in three successive two-shots, the camera getting closer each time. The proximity of their bodies is belied by Lolita's unease and Humbert's deep sense of loss. Refusing her comfort, he evades the touch of her hand, gets up (and out of the frame), and runs madly outside. Humbert appears as a sacrificial figure, inverting the roles of classic melodramas where it is usually the female character who sacrifices herself, like the mother in *Stella Dallas*. Mason's acting is quite subtle and moving and he becomes more of a tragic figure, which for once triggers the spectator's pity. However, this is not a tragic ending. Humbert leaves knowing the name of his rival and tormentor and he intends to avenge himself. Hence the circular structure and the reiteration of part of the murder scene. Lolita is left to her trivial existence, deprived of her nymphet's aura. Contrary to the novel, where she dies in childbirth, Kubrick makes no mention of her death. However, the film ends on the Gainsborough-style portrait of a young woman punctured by Humbert's bullets and hiding Quilty's corpse.

Like Nabokov's novel, Kubrick's film is quite humorous, offering a satirical approach of American society, borrowing from the tropes of the comedy of manners and screwball comedy. This aspect prevails in the first part of the film around the discovery by Humbert of Charlotte Haze's "petit bourgeois" milieu and social mores. The satirical dimension appears from the outset in the visit of the house, filmed in long takes, crane shots, and lateral tracking shots following closely the movements of the two characters, Charlotte leading Humbert through a cramped maze-like space. The mise en scène highlights Charlotte's seductive attempt. Dressed in tight-fitted garments (black leotards, jumper and leopard-skin belt), she strives to stay close to a reticent Humbert, who tries to avoid her and recoils ostensibly from her opulent body. The soundtrack expresses Charlotte's vulgarity. She speaks loudly and continuously (Humbert hardly says a word, simply nodding), flushes the toilet, however asking Lolita to lower the sound of her radio. Kubrick plays with the comic contrast between the refinement of the European intellectual, conveyed by Mason's body language and voice, and the suburban banality and lack of taste of Charlotte. Richard Corliss evokes "Mason's sepulchral beauty, good manners of breeding, understatement, sufferance. And the famous voice: the plummy diction that could make the most egregious proposition like a royal summons."[13] Mason has already proved worldly and cynical in *North by Northwest* (Alfred Hitchcock, 1959), charismatic and mythical in *Pandora and the Flying Dutchman*, (Albert Lewin, 1951), tortured and unbalanced in *Bigger than Life* (Nicholas Ray, 1956).

Charlotte Haze is the prototype of the conformist American middle-class woman who would like to give of herself an image of culture and European sophistication. This tropism is expressed through her artistic choices, the copies of Impressionist masters that adorn her bedroom (Dufy, Monet, Van Gogh) and her obsession of social appearances signified also by her dream of employing a true French maid, the utmost sophistication for her. This fantasy triggers Humbert's anger since the potential maid is supposed to literally take up the place of Lolita (her room), who would then be out of reach, hence the verbal rebellion of the "submissive" husband, defining himself with a hard voice as a "bronzed glamor boy." Charlotte pretends to belong to a cultural elite. She boasts of being the "chairman of the Great Books committee," one of her speakers being Quilty. Her snobbishness and pretention are already stigmatized by Nabokov, who defines her bitingly as: "The definitive artsy-craftsy suburban lady—the culture-vulture, that travesty of Woman, Love and Sexuality."[14] Charlotte's ignorance is attested when she puts on the same level two famous doctors, one real, Dr. Schweitzer, the other fictional, Dr. Zhivago, the hero of Pasternak's eponymous novel (1957). This motif of ignorance and cultural snobbery is present in Hollywood's comedies like George Cukor's *Born Yesterday* (1950).

The satire of American society is manifested in the description of local manners, in particular on the occasion of the school dance where Quilty first appears in the flashback. Charlotte goes to him abruptly, interrupts his dance with dark-clothed Vivian Darkbloom (Marianne Stone), and reminds him of their short affair, but Quilty has a more vivid remembrance of her daughter: "Didn't you have a daughter with a lovely name? Yeah, what was it now? A lovely, lyrical, lilting name like . . . Lolita, Lolita, that's right. Lolita, diminutive of Dolores . . . the tears and the roses." We meet Charlotte's neighbors, John and Jean Farlow (Jerry Stovin, Diana Decker) who beyond their polite behavior, express covertly a kind of loose morality and sexual drive. John puts his hands around Charlotte's waist, suggesting they might "swap partners" while Jean encircles Humbert's wrist, stating: "When you get to know me better, you'll find I'm extremely broad-minded. In fact, John and I, we're both broad-minded." However, Jean averts her eyes when she surprises Humbert naked in his bathtub. This reaction denotes a form of hypocrisy. Humbert appears ill at ease with those sexual innuendoes and he tries to isolate himself, seeking refuge on the balcony from where he observes Lolita as we discover as the camera tracks back upon him.

Charlotte's desperate will to seduce Humbert is comically asserted in the scene where she takes advantage of Lolita's absence to drag, after "a cozy little dinner for two" and pink champagne, a reluctant Humbert into an awkward cha-cha dance. Attired with a "risqué" low-cut leopard-skin dress, Charlotte, under the pretext of teaching Humbert new steps, almost forces him to dance. The scene is filmed in one long take, Humbert, seeking to escape from Charlotte's embrace, being stuck to the wall and hitting, ironically, a copper warming pan (used for bed sheets). This undesired contact may be seen metaphorically as a refusal of the relationship, but also as proleptic of the future wedding. While Humbert looks offscreen with an expression of relief, a reverse-shot reveals Lolita in long shot, seemingly amused. After the wedding, the mood changes but the side-stepping motif recurs in the scene where Humbert finds refuge in the bathroom, locking himself up. Kubrick alternates shots of Humbert writing his diary and vaguely grunting in answer to his wife's queries and shots of Charlotte, waiting behind the door and whining pathetically: "I am lonesome!" This play with proxemics, the invasion of private space, the awkward relation of Humbert with objects he bumps into (the Mexican folding screen), drops (the bullets) or struggles with (the bedroom cot), gets close at times to slapstick. The love triangle is dealt with in a humorous, ironical way where social satire is associated with screwball comedy, with tinges of burlesque.

Kubrick feeds on literary and filmic references taken from the novel, but also on the Hollywood heritage. He deals with genre conventions in various ways, imitating and challenging them, using in particular genre hybridity, incongruous juxtaposition, parody, burlesque, and grotesque distortion. Being unable because of censorship to render the erotic, transgressive dimension of the novel, Kubrick uses innuendo, both verbal and visual, and strategies of indirection. *Lolita* invites the spectator to shift his mode of perception and reading, at times favoring identification with Humbert, at times imparting a critical and ironical distance. The "pervert" motif is toned down by means of film noir tropes. Lolita becomes more of a femme fatale than a nymphet and Humbert more of a victim than a predator; hence the use of melodrama. The foregrounding of Quilty and his many masks introduces a grotesque, at times almost uncanny touch while social satire is expressed through the tropes of the screwball comedy. Kubrick, like Nabokov, plays with the spectator, also using metafilmic allusions (like the film within the film or frame within frame shots) or other allusions to spectatorship (the voyeur motif), but here Humbert loses the privileged status he had in the novel and also his authority as narrator/writer of his own story.

NOTES

1. Alfred Appel, *Nabokov's Dark Cinema* (Oxford: Oxford University Press, 1974).
2. This scene evokes *Scarlet Street* (Fritz Lang, 1945) where Chris Cross (Edward G. Robinson), an old bank clerk, paints the toenails of a much younger Joan Bennett.
3. Lara Delage-Toriel, "Shadow of a Double: Taking a Closer Look at the Opening of Kubrick's *Lolita*," *Miranda* (online journal), Toulouse Jean-Jaures University, no. 3 (2010): 4.
4. Pauline Kael, *I Lost It at the Movies: Film Writings 1954–1965* (New York: Marion Boyars, 1994), 205.
5. See Cristelle Maury's article "Traces du film noir dans *Lolita*, Stanley Kubrick 1962," *Miranda*, no. 3 (2010): 1–14.
6. Cinematographer Oswald Morris stated he used the MGM filters to give *Lolita* the "Hollywood gloss" wished by Kubrick.
7. Vladimir Nabokov, *Lolita: a Screenplay* (New York: Vintage International, 1997), 98.
8. See Anne Paupe's article "La place de la route dans *Lolita* de Nabokov à Kubrick," in *Lolita*, ed. Didier Machu and Taïna Tuhkunen, 239–49 (Paris, Ellipses, 2009).
9. Vladimir Nabokov, *The Annotated Lolita* (London: Penguin, 1995), 74.
10. James Naremore, *On Kubrick* (London: BFI, Palgrave Macmillan, 2007), 107.
11. Jean-Loup Bourget, *Le mélodrame hollywoodien* (Paris: Stock, 1985), 85. My translation.
12. See Anne-Marie Paquet-Deyris's analysis of the scene in *Lolita, Cartographies de l'obsession*, ed. Monica Manolescu and Anne-Marie Paquet-Deyris (Paris: PUF, 2009), 161.
13. Richard Corliss, *Lolita* (London: BFI, 1994), 34.
14. Quoted by Alfred Appel in his introduction to *The Annotated Lolita*, xlvii.

REFERENCES

Appel, Alfred. *Nabokov's Dark Cinema*. Oxford: Oxford University Press, 1974.
Bourget, Jean-Loup. *Le mélodrame hollywoodien*. Paris: Stock, 1985.
Corliss, Richard. *Lolita*. London: BFI, 1994.
Delage-Toriel, Lara. "Shadow of a Double: Taking a Closer Look at the Opening of Kubrick's *Lolita*." *Miranda* (online journal), Toulouse Jean-Jaures University, no. 3 (2010): 1–7.
Kael, Pauline. *I Lost It at the Movies: Film Writings 1954–1965*. New York: Marion Boyars, 1994.
Manolescu, Monica, and Anne-Marie Paquet-Deyris, eds. *Lolita, Cartographies de l'obsession*. Paris: PUF, 2009.
Maury, Cristelle. "Traces du film noir dans *Lolita*, Stanley Kubrick 1962." *Miranda*, n° 3 (2010): 1–14.
Nabokov, Vladimir. *The Annotated Lolita*. London: Penguin, 1995.
Naremore, James. *On Kubrick*. London: BFI, Palgrave Macmillan, 2007.

Chapter Five

History by Candlelight

*How Stanley Kubrick Revolutionized
Depictions of the Past on Film*

Sean O'Reilly

Is the cinema primarily about the future, the present, or the past? In other words, is it an oracle of what is to come, a record of the here and now, or a recollection (or fantasy) of what once was? And is it even possible for film to depict history? In the more than 120-year history of the cinema, and despite its capabilities as a technology firmly rooted in the present, recording events as they happen, many filmmakers have taken up the challenge of depicting, in their narrative (fictional) films, the distant or recent past. This is true in and of every country with a thriving film industry, regardless of how long or interesting that country's history is considered to be. A good example of a country without a particularly long history whose cinema is nonetheless deeply committed to exploring fictionalized depictions of the past is the United States. In Hollywood, almost from the dawn of the film age, many of the industry's most illustrious directors, from D. W. Griffith (*Birth of a Nation*, 1915; *Intolerance*, 1916; etc.) to Victor Fleming (most famously *Gone with the Wind*, 1939) to Kathryn Bigelow (*The Hurt Locker*, 2008; *Zero Dark Thirty*, 2012) and countless others in between, have periodically—and in some cases obsessively—chosen to reject the "here and now" in favor of their often deeply controversial depictions of "there and then." But there is at least one director of equal stature (albeit an American who chose to live most of his life as an expatriate in the United Kingdom and whose obsessive focus on the past was grounded not in American but in European history) whose oeuvre is often misunderstood as being future-focused, and who despite abundant evidence is rarely if ever identified as a "there and then" filmmaker: Stanley Kubrick.

This chapter will show that, contrary to the prevailing view of Kubrick as predominantly forward-focused, he was in fact quite deeply engaged with issues of how to depict the past both in terms of film techniques and in terms of narrative storytelling itself. The chapter will focus on his two historical epics set in the distant past, namely *Spartacus* (1960) and *Barry Lyndon* (1975). Among the thirteen films he made over the course of his life, only three are focused on the future; five, namely one heist, one noir, one black comedy, one horror, and one erotic thriller, are set in the present; and the remaining five, nearly 40 percent of his entire oeuvre, are historical films, including his three films set in the recent past (*Fear and Desire*, 1953; *Paths of Glory*, 1957; and *Full Metal Jacket*, 1987). *Spartacus* and *Barry Lyndon* fall into their own special subcategory of historical films for two reasons. First, only these two films are truly epic in their grandiose scale and ambition, and second, they are set in the distant past (ancient Rome in the former case and eighteenth-century Europe in the latter), unlike the other three, which are firmly grounded in the twentieth-century experience of warfare. In any case, it is odd indeed that Kubrick is so often identified as future-focused when he made just one film (*2001: A Space Odyssey*, 1968) on the distant future, and only two about the near future (*A Clockwork Orange*, 1971; and—arguably—*Dr. Strangelove*, 1964).

Kubrick's commitment to history on film can also be contrasted quantitatively with his efforts at depicting the future. Despite all the attention paid to the (admittedly impressive) innovations in *2001: A Space Odyssey*, he actually spent more years of his career wrestling with new techniques, technologies, and narrative approaches in films like *Barry Lyndon*. Kubrick devoted much of his time and energy to what Hayden White called "historiophoty," which is to say the visual record or depiction of history (contra historiography, the written record of history).[1] This investment of time allowed him to hone his skills at rendering the past on screen, suggesting that Kubrick wrestled more with historiophotic issues (meaning the difficulties, unique to the medium of film and in contradistinction with difficulties facing written history, in narrating historical events or aspects of history "accurately") than with the challenges of how to visualize the future.[2] His two historical epics, then, are not anomalies in a career otherwise devoted to futuristic musings; these two films are also representative of Kubrick, and can offer significant insight into his modus operandi as a director, just as can his more well-known futuristic tales. Far from being overshadowed by *2001*, and without accounting for inflation in the eight years between the two, *Spartacus* was in fact a bigger box office success ($60 million worldwide gross)[3] than *2001* ($41.9 million) when comparing the original theatrical run of each.[4]

Moreover, Kubrick's films about the past have had a major yet largely unrecognized impact on later filmmakers. His contributions to the pool of techniques and storytelling approaches available to historical film directors have been at least as significant as the clever special effects and other innovations he adopted and popularized in *2001*. As such, he should certainly have a prominent place in any discussion about the great historical film directors, and awarding him his rightful position in that conversation will enhance our understanding of historiophoty (the visual display of historical events on screen) and historical films more generally. By comparing two such seemingly disparate epics as *Spartacus* and *Barry Lyndon*, a new conceptualization of historical films will emerge, and Kubrick's own extraordinary contribution to historical storytelling will come into clearer focus.

Proponents of auteur theory—not to mention Stanley Kubrick himself!—have a tendency to dismiss *Spartacus* as irrelevant to any discussion of Kubrick's filmmaking approach. After all, he was merely a director-for-hire in this project, brought in to replace producer and star Kirk Douglas's first choice, Anthony Mann, when Douglas and he clashed over Mann's allegedly deferential treatment of actor Peter Ustinov.[5] As such, Kubrick (in)famously did not have complete or final artistic control over any aspect of the film, including the editing; despite Kubrick's heavy interventions and months of labor in the editing room, Robert Lawrence was officially in charge of editing, and it was he, not Kubrick, who was nominated for Best Editing at the 33rd Academy Awards in 1961. The running length was up to Universal and Douglas's own company Bryna Productions, as was content to a degree; a public campaign to shame the production into removing a scene with homoerotic dialogue and overtones proved successful, convincing the studio, over Kubrick's objections, to cut the offending material entirely.[6]

Kubrick clashed with the producers, Douglas in particular, over the script as well. He exhibited a pronounced tendency in this and many other films (most famously the first half hour of *2001*) to strip the visual story he was telling of any wordiness, which left him deeply dissatisfied with the witty but (to his mind) inconsequential dialogue in much of the hastily written Dalton Trumbo script he inherited. This prompted Kubrick to cut many of Douglas's lines in the first section of the film, to the latter's dismay, and to demand that a big battle scene be inserted, to the consternation of everyone.[7] Kubrick also suggested early in the filming that, despite his problems with the script—which he quipped had led to a movie that "had everything but a good story"[8] and later denounced as "pretty dumb"[9] —he be given primary credit rather than then-blacklisted Dalton Trumbo, to avoid embroiling the production in controversy—and possibly also out of self-aggrandizement. This angered Douglas enough to convince him to make Trumbo's involvement public, forcing the American people to confront the evils of the blacklist system (as is well known, then President-elect John F. Kennedy publicly crossed picket lines to view *Spartacus*, thereby dealing the blacklisting system a deathblow), thus making Kubrick ironically responsible, in a sense, for the ending of the blacklist era itself.

There are various other reasons that are sometimes given to exclude *Spartacus* from the discourse on Kubrick's work. Since Kubrick is widely acknowledged as a genius behind the camera in terms of shot selection, control of lighting, and other aspects of cinematography, a film that did not feature his unique input in this area could conceivably be ignored. And indeed, Kubrick did not have official control over the direction of photography for *Spartacus*. That role was cinematographer Russell Metty's, at least until Kubrick escalated his micromanaging of Metty and simply (and imperiously) commanded him to sit silently in his chair and let Kubrick do everything himself. Yet despite this highhanded attempt to seize authorial control over the project, it was still Metty rather than Kubrick who went home with an Academy Award in 1961 for Best Cinematography—Color.[10]

Nonetheless, to dismiss this film as somehow un-Kubrickian would be a mistake. For one thing, it is stylistically consistent with both his earlier and later films. His trademark meticulousness and sense of visual composition is on full display in *Spartacus*, during which he numbered each actor playing a slave corpse so he could call out instructions while filming to each individual, thereby getting their bodies into exactly the sort of tableau he wanted.[11] Kubrick also used similar techniques for immersive, rapid-editing melee fight scenes in this and many other films, and arranged for essentially the same reverse tracking shots, of Ustinov's character Batiatus ambling about the mines, that he had used to show Dax (Douglas) and Broulard (Adolphe Menjou) on their trench-walks in the 1957 World War I film *Paths of Glory*.[12]

Not coincidentally, that Kubrick-directed film had also starred Kirk Douglas, on the strength of which experience the star had asked Kubrick to join his sword-and-sandals epic in the first place. But their collaboration did not survive *Spartacus*, a pattern which was to repeat many times over the course of Kubrick's tempestuous career.[13] Indeed, only one actor (Philip Stone), and a minor character actor with bit parts at that, is known to have appeared in three consecutive Kubrick films.[14] His detractors tended to end up thinking very little of him personally, even as they perhaps reluctantly continued to acknowledge his brilliance, and Douglas was emblematic of that trend. He seems to have soured against Kubrick as a person during the aforementioned early discussions about who would receive screenwriting credit, professing shock in his second autobiography that Kubrick claimed he would feel no shame in taking sole credit even though he was joining the project after it had already started and feeling not a bit chagrined that, in so doing, he would be depriving Trumbo of any credit at all.[15] Regardless, although Kubrick himself created a narrative where the experience of making *Spartacus* was so bad it had permanently soured him on the entire Hollywood system, the truth is his often cantankerous relations with his cast and crew on this film were not exceptional but rather form a telling continuity with the rest of his career.

Furthermore, and like many of his more famous films, *Spartacus* also constituted an ambitious series of "firsts" for Kubrick. For one thing, it was the largest film, in terms of budget, sheer scale, and in every other respect, he had ever worked on; indeed, by some accounts it was actually the most expensive film ever made up until that point in the United States.[16] It was also Kubrick's first time to shoot in color, as well as his first foray into the widescreen format. He was evidently determined to make the most of both these two new mediums, insisting on a truly grandiose, almost awe-inspiring scale for the battle sequence; as noted above, this was something he had demanded be added to the script, which initially contained no such large-scale sequence. This is a significant detail, as it speaks to Kubrick's desire for historical verisimilitude, since focusing on a handful of principals on a studio lot is a far cry from filming thousands of extras preparing for combat, as he wished to do.

Kubrick also faced the challenge of what to him was a new and unfamiliar widescreen format. But he rose to this challenge in impressive form, meticulously filling up the mammoth Super 70 Technirama widescreen frame (projected via 70mm film at an anamorphic aspect ratio of 2.35:1, this was a truly huge widescreen format for its time) with the lush rolling hills of Europe as a background and also placing into the frame over 8000 Spanish active-duty soldier-extras, colorfully dressed up as Roman Legionnaires and all marching in lock-step. There is certainly something extraordinary in hiring soldiers of Franco's Spain—which in 1960 was the only openly fascist country on earth—to appear as extras in a film intended by its blacklisted screenwriter and many of its stars to denounce McCarthyism, personified by Laurence Olivier's Crassus and by extension his legions, as the worst sort of fascism and instead to celebrate an almost utopian vision of freedom and communal living. But in this, too, the film is representative of Kubrick's desire to court controversy, so apparent in his later post-Hollywood successes.

Finally and most importantly for our purposes, with *Spartacus* Kubrick also revealed something quite telling about his approach toward historiophoty. He repeatedly disowned the film, and over the years he gave a wide variety of reasons as to why, but one of them stands out: its historical inaccuracies. The fact that he railed against the script is well known, but what exactly was the source of the script's stupidity to Kubrick? The answer is in the rest of Kubrick's statement, made during an interview with Michel Ciment: "[it] was rarely faithful to what is known about Spartacus."[17] One of the primary irritations, to Kubrick, of the entire project was—it seemed to him, at least—that he was the only one committed to an accurate retelling of history on screen. Trumbo, Douglas, and Olivier intended to use the film as a thinly veiled allegory on McCarthyism, fabricating dictatorial ambitions for Crassus and inventing a crucifixion for Spartacus himself that was as messianic as it was contrary to known fact.[18] Ustinov and Charles Laughton (Gracchus), for their part, seemed interested only in dazzling audiences with their rapid-fire wit in their dialogue. Kubrick alone cared, it seemed, about the actual historical saga of Spartacus. He was particularly upset that the film and its script altered history to insinuate Spartacus had been outmaneuvered by Crassus and "the silly contrivance of a pirate leader" and became thereby trapped in Italy, whereas it is well known that Spartacus twice could have escaped out of Italy to the north during the Third Penile War, instead choosing—for reasons that remain shrouded in mystery—to turn back and confront the power of Rome directly; to Kubrick, this question was the most interesting one the film could ask and seek to answer, but his lack of complete control over the project meant he was prevented from doing so.[19] This sense of disillusionment caused him to abandon Hollywood—and America itself—permanently, yet the against-all-odds success of *Spartacus* and his string of later successes ensured that the next time Kubrick set his sights on an historical epic, he would have complete control over that project. What sort of film would emerge from Kubrick's exacting vision of how to depict the past? The answer would not come until 1975, fifteen years later, with *Barry Lyndon*.

Kubrick in the early 1970s was still in the afterglow of his three triumphs from 1964–1971, and consequently was bestriding the cinematic world like a colossus, but he was still subject to the vicissitudes of fate. Whatever his towering reputation, he remained dependent on studio funding for his projects, whose ambitions were far beyond the shoestring budgets of his earliest independent efforts. Unfortunately for his long-cherished ambition to make a biopic about Napoleon, about whom he had allegedly read hundreds of books in preparation, the inability of *Waterloo* (Sergei Bondarchuk, 1970) to recoup its enormous budget meant no studio was willing to green-light another Napoleon project so soon. It was in this period of frustrated ambition that Kubrick took up William Makepeace Thackeray's rather obscure 1844 novel *The Luck of Barry Lyndon* instead. More famous for its alleged continuity—both based on first-person novels about not very nice young men, both of whose endings were altered by Kubrick in similar ways, etc.—with *A Clockwork Orange*, the film project immediately preceding it, few have thought to compare this stately film with the savage sword-and-sandals epic *Spartacus*.

Yet there are many structural and production similarities between these two films. First, they had similarly huge budgets ($12 million for *Spartacus* and $11 million for *Barry Lyndon*, unadjusted for inflation).[20] They are also almost exactly the same running length (184 minutes for *Spartacus* and 187 for *Barry Lyndon*), and Kubrick's only two films over three hours long. This suggests—and a careful examination of the editing style, average shot length, and so forth would seem to confirm—that the overall pace of each film is, broadly speaking, equivalent, though *Barry Lyndon* is somewhat slower in average shot length. This stately pace was at the time referred to by some nonplussed commentators as "glacial," but some critics, at least, have begun to soften toward ultra-long films only recently, in the last couple of decades, as so-called "slow cinema" began to gain a following along with various other cultural movements stressing a more languid pace.[21]

Second, both films have an uneasy ontological status within Kubrick's oeuvre. *Spartacus* was intentionally left out of some scholars' and critics' appraisals of Kubrick's body of work over the years, with detractors arguing (unconvincingly) it had nothing to contribute to an understanding of Kubrick's approach to the cinema.[22] So too *Barry Lyndon* languished in obscurity for at least thirty years after its original release, with critics sometimes discussing Kubrick's career by focusing on *A Clockwork Orange* and then jumping right to *The Shining*, without any mention of the intervening *Barry Lyndon* at all; even studios like Warner Bros. contributed to this strange erasure a few years after Kubrick's death in 1999, by releasing a Stanley Kubrick DVD collection that did not include the 1975 film![23]

Third, music in the two films plays a surprisingly similar role. This is true even though *Spartacus* was a project not totally under Kubrick's authorial control and thus featured the work of a Hollywood composer (Alex North), whereas in *Barry Lyndon*, Kubrick was able to exert total executive control over the music and followed up on his tactic, first and most dramatically shown in *2001*, of using preexisting music instead of original compositions. The key similarity is that in both films, music was used to take the place of expository dialogue, setting the tone in some of the emotionally charged wordless scenes that a more quotidian director might have chosen to fill up with dialogue instead.[24] But given his greater control over the 1975 film, Kubrick was able to go one step further, creating a sort of "historiophony" in addition to his concerted effort at historiophotic accuracy, discussed in more detail below. He arranged that the music appearing in the film would be (nearly) authentic to the late-eighteenth-century spatiotemporal setting, though some is actually from the early nineteenth century instead, and played on period and country-appropriate instruments such as the Irish bodhrán, Uillean pipes, and so forth.[25]

Fourth, as is perhaps to be expected of two films of such tremendous scale and ambition, the landscape on display is deeply significant, coming to function almost as a kind of main character in a sense. In the case of *Spartacus*, it is the rolling hills of "Italy" though in reality, this is mostly the studio lot, supplemented at Kubrick's insistence with scenes shot in Spain to get that grandeur of scale. In *Barry Lyndon*, a film shot almost entirely on location, mostly in Ireland, but also in England, Scotland, and some exteriors in Germany, it is the verdant fields and quaint castles and estates of Ireland that the camera so lovingly devours. That picturesque quality has even led some critics to conclude *Barry Lyndon* is the "most visually beautiful film ever made."[26] The sense of landscape as painterly,[27] reproduced ever so faithfully, is no accident; the film crew, especially cinematographer John Alcott, who in 1976 went on to win the Academy Award for Best Cinematography for his work on *Barry Lyndon*, and Kubrick himself, conducted a great deal of research into how to recreate the visual look both of specific locations and how to create a sort of static tableaux cinematographic style more generally.[28]

Kubrick supplemented this lush landscape by populating it in many scenes with a huge number of extras playing soldiers all marching in lockstep, just as he had with *Spartacus*. He also focused the story in each film on a singular larger-than-life character, in both cases played by a then-prominent American actor, though Douglas's career continued to flourish despite or perhaps even because of his performance in *Spartacus*, while Ryan O'Neal's appears to have been derailed by *Barry Lyndon*, for which he received a Harvard Lampoon Award for Worst Actor.[29] But where in *Spartacus* Kubrick was just beginning to formulate a historiophotic strategy featuring complex movements of extras among other elements, in *Barry Lyndon* that strategy is fully developed and yields far more impressive results.

Fifth, just as *Spartacus* had featured a number of firsts for Kubrick, notably his shift to color and to widescreen format, *Barry Lyndon* has Kubrick breaking new technical and narratological ground. Most famously, *Barry Lyndon* became the first film ever made to attempt to use, in many of its scenes, only natural, period-appropriate lighting, including at night. As is well known, this was only possible thanks to NASA's commissioning of a special ultra-lowlight camera Zeiss lens for use during the moon landings, which Kubrick adapted so as to be able to shoot by candlelight. This puts *Barry Lyndon* in the illustrious company of *2001*, as these two films were the most technically ambitious and groundbreaking of Kubrick's career; it is worth noting, moreover, that while *2001* famously shows a rather distant future, it also spends quite a lot of screen time depicting the remote past, meaning that the two films have more in common than may be apparent at first glance. But in any case, many Kubrick admirers[30] breathlessly note the fact of the "moon camera" having been used in *Barry Lyndon*, praise the director for attempting a new technical feat, and leave the matter at that; in doing so, they miss the point entirely. What is significant is not *what* Kubrick did (using a camera capable of recording the play of emotions across characters' faces even in low light) but *why*.

Here is where the misconception of Kubrick as future-oriented has done the most damage. In such a view, what is noteworthy is Kubrick's clever adaptation of a futuristic device (the space camera). In reality, Kubrick's great achievement is not the use of a new type of camera, but his comprehensive dedication to total verisimilitude and historiophotic accuracy, or in other words, his attempt to show what might be called, following Leopold von

Ranke, *wie es eigentlich gewesen*, which can be translated as "how things really were."[31] Kubrick's great insight was his reframing of this story as a sort of moving painting, a window into that time period nearly 200 years gone, utterly rejecting the too-bright lights and colors of the various fantasies about the past that had come to dominate the world cinema's approach to the "costume drama" or "period piece" in favor of a relentlessly realistic viewing experience.

This approach also extended beyond the visual. Rather than preserve the unreliable first-person narrator of the Thackeray novel, Kubrick transformed the narration into an impersonal third-person register. He refused to keep the novel's juxtaposition between Barry's deeds and his unreliable commentary on those deeds, saying in an interview with Michel Ciment that an untrustworthy narrator would not work well in a movie because "of course, in a film you have objective reality in front of you all the time," showing he was keenly aware of film's historiophotic potential.[32] He went so far as to make the narrator rather coldly distant in his commentary, even as the smooth baritone of the narrator (voiced by Michael Hordern) with his posh British accent is so stereotypically trustworthy that the experience of listening to him speak can cause the opposite reaction in viewers: suspicion. In using such an impersonal narrator, he denied viewers the chance to immerse themselves in the story. Meanwhile, with his similarly cold and often intentionally gloomy visual approach, he forced viewers to become aware of their own visual assumptions, ensuring that viewers would never encounter what John Fiske has called the "recognition effect" in *Barry Lyndon*.[33]

According to the idea of the recognition effect, the way viewers evaluate the historical accuracy of a film is not based on the factual claims the film or its dialogue may make about the past. Instead, it simply and primarily has to do with whether the image being shown looks similar to other foundational images of that time and place (regardless of their accuracy).[34] Thus, perhaps one reason for the lukewarm critical and general audience response, especially in the United States, to *Barry Lyndon* when it was first released, and for decades afterward, is not about the editing pace or the content per se; the crucial issue is that viewers could not recognize it as late 1700s Ireland/England, in the sense that it does not look like what people had come to expect of a ca. 1800 period piece. Yes, the characters may be dressed in the right costumes, but if it is a tale of adventure, why did the actors sit around so listlessly on camera, doing so little and making such a sorry spectacle of their ennui? Time itself, rather than progressing relentlessly, is agonizingly slow, suggesting even in his editing pace Kubrick is reminding us of something important regarding the essence of eighteenth-century life.[35] And why show us these characters and their boring lifestyle, languishing in what, to our eyes—long accustomed to the too-bright artificial lighting of Hollywood which is used for period pieces—seem to be dark, shadowy rooms all day?

Astute viewers will note a number of occasions in interiors where the shadows cast by the actors seem to be in the wrong places, but in reality, they only appear wrong because we are collectively so used to the shadow-banishing effects of artificial supplemental lighting, so much so that natural lighting appears "wrong" to us. Ironically, by showing the bygone world as it really would have looked, Kubrick is denying viewers that comfortable reinforcement of our visual assumptions that is the bedrock of our recognition of what we believe to be "accurate."

Kubrick's commitment to reproduce the actual look of the early 1800s life of leisure is all the more remarkable due to its implications for film theory as it relates to historical films. This sort of accurate depiction actually calls into doubt Robert Rosenstone's fundamental assumption about historical films: that "on the screen, history must be fictional in order to be true!"[36] Rosenstone is certainly correct to say that what we see on screen is not literally true; in the case of *Barry Lyndon*, the American actor Ryan O'Neal is not actually the Irish rogue Redmond Barry, and besides, Redmond Barry is a fictional character from a Thackeray novel. But in another sense, what we see when we watch *Barry Lyndon* actually *is* "true" and not precisely fictional, because it is subject to none, or at least far less, of the usual apparatus of cinema; notably absent is all the extra lighting to make actors' faces legible and the use of close-ups to divorce actors from their context so as to draw attention to their brightly lit faces within the larger mise en scène (a technique that is very seldom used in *Barry Lyndon*).

We see, instead, the actors positioned (often asymmetrically) in tableaux within a cavernous space, exactly—and at exactly the same level of gloom—as people living in that time would have seen each other. This makes the experience of watching *Barry Lyndon* nearly unique in all the thousands of historical films the world cinema has produced: almost alone among those myriad films, *Barry Lyndon* actually offers something experientially accurate. It turns out that watching a story that is lit naturally, and seeing this period of history reenacted by candlelight, has more to offer than proof of technical accomplishment in using the moon camera, which was only the medium for Kubrick's message. It was the *experience* of seeing history by candlelight that is the film's most important message, and Kubrick's greatest historiophotic contribution.

NOTES

1. Hayden White, "Historiography and Historiophoty," *American Historical Review*, vol. 93, no. 5, (December 1988): 1193–99.
2. Ibid.
3. *The Numbers*, https://www.the-numbers.com/movie/Spartacus#tab=summary (accessed December 19, 2019).

4. Alex B. Block and Lucy A. Wilson, *George Lucas's Blockbusting: a Decade-by-Decade Survey of Timeless Movies Including Untold Secrets of Their Financial and Cultural Success* (New York: IT Books, 2010), 434.

5. Mark Frankel, "Spartacus," *Turner Classic Movies*, February 20, 2019, http://www.tcm.com/this-month/article/17971%7C0/Spartacus.html (accessed December 19, 2019).

6. It was reinserted into the rerelease issued some thirty years later, but the soundtrack had degraded too much to be usable and Laurence Olivier had recently died, forcing the production to take the highly unusual step of hiring an Olivier impersonator—none other than Anthony Hopkins!—to rerecord Olivier's lines as Crassus. Frankel, n.d.

7. Larry Ceplair and Christopher Trumbo, *Dalton Trumbo: Blacklisted Hollywood Radical* (Lexington, KY: University Press of Kentucky, 2015), 393.

8. David James, "Spartacus: How the Film Kubrick Hated Made Him," *Orca Beacon*, November 4, 2018, http://orcabeacon.com/index.php/2018/11/04/spartacus-how-the-film-kubrick-hated-made-him/ (accessed December 19, 2019).

9. Henry Sheehan (quoting Michel Ciment's interview with Kubrick) mentions this "pretty dumb" comment. See Sheehan, "Kubrick's Personal Stamp on 'Spartacus,'" *Scraps from the Loft*, June 10, 2016, https://scrapsfromtheloft.com/2016/06/10/kubricks-personal-stamp-spartacus/ (accessed December 19, 2019).

10. In addition to the aforementioned 1961 Oscar win for Best Cinematography (Color) and a nomination for Best Editing, *Spartacus* also won Academy Awards for Best Supporting Actor (Peter Ustinov), Best Costume Design, and Best Art Direction, with Alex North's score earning a nomination for Best Music.

11. Paul Duncan, *Stanley Kubrick: Visual Poet, 1928–1999* (Cologne: Taschen, 2011), 69–71.

12. Ibid., 62.

13. This pattern holds true for most actors and crew members who ever worked with Kubrick; it was rare for an actor or crew member to appear in more than one or at most two of his films, with one of the only exceptions being composer Alex North, whose scores had served Kubrick well in *Spartacus* and *Dr. Strangelove*; Kubrick peremptorily and quickly discarded the completed score North had made for *2001*, apparently without even informing North he had done so, and perhaps unsurprisingly, the two would never work together again.

14. Christine L. Gengaro, *Listening to Stanley Kubrick: The Music of His Films* (Lanham, MD: Scarecrow, 2012), 175. Stone appeared in *A Clockwork Orange* (as Alex's father), *Barry Lyndon* (as Graham, one of Lady Lyndon's advisors), and *The Shining* (as the previous caretaker before Jack).

15. Kirk Douglas, *Let's Face It: 90 Years of Living, Loving, and Learning* (Hoboken, NJ: John Wiley & Sons, 2007), 78–79.

16. There seems to be consensus that, at the very least, it was the most expensive film Universal had ever bankrolled. See Duncan L. Cooper, "Who Killed the Legend of *Spartacus*? Production, Censorship, and Reconstruction of Stanley Kubrick's Epic Film," in Martin M. Winkler ed., *Spartacus: Film and History*, 14–55 (Hoboken, NJ: Blackwell, 2007), 22.

17. Gengaro, 34.

18. Spartacus was not among the slaves so infamously and cruelly crucified all along the Appian Way, since he was known to have been killed in the final battle; for more on the historical inaccuracies of the film, see William J. Duiker and Jackson J. Spielvogel, *World History vol. 1, Sixth Ed.* (New York: Wadsworth, 2010), 145.

19. Duncan L. Cooper, "Dalton Trumbo versus Stanley Kubrick: The Historical Meaning of Spartacus," in Martin M. Winkler, ed., *Spartacus: Film and History*, 56–64 (Hoboken, NJ: Blackwell, 2007), 57.

20. Thomas Allen Nelson, *Kubrick: Inside a Film Artist's Maze* (Bloomington, IN: Indiana University Press, 2000), 167.

21. Maria Pramaggiore, *Making Time in Stanley Kubrick's Barry Lyndon: Art, History, and Empire* (New York: Bloomsbury, 2014), 22.

22. A representative example is William Fitzgerald, among whose more memorable excoriations of *Spartacus* are that the film had a "nauseous incontinence" and was an "embarrassment"; more tellingly, he notes that it "tends to feature more as an episode in the biography of Kubrick than

as a part of his filmography." See Fitzgerald, "Mucking out the Bullshit: Kubrick, Spartacus and Full Metal Jacket," *Open Democracy*, November 14, 2011, https://www.opendemocracy.net/en/mucking-out-bullshit-kubrick-spartacus-and-full-metal-jacket/ (accessed December 19, 2019).

23. Pramaggiore, 21–22.
24. Gengaro, 149.
25. Ibid., 159.
26. Mark Crispin Miller has claimed this, as reported in Pramaggiore, 23.
27. Likely based upon the landscapes of Thomas Gainsborough, William Hogarth, and others; see Nelson, 184.
28. Gengaro, 175.
29. "'Barry Lyndon' Caught on Lampoon's Spear," in *New York Times*, May 21, 1976, 82.
30. For example, see Neil Oseman's blog on the cinematography in *Barry Lyndon*: "BARRY LYNDON": THE FULL STORY OF THE FAMOUS F/0.7 LENSES," *Neiloseman.com*, http://neiloseman.com/barry-lyndon-the-full-story-of-the-famous-f0-7-lenses/ (accessed December 19, 2019).
31. Felix Gilbert, "Historiography: What Ranke Meant," in *The American Scholar*, vol. 56, no. 3 (Summer 1987), 393–97.
32. For a reprinting of this snippet of the Ciment interview, see David L. Kranz and Nancy C. Mellerski, eds., *In/Fidelity: Essays on Film Adaptation* (Newcastle upon Tyne, U.K.: Cambridge Scholars, 2008), 42.
33. John Fiske, *Television Culture* (New York: Routledge Classics, 2010 [1987]), 30.
34. Indeed, the visual assumptions viewers bring to bear when evaluating historical films are quite often thoroughly inaccurate. A notorious example is the 1995 film *Braveheart*, in which the Scottish warriors are all wearing kilts, Scotland's most iconic form of dress, even though kilts were not worn in the early fourteenth century. See Simon Johnson, "Scots Fought in Bright Yellow War Shirts Not Braveheart Kilts," *The Telegraph*, June 28, 2009, https://www.telegraph.co.uk/news/uknews/scotland/5675615/Scots-fought-in-bright-yellow-war-shirts-not-Braveheart-kilts.html (accessed December 19, 2019). According to the theory of the recognition effect, though, if the film had dared to show a sartorially accurate version of 1300s Scotland, it would have instead violated what people "know" about Scotland's past, and clashed with their visual expectations, denying them the chance to say, "yes, that's how it was" and leaving them confused, probably convinced the film was "inaccurate" and possibly ready to spread negative word of mouth. There are easy-to-grasp commercial reasons for film projects subject to studio funding and the usual constraints of the studio system to avoid this sort of too-accurate depiction, needless to say. Perhaps only Kubrick, with his towering reputation, could "get away with" showing the past as it actually would have looked!
35. *Barry Lyndon* can be conceived of as all about time. Contra *2001: A Space Odyssey*, it has even been memorably described as a "time odyssey" and its viewers as "voyeurs of time" by Thomas A. Nelson in his book *Kubrick: Inside a Film Artist's Maze*, 166 and passim.
36. Robert Rosenstone, "The Historical Film: Looking at the Past in a Postliterate Age," in Marcia Landy, ed., *The Historical Film: History and Memory in Media*, 50–66 (New Brunswick, NJ: Rutgers University Press, 2000), 61.

REFERENCES

"'Barry Lyndon' Caught on Lampoon's Spear." *New York Times*, May 21, 1976.
Block, Alex B., and Lucy A. Wilson. *George Lucas's Blockbusting: A Decade-by-Decade Survey of Timeless Movies Including Untold Secrets of Their Financial and Cultural Success*. New York: IT Books, 2010.
Ceplair, Larry, and Christopher Trumbo. *Dalton Trumbo: Blacklisted Hollywood Radical*. Lexington, KY: University Press of Kentucky, 2015.
Cooper, Duncan L. "Who Killed the Legend of *Spartacus*? Production, Censorship, and Reconstruction of Stanley Kubrick's Epic Film." In *Spartacus: Film and History*, edited by Martin M. Winkler, 14–55. Hoboken, NJ: Blackwell, 2007.

———. "Dalton Trumbo versus Stanley Kubrick: The Historical Meaning of Spartacus." In *Spartacus: Film and History*, edited by Martin M. Winkler, 56–64. Hoboken, NJ: Blackwell, 2007.
Douglas, Kirk. *Let's Face It: 90 Years of Living, Loving, and Learning*. Hoboken, NJ: John Wiley & Sons, 2007.
Duiker, William J., and Jackson J. Spielvogel. *World History vol. 1, Sixth Ed.* New York: Wadsworth, 2010.
Duncan, Paul. *Stanley Kubrick: Visual Poet, 1928–1999*. Cologne: Taschen, 2011.
Fiske, John. *Television Culture*. New York: Routledge Classics, 2010 (1987).
Fitzgerald, William. "Mucking out the Bullshit: Kubrick, Spartacus and Full Metal Jacket." *Open Democracy*, November 14, 2011. https://www.opendemocracy.net/en/mucking-out-bullshit-kubrick-spartacus-and-full-metal-jacket/.
Frankel, Mark. "Spartacus." *Turner Classic Movies*, February 20, 2019. http://www.tcm.com/this-month/article/17971%7C0/Spartacus.html.
Gengaro, Christine L. *Listening to Stanley Kubrick: The Music of His Films*. Lanham, MD: Scarecrow, 2012.
Gilbert, Felix. "Historiography: What Ranke Meant." *The American Scholar*, vol. 56, no. 3 (Summer 1987): 393–97.
James, David. "Spartacus: How the Film Kubrick Hated Made Him." *Orca Beacon*, November 4, 2018. http://orcabeacon.com/index.php/2018/11/04/spartacus-how-the-film-kubrick-hated-made-him/.
Johnson, Simon. "Scots Fought in Bright Yellow War Shirts Not Braveheart Kilts." *The Telegraph*, June 28, 2009. https://www.telegraph.co.uk/news/uknews/scotland/5675615/Scots-fought-in-bright-yellow-war-shirts-not-Braveheart-kilts.html.
Kranz, David L., and Nancy C. Mellerski, eds. *In/Fidelity: Essays on Film Adaptation*. Newcastle upon Tyne: Cambridge Scholars, 2008.
Nelson, Thomas Allen. *Kubrick: Inside a Film Artist's Maze*. Bloomington, IN: Indiana University Press, 2000.
Oseman, Neil. "BARRY LYNDON": The Full Story of the Famous F/0.7 lenses." *Neiloseman.com*. http://neiloseman.com/barry-lyndon-the-full-story-of-the-famous-f0-7-lenses/.
Pramaggiore, Maria. *Making Time in Stanley Kubrick's Barry Lyndon: Art, History, and Empire*. New York: Bloomsbury, 2014.
Rosenstone, Robert A. "The Historical Film: Looking at the Past in a Postliterate Age." In *The Historical Film: History and Memory in Media*, edited by Marcia Landy, 50–66. New Brunswick, NJ: Rutgers University Press, 2000.
Sheehan, Henry. "Kubrick's Personal Stamp on 'Spartacus.'" *Scraps from the Loft*, June 10, 2016. https://scrapsfromtheloft.com/2016/06/10/kubricks-personal-stamp-spartacus/.
"Spartacus." *The Numbers*. https://www.the-numbers.com/movie/Spartacus#tab=summary.
White, Hayden. "Historiography and Historiophoty." *American Historical Review*, vol. 93, no. 5. (December 1988): 1193–99.

Chapter Six

Intertextuality, Distortion, and Echoes of World War II in Stanley Kubrick's War Films

Guillaume Mouleux

From the onset of Kubrick's career as a filmmaker, picturing war was a predominant theme declined through various onscreen historical contexts that include the deliberately unspecified setting of *Fear and Desire* (1953), World War I in *Paths of Glory* (1957), the Cold War in *Dr. Strangelove* (1964) and the Vietnam War in *Full Metal Jacket* (1987). However, in spite of its absence from this list, the Second World War and more specifically its visual corpus as a whole stands out as a considerable influence in shaping these movies, which shall come as no surprise considering that it was the very period during which young Stanley Kubrick grew up and developed his own visual culture and references through regular attendance at local theaters.[1] This resulted in a large number of direct or indirect references, as well as frequent common themes or approaches that all contribute to specifically link World War II imagery with the Kubrickian universe, although these references were sometimes used in the exact opposite direction in order to convey a more balanced—and critical—vision of war.

A major landmark of World War II–era Hollywood feature films, the notions of conversion and redemption aimed at establishing a narrative of the United States' conversion from isolationism to interventionism while insisting dramatically on the possibility of redeeming through heroism.[2] Sometimes marked with religious overtones, the theme had already been occasionally developed before the attack on Pearl Harbor in movies such as William Keighley's *The Fighting 69th* (1940), in which an undisciplined soldier becomes a war hero. After the involvement of American troops in the conflict, though, it became prominent in many films. In the allegorical *Tarzan Tri-*

umphs (Wilhelm Thiele, 1943), the "ape man" played by Johnny Weissmuller embodies the evolution of the American public opinion regarding international affairs from 1776 on. The cynical bartender played by Humphrey Bogart in *Casablanca* (Michael Curtiz, 1942) first states that "the problems of the world are not in [his] department" before he finally joins the Allies. *Margin For Error* (Otto Preminger, 1943) revolves around a former Nazi who finally joins the U.S. Army, while the main character in *Mr. Lucky* (H. C. Potter, 1943) is a draft-dodging gangster who suddenly decides to join the navy after he attempted to scam a war-related charity.

Although present in Kubrick's movies, the notion of conversion strongly differs in aspect, as its triggering is forced and its result either unachieved or unsatisfactory. *Paths of Glory* shows elite officers trying to forcefully convert their troops to a suicidal form of heroism through setting examples with the arbitrary execution of three of them. The first part of *Full Metal Jacket* illustrates the process supposed to convert each of the recruits into "a weapon, a minister of death, praying for war," as announced by Sergeant Hartman (Lee Ermey) at the very beginning of the movie. This baptism materializes with their initial head shaving reminiscent of a tonsure[3] and the change of their legal identities into war names (illustrating Hartman's paternal ascendency over them), but also with their subsequent own adoption of war mottos supposed to reflect their new identities, histories, and destinies. These formulas are not devoid of paradoxes or references: Joker (Matthew Modine)'s "Born to kill" ironically coexists with the peace symbol on his helmet, while Animal Mother (Adam Baldwin)'s "I am become Death" evokes words from the *Bhagavad Gita* reportedly quoted by Robert Oppenheimer after the first successful experimental detonation of an atomic bomb.[4] The movie, however, also shows the side effects of the process with Pyle (Vincent D'Onofrio)'s mental breakdown and its ultimate consequences. The intimacy he develops with his rifle reveals only a partial understanding and application of the "Rifleman's Creed": while he follows the injunction to consider that "[his] rifle is [his] best friend" and "[his] life," he eventually forgets the necessity to "master it" and "master [his own] life." To a certain extent, the underlying message is reminiscent of *2001: A Space Odyssey* (1968), as in both films the cult of a technological (or for the matter technical) prosthesis incidentally leads to the superseding of humanity and relegates humans to the status of nuanceless and senseless artifacts.[5] Paradoxically, its non-explicit nature in *Full Metal Jacket* has led to criticism of the film as supposedly praising the elevation of technique and technology over human values.[6] *Fear and Desire* and *Dr. Strangelove* show the results of the conversions of Sidney (Paul Mazursky) and General Jack D. Ripper (Sterling Hayden) from discipline to madness—although through different processes as Sidney's results from an onscreen traumatic experience while Ripper's precedes the beginning of the film. While the idea of redemption and its pairing with heroism was an essential part of the process in World War II films, the very concept was made irrelevant in Kubrick's movies by the absence of both an original sin (or anything perceived as such) *and* heroism combined within a same character: even Pyle's killing of the tyrannical Sergeant Hartman cannot be seen as an act of bravery, but only as the result of madness; it also fails to spare effectively his comrades-in-arms more abuse, as the training period was over and the men were bound for action on the following day.

The motivations for war expressed in Kubrick's films also strongly differ from the cinematographic canons of the World War II era, although again not without evocations. While the defense and global spreading of the "four freedoms" exhorted by Roosevelt as well as the dangers put forward by the Office of War Information (especially through Frank Capra's series of documentary films generically known as "Why We Fight") were central in war movies from the early 1940s, Kubrick often tended to depict heroism as more closely linked to personal ambition than collective values. A strange surrogate for Mac (Frank Silvera)'s expectation of a dull life outside the service in *Fear and Desire*, the quest for honors appears all the more disturbing and perverse when it takes the shape of heroism by proxy in *Paths of Glory*, where the generals are so obsessed by the sacrifice of others for their own advancements that Dax (Kirk Douglas)'s refusal to profit from this logic appears utterly incomprehensible in their eyes. The same paradoxical vision of war being decided by non-combatants is also hinted at in *Dr. Strangelove*, when the "gentlemen" in the military command center are told that "you can't fight in here, this is the war room." In *Full Metal Jacket*, the pseudo-documentary sequence shows Joker define his motivations ironically as some kind of absurd war tourism: "I wanted to meet interesting and stimulating people of an ancient culture . . . and kill them. I wanted to be the first kid on my block to get a confirmed kill"—a derisory motivation that hints at unspeakable (and possibly unconscious) real motives while entirely silencing the elephant in the room: in the Vietnam War, many soldiers were not volunteers but draftees and had no choice but to be there.[7] In Kubrick's view, though, personal motivations in wartime were a fool's game in which not even recognition was to be expected. A scene from Michael Curtiz's 1942 *Captains of the Clouds*, in which the Texan origin of a volunteer who had joined the Royal Air Force before Pearl Harbor was warmly greeted by a high-ranked British air officer ("one of our most loyal provinces! . . . we thank you for coming up here and helping us"), is both convoked and reversed in *Full Metal Jacket* through Sergeant Hartman's reaction to one of the recruits coming from the same state: "Holy dogshit! Texas! Only steers and queers come from Texas, Private Cowboy! And you don't look much like a steer to me so that kinda narrows it down!"[8]—a line that does not originate from Gustav Hasford's novel *The Short-Timers*, which inspired the movie.[9]

Coherently with the communicational failure that dominates the entire plot, *Dr. Strangelove* illustrates dramatically diverging motivations. The men aboard the bomber are given an emotionally charged motivational speech reminiscent both visually and in content of a scene of Howard Hawks's 1944 *Air Force*, in which the crew are invited to look at the damages caused by the attack on Pearl Harbor as a motivation to fight, as "something [they]'ll want to remember"; conversely, the sexual dimension of General Ripper's motivations are made explicit, not only when he links it with his growing sexual impotence but most importantly when he describes the supposed fluoridation of water as the introduction of a "foreign substance . . . into our precious bodily fluids without the knowledge of the individual, and certainly without any choice," a rhetoric that reminds of the use of rape as a propaganda argument in World War II.

In that regard, not only have the scenes involving actress Virginia Leigh in *Fear and Desire* resulted in the movie being occasionally marketed as a sexploitation picture,[10] they also linked the film with the wartime imagery of sexual violence, although with a noteworthy variation: on this occasion, violence originates from the heroes—not the enemy. The contrast is all the more striking in the scene in which Mac subdues the young woman, which is an exact staging of a 1940s poster from the War Production Board that showed a Japanese soldier overpowering a white woman from behind.[11] As often during the war, the racial dimension was meant to be all the more shocking in the profoundly segregated American society, and its 1950s onscreen rendition by Kubrick echoed this in having the role of the aggressor played by the only non-white performer in the cast, Jamaican-born actor Frank Silvera. The same question of sexual violence is evoked in the final scene of *Paths of Glory*, when the young German woman (Christiane Kubrick, credited as "Susanne Christian") is made to sing in front of an initially hostile crowd of soldiers before their attitudes change and sympathy brings them to tears—a scene Kubrick conceived as a late addition in the writing process;[12] the same occurs in *Full Metal Jacket*, considering the stark contrast between T.H.E. Rock (Sal Lopez)'s bawdy remark ("no more boom-boom for this baby-san") on the agonizing female sniper (Ngoc Le) and his sad look while pronouncing these words:[13] in both cases, the prevalence of emotion over any sexualized dimension is affirmed.

The Freudian causal link between sex and violence was not entirely denied, though: in *Dr. Strangelove*, not only does Ripper implicitly justify his actions by his own fear of sexual dysfunction, but the very first scene of the film essentially rests on the phallic appearance of military devices,[14] a common theme among the most daring World War II animated short cartoons such as Tex Avery's 1942 *Blitz Wolf*. With various degrees of subtlety (or lack thereof) ranging from "Captain Mandrake" (Peter Sellers) to "General Turgidson" (George C. Scott), the comical innuendo-laden names of many characters only confirm this impression, and the fact that all the other characters end up relying (finally to no avail) on Mandrake, a character named after a supposed aphrodisiac, makes the metaphor of international impotence to prevent a world catastrophe all the more explicit. *Full Metal Jacket* has also been analyzed as a sort of coming-of-age story focusing on masculinity and its achievement through violence. In this perspective, Joker's mercy kill of the female sniper is seen as embodying his successful conquest of virility. As for his sarcastic rendition of John Wayne at the very beginning ("Is that you, John Wayne? Is this me?"), it appears as an announcement of the very quest for identity that is to follow.[15] One may notice that while John Wayne was undeniably the onscreen archetype of a certain vision of masculinity, he is also remembered as the iconic star of many war films shot during World War II or representing it afterward, hinting at another war era reference.

Already present in Hasford's original novel, the depiction of an Asian woman as a dangerous enemy combatant in *Full Metal Jacket* is also reminiscent of the World War II image of the Eastern enemy of the time, the Japanese, who were then often depicted in the American popular culture and media as so radicalized a population that, in the words of Colonel Harry F. Cunningham, "there [were] no civilians in Japan" in the eyes of many Americans—including within the War Department.[16] However, in other regards, the portrayal of the enemy in Kubrick's movies drastically departs from its counterpart in World War II cinema. In the 1940s, the enemy was defined by its otherness, essentially on an ideological basis; oppositely, Kubrick's films insist on his sameness, on the idea of an enemy within or from the inside. In *Fear and Desire*, not only do the aforementioned scenes featuring the unnamed female character blur the line between heroes and savages, but, most importantly, the two enemy commanding officers and the two heroes who eventually kill them are played by the same pair of actors. Suddenly, this apparent collision challenges the viewer's previous experience of the movie by putting both sides on an equal footing, questioning the sympathy that the viewer is likely to have developed for the main characters from the beginning of the movie. In *Dr. Strangelove*, while the Americans and Soviets appear similarly mad and privately demonstrate the same taste for a certain kind of debauchery, the U.S. president's scientific adviser shows disquieting signs of resurging Nazism both in words and gestures, hinting at the influence of an enemy ideology acting from the inside, which consequently leaves little if any chance to "prevail in peace and freedom from fear" if there is no clear-cut dividing line between supposedly incompatible ideologies.

The enemy, however, was not the only one to see its nature questioned on the silver screen. A striking element in *Full Metal Jacket* is how the film stresses the training period of the recruits in Parris Island, a sequence that occupies less than 20 percent of *The Short-Timers* but was expanded in adaptation so as to finally take up almost 40 percent of the total running time of Kubrick's motion picture. This choice did not only depart from the Vietnam War movie subgenre as defined by such films as Michael Cimino's *The Deer Hunter* (1978), Francis Ford Coppola's *Apocalypse Now* (1979) or

Oliver Stone's *Platoon* (1986); it also resurged the tradition of the "draft movies" that had emerged following the Selective Service and Training Act of 1940. Popularized by films such as Howard Hawks's *Sergeant York* (1941), Raoul Walsh's *They Died With Their Boots On* (1941), or H. Bruce Humberstone's *To the Shores of Tripoli* (1942), the draft movie subgenre focused extensively on the training of recruits in army boot camps and, most importantly, on the slow acquisition of a collective discipline by talented individuals—a necessary step for them to merge into a collective military entity. As with "platoon movies," which depicted the subsequent important step of the recruits' experience of war, the concept behind draft movies was to portray the U.S. armed forces as the embodiment of an American ideal based on the overcoming of differences and on the successful union of various talents, personalities, and backgrounds, illustrating the national mottos "*E pluribus unum*" and "united we stand." The first part of *Full Metal Jacket*, however, resolutely departs from the stereotype and illustrates the failure of the system: although a talented sniper, Pyle never fully manages to adapt and does not blend in the collective model imposed by the institution, which finally breaks him.

Certainly the most quintessential subcategory in the war film genre, the classic platoon movie may be characterized by three main elements: the successful coexistence of originally hardly compatible archetypal characters, eventually evolving into a strongly binding comradeship; the advent of heroic actions; finally, the prevalence of discipline that made all of the above possible. In many regards, however, Kubrick's various takes on the genre differed strongly from the original model and its ensuing expectations.[17]

While World War II platoon movies praised the success and harmony of groups of soldiers characterized by their social, ethnic, and occasionally even racial (such as in Ted Garnett's *Bataan*, 1943) diversities, Kubrick's portrayal of such questions was more mixed in *Full Metal Jacket*, where racial tensions are apparent, first when Hartman gives a black recruit the nickname of "Snowball" (Peter Edmund) before going on a racially tainted rant on food stereotypes, then when Animal Mother insists on going with a young prostitute before a black soldier and jokingly adds a racist remark. Although truer to a Whitmanian ideal, comradeship in *Fear and Desire* eventually proves inefficient: although Corby (Kenneth Harp) and Fletcher (Steve Coit) volunteer to go back in order to retrieve Mac and Sidney, the reunion of the four men proves impossible as Mac is already dead and Sidney appears irreversibly mad. In other circumstances, comradeship also appears limited in extent and not exempt from dilemmas—a point that is to be developed later on.

Heroism is also quite questionable. In *Paths of Glory*, Dax's inability to save the lives of the three soldiers in spite of his efforts is reminiscent of the unsuccessful attempt of the central character of William Wellman's 1943 *The Ox Bow Incident* to save three innocent men from being lynched on unconvincing grounds: in both cases, the hero does not manage to fulfill the viewer's expectations, and logic and justice fail to prevail in front of superior powers—ambition and selfishness in one case, demagogy and mob mentality in the other. The failure of all attempts to save the world in *Dr. Strangelove* goes as far as to question the military institution and its capacity to fulfill its mission, a theme that was totally unimaginable in World War II Hollywood cinema but was becoming a trend in the 1960s: released a few months after *Dr. Strangelove*, Arthur Hiller's romantic dark comedy *The Americanization of Emily*, the action of which is set during the Second World War (and which also plays on the visual codes of World War II films), testifies of the same questioning as to the trustworthiness of the U.S. military institutions, which are portrayed as cynically focusing more on which branch of the armed forces would be able to claim the first dead in the Normandy landings than on sparing their men's lives. Heroism in *Full Metal Jacket* is difficult to be found, while in *Fear and Desire* the mission, which results in the successful assassination of an enemy general, is somehow tainted, not only by its suicidal nature but also by the fact that it explicitly derives from hubris and ambition—not genuine, disinterested sacrifice.

But the failure of heroism most importantly illustrates and derives from the collapse of authority, that in turn entails that of the discipline that it is supposed to impose. In *Fear and Desire*, Sergeant Mac softly overthrows Lieutenant Corby to impose his own agenda, revealing the unstable nature, the weakness, and consequently the unreliability of the supposedly established hierarchy within the small group. *Dr. Strangelove* also focuses on the unreliability of authority figures who are not only challenged by Ripper's actions but also prove unable to live up to that challenge. The constant ridicule of the men in charge only stresses their own powerlessness in front of the dehumanized, machine-driven system that they chose to implement—and yet that is about to bring about the very global destruction that it had precisely been designed to prevent. While hinting at a certain level of insanity for delegating such powers out of human control,[18] the movie also challenges the view of a disembodied system through a criticism of the dangers of all-powerful individuals.[19] Absurdity and incompetence also appear through the choice by the U.S.S.R. to have kept the "Doomsday device" a secret in the first place, irrationally rescinding its deterring potential.[20] In *Full Metal Jacket*, power is depicted as a source of abuse: not only does Sergeant Hartman tyrannize the recruits in the first part of the movie, but the lesson seems to have had a lasting traumatic effect when, by the end of the film, Joker emphatically rejects the mere idea of coveting authority: "I'm not trying to run this squad." *Paths of Glory*, finally, provides the most crooked example of power being abused at all levels. While General Mireau (George Macready) is willing to have innocent men shot to preserve his reputation as a leader and Lieutenant Roget (Wayne Morris) seizes the opportunity to get rid of an embarrassing witness, General Broulard (Adolphe Menjou)'s Pilate-like attitude fails to reestablish the situation; although inefficient in exercising justice, the military institution, however, keeps its rigidity in preventing Dax from saving the day. Visually, the settings also encourage doubt and defiance: *Paths of Glory*'s checkered-floored military courtroom and *Dr. Strangelove*'s war room equipped with a large table, which Kubrick himself reportedly compared with a poker table,[21] indicate both irresponsibility and cynicism. In both cases, not only are the leaders merely gambling with the future, but, most importantly, they do it at the cost of other people's lives.

In a number of aspects, Kubrick's onscreen war experience highlights irreconcilable contradictions between some of these notions. While the soldiers in *Paths of Glory* show both comradeship and discipline, the latter eventually prevails and the firing squad performs its duty in spite of all the sympathy previously expressed to the men about to be executed, remarkably predating the Milgram and Stanford experiments by a few years.[22] In a different context, *Full Metal Jacket* features a comparable situation when Joker seems to hesitate between two contradictory allegiances—to Pyle, and to the rest of the group that has decided to punish him; while the inducement to harm Pyle does not come from a legitimate authority, Joker's choice to obey it still does coincide with the climate of violence and terror instituted by Hartman. Blind obedience and its absurdity are also made obvious in *Dr. Strangelove* when bureaucratic rules obstruct the communication of the recall code. Although apparent on the screen, these dilemmas remain unaddressed, leaving the viewer to contemplate the apparent normality of each of these situations as just as many illustrations of Hannah Arendt's "banality of evil" applied to the American war experience.

While Kubrick's affirmed will to portray universal stories pertaining to humanity as a whole beyond cultural borders has been well documented, the manner in which his movies depict the confrontation of his characters with wartime situations is reminiscent of a typically American question: that of the dialectic between innocence and experience (respectively described in Emerson's words as the "party of Hope" and the "party of Memory")[23] as a defining element of the American identity.[24] To a certain extent, Sidney, Pyle, or the three men executed in *Paths of Glory* all appear as possible embodiments of the American Adam, whose innocence is eventually corrupted by the hardships of experience. *Full Metal Jacket* is particularly rich in such evocations and metaphors: while the opening scene in which the recruits have their heads shaven may appear as merely realistic and utilitarian, it also evokes the rituals surrounding a child's first haircut in many societies around the world, including the Jewish tradition of *upsherin* (or *chalaka*), which is sometimes interpreted as symbolizing a boy's entry into an active role in society.[25] Conversely, the progressive loss of the characters' innocence all along the movie, which climaxes with Joker's mercy killing of the sniper, ultimately leads to the final scene in which the hostile or sometimes bawdy cadences heard at various moments during the first part the film are replaced by a collective rendition of the "Mickey Mouse Club" theme song (also turning for the occasion the hierarchical call-and-response format into an egalitarian symbol of union and harmony). This surreal and regressive moment seems a desperate supplication by the troops for the return of childhood and innocence into their lives, just as they are marching together toward a group of buildings in flames that resembles a visual evocation of hell.[26] This scene also shows an attempt by the characters to react to the traumatic experience of the war, hence opposing the idea of a return to the starting point and of the apparently unopposed continuing experience of the war that seemed to accompany the singing of "God Bless America" in the very last scene of Cimino's *The Deer Hunter*, but also the many World War II movies that ended with comparable scenes involving patriotic songs or prayers for victory.

This offset musical evocation also has much in common with the use of Vera Lynn's 1939 success "We'll Meet Again" at the end of *Dr. Strangelove*, as both scenes convoke musical elements from a reassuring past: set and released at the height of Cold War tensions, *Dr. Strangelove* suddenly brings the contemporary viewer back to a past war (the issue of which was already known to be favorable), while the soldiers of *Full Metal Jacket* sing a song evocative of a careless childhood. Both songs involve a childish denial of the situation, which is not only shown but also exposed as such: in addition to the manner in which the movie portrays the persisting influence of the supposedly defeated Nazi ideology, thereby questioning the effective outcome of World War II, the final atomic catastrophe in *Dr. Strangelove* actually leaves little if any chance to ever "meet again"; in *Full Metal Jacket*, the singing of the Disney-themed song, the lyrics of which include perceivable military metaphors such as "Forever let us hold our banner high" or several appearances of the word "marching," represents a final attempt to disarm the situation as well as to escape the actual context in which the men are actually marching—an attempt that is ultimately voided when the end credits unroll to the music of the Rolling Stones' "Paint It Black," suddenly making the absence of any possible escape explicit and reminiscent of the well-known ending of the Vietnam War for the United States. These apparent regressive behaviors contribute to create the "superficial universe where evil and negative things are deprived of depth" of kitsch,[27] while the accompanying denial of the obvious death and dangers inherent to these situations evokes Milan Kundera's vision of kitsch not only as "a world in which shit is denied and everyone behaves as if it did not exist,"[28] but also as a "permanent social request"[29] aimed at preserving the illusion of a supposedly perfect world. Although nothing indicates whether Kubrick ever read Kundera's *The Unbearable Lightness of Being* (a novel whose first English translation had come out in 1984, three years prior to the release of *Full Metal Jacket*), such a parallel gives an interesting hindsight on Kubrick's displacement of the murder-suicide scene that concludes the first part of the story from the squad bay in Hasford's novel to the latrines in the movie, denying the characters—and the viewers—the possibility to take refuge in denial in front of a particularly graphic scene.

Seemingly censored by these attempts at softening the message, the onscreen experience fails at successfully fulfilling a memorial duty, but neither does it manage to regain the authenticity of innocence. Actually, the very possibility of an authentic innocence in the eyes of Kubrick can even be doubted considering the director's own words on the nature of Man as an "ignoble savage" (instead of a noble one) and his denunciation of "Rousseau's romantic fallacy that it is society which corrupts man" (instead of the other way around) as a "pessimistic" and "hopeless" philosophy.[30] In such a paradigm, is there any possibility—even in retrospect—for such a thing as a "*Good* War"? In the end, Kubrick's position regarding innocence and experience appears closer to the third side defined by R. W. B. Lewis in his 1955 essay *The American Adam*: the "party of Irony," as neither hope or memory seem to be adequately served in his films—although they appear to lean much more toward the struggling, almost doomed "American as Laocoön" than the hopeful, Emersonian American as Adam.[31]

However, as ironic as it may be, Kubrick's art also owes a lot to memory through the ideas of repetition and variation, two notions that are inherent to the very concept of movie genre. In such a codified cinematographic category as the war film, repetitions and variations are all the more crucial to understand the full dimension of the message delivered onscreen. In Kubrick's universe, which is known for the heavy underlying influence of various philosophical references, these two notions are of course to be analyzed through several thoughts and theories revolving around them.

The very existence of genres in the cinematographic domain, as well as Kubrick's if only partial adherence to them in the films of the corpus examined here, both evoke Walter Benjamin's idea that "The uniqueness of a work of art is inseparable from its being imbedded in the fabric of tradition."[32] But the said "tradition" here goes beyond the sole artistic dimension, and Kubrick's references not only addressed his predecessors behind the camera but also the entire American society of his youth through a thorough questioning of the messages delivered at the time by the overall wartime iconography and discourse. While recently some critics and scholars have pointed out that Kubrick's movies are "neither anti-war nor pro-war,"[33] the balanced critical approach involved in these films departs strongly from the hagiographic style that was the rule in the 1940s—and extended much later, considering movies such as John Wayne's 1968 *The Green Berets*. To a certain extent, the Jungian duality of the shadow explicitly evoked in *Full Metal Jacket* is not only relevant in describing the onscreen soldiers or their real-life counterparts, but also the very genre movie that developed this parallel.

The aforementioned extensive use of irony by Kubrick can also be paralleled with Gilles Deleuze's view of repetition through irony and humor as two ways of "overturning the law,"[34] the said "law" being here the flattering norm that applied to 1940s war-related motion pictures. Such an analysis allows the corpus considered here to divide into two equal parts: *Fear and Desire* and *Paths of Glory* are only very implicitly ironic and identifying them as such requires prior knowledge of the genre paradigms inherent to war films, while Kubrick's following two war movies displayed blatant irony understandable even outside of the codes of the genre. While it illustrates Soren Kierkegaard's vision of repetition as intrinsically linked with renewal, this concurringly chronological divide also coincides with Karl Marx's vision of the second iteration in a historical repetitive process as necessarily farcical in nature, the tragedy-laden first two films giving way to the comedic *Dr. Strangelove* and the bittersweet (yet not devoid of occasional comical shifts) *Full Metal Jacket*.

Quite expectedly considering the strong influence exercised by Nietzsche's philosophy on Kubrick's work, the philosopher's idea of "eternal return" as introduced in aphorism #341 of *The Gay Science*[35] is of course also relevant here, with the depiction of a strictly similar phenomenon (war) through a focus that actually evolves. While *Paths of Glory* is the sole of the four films considered here to present an apparently circular structure, with Dax and his men bound to return to the front the next day, the radical evolutions induced by the endings of the three other films still manage to make repetition and irreversible change coexist. While the last scene of *Fear and Desire* affirms the definite impossibility of Mac and Sidney ever returning to their previous states, it also inscribes itself into the universal and repetitive circle of wars when Corby replies to Fletcher's overt doubt to be "built for" facing the death and madness induced by conflicts with the words "nobody ever was." In spite of its apocalyptic ending, *Dr. Strangelove* also stages the return of the Nazi ideology—and its possible triumph, should the survivors of the nuclear holocaust indeed be selected according to Strangelove's criteria. Finally, *Full Metal Jacket*'s closing invocation of childhood manages to hint at the endless recruiting cycle at the heart of the military system: as the traumatized soldiers sing a song that each of them knew as a child, it is understated that every child may as well one day be turned into a traumatized soldier. The film also insists on the irreversibility of the transformations induced by the war experience. But as in Nietzsche's logic, as the "change" induced by the very conscience of this eternally repetitive nature weighs upon the subject (here the filmmaker), the very observation of these similarities eventually induces the failure of *identical* repetition, and *Full Metal Jacket*, the last in this series of iterations of a supposedly similar object (the war film), is sometimes seen as not being a war movie but instead a film "on the representation of war and on the *analogy between all techniques of indoctrination*"[36] in the words of Jordi Vidal, consequently also involving a transformation of the film into a metarepresentational object.

While the visual universe of the Second World War was of course heavily influential on his way of picturing war, Kubrick managed to avoid letting these references confine his own depictions to a preexisting and dated model. Conversely, his sparing use of subtle references allowed him to provide points of references, which resulted in the highlighting of changes and evolutions both in the American society's relation to war and in the depiction of armed conflicts on the silver screen from the 1940s on. If the resulting movies were obviously not in the continuity of the World War II imagery or rhetoric, neither were they in radical or systematic opposition with them, but the products of an evolving artistic and thinking process that had taken these as one of its origins and recognized them as such. Through sophisticated combinations of intertextuality and novelty, creation and distortion, understated shadows and audible echoes, Stanley Kubrick not only contributed to the development of the war film genre; he also provided markers that allowed to measure that very evolution.

NOTES

1. Gene D. Phillips, "Early Works," in *The Stanley Kubrick Archives*, ed. Alison Castle, 268–76 (London: Taschen, 2008), 268.

2. Guillaume Mouleux, "La formation de la 'meilleure des générations': propagande et société aux États-Unis durant la Deuxième Guerre Mondiale" (PhD diss., Université Sorbonne Paris Cité/Université Paris Diderot–Paris 7, 2018), 168–93. My doctoral dissertation develops the observation that in classic 1940s Hollywood war tropes, redemption through heroism had to be ultimately accompanied by the protagonist's sacrificial death whenever his conversion had only followed an "original sin" on his part that was not only ideologically objectionable but had also unwillingly caused the death of an ally. Lary May insists on another kind of conversion in movies from the same era, one that was aimed at shaping the postwar white consumer society: see Lary May, *The Big Tomorrow: Hollywood and the Politics of the American Way* (Chicago, IL: The University of Chicago Press, 2000), chap. 4 .

3. An equally interesting analysis of the onscreen shaving of the recruit's heads at the beginning of the film was suggested by film critic Terrence Rafferty, according to whom the scene represents a preoperative routine before the proper training, which was supposed to act as "an operation on their brains, a procedure that excises, with laserlike precision, all traces of humane and civilized impulses and implants in their place the hard instincts of killers." See Terrence Rafferty, *"Full Metal Jacket," The Nation*, August 1, 1987: 98–99, https://www.thenation.com/article/full-metal-jacket/ (accessed 18 December 2019).

4. Susan White, "Kubrick and Death," in *Death in Classic and Contemporary Film: Fade To Black*, ed. Daniel Sullivan and Jeff Greenberg, 167–83 (New York: Palgrave Macmillan, 2003), 169.

5. Jordi Vidal, *Traité du combat moderne: films et fictions de Stanley Kubrick* (Paris: Allia, 2005), 130.

6. Greg Jenkins, *Stanley Kubrick and the Art of Adaptation: Three Novels, Three Films* (Jefferson, NC: McFarland & Company, 2007), 109–10.

7. While the proportion of draftees was significantly lower among the Marines, it still amounted to 42,600 (approximately 10 percent of the total number of Marines deployed in Vietnam). See John Prados, "The Marines' Vietnam Commitment," *Naval History Magazine* 29, no. 2 (April 2015): 16–25, https://www.usni.org/magazines/naval-history-magazine/2015/april/marines-vietnam-commitment (accessed 18 December 2019).

8. While the "steers and queers" line had already been used in Taylor Hackford's 1982 award-winning film *An Officer and a Gentleman*, the remark in Hackford's movie applied to a recruit from Oklahoma, making the shift to Texas (and the accompanying parallel with *Captains of the Clouds*) all the more relevant.

9. Gustav Hasford, *The Short-Timers* (New York: Harper & Row, 1979).

10. Vincent LoBrutto, *Stanley Kubrick: A Biography* (New York: Da Capo Press, 1999), 90.

11. The original poster (ca.1942–1943) is registered in the U.S. National Archives Catalog under National Archives Identifier (NAID) 534105 and Local Identifier 179-WP-256.

12. Michael Herr, *Kubrick* (London: Picador, 2001), 47–48.

13. This very short sequence is also absent from the original novel by Hasford.

14. In another Freudian ambiguity, the scene that shows an aircraft being refilled by an air tanker has been interpreted both as a visual metaphor for sexual intercourse and as "a mother giving suck to her infant." See Alexander Walker, Sybil Taylor, and Ulrich Ruchti, *Stanley Kubrick, Director* (New York: W. W. Norton & Company, 2000), 121.

15. Paula Willoquet-Maricondi, "Full Metal Jacketing, or Masculinity in the Making," in *Depth of Field: Stanley Kubrick, Film, and the Use of History*, ed. Geoffrey Cocks, 218–41 (Madison, WI: University of Wisconsin Press, 2006), 220–26. Also according to Willoquet-Maricondi (op. cit., 221–22), Kubrick "forces his audience to re-examine . . . the central myths that continue to define 'America' by defining masculinity."

16. See Ronald Takaki, *Hiroshima* (Boston, MA: Little, Brown and Company, 1995), 28–29.

17. Another way in which Kubrick departs from the Vietnam movie subgenre in *Full Metal Jacket* is of course his focus on urban warfare, instead of the expected jungle setting of previous Vietnam movies—which was itself reminiscent of World War II depictions of the war in the Pacific.

18. Elizabeth F. Cooke, "The Dialogue of Fear in *Fear and Desire* and *Dr. Strangelove*," in *The Philosophy of Stanley Kubrick*, ed. Jerold J. Abrams, 9–31 (Lexington: The University Press of Kentucky, 2007), 10. This aspect is of course to be related with one of the major themes in *2001: A Space Odyssey*, which was to come out four years later.

19. Sam Azulys, *Stanley Kubrick: une odyssée philosophique* (Chatou: les éditions de la transparence, 2011), 110.

20. Glenn Perusek, "Kubrick's Armies: Strategy, Hierarchy, and Motive in the War Films of Stanley Kubrick," in *Depth of Field: Stanley Kubrick, Film, and the Use of History*, 77–100, 78.

21. Michel Ciment, *Kubrick* (Paris: Calmann-Lévy, 2004), 208.

22. Stanley Milgram, "Behavioral Study of Obedience," *Journal of Abnormal and Social Psychology* 67, no. 4 (1963), 371–78.

23. R. W. B. Lewis, *The American Adam* (Chicago, IL: The University of Chicago Press, 1955), 7.

24. Gaylord C. LeRoy, "American Innocence Reconsidered," *The Massachusetts Review* 4, no. 4 (Summer, 1963): 625.

25. Amy K. Milligan, "Hair Today, Gone Tomorrow: Upsherin, Alef-Bet, and the Childhood Navigation of Jewish Gender Identity Symbol Sets," *Children's Folklore Review* 38 (2017): 7–26. Milligan explains how the *upsherin* marks a little Jewish boy's passage from infancy to childhood and from being cared for by his mother to being "educated and raised under male leadership," as well as the beginning of his formal religious education. In the film, this description relates respectively with the young recruits' transition into adulthood, the eminently virile manner in which Hartman exercises his authority, and the military mystique that he tries to convey. It may also explain the renaming of the character as "Hartman" (a rather common name among Ashkenazi Jews), instead of "Gerheim" in Hasford's novel—although the character retains his declared attachment to the Virgin Mary. See also Yoram Bilu, "From Milah (Circumcision) to Milah (Word): Male Identity and Rituals of Childhood in the Jewish

Ultraorthodox Community," *Ethos* 31, no. 2 (June 2003), 172–203. Bilu specifically insists on the conforming dimension of the traditional ceremony, following which "the little boy . . . becomes a miniature replica of his father. He is granted, as the participants say, 'the figure of a Jew.'" This idea can be paralleled with the uniformity in appearance conferred to the recruits as a symbol of their incorporation into the Marines with the aim to have them ultimately reproduce the model of their instructor, endowed with a father-figure role. Although Kubrick originated from a nonreligious Jewish background, such a reference in *Full Metal Jacket* is consistent both with Milligan's depiction of the existence of *upsherin* as "familiar to most contemporary Jews, even among more liberal Jewish movements" who do not practice it and with Nathan Abrams's view of the Jewish cultural experience as central to Kubrick's work especially after 1967 (Nathan Abrams, "A Hidden Heart of Jewishness and Englishness: Stanley Kubrick," *European Judaism* 47, no. 2 [Autumn 2014], 69–76). The ambiguity of Kubrick's relation to his own Eastern European Jewish roots is also repeatedly illustrated in Michael Herr's *Kubrick*.

26. In such a setting, the mention by Joker's voiceover of the fact that the men are heading toward a river to set in for the night evokes the Styx and only adds to this impression.

27. Jean Robelin, "Le kitsch ou l'authenticité de l'inauthentique," *Noesis* 22–23 (2014): 203–17, https://journals.openedition.org/noesis/1902, accessed 18 December 2019. Translation is mine.

28. Milan Kundera, *L'insoutenable légèreté de l'être*, translated from Czech by François Kérel and revised by the author (Paris: Gallimard, 1987), 311. Translation from French to English is mine.

29. Milan Kundera, *Les testaments trahis* (Paris: Gallimard, 1993), 170–71. Translation is mine.

30. Stanley Kubrick, "Now Kubrick Fights Back," *The New York Times* (February 27, 1972), Section 2: 1, 11.

31. Lewis, *The American Adam*, 197. The image of Laocoön, a mythological Trojan priest who was—in some versions of the myth—killed by the very god he served, is all the more relevant when considering *Full Metal Jacket* and Hartman's wish to turn each recruit into a "minister of death, praying for war."

32. Walter Benjamin, "The Work of Art in the Age of Mechanical Reproduction," in *Illusions*, translated by Harry Zohn and edited by Hannah Arendt, 217–51 (New York: Schocken Books, 1968), 223.

33. Philip Kuberski, *Kubrick's Total Cinema: Philosophical Themes and Formal Qualities* (London: Continuum, 2012), 52.

34. Gilles Deleuze, *Difference and Repetition*, translated by Paul Patton (New York: Columbia University Press, 1994), 5.

35. Friedrich Nietzsche, *The Gay Science*, translated by Walter Kaufmann (New York: Vintage Books, 1974), 273–74.

36. Vidal, *Traité du combat moderne*, 84. Translation is mine, italics are the author's.

REFERENCES

Abrams, Nathan. "A Hidden Heart of Jewishness and Englishness: Stanley Kubrick." *European Judaism* 47, no. 2 (Autumn 2014): 69–76.

Azulys, Sam. *Stanley Kubrick: une odyssée philosophique*. Chatou: les éditions de la transparence, 2011.

Benjamin, Walter. "The Work of Art in the Age of Mechanical Reproduction." In *Illusions*, translated by Harry Zohn and edited by Hannah Arendt, 217–51. New York: Schocken Books, 1968.

Bilu, Yoram. "From Milah (Circumcision) to Milah (Word): Male Identity and Rituals of Childhood in the Jewish Ultraorthodox Community." *Ethos* 31, no. 2 (June 2003): 172–203.

Ciment, Michel. *Kubrick*. Paris: Calmann-Lévy, 2004.

Cooke, Elizabeth F. "The Dialogue of Fear in *Fear and Desire* and *Dr. Strangelove*." In *The Philosophy of Stanley Kubrick*, edited by Jerold J. Abrams, 9–31. Lexington, KY: The University Press of Kentucky, 2007.

Deleuze, Gilles. *Difference and Repetition*, translated by Paul Patton. New York: Columbia University Press, 1994.
Hasford, Gustav. *The Short-Timers*. New York: Harper & Row, 1979.
Herr, Michael. *Kubrick*. London: Picador, 2001.
Jenkins, Greg. *Stanley Kubrick and the Art of Adaptation: Three Novels, Three Films*. Jefferson, NC: McFarland & Company, 2007.
Kuberski, Philip. *Kubrick's Total Cinema: Philosophical Themes and Formal Qualities*. London: Continuum, 2012.
Kubrick, Stanley. "Now Kubrick Fights Back." *The New York Times*, February 27, 1972, Section 2: 1, 11.
Kundera, Milan. *L'insoutenable légèreté de l'être*, translated from Czech by François Kérel and revised by the author. Paris: Gallimard, 1987.
———. *Les testaments trahis*. Paris: Gallimard, 1993.
LeRoy, Gaylord C. "American Innocence Reconsidered." *The Massachusetts Review* 4, no. 4 (Summer, 1963): 623–46.
Lewis, R. W. B. *The American Adam: Innocence, Tragedy and Tradition in the Nineteenth Century*. Chicago, IL: The University of Chicago Press, 1955.
LoBrutto, Vincent. *Stanley Kubrick: A Biography*. New York: Da Capo Press, 1999.
May, Lary. *The Big Tomorrow: Hollywood and the Politics of the American Way*. Chicago, IL: The University of Chicago Press, 2000.
Milgram, Stanley. "Behavioral Study of Obedience." *Journal of Abnormal and Social Psychology* 67, no. 4 (1963): 371–78.
Milligan, Amy K. "Hair Today, Gone Tomorrow: Upsherin, Alef-Bet, and the Childhood Navigation of Jewish Gender Identity Symbol Sets." *Children's Folklore Review* 38 (2017), 7–26.
Mouleux, Guillaume. "La formation de la 'meilleure des générations': propagande et société aux Etats-Unis durant la Deuxième Guerre Mondiale." PhD diss., Université Sorbonne Paris Cité/Université Paris Diderot–Paris 7, 2018.
Nietzsche, Friedrich. *The Gay Science*, translated by Walter Kaufmann. New York: Vintage Books, 1974.
Perusek, Glenn. "Kubrick's Armies: Strategy, Hierarchy, and Motive in the War Films of Stanley Kubrick." In *Depth of Field: Stanley Kubrick, Film, and the Uses of History*, edited by Geoffrey Cocks, 77–100. Madison, WI: University of Wisconsin Press, 2006.
Phillips, Gene D. "Early Works." In *The Stanley Kubrick Archives*, edited by Alison Castle, 268–76. London: Taschen, 2008.
Prados, John. "The Marines' Vietnam Commitment." *Naval History Magazine* 29, no. 2 (April 2015): 16–25. https://www.usni.org/magazines/naval-history-magazine/2015/april/marines-vietnam-commitment.
Rafferty, Terrence. "*Full Metal Jacket*." *The Nation*, August 1, 1987: 98–99. https://www.thenation.com/article/full-metal-jacket/.
Robelin, Jean. "Le kitsch ou l'authenticité de l'inauthentique." *Noesis* 22–23 (2014): 203–17. https://journals.openedition.org/noesis/1902.
Takaki, Ronald. *Hiroshima*. Boston, MA: Little, Brown and Company, 1995.
Vidal, Jordi. *Traité du combat moderne: films et fictions de Stanley Kubrick*. Paris: Allia, 2005.
Walker, Alexander, Sybil Taylor, and Ulrich Ruchti. *Stanley Kubrick, Director*. New York: W. W. Norton & Company, 2000.
White, Susan. "Kubrick and Death." In *Death in Classic and Contemporary Film: Fade To Black*, edited by Daniel Sullivan and Jeff Greenberg, 167–83. New York: Palgrave Macmillan, 2003.
Willoquet-Maricondi, Paula. "Full Metal Jacketing, or Masculinity in the Making." In *Depth of Field: Stanley Kubrick, Film, and the Uses of History*, edited by Geoffrey Cocks, 218–41. Madison, WI: University of Wisconsin Press, 2006.

Part II

Master of Chaos and Transgression

Chapter Seven

The Philosophy of War in *Dr. Strangelove*

Jerold J. Abrams

Stanley Kubrick's *Dr. Strangelove, or: How I Learned to Stop Worrying and Love the Bomb* (1964) is a satirical black comedy about global nuclear annihilation at the height of the Cold War.[1] *Dr. Strangelove* is also a brilliant illustration of the ancient Greek pre-Socratic philosopher Heraclitus's view of war as a cyclical and never-ending game. In Heraclitus's philosophy, the very structure of existence is "war," understood ontologically as continuous "becoming" (or change). All things in nature undergo continuous change within this never-ending cycle of creation and destruction according to the "*logos*" (which means word, language, and order). All things in civilization also undergo continuous change according to this universal cycle of creation and destruction. But within civilization human beings are both part of the *logos* (language), and they possess language as a power unique to the species. As "war" takes the form of "becoming" in nature, in civilization becoming takes the form of actual wars between villages, cities, and states, which wield language (*logos*) as an instrument of power. The supreme masters of language (instrumental rationality) within these actual wars consequently become the supreme masters of war itself. They master war as a vast rational and strategic game and command soldiers and artillery as instruments of battle. These masters of instrumental rationality know that the history of war is not an unfortunate succession of particular wars pervaded by contingency on the way to an ideal condition of ultimate peace, but instead that war is universal, necessary, cyclical, and permanent, because war is being itself, and that the end of each war is simply the beginning of the next. Cultures, positions, alliances, strategies, technologies, and spoils in war have always and will always change from one war to the next, but war itself does not change and will never change. In *Dr. Strangelove* this philosophy of cyclical and unending war appears in the historically seamless and seemingly inevitable transition from World War II to the Cold War to nuclear war to the Mineshaft War, which begins at the end of the film.

A preliminary summary of the film will be helpful. The opening shot of *Dr. Strangelove* closely resembles Leni Riefenstahl's opening shot sequence in her black-and-white Nazi propaganda film *Triumph of the Will* (1934), commissioned by Adolf Hitler himself.[2] *Dr. Strangelove*, like *Triumph of the Will*, begins in the sky above the clouds in an airplane from a window gazing upon the horizon. In *Triumph of the Will* the camera takes the perspective of Adolf Hitler seated in the cockpit of a plane that then descends through the clouds to land at the 1934 Nazi Party Congress in Nuremberg, Germany, where Hitler will mobilize a nation for war. In *Dr. Strangelove* the above-the-clouds shots of midair refueling establish the presence of U.S. Air Force bombers prepared to drop megaton nuclear bombs on the U.S.S.R., should the pilots receive orders to attack.

From Burpelson Air Force Base, Brigadier General Jack D. Ripper (Sterling Hayden), Commander of the Strategic Air Command 843rd Bomb Wing sends to all of the bombers "Wing Attack Plan R," according to which the bombers will strike the U.S.S.R. with nuclear warheads. Ripper believes the U.S.S.R. has introduced "fluoridation" in 1964 to poison the earth's drinking water, and successfully degraded the mental capacities of the president of the United States, Merkin Muffley (Peter Sellers) and the generals of the War Room. Ripper reasons that upon discovery of a first strike, and an imminent Soviet counterstrike, the president will have no choice but "total commitment" of the U.S. nuclear arsenal against the U.S.S.R. to secure victory.

U.S.A.F. Chief of Staff General Buck Turgidson (George C. Scott) informs the president of Ripper's initiation of Attack Plan R, and that Ripper alone possesses the recall code. The president requests Soviet ambassador Alexei de Sadeski (Peter Bull) to join him in the War Room, and then call to inform Soviet Premier Demitri Kissoff of Plan R so that the Soviets can shoot down the U.S. bombers. But the premier informs the ambassador, who then informs the president, of the U.S.S.R.'s secret Doomsday Machine. The Doomsday Machine is a network of Cobalt-Thorium-G nuclear bombs (designed for augmented radiation) set to detonate automatically and irrevocably by computer should any bomb fall inside the U.S.S.R. But the Doomsday Machine only functions as a mechanism of absolute deterrence against any first strike, by the United States or U.S.S.R., if both sides know about it. Unfortunately the U.S.S.R. failed to announce the Doomsday Machine, so now the president's first plan is irrelevant: shooting down bombers carrying nuclear bombs will trigger the device.

A second plan is needed. The president must capture Ripper to extract the recall code by torture to recall all the bombers. As U.S. troops take Burpelson, Ripper shoots himself to escape torture and secure victory, but Royal Air Force Group Captain Lionel Mandrake (Peter Sellers) soon deciphers and sends the recall code to the president. The president then successfully recalls all the bombers but one, which will eventually drop its bomb inside the U.S.S.R. and thereby trigger the Doomsday Machine. Inside the War Room the naturalized German Nazi scientist and strategy advisor Dr. Strangelove (Peter Sellers) informs the president and War Room that an elite society of men like themselves, along with the most beautiful and intelligent American women, at a ratio of ten women to every man, must descend to pre-established habitable underground mineshaft cities. Underground the survivors will repopulate their numbers for the duration of a century, awaiting dissipation of radiation levels, at which time the only partially reconstituted nation will retake the surface to fight the Soviets. But the U.S.S.R. has also established its mineshaft cities and will plan to repopulate their numbers to fight the United States after a century underground. The United States and U.S.S.R. also both know that more mineshaft space is necessary for a greater number, which will secure either side's advantage. So each side must immediately begin capturing the other's limited mineshaft space. So in the very moment the Cold War ends with the outbreak of nuclear war, the Mineshaft War has already begun, and the Mineshaft War will end in one century when the surface war begins. Presumably, once that war ends another war will begin. War in *Dr. Strangelove* is perpetual, cyclical, universal, and necessary, as it is in Heraclitus's philosophy.

Heraclitus's writings survive only in fragments, but together they reveal the outlines of a unified philosophy. "It is wise," writes Heraclitus, "listening not to be me but to the report: to agree that all things are one."[3] The word "report" is a translation of the Greek word "*logos*," which may also be translated as "word" or "language" or "ordering." According to the *logos* (the report), all things are one, but the "one" is also self-opposed and volatile.[4] As Heraclitus writes, "The ordering, the same for all, no god nor man has made, but it ever was and is and will be: fire everliving, kindled in measures and in measures going out."[5] Here Heraclitus claims that the universe is uncreated, eternal, and perpetually self-transforming according to the *logos*, which is fire-everliving.[6] This fire everliving, in human history, takes the form of conflict, violence, and war.

In establishing this philosophical view of human history, Heraclitus openly opposes Homer: "Homer was wrong when he said, 'Would that Conflict might vanish from among gods and men!' (*Iliad*, XVIII.107). For there would be no attunement without high and low notes, nor any animals, male and female, both of which are opposites."[7] Homer wills that conflict disappear among men and women, and even among the gods of Olympus, such as Zeus, Hera, Athena, Apollo, and so on. But, according to Heraclitus, conflict is the necessary condition of all "attunement" among humans, among the gods, and even among the animals, for "all things come to pass from conflict."[8] If all things come to pass from conflict, and conflict were to end, then nothing would come to pass. To will that conflict and war should come to an end is to will that being would come to an end, because being is war. Heraclitus explains that the ordering of the universe requires conflict with his famous image of the lyre and the bow and the reconciliation of the high notes and the low notes in musical attunement.[9] Plato in the *Symposium* notes this image of the lyre in Heraclitus's philosophy: "The one, he says, 'being at variance with itself is in agreement with itself' 'like the attunement of a bow or a lyre.'"[10] Plato then comments: "Heraclitus probably meant that an expert musician creates a harmony by resolving the prior discord between high and low notes."[11] As a bow acts on a lyre to create musical attunement by reconciliation of low notes and high notes, the *logos* creates ontological attunement with itself by dividing itself (as if into bow and lyre) and continuously reconciling its opposing elements, while at the same time undoing that reconciliation with perpetual introduction of discord.

In addition to dismissing Homer's desire for an end of war, Heraclitus also dismisses the poet's pantheon of anthropological gods, replacing them with war: "War is father of all and king of all; and some he has shown as gods, others men; some he has made slaves, others free."[12] W. K. C. Guthrie in "Flux and *Logos* in Heraclitus" comments on this fragment: "By calling War 'father and king of all,' Heraclitus deliberately recalls Homer's titles for Zeus, and so suggests that War, not Zeus, is the supreme god."[13] War is not literally a god or a father or a king, but the supreme principle of the universe, the *logos*.[14] But this supreme principle, according to Heraclitus, shows some men to be "gods."[15] These men are not literally gods either but godlike warriors and masterminds of war.[16] The godlike men of war are "free" because they stand above all other men whom they use as "instruments" and "slaves" in their mastery of war.[17] Any such godlike man is virtually equivalent to an army: "One man is ten thousand, if he is the best."[18]

Even though the mastermind of war moves men in war by thought as instruments, this superior man is also a kind of instrument. Like all men he is an instrument of the *logos* because he is a part of the *logos*. But the mastermind is a purer and naturally fine-tuned conduit (or medium or vehicle) of the *logos*, a virtually superhuman vehicle of war. The greater his union with the *logos*, and the greater his self-understanding as a conduit of war, the greater his freedom and power over all other instruments. If the universe is an unconscious game of war, the mastermind is the truest human (or superhuman) expression of the universe because he is war itself become self-conscious. He takes himself to be the supreme embodied instrument of the ultimate game.

In one of his most important fragments, Heraclitus describes war as a child playing a game against itself, for all time: "Lifetime is a child at play, moving pieces in a game. Kingship belongs to the child."[19] Here Heraclitus claims human life (or even existence itself) to be one child and king who plays a game whose rules are his own, and whose game is the becoming of all things. Charles H. Kahn in "A New Look at Heraclitus" comments on this fragment: "Life-time (*aiôn*) is the royal player, moving pieces back and forth in a game whose rules are those of the cosmos. It is War, the struggle of opposing tendencies up and down, which assigns everyone his place: god or man, slave or free."[20] As a father begets a child, a king begets a king; and as fire begets fire, war begets war. In Heraclitus's philosophy, king, war, game, fire, language, father, and child are all one. This child is one child because all things are one, but the child is also self-opposed because all things are self-opposed. These two sides of the child are opposed only through the game they play, which is war, although they are only one child because the universe is the one game of war. If the child's game of war may be compared to chess, then the one child divides itself into black and white. Black has one king, and white has one king. Each king is a mastermind, and all the other pieces on the board are instruments of either king: pawn, rook, knight, bishop, queen. Neither king moves much in the game, but each moves all his other pieces against his opponent. The white king wins only by destroying the other, but destruction of the other king or "child" by necessity creates from itself a new black king as an opposite to play the game again. Each game's end begins another game.[21]

Like no other film, *Dr. Strangelove* illustrates this philosophy of war as a cyclical and never-ending game. First, *Dr. Strangelove* begins at the height of the Cold War, named for its opposition to World War II. World War II was a "hot war" because Axis and Allies fought one another with gunfire, tanks, rockets, and bombs. The Cold War was "cold" because the United States and the U.S.S.R. did not attack one another with artillery and bombs, but instead "fought" by means of espionage and increasing threat of destruction from maximization of nuclear stockpiles. As Heraclitus claims each thing becomes its opposite through war, the hot war of World War II, culminating in nuclear destruction, transformed into a cold war. As "cold warms up," writes Heraclitus, "warm cools off."[22] Cold can never stave off hot for long, any more than hot can stave off cold: "Fire coming on will discern and catch up with all things."[23] In *Dr. Strangelove*, terror and madness mount in the Cold War with the ever-increasing threat of mutually assured nuclear destruction, until finally fire catches up with both sides.

Second, the positions on the gameboard of the world changed from World War II to the Cold War. In World War II, "The Big Three," i.e., England, the United States, and the U.S.S.R., led the Allies against Germany, Japan, and Italy.[24] After World War II ended, the United States and the U.S.S.R. broke their alliance and became enemies. As Heraclitus writes, opposites become their opposites in a continuous movement of transposition, in a never-ending game of war: "For these transposed are those, and those transposed again are these."[25] But the transposition of opposites in World War II, and in *Dr. Strangelove*, entails more than the altering of sides. The sides themselves in the Cold War reduce in number and expand in size. In World War II, three nations fought three nations, each with its own allies, but in the Cold War one "bloc" fought another, and all other countries effectively became instruments on either side of the game. The Soviets led the Eastern Bloc, and the United States led the Western Bloc. As Heraclitus's "child" plays for absolute conquest over himself in the game of war, in the Cold War the species divided itself into two halves with each playing for absolute conquest of the other.

Third, at the end of World War II, the United States in Operation Paperclip extracted about sixteen hundred Nazi rocket scientists and engineers from Germany to America to fight the U.S.S.R. At the same time, the U.S.S.R. in Operation Osoaviakhim extracted about two thousand Nazi rocket scientists and engineers from Germany to Russia to fight the United States.[26] According to Annie Jacobsen in *Operation Paperclip: The Secret Intelligence Program that Brought Nazi Scientists to America*, "The CIOS [Combined Intelligence Objectives Subcommittee] Black List for rocket research included one thousand names of scientists and engineers slated for interrogation. Wernher von Braun was at the top of that list."[27] Von Braun was at the top of the list partly for his work on the V-2 (*Vergeltungswaffe* 2) long-range ballistic missile. He surrendered to the Americans in May 1945, became a U.S. citizen, and soon began working for the army and the NASA Space Program.

Kubrick based the character of Dr. Strangelove on von Braun. As David Hughes writes in *The Complete Kubrick*, "[Peter] Sellers later revealed that the model for Strangelove was Werner von Braun—the German rocket pioneer who worked on the US space programme."[28] Jacobsen in *Operation Paperclip* similarly recognizes von Braun as the primary source of the character of Dr. Strangelove: "Filmmaker Stanley Kubrick created a von Braun–inspired character in his black comedy *Dr. Strangelove* in which a mad scientist famously gets out of his wheelchair and cries, "*Mein Führer*, I can walk!"[29]

But even though he based his Cold War film on actual U.S. military operations and an actual Nazi scientist, Kubrick also clearly based *Dr. Strangelove* on another satirical black-and-white film: namely, Charlie Chaplin's *The Great Dictator* (1940). In fact, several elements of Chaplin's *Great Dictator* can be seen in Kubrick's *Dr. Strangelove*. First, the timing of each film's release is important. As Chaplin satirizes Nazi Germany and fascist Italy right in the middle of World War II, Kubrick satirizes the United States and the U.S.S.R. right in the middle of the Cold War. Second, both directors invent absurd names for the characters they mock. Chaplin baptizes his spoofs of Hitler and Benito Mussolini, respectively, with "Adenoid Hynkel," Dictator of Tomania, and "Signor Benzino Napoloni," Dictator of Bacteria (Jack Oakie), while Kubrick's film is populated with equally preposterous names: Dr. Strangelove, Merkin Muffley, Colonel Mandrake, Jack D. Ripper, King Kong, and Bat Guano.

Third, in both *The Great Dictator* and *Dr. Strangelove* these absurdly named leaders of powerful countries also behave ridiculously. In his own war room, Adenoid Hynkel's argument with Benzino Napoloni soon leads to a food fight. The scene is clearly referenced in *Dr. Strangelove* when General Turgidson attacks the Soviet ambassador at the food table for photographing the Big Board with a smuggled miniature spy camera. The president, who is as weak and uninformed as Ripper knew him to be, scolds the general and the ambassador: "Gentleman, you can't fight in here! This is the War Room!" The irony of the line lies in the president's implication that the War Room is no place for battle because violence can only impede rational deliberation. Kubrick also shot a food-fight scene in the War Room for *Dr. Strangelove*, like the one from *The Great Dictator*, but ultimately cut the scene from the film.[30] Images of the food-fight scene appear in *The Stanley Kubrick Archives*.[31]

Fourth, in both *The Great Dictator* and *Dr. Strangelove* the central character plays opposing roles. Chaplin wrote and directed *The Great Dictator*, but he also played the Jewish Barber of Tomania, and the fascist anti-Semitic dictator Adenoid Hynkel. In *Dr. Strangelove* Sellers plays the British Colonel Mandrake, the American President Muffley, and the German Nazi scientist Dr. Strangelove. According to Gene D. Phillips in "*Dr. Strangelove, or: How I Learned to Stop Worrying and Love the Bomb*," Kubrick originally planned for Sellers to play the fourth role of Major T. J. "King" Kong, who commandeers the B-52 Stratofortress to deliver a megaton nuclear bomb into Russia. But already playing Muffley, Mandrake, and Dr. Strangelove, Sellers declined to play King Kong; and the role went to Slim Pickens, who is excellent as the twangy-voiced bomb-riding cowboy.[32] In casting Sellers in these three roles (Muffley, Mandrake, and Strangelove), Kubrick illustrates the Heraclitean underlying interchangeability of positions in the game of war, just as Chaplin reveals the interchangeability of the positions of Adenoid Hynkel and the Barber of Tomania. As one actor may play Adenoid Hynkel and the Barber, and another actor may play Mandrake, the president, and Dr. Strangelove, one man (perhaps any man)—under certain circumstances—may become a barber or dictator, a president or a Nazi scientist.

One could also argue that Sellers plays still more than these three characters. Dr. Strangelove is after all one man divided in two, not unlike the one child divided into two children, in Heraclitus's philosophy. One man is the German Nazi scientist *Herr Doktor Merkwürdigliebe*, while the other is the American scientist Dr. Strangelove. During World War II *Merkwürdigliebe* worked for Adolf Hitler to conquer Europe, but then became an American citizen and changed his name to "Strangelove" (which is the English translation *Merkwürdigliebe*). But despite changing his name, becoming a U.S. citizen, and working for the president to fight the U.S.S.R., Dr. Strangelove remains conflicted between his loyalty to the United States and his loyalty to the Nazi Party.[33]

As Dr. Strangelove sits in his wheelchair in the U.S. War Room, the metaphor for Operation Paperclip is vivid in two ways. After breaking Germany's back in World War II, the United States effectively extracted Germany's brain in Operation Paperclip. Germany, personified in Dr. Strangelove, can no longer walk or run militarily, but its brilliant mind now serves the United States against the U.S.S.R. Dr. Strangelove's separation into Nazi and American therefore appears as a horizontal division: his upper half is American, and his lower half is German. Dr. Strangelove is also vertically divided: his left arm and hand are loyal to the United States, but his right arm and hand are loyal to Nazi Germany. Dr. Strangelove wears a black glove on his right hand resembling perhaps the black leather gloves of the Nazi *Luftwaffe Fallschirmjager*, and perhaps also the black-gloved hand of the mad scientist Rotwang (Rudolph Klein-Rogge) in Fritz Lang's 1927 film *Metropolis*.

But even though *Dr. Strangelove* recasts and transposes so many themes and characters from *The Great Dictator*, ultimately Kubrick's philosophy is very different from Chaplin's. Nowhere is this difference more apparent than at their endings of their two films. At the end of *The Great Dictator*, Adenoid Hynkel gives his last speech: "I'm sorry, but I don't want to be an emperor. That's not my business. I don't want to rule or conquer anyone." All should be free and at peace, says Adenoid Hynkel. All should unite and be happy: "In this world there is room for everyone. And the good earth is rich and can provide for everyone. The way of life can be free and beautiful, but we have lost the way." We have lost the way, says Hynkel, because of "greed" and "hate" and all the "machinery" of the world that could be used for good, but instead is used for war. Eventually, however, says Hynkel, war will come to an end. "The hate of men will pass, and dictators die, and the power they took from the people will return to the people."

Dr. Strangelove, by contrast, ends with the recognition of the inevitability of global nuclear annihilation, and the eternal perpetuation of war. As the War Room accepts the imminent murder of billions, the president and the generals consider what must be done to ensure their survival. Dr. Strangelove alone has already anticipated and thought through the war game to its end, and informs the War Room about the next steps. Listening to Dr. Strangelove's plan for mineshaft civilization, Ambassador Sadeski appears quickly to exchange Soviet communism for post-apocalyptic American dictatorship: "I must confess you have an astonishingly good idea there, Doctor." Ambassador Sadeski then slips away from the discussion, among the president and generals in the War Room, to secretly photograph the Big Board. Even while planning to inhabit an American mineshaft city, Ambassador Sadeski also plots to continue to spy for the U.S.S.R. during the Mineshaft War.

Dr. Strangelove, Ambassador Sadeski, and General Turgidson all understand that war is perpetual and none so much as pauses learning of the activation of the Doomsday Machine, but instead immediately begins planning the next move in the game, as if annihilation were simply one more moved played on the board. They also understand that they must think quickly because the U.S.S.R. is also thinking through the strategy of the war game as it is played. For not only have the United States and the U.S.S.R. both created underground mineshaft cities, each side *knows* the other has created these mineshaft cities, *and* that after a century the next war will take place. The United States and the U.S.S.R. also know that whichever side possesses more underground space will be able to support a larger population and therefore a larger army. As General Turgidson claims, the United States must prevent the U.S.S.R. "from taking over other mineshaft space, in order to breed more prodigiously than we do, thus knocking us out from superior numbers when we emerge." Both sides must breed prodigiously, but mineshaft space is limited, so each side will immediately begin seizing mineshaft space from the other. The Mineshaft War is a zero-sum game: increasing U.S. mineshaft space means decreasing U.S.S.R. mineshaft space. The Mineshaft War is also a game of global strategic positioning. Space taken by the United States close to the U.S.S.R. will be advantageous for the United States, and space taken by the U.S.S.R. close to the United States will be advantageous for the U.S.S.R., a game analogous to positioning nuclear missiles in the Cold War. Dr. Strangelove has already thought through the entire game of the Mineshaft War, how to take U.S.S.R. mineshaft space, the most valued positions, and the attack timeframe following dissipation of radiation. "Sir, I have a plan!" Suddenly, Dr. Strangelove stands from his wheelchair. "*Mein Führer*! I can walk!" Nazi Germany is no longer paralyzed. Earlier the president declared, "I will not go down in history as the greatest mass murderer since Adolf Hitler!" Now the president knows he will indeed go down in history as a far worse mass murderer than Hitler, and Dr. Strangelove recognizes the president as the new American Nazi *Führer*.

The film cuts to a sequence of mushroom clouds over the Soviet Union, one after another, all set to Vera Lynn's version of "We'll Meet Again." Once the blue skies in a hundred years drive the dark nuclear clouds away, the United States and the U.S.S.R. will "meet again" in a new war, and another war after that war, in a never-ending cycle of war, a game that plays itself forever. The end of the game is always the beginning of the game, a game without beginning or end, as the beginning of a circle is the end of the circle, and the end of the circle its beginning. As Heraclitus writes, "The beginning and the end are shared in the circumference of a circle."[34] War is cyclical and never-ending. Each war ends as the next war begins, and all wars are one war, one game. The pieces on the board of the world may change their alliances and positions and weapons and strategies, but the game will no more come to an end than being itself will disappear. The true masterminds of war, the philosopher warriors whom Heraclitus identifies as gods and kings on earth who play the ultimate game, know the game will never end but always prepare for the next game and the one after that.

That is the philosophy of Kubrick's *Dr. Strangelove*, and one that Kubrick would advance once again in his next war film, *Full Metal Jacket* (1987). At a Vietnamese mass grave, Pogue Colonel (Bruce Boa) questions Sergeant J. T. "Joker" Davis (Matthew Modine) about his uniform and helmet. Joker wears a peace symbol on his chest, and "Born to Kill" is written on his helmet. The colonel demands to know the meaning of the contradiction, only one side of which is acceptable. "I think I was trying to suggest something about the duality of man, sir!" says Joker. Perplexed by a philosophical response, and suspecting himself well out of his depth, the colonel demands to know whose side Joker is on. "Our side, sir!" responds Joker. The colonel asks Joker if he loves his country. "Yes, sir!" says Joker. The colonel then asks Joker if he's ready to "get with the program" and "come on for the big win." "Yes, sir!" says Joker. Moderately satisfied, the colonel gives Joker some last words of advice: "It's a hardball world, son. We've got to try to keep our heads until this peace craze blows over." "Aye-aye, sir!" says Joker. Joker may be philosophically conflicted, but the colonel is not. The "Peace Movement" and its opposition to the war and all wars, during the 1960s in America, is nothing but a "craze," which will soon blow over. Peace symbols like the one on Joker's uniform are symptoms of an unfortunate if widespread delusion about the universe, what it has always been, and what it will always be. War is eternal.

NOTES

1. I am very grateful to Elsa Colombani and Antonio Sanna for helpful comments on an earlier draft of this chapter. Of course, any mistakes that remain are my own.
2. Following an opening shot of an eagle and swastika, *Triumph of the Will* announces itself as a "documentary of the Reich party congress." The effect of the film on the people of Germany would be powerful, mobilizing them toward unspeakable horror.
3. Heraclitus, Fragment XXXVI, in Charles H. Kahn, *The Art and Thought of Heraclitus* (Cambridge: Cambridge University, 1979), 45. All further references to Heraclitus are to this edition.
4. The unity and opposition of the *logos* may be seen in the structure of language. For example, one thinks oneself singular, but all thought is linguistic, and language is dialogical: to think at all is to dialogue with oneself, as speaker and hearer, and to presuppose the opposition of thought into speaker and hearer, even within one's own mind. Language itself is also one thing, but again language is always dialogical, self-opposed, and always flowing, and differentiating itself through its flowing.
5. Heraclitus, Fr. XXXVII, 45.

6. This point about flowing and becoming also appears in Heraclitus's best-known fragment: "One cannot step twice into the same river, nor can one grasp any mortal substance in a stable condition, but it scatters and again gathers; it forms and dissolves, and approaches and departs" (Fr. LI, 53). One cannot step into the same river twice because the water of the river is always flowing, always changing, always moving. Like the water of a rushing river, all things in being flow, all things move (*panta rhei*).

7. Heraclitus, Fr. LXXXI, 67. See also W. K. C. Guthrie in "Flux and *Logos* in Heraclitus," in *The Pre-Socratics: A Collection of Critical Essays*, ed. Alexander P. D. Mourelatos, 197–213 (Princeton, NJ: Princeton University Press, 1993): "In saying that justice (or right) is strife he probably shows himself aware also of Anaximander's teaching," writes Guthrie, "which branded the warfare of the opposites as a series of acts of injustice. On the contrary, retorts Heraclitus, it is the highest justice" (198). What he opposes in Anaximander's philosophy, Heraclitus more vehemently opposes in Homer's poetry; and opposing Homer, Heraclitus also appears to establish their opposition as expressing the *logos* itself.

8. Heraclitus, Fr. LXXV, 63.
9. Ibid., Fr. LXXVII, 65.
10. Plato, *Symposium*, in *Complete Works of Plato*, ed. John M. Cooper, 457–505 (Indianapolis, IN: Hackett, 1997), 187a–b, 471.
11. Ibid., 187a–b, 471.
12. Heraclitus, Fr. LXXXIII, 67.
13. Guthrie, "Flux and *Logos* in Heraclitus," 197.
14. In Cormac McCarthy's novel *Blood Meridian, or The Evening Redness in the West* (New York: Random House, 1992), Judge Holden articulates his Heraclitean philosophy: "It makes no difference what men think of war, said the judge. War endures. As well ask men what they think of stone" (259); and "War is the ultimate game because war is at last a forcing of the unity of existence. War is god" (261).
15. Heraclitus, Fr. LXXXIII, 67.
16. Ibid.
17. Ibid.
18. Ibid., Fr. LXIII, 57.
19. Ibid., Fr. XCIV, 71.
20. Charles H. Kahn, "A New Look at Heraclitus," *American Philosophical Quarterly*, vol. 1, no. 3 (July 1964), 200.
21. Friedrich Nietzsche in *Thus Spoke Zarathustra*, trans. Walter Kaufmann (New York: The Modern Library, 1995) adopts Heraclitus's image of the child and the game: "The child is innocence and forgetting," writes Nietzsche, "a new beginning, a game, a self-propelled wheel, a first movement, a sacred 'Yes'" (23).
22. Heraclitus, Fr. XLIX, 53.
23. Ibid., Fr. CXXI, 83.
24. In World War II the U.S.S.R., the United States, and England allied against Germany, Japan, and Italy. Italy surrendered on September 3, 1943. Germany surrendered on May 7, 1945. The war ended with Japan's surrender on August 15, 1945. Japan attacked Pearl Harbor on December 7, 1941. The Allies landed in Normandy on June 6, 1944, D-Day (Operation Neptune and Operation Overlord). The United States dropped the nuclear bomb, codename "Little Boy," on Hiroshima on August 6, 1945, and the nuclear bomb, codename "Fat Man," on Nagasaki on August 9, 1945.
25. Heraclitus, Fr. XCIII, 71.
26. See Annie Jacobsen, *Operation Paperclip: The Secret Intelligence Program that Brought Nazi Scientists to America* (New York: Little, Brown and Company, 2014): "Through their own version of Operation Paperclip, a parallel exploitation program called Operation Osoaviakhim, the Soviets captured German chemist Dr. von Bock and members of his team" (285).
27. Ibid., 68.
28. David Hughes, *The Complete Kubrick* (London: Virgin, 2000), 128.
29. Jacobsen, *Operation Paperclip*, 399.

30. Gene D. Phillips, "*Dr. Strangelove, or: How I Learned to Stop Worrying and Love the Bomb*," in Alison Castle, ed., *The Stanley Kubrick Archives*, 300–47 (Hohenzollernring: Taschen Publishing, 2018), 312.

31. Phillips, "*Dr. Strangelove*," 326–31.

32. According to Phillips in "*Dr. Strangelove*," "Kubrick was disappointed that Sellers declined to play the fourth part," writes Phillips, "since, in his view, that would have meant that almost everywhere the viewer looks, there is some version of Peter Sellers holding the fate of the world in his hands" (312).

33. Still another opposite is suggested in the film. Dr. Strangelove would appear to have a counterpart in the U.S.S.R. similarly extracted in Operation Osoaviakhim. Such a German-Russian scientist would be capable of designing the Doomsday Machine and planning for underground survival during a century-long nuclear winter.

34. Heraclitus, Fr. XCIX, 75.

REFERENCES

Abrams, Jerold J., ed. *The Philosophy of Stanley Kubrick*. Lexington, KY: University Press of Kentucky, 2007.

Castle, Alison, ed. *The Stanley Kubrick Archives*. Hohenzollernring: Taschen Publishing, 2018.

Cooke, Elizabeth F., "Understanding the Enemy: The Dialogue of Fear in *Fear and Desire* and *Dr. Strangelove*." In *The Philosophy of Stanley Kubrick*, edited by Jerold J. Abrams, 9–31. Lexington, KY: University Press of Kentucky, 2007.

Guthrie, W. K. C. "Flux and *Logos* in Heraclitus." In *The Pre-Socratics: A Collection of Critical Essays*, ed. Alexander P. D. Mourelatos, 197–213. Princeton, NJ: Princeton University Press, 1993.

Hughes, David. *The Complete Kubrick*. London: Virgin, 2000.

Jacobsen, Annie. *Operation Paperclip: The Secret Intelligence Program that Brought Nazi Scientists to America*. New York: Little, Brown and Company, 2014.

Kahn, Charles H. *The Art and Thought of Heraclitus*. Cambridge: Cambridge University, 1979.

Kolker, Robert. *The Cinema of Loneliness*. New York: Oxford University Press, 2011.

McCarthy, Cormac. *Blood Meridian, or The Evening Redness in the West*. New York: Random House, 1992.

Nietzsche, Friedrich. *Thus Spoke Zarathustra: A Book for None and All*. Translated by Walter Kaufmann. New York: The Modern Library, 1995.

Plato. *Symposium*. In *Complete Works of Plato*, ed. John M. Cooper. Indianapolis, IN: Hackett, 1997.

Singer, Irving. *Three Philosophical Filmmakers: Hitchcock, Welles, Renoir*. Cambridge: MIT Press, 2008.

Chapter Eight

Stanley Kubrick and the Cinema of Chaos

The Theater of War

William Gombash

The films of Stanley Kubrick are often about protagonists who endeavor to achieve an advantageous position through intricate and well-ordered plans but are ultimately stymied or defeated by forces beyond their control. This is evident in the disastrous consequences including the plans of Johnny Clay in *The Killing* (1956) to commit the perfect crime, the generals in *Paths of Glory* (1957) to attack the Ant Hill, the strategic planners in *Dr. Strangelove* (1964) to design the ultimate deterrence to nuclear war, the computer engineers to create an infallible computer in *2001: A Space Odyssey* (1968), Barry Lyndon's aspirations for wealth and noble title (*Barry Lyndon*, 1975), and Gunnery Sergeant Hartman's training to create the perfect Marine in *Full Metal Jacket* (1987). Those who venture to rule by their own sense of order inevitably fail because unforeseen circumstances create a state of disorder and chaos. Losing control of their circumstances, the protagonists cannot adjust to the confounding variables that are interfering with their plans. As a result, they cannot create a new order out of the disorder: their plans have failed; there is no turning back. The chaotic failures of these planners particularly stand out in Kubrick's war films, and most significantly in *Paths of Glory*, *Dr. Strangelove or: How I Stopped Worrying and Love the Bomb*, and *Full Metal Jacket*.

The second law of thermodynamics "states that everything in the entire universe began with structure and value and is irrevocably moving in the direction of random chaos and waste."[1] In addition, "whenever a semblance of order is created anywhere on Earth or in the universe, it is done at the expense of causing an even greater disorder in the surrounding environment."[2] For planners endeavoring to reduce the chaotic variables that interfere with planned outcomes there may be "relationships hidden in the data"[3] particularly in catastrophic phenomena such as wars.[4] On the field of battle variables such as "complexity, diversity, randomness, ductility, counterintuitive, and tangle"[5] can foil the efforts of even the best strategic and tactical planners. To control these variables and to cut through "the noise" one must be able to recognize and control these variables by observing the system from the "micro-level."[6] According to George E. Mikhailovsky and Alexander P. Levich, "If, on the other hand, the observer is located at the macro-level, he as 'commander-in-chief' is interested in the total disposition of troops and their fighting spirit and not in relations between the two individual soldiers, their fears and ideals."[7] However, for the commander-in-chief, the ability to evaluate the chaos of battle at the micro-level as well as the macro may be the difference between defeat or victory. By nature war is "multidimensional," "paradoxical," and "polymorphous" and therefore developing a successful strategy requires significant "analytical tools."[8] The sound strategy in war does not guarantee success—for even the best commander cannot see or account for every chaotic variable that could spell defeat—but a sound strategy is better than an unsound strategy in terms of reducing the effects of chaos.

Like war, the game of chess is often about loss and uncertainty. Initially, all of the pieces are in a state of order, in designated places, only to have that order broken down once the game begins. From one move to the next, as pieces are lost or sacrificed, sometimes on purpose, the winner emerges from a state of disorder more advantageous than that of his opponent. Chess is a game of chaos from which one can achieve victory.[9] Before Kubrick became a filmmaker, he made a small living hustling games of chess in Washington Square in New York City. Among the regulars who frequent this chess world is the term "'potzer'—a relatively weak player with an inflated ego."[10] More commonly spelled "patzers," these players are easily defeated because they think that they are smarter than they really are; they tend to lose matches because they are readily deluded and prone to be distracted. Even in the face of overwhelming odds, they do not know when to give up. In Kubrick's war films, military leaders are often presented as patzers: they lack the foresight of the chess grandmaster to look many moves ahead during the chaos of battle and are therefore defeated.

Such is the case in *Paths of Glory*, which takes place during World War I. The Great War was often referred to by historians such as Basil Liddell Hart and Barbara Tuchman as a series of battles resulting in chaos, disorder, and stalemate led by incompetent generals. The generals were largely incompetent because they had no understanding of strategy. At the very beginning of the war the German and French plans failed and resulted in four years that would suck "up lives at a rate of 5,000 and sometimes 50,000 a day."[11] The generals who formulated the strategies were sometimes referred to as "donkeys"[12] or in Siegfried Sassoon's poem "The General" as "incompetent swine."[13] In "The General," the soldiers Harry and Jack were killed "by his plan of attack."[14]

It appears fitting then that the two French generals at the heart of *Paths of Glory* should be depicted by Kubrick as patzer-like characters. In the film, General Broulard (Adolph Menjou)'s and Major General Mireau (George Macready)'s plans lead to a tactical defeat and the needless deaths of thousands of French soldiers on the battlefield, as well as the execution of three French soldiers by firing squad. When conceiving their plan, both generals are too far removed from the battlefield, unable to catch the details that might have avoided failure, as if playing a game of chess without being able to see the board. Because they possess a patzer's arrogance, they assume that they can move pieces around to checkmate the enemy. To further complicate the plan of attack, Broulard informs Mireau that there will be no replacements for the soldiers he has lost in previous attacks or sufficient artillery to soften up the enemy defenses. This adds to the chances of failure: Mireau is starting a chess game with some of his pieces missing. All of these variables add up to chaos and defeat. Deluded by their ambitions for glory, Mireau and Broulard lack the ability to see the game many moves into the future. As the two generals walk through one of the great rooms of the elegant chateau Mireau uses as headquarters, they recede into the distance, their size becoming smaller as if Kubrick were showing us their future insignificance and their failure to measure up to the great upcoming battle.

A recurring theme in the films under discussion is that the locations prior to the battles are well ordered, with the elements of the set design perfectly arranged like chess pieces at the beginning of the match. For example, one of the frames of the chateau where Broulard and Mireau meet to discuss their plans for the attack on the Ant Hill is an overhead shot of the tiled floor that looks like a chessboard. In addition, all of the furnishings, rugs, and paintings are meticulously arranged for maximum aesthetic effect, prompting Broulard's admiration. Kubrick strikingly represents the opposition between order and chaos, between the generals' blindness and the reality of the field. From Mireau's elegant chateau Kubrick cuts to a series of trenches where the common French soldier must live. As Mireau walks through the trench inspecting the troops he seems oblivious to the effects of war that surround him—the bandaged soldiers, the mud, the dirt. Outside the trenches, Mireau is equally unaware of the chaos caused by previous failed plans—the dead bodies, broken equipment, and shell holes filled with stagnant water. Even when confronted with these harsh realities Mireau cannot see beyond the plans created in his neatly organized headquarters.

Colonel Dax (Kirk Douglas), one of Mireau's infantry commanders, tries to warn the patzer of the futility of his plan by having him look at the Ant Hill through a powerful pair of binoculars in order to impress upon him the defensive strength of the German position. But Mireau states rather blithely: "Well, I've seen much more formidable objectives." Dax, unlike Mireau, lives in the trenches. On a daily basis he sees the war on a micro level and therefore understands the elements of chaos that can foil a battle plan, and that indeed come to confound Mireau's plan once the battle begins: the weather is too good, the Germans are not taken by surprise, casualties are higher than expected, one of the companies did not leave the trenches because the commanding officer was killed as the attack began. Kubrick uses long tracking shots to follow the chaos of battle. Within these frames the terrain of no man's land is revealed, consisting of shell holes, destroyed equipment, and dead soldiers; that bears little resemblance to the tiled floors of Mireau's elegant chateau.

During the assault on the Ant Hill, the soldiers fail to execute the general's plan due to a myriad of unforeseen circumstances. In his book *On War* (1832), Carl von Clausewitz refers to the chaos that can happen in armed conflicts as Friction of War.[15] According to Clausewitz, "So in War, the influence of an infinity of petty circumstances, which cannot be properly described on paper, things disappoint us, and we fall short of the mark."[16] Within this chaos that is the Friction of War the only way to avoid total defeat is to have a leader "the strong will of a proud spirit" that "stands prominent and commanding in the middle of the Art of War."[17] Unfortunately, Mireau does not possess the leadership qualities to overcome the Friction of War. He does not understand that, as in chess, "one cannot control everything,"[18] and is checkmated like a patzer. Not knowing when to give up, he decides to play another game of chess.

The second game of chess involves Mireau court martialing three of his soldiers for cowardice under fire, hoping that the trial will deflect the blame on them. Mireau seemingly has planned every move in advance to win this match, and win he does: the proceedings are arranged in such a way that the defendants' guilt is a fait accompli, and the moves that Dax, the accused soldiers' defense attorney, can use for an adequate defense are deliberately restricted. After the soldiers' execution, Mireau's reputation seems safe. However, unbeknownst to him, Broulard has his own plan to protect himself against being implicated in the Ant Hill disaster, and thus sets in motion a third chess game. Broulard informs Mireau that "There'll have to be an inquiry" to clear his name. Just as the fate of the executed soldiers was sealed in advance, Mireau's destiny is rigged by Broulard who knows full well that the inquiry will not exonerate him. Broulard indicates as much when he tells Dax that "France cannot afford to have fools guiding her military destiny." In other words, Broulard is informing Dax that patzers like Mireau who interfere with his chess matches with the French politicians and the press must be eliminated. Mireau loses this final chess game and his military career, because he could not foresee the destructive forces that led to his demise. To avoid the humiliation of an inquiry there is a "fair certainty that he will 'honorably' blow his brains out before things get that far."[19] The irony is that Mireau will be the last casualty of his own plan to take the Ant Hill.

Although *Paths of Glory* was about World War I, it was produced during the Cold War at a time when the United States and the Soviet Union engaged in a chess match of nuclear brinksmanship. During the Cuban Missile Crisis of 1962 "nuclear war was barely avoided and the slightest mistake could have sparked a nuclear conflict that neither the United States nor Russia intended."[20] Fortunately, those slightest mistakes and chaos were avoided and the world was spared from a nuclear holocaust. A little over a year after the Cuban Missile Crisis, *Dr. Strangelove* was released. The film explores how nuclear destruction leading to the deaths of most of the world's population and the destruction of the planet is begun through a series of chaotic unintended consequences.

The next to last line in *Dr. Strangelove* is stated by Dr. Strangelove (Peter Sellers) himself. Rising from his wheelchair, he says to the president of the United States: "I have a plan." The irony of the line is twofold: the film itself is about to end, while in the diegesis the population of the earth is about to die because the competing plans from the United States and the Soviet Union, created by patzers at the highest chain of command, have completely failed. They failed because the Soviet and American patzers did not foresee how their plans to create order within the Friction of War—in this case the Cold War—could only lead to the chaos and waste of nuclear annihilation. The American patzers who created Plan R and the Soviet patzers who created a plan associated with the Doomsday Machine, both without knowledge of the others' plan, compounded the chances for chaos because the unforeseen combination variables between the two plans set in motion events beyond their control. There were, according to Soviet Ambassador to the United States de Sadeski (Peter Bull), those on the Russian side who "fought against it" and could foresee the dangers of a plan that had failure written all over it, but they remained unheard. As previously seen with Mireau, patzers do not listen to reason. The Americans must, however, be equally held responsible since they were blind to the possibility that their "Plan R" was seriously flawed. When President Muffley (Peter Sellers) chastises General Turgidson (George C. Scott) because a contingency policy in Plan R inadvertently allows a mentally disturbed lower echelon commander General Ripper (Sterling Hayden) to start a nuclear war without proper cause, Turgidson foolishly defends the plan as a patzer would, alleging a "slip up."

As previously seen in *Paths of Glory*, Kubrick visually represents his settings as places of order only to transition to a setting that displays chaos.

As Alexander Walker writes, "The film begins with almost lethargic calm in each of the three locations."[21] In the first setting, at Burpleson Air Force Base, we first see Group-Captain Lionel Mandrake (Peter Sellers) surrounded by computers that "produce a murmur of order and routine."[22] Although not as elegant as Mireau's headquarters, Brigadier General Jack D. Ripper's office is nonetheless neat and orderly. It is in this isolated ordered environment that Ripper devises his own game of chess, without the sanction of higher command. A plan of order, like the ones of Broulard and Mireau, that will unleash chaos. The second setting is a B52 Bomber fully loaded with two hydrogen bombs. Within the plane, there is an air of calm: the crew is unaware of Ripper's plan that will make them unwitting pawns in the destruction of the planet and therefore acts disconnected with the potential destructive power under their command. The members of the crew are all seated in their designated position and acting nonchalantly (reading a magazine, eating a sandwich, playing card tricks). Similar to the computer room at Burpleson, the only sound is from a steady white noise, in this instance, the drone from the engines. The third setting is the War Room, where the president of the United States, as well as his cabinet and the Joint Chiefs of Staff, meet in the event of an emergency. They all sit in their designated places in a perfect circle. Order is essential in the War Room. When General Turgidson and Ambassador de Sadeski scuffle on the floor after Turgidson catches de Sadeski trying to take pictures of the big board with a tiny spy camera, President Muffley is incensed at the behavior. "You can't fight in here!" Muffley screams like a schoolmaster trying to discipline two boys, "This is the War Room." The irony is that while Muffley is trying to gain control inside the War Room, he is increasingly losing control over events in the outside world.

As the film progresses the visual evidence of the chaos increases. During the fight for Burpleson, Kubrick's cinema verité camera work captures the chaos of the fighting between the soldiers invading the base and the airmen defending it. For example, a long shot—in which Kubrick uses a telephoto lens to compress the image, making the background appear to be closer to the foreground—shows a soldier with a rifle in the foreground firing his ammunition, while closer to the middle ground a vehicle is burning. In the background, a building with the sign Burpleson Air Force Base is being hit with bullets. However, the most dominant element in the frame is a sign that reads KEEP OFF THE GRASS, which represents a demand for order that is no longer possible. Meanwhile, inside Ripper's once well-ordered office, the contents are torn apart by bullets. Eventually, the men who are guarding the base surrender and Ripper, realizing that he is about to get captured, complains like Mireau that his men have let him down. Ripper, his failure greater than all, commits suicide—which Mireau considered—and turns himself into another victim of bad planning and chaos.

At the beginning of the film the B52 is a well-ordered, highly complex technological machine. As part of this system, once war has been declared, all communications must go through the CRM 114 Discriminator that allows the plane to receive coded messages from Strategic Air Command Headquarters. When the order to attack is received through the discriminator, Kubrick zooms in on the device, the extreme close up shot emphasizing its overall importance. When Lieutenant Goldberg (Paul Tamarin) sets the code prefix into the CRM 114, Kubrick once again zooms into the device, which from this point forward will be the only means to communicate with the B52. In both instances, the device acts as a central piece in a well-ordered system and is meant to function perfectly in the event of war. But the patzers who designed it did not account for the consequences should the device be damaged or destroyed. When the B52 survives a near miss from a Soviet surface-to-air missile, the crew assesses the damage and the camera zooms again into the discriminator to show that it has been destroyed: the B52's well-ordered system has been reduced to a state of chaos. As a result, the B52 does not hear the recall message sent out to the surviving planes, does not return as ordered, and drops the bomb that sets off the Doomsday Machine. By forgetting to incorporate a redundancy into the communication system to compensate for a potential failure, the designers acted like patzers. When a player loses one piece in a chess game, he can still win the match. However, because of this one seemingly insignificant failure of one piece, the entire strategic plans of both the Soviet Union and the United States falls apart.

Back at the War Room, all of the players have left their designated seats and have given in to a state of disorder while the world faces total annihilation. The patzers have given up any sense of protocol: Turgidson has taken off his jacket, Muffley is having a drink. Dr. Strangelove's true nature resurfaces when he channels Hitler, rising from his wheelchair and emphatically stating: "Mein Führer, I can walk!" Just like Hitler died in a bunker as the Soviet army was closing in on him, the War Room men are trapped in their own bunker, victims of their own incompetence, as the Soviet Doomsday Machine is triggered. Kubrick ends the film with a montage of nuclear explosions, demonstrating the insane power placed in the hands of world leaders, who, if they turn out to be patzers and fools, will effectively destroy the world. While wars used to oppose one side to another, ending with a winner and a loser, the nuclear age leaves both sides checkmated.

Kubrick expanded his criticism of war and the inaptitude of the men leading them in *Full Metal Jacket*. Dorian Harwood, who played Eightball in the film, related a conversation he had with the director regarding what motivated him to make a film about Vietnam: "He told me that he was doing this film as an answer to *Rambo*."[23] Apparently, Kubrick objected to the film's glorification of war. "And he wanted," Harwood continued, "to show what war was really like."[24] The films starred Sylvester Stallone as a disillusioned Vietnam veteran who finds it hard to adjust to civilian life. In *First Blood* (Ted Kotcheff, 1982), the first of the *Rambo* series, Rambo angrily complains to his former commanding officer Colonel Trautman (Richard Crenna) that despite his best efforts as a soldier he was denied victory because of the interference of the people who ran the war: "And I did what I had to do to win, but somebody wouldn't let us win!"[25] That specific line must have sounded absurd to Kubrick, whose conception of war was an exercise in chaos. In *Full Metal Jacket*, the filmmaker counters the false propaganda that *First Blood* posits, that the war could have been won had the soldiers been allowed to fight like Rambo. Though the two films coincide in "the war run by patzers" theme, Kubrick's depiction differs in that the individual soldier was incapable of winning the war. Structured in two parts, *Full Metal Jacket* tells the story of how to lose a war, from the training of the troops to their actual fighting in Vietnam.

Based on the ribbons on his chest, drill instructor Gunnery Sergeant Hartman (R. Lee Ermey), in charge of Marine training, is a decorated veteran of the Korean and Vietnam wars. However, Kubrick showed us in *Paths of Glory* and *Dr. Strangelove* that highly decorated military leaders could also be patzers. Hartman's authority is established early on: while the recruits remain at attention he strides about the barracks waiting to pounce on anyone he perceives as weak. His obscenity-laced monologues are primarily focused on the doctrine that the recruits will not pass muster as a Marine until they learn everything that Hartman can teach them. Hartman is a patzer at the micro level. He has no control over the strategy in Vietnam. He teaches the recruits how to maintain order within their small area of the war, which may only have a radius of a few hundred yards. However, control, regardless the size of the battlefield, is only an illusion. Hartman's prescriptive training that is taught in the peaceful surroundings of the training camp is inadequate protection in combat. They will learn "by the numbers," he tells them. However, during the Friction of War those might not be the right numbers given the myriad equations that are possible in combat. The recruits are programmed to keep neat footlockers, make their bunks with a four-inch fold, and keep their boots shined. What do these tasks have to do with survival in the chaos of combat? Hartman stresses to his recruits that "Marines are not allowed to die without permission." Are the recruits to infer that the life and death of Marines are totally within the command of their superiors? Are their superiors fully aware of how to direct Marines during combat to help them avoid the elements that are part of the chaos of war? Does this mean that when a Marine dies in combat, because of his training, he only does it because he is ordered to do it? Unfortunately, the recruits will later discover that this order will be hard to follow once they get to Vietnam.

Once again, the mise en scene of the well-ordered versus chaotic environment plays a significant role in illustrating the contrast between what the planners want and what awaits those who must fight within the Friction of War. The barracks occupied by the Marine recruits is absolutely spotless and organized. In a number of the shots the composition is nearly symmetrical further emphasizing the order of the environment. When the Marines jog through Parris Island in tight formation they pass lawns that are as neatly manicured as those in Burpleson Air Force base before it was attacked. When Joker (Matthew Modine) and Cowboy (Arliss Howard) are cleaning the head, the bathroom, both in terms of lighting and composition, presents a sense of security and order. Unfortunately, this training has no value in terms of their survival in the dangerous chaos of Vietnam.

According to Hartman, the United States has a plan to win the war in Vietnam: "Chaplain Charlie," he tells the recruits, "will tell you about how the free world will conquer Communism with the aid of God and a few marines!" However, the strategy to win in Vietnam was primarily under the command of Robert McNamara, who was Secretary of Defense from 1961 to 1968. McNamara would later admit that this anti-Communist strategy in Vietnam was a mistake and not properly thought out: "One reason the Kennedy and Johnson administrations failed to take an orderly, rational approach to the basic questions underlying Vietnam was the staggering variety and complexity of other issues we faced."[26] In other words, Joker and his fellow platoon recruits go to Vietnam in 1967 ill equipped to survive, not just because of Hartman but also because the patzer strategic planners like McNamara are too far away to understand how to develop a successful plan for the Marines to follow.

While in the field, Joker encounters a U.S. Army colonel. In at least one version of the script (1985), the character is referred to as a "poge colonel (Bruce Boa)."[27] A "poge," sometimes spelled "POG" or "pogue," is a derisive term for someone in the military who has not seen combat.[28] Because Joker is wearing a peace symbol button, the colonel assumes that Joker is not a fully committed warrior and tells him: "Why don't you jump on the team and come on in for the big win?" The words of the poge colonel sound more like a pep talk given to players before an athletic contest than a rational military strategy. The colonel embodies the patzers who, far behind the lines, have little clue of the reality of combat and yet are pushing the notion that "winning" is the goal to the soldiers who are actually fighting the war.

Although essentially a work of fiction, there is a great deal of veracity to *Full Metal Jacket*. The film is based on the semi-autobiographical novel *Short-Timers* (1979) by Gustav Hasford, who was a Marine Vietnam veteran, and the script was co-written by Michael Herr, a combat correspondent during the years the film takes place. According to the latter, a common joke among Marines was "What is the difference between the Marines and the Boy Scouts? The Boy Scouts have adult leadership."[29] Herr also noted that Marine operations were likely to fail in Vietnam: "Something almost always went wrong somewhere, somehow. It was always something vague, unexplainable, tasting of bad fate, and the results were always brought down to their most basic element—the dead Marine."[30] Far from the order advocated by the military leaders during training, war on the field is nothing but chaos and death.

No scene better illustrates the chaos that Herr describes than when Joker joins the Lusthog Squad during the battle for the city of Hue, during the Tet offensive. As they enter Hue, part of the squad is decimated by a sniper (Ngoc Le), a young woman, hidden in one of the buildings. Although they have superior firepower, the Marines are at a disadvantage and can only witness the damage: this scenario was never part of their training. All the order the Marines were taught—how to march, make their beds, and clean the head—has no use in this rampageous situation. According to Peter Hyams, who was a war correspondent in Vietnam, the sniper scene in *Full Metal Jacket* encapsulated the futility and chaos of Vietnam, and he greatly admired the film's verisimilitude: "If you want the lesson of Vietnam it is that one girl, being up in a building holding off a company of American soldiers knowing she is going to die. And her job is somehow to disrupt . . . kill and basically delay . . . the progress of a company of American soldiers. That, was Vietnam."[31] Much like with the CRM 114, one unforeseen element could render American plans ineffective.

Full Metal Jacket does not end with a victory parade with a band playing some patriotic tune. Instead the final scene presents Joker and the rest of the Hue survivors marching through the burning city, singing the theme of the Mickey Mouse Club—"Who's the leader of the club that's made for you and me?" The song, Joker's final spoken narrative—"I'm in a world of shit"—and the burning city of Hue conclude Kubrick's statement on the chaos war creates and who must be held responsible for it. The Mickey Mouse song is not about patriotism or victory. In this context, the song is an ode to the dubious goals and the fanciful strategies of the patzers who planned the war. When it comes to the war in Vietnam, Joker does not care who won the chess match, who's been checkmated, or if it is all one big stalemate. All he cares about is that whatever chess piece he may represent he has not been captured and therefore he gets to leave the board alive.

Unlike in *Paths of Glory* and *Dr. Strangelove*, high-echelon patzers are not shown in *Full Metal Jacket* (with the possible exception of the poge colonel). However, their invisible hand, like General William Westmoreland's, commander of U.S. forces in Vietnam from 1964 to 1968, is clearly evident. Even though he is never seen or referred to in Kubrick's film, his imprint on the narrative along with McNamara's is unmistakable. According to Herr, in an article he wrote after reporting the chaos that was the Tet Offensive:

It became finally clear that General Westmoreland did not understand this war ("This is a different war than Americans have ever been asked to fight," he told the Examining Angels. "How is it different?" they asked. "Well, you know, it's just . . . different"), and he was asked to leave it. The immediate official response was manic; after years and years of posing along the rim, the Mission joined hands and leapt through the Looking Glass. It was as though Swift's vault had been plundered to meet the public doubt.[32]

Army Lieutenant General Harold G. Moore, a Vietnam veteran and author, believed that Westmoreland's formula for victory was flawed and could never achieve victory. He quotes Clausewitz to explain why Westmoreland and other strategists failed in Vietnam. "No one starts a war—or rather, no one in his senses ought to do so—without first being clear in his mind what he intends to achieve by that war and how he intends to conduct it."[33] The end result of this lack on the part of leadership of, in the words of Clausewitz, "the strong will of a proud spirit"[34] during the friction of war was "the lives of 58,000 young Americans" and a "humiliating defeat on a nation that had never lost a war."[35]

After the release of *Dr. Strangelove* an interviewer told Kubrick that some viewers felt that he "seemed curiously aloof and detached and unmoved by the annihilation of mankind."[36] Kubrick strongly disagreed, replying "that the only immorality is that which endangers the species; and the only absolute evil, that which threatens annihilation."[37] Kubrick, in his films, does not want the patzers to win. He recognizes the chaos and waste they contribute to through their lack of foresight when engineering their plans. Kubrick even believed in a "possibility of curing it"[38] meaning that there are ways to mitigate against their influence and contribution to waste. Unfortunately, the patzers in *Paths of Glory*, *Dr. Strangelove*, and *Full Metal Jacket* who led others into a battle they could not win, are irredeemable. It is doubtful, had Hartman been alive to see how his recruits suffered and died because his plan was flawed, that he would have seen the error of his ways: a patzer never admits to having lost the game due to his own mistake. The Soviet and American experts, when the world is about to end, are too busy thinking about how to save themselves to accept their own role in the impending death of the planet. When Dax pleads that the attack on the Ant Hill was doomed from the start, General Mireau responds: "If it was impossible, the only proof of that would be their dead bodies lying in the trenches." In other words, if only one soldier out of an entire regiment survived, the plan was not "impossible." These are the words of a patzer, and like all patzers in Kubrick's war films, those words brand them as self-interested cynics who are blind to the fact that they have been checkmated before the match even starts.

NOTES

1. Jeremy Rifkin with Ted Howard, *Entropy: A New World View* (Toronto: Bantam Books, 1980), 6.
2. Ibid.
3. J. A. Tenreiro Machado, Carla M. A. Pinto, and A. Mendes Lopes, "Power Law and Entropy Analysis of Catastrophic Phenomena," *Mathematical Problems in Engineering* (January, 2013): 1–10.
4. Ibid., 1.
5. George E. Mikhailovsky and Alexander P. Levich, "Entropy, Information and Complexity or Which Aims the Arrow of Time?" *Entropy* 17, no. 7 (2015): 4863–90.
6. Ibid.
7. Ibid.
8. David J. Lonsdale, "Strategy: The Challenge of Complexity," *Defence Studies* 7, no. 1 (March 2007): 42–64, 42.
9. Rudolf Spielmann, *The Art of Sacrifices in Chess* (New York: Dover Publications, 1995), 2.
10. Jeremy Bernstein, "How about a Little Game," *The New Yorker*, November 12, 1966, https://www.newyorker.com/magazine/1966/11/12/how-about-a-little-game (accessed July 19, 2019).
11. Barbara W. Tuchman, *The Guns of August* (New York: Ballantine Books, 1990), 438.
12. Alan Clark, *The Donkeys* (New York: William Morrow and Company, 1962), 6.
13. Siegfried Sassoon, *War Poems* (Mineola, NY: Dover Publications, Inc., 2018), 58.
14. Ibid.
15. Carl von Clausewitz, *On War*, trans. J. J. Graham (New York: Barnes & Noble, 2004), 61.
16. Ibid.
17. Ibid.
18. Achilleas Zographos, *Music and Chess: Apollo Meets Caissa* (Milford, CT: Russell Enterprises, Inc., 2017), 60.
19. Alexander Walker, Sybil Taylor, and Ulrich Ruchti, *Stanley Kubrick, Director: A Visual Analysis* (New York: W. W. Norton and Company, 1999), 100.
20. Sam Nunn, "Away from a World of Peril," *Survival (00396338)* 54, no. 1 (2012) 234–44.
21. Alexander Walker, *Stanley Kubrick Directs* (New York: Harcourt, Brace, Jovanovich, 1971), 168.
22. Ibid.
23. *Full Metal Jacket: Between Good and Evil*, directed by Gary Leva (Burbank: Warner Home Entertainment, 2007), Blu-ray.
24. Ibid.
25. *Rambo: First Blood*, directed by Ted Kotcheff (Los Angeles: Orion Pictures, 1982), Blu-ray.
26. Robert S. McNamara with Brian Van De Mark, *In Retrospect: The Tragedy and Lessons of Vietnam* (New York: Vintage Books, 1995), xvii.
27. Stanley Kubrick and Michael Herr, *Full Metal Jacket*, Screenplay, 1985, http://www.visual-memory.co.uk/amk/doc/0065.html (accessed July 15, 2019).
28. Ben Brody, "U.S. Military Lingo: The (almost) Definitive Guide, National Public Radio," December 4, 2013, https://www.npr.org/sections/parallels/2013/12/04/248816232/u-s-military-lingo-the-almost-definitive-guide (accessed July 31, 2019).
29. Michael Herr, *Dispatches* (New York: Avon, 1977), 101.
30. Ibid., 102.
31. *Full Metal Jacket: Between Good and Evil*.
32. Michael Herr, "Hell Sucks," *Esquire*, August 1968, 66–69, and 108–10, 66.
33. Harold G. Moore and Joseph Galloway, *We Were Soldiers Once . . . and Young: The Battle That Changed the War in Vietnam* (New York: Random House, 1992), 374.
34. Clausewitz, *On War*, 61.

35. Moore and Galloway, *We Were Soldiers Once . . . and Young*, 374.
36. Norden, Eric, "Playboy Interview: Stanley Kubrick," in *Stanley Kubrick Interviews*, ed. Gene D. Phillips, 47–74 (Jackson, MS: University Press Mississippi, 2001), 68.
37. Ibid.
38. Ibid.

REFERENCES

Bernstein, Jeremy. "How about a Little Game." *The New Yorker*, November 12, 1966. https://www.newyorker.com/magazine/1966/11/12/how-about-a-little-game.

Brody, Ben. "U.S. Military Lingo: The (almost) Definitive Guide, National Public Radio." *Npr*, December 4, 2013. https://www.npr.org/sections/parallels/2013/12/04/248816232/u-s-military-lingo-the-almost-definitive-guide.

Clark, Alan. *The Donkeys*. New York: William Morrow and Company, 1962.

Clausewitz, Carl von. *On War*, trans. J. J. Graham. New York: Barnes & Noble, 2004.

Full Metal Jacket: Between Good and Evil. Directed by Gary Leva. Burbank: Warner Home Entertainment, Inc., 2007, Blu-ray.

Herr, Michael. "Hell Sucks." *Esquire*, August 1968, 66–69, and 108–10.

———. *Dispatches*. New York: Avon, 1977.

Kubrick, Stanley, and Michael Herr. *Full Metal Jacket*, Screenplay, 1985. http://www.visual-memory.co.uk/amk/doc/0065.html.

Lonsdale, David J. "Strategy: The Challenge of Complexity." *Defence Studies* 7, no. 1 (March 2007): 42–64.

Machado, J. A. Tenreiro, Carla M. A. Pinto, and A. Mendes Lopes. "Power Law and Entropy Analysis of Catastrophic Phenomena." *Mathematical Problems in Engineering* (January, 2013): 1–10.

McNamara, Robert S., and Brian Van De Mark. *In Retrospect: The Tragedy and Lessons of Vietnam*. New York: Vintage Books, 1995.

Mikhailovsky, George E., and Alexander P Levich. "Entropy, Information and Complexity or Which Aims the Arrow of Time?" *Entropy* 17, no. 7 (2015): 4863–90.

Moore, Harold G., and Joseph Galloway. *We Were Soldiers Once . . . and Young: The Battle That Changed the War in Vietnam*. New York: Random House, 1992.

Norden, Eric. "Playboy Interview: Stanley Kubrick." In *Stanley Kubrick Interviews*, edited by Gene D. Phillips, 47–74. Jackson, MS: University Press of Mississippi, 2001.

Nunn, Sam. "Away from a World of Peril." *Survival (00396338)* 54, no. 1 (2012): 234–44.

Rambo: First Blood. Directed by Ted Kotcheff. Los Angeles: Orion Pictures, 1982, Blu-ray.

Rifkin, Jeremy, with Ted Howard. *Entropy: A New World View*. Toronto: Bantam Book. 1980.

Sassoon, Siegfried. *War Poems*. Mineola, NY: Dover Publications, Inc., 2018.

Spielmann, Rudolf. *The Art of Sacrifices in Chess*. New York: Dover Publications, 1995.

Tuchman, Barbara W. *The Guns of August*. New York: Ballantine Books, 1990.

Walker, Alexander. *Stanley Kubrick Directs*. New York: Harcourt, Brace, Jovanovich, 1971.

Walker, Alexander, Sybil Taylor, and Ulrich Ruchti. *Stanley Kubrick, Director: A Visual Analysis*. New York: W. W. Norton and Company, 1999.

Zographos, Achilleas. *Music and Chess: Apollo Meets Caissa*. Milford, CT: Russell Enterprises, Inc., 2017.

Chapter Nine

Joker's Ideological Becoming

The Limits of Irony in Full Metal Jacket

James R. Britton

Stanley Kubrick's *Full Metal Jacket* (1987) contains two separate but related stories, the first a tightly focused narrative set on Parris Island, the second a meandering sequence of scenes set during the Vietnam War. Holding these sections together is the character Joker (Matthew Modine), whose perspective viewers follow as the film progresses. Joker's role may not be immediately clear, but his presence in every scene establishes him as the central, if not the most compelling, character, and the audience follows his perspective, seeing what he sees and perhaps feeling what he feels. In short, Kubrick uses Joker's point of view to shape our understanding of what it means to be a Marine during the Vietnam era.[1]

Kubrick uses Joker and other characters to reveal the ideological force of Marine masculinity, a form of identity rooted in patriarchal notions of manhood and interwoven with larger elements of American identity.[2] Tellingly, while Joker does not directly resist this force, he uses irony to question it. This chapter will examine Joker's use of irony, which is related to but not identical to the larger ironies Kubrick offers, and which sets Joker apart from other characters. This discussion of irony is informed by Linda Hutcheon's argument "that irony happens because what could be called 'discursive communities' already exist and provide the context for both the deployment and attribution of irony."[3] In *Full Metal Jacket*, these communities include the recruits on Parris Island, Marines in Vietnam, and even the film's viewers. Hutcheon explains that irony "happens in the space between (and including) the said and unsaid. . . . The said and the unsaid coexist for the interpreter, and each has meaning in relation to the other because they literally 'interact' . . . to create the real 'ironic' meaning."[4] Joker employs such irony to resist the pull of Marine masculinity, but as the film progresses irony proves insufficient, and he must develop other strategies to engage meaningfully with the world and preserve a sense of self.

While Joker's central role becomes clear as the narrative progresses, two other characters, Drill Sgt. Hartman (R. Lee Ermey) and recruit Leonard Lawrence (Vincent D'Onofrio), whom Hartman immediately renames "Gomer Pyle," dominate the Parris Island section. These characters shape and drive the narrative: Hartman provides the ideological context while Pyle forces the action through his physical ineptitude, childishness, and, most crucially, inability to psychologically negotiate Hartman's demands. Throughout this section, however, Joker's relationship to the events of basic training, particularly to Hartman's words and Pyle's actions, guides our understanding. Although Pyle draws attention as the recruit most out of place, Joker is also an outsider despite his success as a recruit. In fact, Joker is the first to set himself apart from other recruits, not through his failings, like Pyle, but by invoking John Wayne, the first instance of a recruit speaking not in response to Hartman's questions. This ambiguous outsider status emerges as a critical element shaping Kubrick's representation of the Vietnam War as the film progresses.

Joker's reference to John Wayne—"Is that you John Wayne? Is this me?"—ironically contextualizes the Marine project.[5] That his first words in the film take the form of caricature provides insight into his mindset, establishing that he arrives at basic training with a skeptical nature. John Wayne's status representing American mythologies, particularly those related to manhood and war, would be familiar to the recruits. By invoking Wayne, Joker offers commentary that could be satirical, even if the precise meaning is unclear. While recruits may respond to the Wayne myth, the Marines in Vietnam certainly did not, so basic training serves as a potential transitional stage in this regard. Joker's words also suggest questions of identity—"Is this me?"—that would presumably be answered through the recruits' experience at Parris Island.

Despite the film's highly ironic content, *Full Metal Jacket* is not a satire. In describing the relationship between satire and irony, Paul Simpson explains that "satire is characterized by multiple forms of irony and that, moreover, ironic phases sit in the spaces between discursive positions in satire."[6] While Joker's use of irony, particularly sarcasm in the Vietnam section, and Kubrick's inclusion of ironic situations suggest a satirical approach, satire never fully emerges. Kubrick's choice here is interesting given the qualities of many of the characters, particularly those in positions of authority. Despite similar representations of military authority, *Full Metal Jacket* never becomes a full-on satire like *Dr. Strangelove* (1964), as the presentation of the characters in each film makes clear. The broad satire of *Dr. Strangelove* has viewers laughing at the characters while feeling disconcerted by their actions. Although Jack D. Ripper's (Sterling Hayden) apparent mental illness, which sets the stage for nuclear war, and Buck Turgidson's (George C. Scott) childish enthusiasm for that war are terrifying, Kubrick presents their behavior as comically absurd.[7] Superficially, *Full Metal Jacket*'s Sgt. Hartman's attitude and demeanor could make him a character much like Ripper, but in the hands of Kubrick and actor R. Lee Ermey, he becomes a figure taken seriously by both the recruits and audience alike. Like the *Dr. Strangelove* characters, he is frightening, and he is comic, but viewers are less likely to laugh at him as a comic figure than to laugh at what he says, despite the misogynistic, racist, and homophobic elements of his discourse.[8] Kubrick uses him not to point out the absurdity inherent to basic training but instead to reveal the psychology animating Marine identity. Hartman serves not as part of the context for the first half of the film; he creates and represents the context, embodying the belief system and meaning of basic training. It is as if the Marine recruits live in his imagined world, a world they must become part of before they can move on, carrying his belief system or some part of it to Vietnam.

Throughout the psychologically charged, emotionally wrenching, and physically grueling contexts of both sections, Joker must establish a means to maintain his sense of self. At times, he turns to irony, while at others he attempts to negotiate an ethical path forward through engagement, such as when he instructs Pyle or kills the wounded sniper near the film's end. Joker's behavior and decisions reveal his efforts to preserve his emerging moral code while confronting the systematic effort to break down and reconstruct recruit identity.[9] To understand Joker, Bakhtin's discussion of authoritative discourse and internally persuasive discourse from "Discourse in the Novel"[10] is illuminating. Joker and the other recruits, largely recent high school graduates still developing an understanding of the world, encounter what Bakhtin calls "authoritative discourse,"[11] which Hartman controls and deploys as a means of indoctrination. Bakhtin explains that authoritative discourse "demands our unconditional allegiance. . . . It enters our verbal consciousness as a compact and indivisible mass; one must either totally affirm it, or totally reject it. It is indissolubly fused with its authority—with political power, an institution, a person—and it stands and falls together with that authority."[12] Within the context of basic training, Hartman embodies authoritative discourse, his words and actions representing a form of masculinity related to but not identical to American identity more generally. We see this in Hartman's commitment to the construct of Marine identity, in his attempts to remake the recruits in that image, and in his demands for "unconditional allegiance" to this vision. Hartman exists to indoctrinate recruits, to remake them as killing machines, using an amalgamation of religion, patriotism, homophobia combined with homoeroticism, masculinized violence, and sexualized technology. He employs an array of tools to achieve this, almost all rooted in language. He renames the characters, berates them with imaginative and demeaning invective, and has them sing repetitive marching songs to enforce the Marine ethos. In this way, the discourse Hartman advances emerges from both the language he employs and the institutional authority he represents, which combine to form a pervasive and persuasive argument for the recruits to become the kind of Marine he envisions.

Initially, Joker implicitly mocks Hartman's authority when he references Wayne. Is Joker suggesting that Hartman is a Wayne figure, with Kubrick using Wayne to allude to tropes of American masculinity? Does Joker invoke Wayne to undermine Hartman's attempt to establish basic training as his domain? Whatever the answer, Joker's is at best a halting, un-sustained resistance, as he generally conforms to Hartman's expectations. While the conformity is never complete, Joker, perhaps unaware, adopts elements of Hartman's instruction. After Joker impersonates John Wayne, Hartman tells him, "Hell, I like you. You can come over to my house and fuck my sister," before punching Joker in the stomach. Hartman then shouts "You little scumbag! I got your name! I got your ass! . . . You will learn by the numbers! I will teach you!" Following this early application of the authoritative discourse of Marine masculinity, Joker not only conforms but also internalizes elements of the discourse, later parroting Hartman's language when he jokes about having sex with Cowboy's sister and, more significantly, when he repeats Hartman's "Mary Jane Rottencrotch" and "world of shit" as the film ends.

During basic training, Joker resists Hartman's expectations on one other occasion, by choosing to be a military journalist, not a warrior. However, despite his gestures of conformity and desire to become a killing machine, Joker's relationship with Pyle suggests an attempt to maintain an identity separate from Marine masculinity, an act of ideological resistance within a context where such resistance may be near impossible. This is part of an internal psychological struggle that Joker experiences, one that will determine who he will be. As a young man, Joker is developing a personal worldview, engaged in what Bakhtin calls "an individual's ideological becoming,"[13] which is informed by the values he brought with him to basic training, those advanced by Hartman, and whatever subsequent influences he encounters as he matures. Unsurprisingly, these forces often work in opposition. Bakhtin explains that

> The tendency to assimilate others' discourse takes on an even deeper and more basic significance in an individual's ideological becoming. . . . Another's discourse performs no longer as information, directions, rules, models and so forth—but strives rather to determine the very bases of our ideological interrelations with the world, the very basis of our behavior.[14]

From this perspective, fully submitting to Hartman's worldview would lead Joker to replicate Hartman's authoritative discourse and thus represent the Marine masculinity Hartman hopes to reproduce. As Bakhtin describes it, another form of discourse operates alongside authoritative discourse, internally persuasive discourse, which is

> tightly interwoven with "one's own" word ... the internally persuasive word is half-ours and half-someone else's. Its creativity and productiveness consist precisely in the fact that such a word awakens new and independent words, that it organizes masses of our words from within, and does not remain in an isolated and static condition. It is not so much interpreted by us as it is further, that is, freely, developed, applied to new material, new conditions.... Our ideological development is just such an intense struggle within us for hegemony among various verbal and ideological points of view, approaches, directions, and values.[15]

Joker experiences such development as he struggles to maintain self-determination and self-definition. On Parris Island, Joker confronts the danger that Hartman's authoritative discourse could become his own, leaving little psychological space to develop a more nuanced personal set of values.

Joker's method of helping Pyle underscores his attempt to maintain a sense of self separate from what Hartman teaches. When Hartman assigns Joker as Pyle's personal instructor—making him more a parent to Pyle than a peer—he performs the task with kindness and decency. The subsequent scenes present the clearest instances of human connection in the film, the only such examples Kubrick offers. Joker patiently helps Pyle through the obstacle course, shows him how to lace shoes, teaches him to make his bunk, and guides him through rifle drills. Joker's genuine engagement, his patient efforts to help Pyle despite the frustrations that must have accompanied them, represent a version of Joker's character not seen elsewhere until the film's end.

However, when Pyle's continued failures prompt Hartman to punish the whole company one time too many, the recruits in turn punish Pyle, with Cowboy (Arliss Howard), Joker's closest friend, taking the lead. With Pyle gagged and pinned to his bunk, each recruit strikes him with a bar of soap wrapped in a towel. When it's Joker's turn, he hesitates, reluctant to join the brutality (he will later again hesitate at a crucial moment), but at Cowboy's urging, he strikes Pyle not once but six times. As Susan White observes, this is "the first moment of [Joker's] moral collapse."[16] Here, Joker can remain true to the sense of self he hopes to maintain—that is, as the person who helps Pyle and remains separate from the narrow sense of manhood advanced by Hartman—or he can submit to the larger corporate values of Marine masculinity.

This scene represents a transitional moment for Pyle, who becomes psychologically broken. Michele Pavan Deana notes, "Leonard's insanity and final reaction thus become only a consequence of his isolation from the group—the real turning point for Leonard is when his comrades-in-arms beat him up."[17] The beating tips him into mental illness and, not coincidentally, makes him a much better recruit, one on the path to becoming a killer, although not the kind that Hartman intends. The scene is similarly pivotal for Joker in that for him, unlike the others, it represents a moral choice—not a rote act of falling in line with expected behavior—with him *choosing* conformity. As Pyle sobs in his bunk, Joker, in the bunk below, closes his eyes and covers his ears, struggling emotionally with Pyle's despair and his own role in the assault. Joker's involvement is a submission to Hartman, as he conforms to certain values and expectations of his fellow Marines, perhaps against his better judgment. Beyond this moment, however, viewers are only fleetingly made aware of Jokers's struggle. In the hands of another director, this struggle might be made transparent, perhaps even highlighted, but Kubrick refuses to offer such simple—and simplifying—clarity.

While it is unclear how this participation impacts Joker, the effects on Pyle become evident, as he transforms from an inept loser to an expert marksman whom Hartman almost praises; at the same time, he descends into mental illness, having internalized and distorted Hartman's instruction. Joker notes that Pyle has started talking to his gun, but the depth of Pyle's mental illness is not revealed until this section's final scene, when Pyle performs a Marine rifle drill in the latrine before misdirecting his newfound violent impulses by killing Hartman and himself. Here, Joker plays the role of observer, watching as Hartman, in characteristic authoritarian mode, demands that Pyle put down his weapon. It is tempting to argue that by this point Pyle is beyond listening to reason, and while this is likely the case, he reacts to an entirely unreasonable situation, one designed to strip him and the other recruits of their identities and replace them with a narrow and corrosive version of masculinity. Richard Rambuss explains that Kubrick offers "a nearly clinical preoccupation . . . with how men—boys, really—are made into soldiers, specifically into marines, into deindividuated, readily replaceable cogs."[18] Pyle's inability to become one of these cogs is the heart of the matter. He could neither conform nor escape, other than through insanity and suicide. While others adapted, Pyle lacked the necessary mental and physical resources. In this moment, Pyle has not failed to internalize Hartman's teachings but has mutated them, making his enemy not the Vietnamese other but, instead, Hartman himself, the embodiment of Marine culture.

The shift from Parris Island to Vietnam is abrupt, disorienting, and full of meaning. On this transition, Gruben aptly notes that as viewers "we are still reeling from the violence when we suddenly jump to a busy square in Da Nang, like waking up from a nightmare into another nightmare."[19] Having just witnessed Pyle kill Hartman and himself, viewers now face a strikingly different world. This opening fades into an urban setting; as the camera follows a Vietnamese prostitute, whose strutting parodies female sexuality, Joker and a new character, Rafterman (Kevyn Major Howard), come into focus, all with Nancy Sinatra's "These Boots are Made for Walkin'" playing on the soundtrack.[20] While months have passed since the murder-suicide, it is nonetheless surprising how little Joker seems changed by the experience. If the film has transitioned from one nightmare to another, Joker shows no sign that either has affected him. The controlled setting and the focused narrative of the first half diffuses, with the war depicted as absent of coherent meaning, a world where Hartman's teaching may offer Marines a way to operate but not to understand, particularly in moral terms. Whatever it lacked, Parris Island provided a consistent worldview, even if the worldview was rooted in ideological fantasy. In Vietnam, the rules for behavior and the meaning of the Marines' actions are far less clear.

Kubrick's heavier use of irony as a means of representation becomes apparent in this section's opening moments. Despite Hartman's reliance on iterations of the virgin-whore dichotomy, Parris Island lacked any real female presence. In contrast, the Vietnam section opens with a song of female empowerment, although one that conforms to rather than challenges patriarchal norms. Here, a Vietnamese prostitute (Papillon Soo Soo), a woman questionably empowered at best, offers her services to Joker and Rafterman. And yet, the seizing of authority expressed in the line "one of these days these boots are going to walk all over you"[21] is later far more effectively enacted by the young female sniper (Ngoc Le) at the film's end, a character who better represents Hartman's killing machines than any Marine in the movie.

What follows is a meandering sequence of scenes tracing Joker's experience of Vietnam and communicating the unfocused nature of the American mission. No longer a recruit, Joker now participates in war, a participation complicated by his role writing for *Stars and Stripes*, which places him as an observer who represents, or more accurately, misrepresents, the war for others. In fact, the film presents misinformation as *Stars and Stripes*' reason for being, reflecting Kubrick's observation that "the Vietnam War . . . was manipulated in Washington by hawk intellectuals who tried to fine-tune reality like an advertising agency, constantly inventing new jargon like 'kill ratios,' 'hamlets pacified,' and so forth."[22] In his role at *Stars and Stripes*, Joker must participate in this manipulation, which he clearly finds distasteful.

The nature of this misinformation becomes apparent during a meeting of the newspaper's staff, where a banner hanging in the background reads "First to go, last to know" and "We will defend to the death our right to be misinformed." During this meeting, the editor, Lieutenant Lockhart (John Terry), dismisses Joker's question about the North Vietnamese calling off the Tet holiday, instead emphasizing the need to create bogus stories and report on Ann-Margret's upcoming visit. During their next meeting, after the Tet Offensive has begun, proving Joker's question relevant, Lockhart explains that Tet is "a huge shit sandwich" that will affect all of them. In a response that prompts laughter from the other correspondents, Joker asks, "Sir, does this mean that Ann-Margret's not coming?" a use of irony that emphasizes the nature of *Stars and Stripes*' mission. Joker's approach here corresponds to Hutcheon's idea "that irony happens as part of a communicative process; it is not a static rhetorical tool to be deployed, but itself comes into being in the relations between meanings, but also between people and utterances and, sometimes, between intentions and interpretations."[23] The situational and discursive nature of Joker's comment is crucial, as he sarcastically but indirectly highlights for his colleagues the absurdity of their military journalism, implicitly challenging Lockhart's legitimacy. Here, Joker's ironic commentary overlaps with the film's use of irony, as Kubrick includes this scene to illustrate a fundamental failing of the American project in Vietnam, the focus on public relations.

Joker's attitude toward the distorted representation of the war, and his willingness to voice it, demonstrates that he understands the hypocrisy linked to the American presence in Vietnam. From one colonel's perspective, Joker struggles in "getting with the program," which is less about Joker's behavior than his resistance to full ideological buy-in. The most direct example of this occurs when Joker is confronted a second time—the first was by Lieutenant Lockhart—about wearing a peace symbol. When the colonel asks about the meaning of Joker wearing the peace symbol while having "Born to Kill" on his helmet, Joker explains, "I think I was trying to suggest something about the duality of man, sir. . . . The Jungian thing, sir?" Unimpressed, he orders Joker to remove the button. With little interest in Jung's duality of man, the colonel represents a single-minded, unnuanced, and narrow vision. The irony of the peace symbol combined with "Born to Kill" is either lost on him or simply irrelevant to America's mission. As Hutcheon observes, "If we considered irony to be formed though a relation both between people and between meanings—said and unsaid—then . . . it would involve an oscillating yet simultaneous perception of plural and different meanings."[24] Joker seeks not the narrow vision offered by Hartman and this colonel but a more nuanced understanding of the world, one that synthesizes elements of Marine teachings with his own personal beliefs, one including room for the simultaneous drives for violence and peace. The colonel, in contrast, finds violence alone sufficient.

While wearing the peace symbol signifies slight resistance at best, it illustrates Joker's effort to claim some control over his own identity, and to represent it for others to see, a representation linked to the antiwar efforts at home, signifying the larger national duality of American identity. While

Joker performs the duties expected of him, his failure to fully internalize Marine beliefs shows that, at least from the colonel's perspective, he is not a team player, but instead he sides with the peaceniks at home. Moreover, the emphasis on the duality of man underscores Joker's ongoing resistance to Hartman's teaching.

It would be an oversimplification, however, to suggest that Joker fully rejects Hartman's worldview, as he expresses a desire for battle. While the correspondents relax in their bunks, Joker says he wants to "Get back in the shit," complaining that he "ain't heard a shot fired in anger in weeks." Perhaps this is prompted by boredom, but it also suggests that Joker feels compelled to fight, to be a part of the real war. This becomes further complicated when the camp is subsequently attacked. With the others, Joker runs outside to defend the camp, hunkering down in a bunker with an M-60 machine gun, ready to fight. Despite his desire to get "in the shit" and his subsequent participation in the short battle, his ambivalence becomes clear when right before the battle he says, "I hope they're just fucking with us. I ain't ready for this shit."

A soldier's ambivalence about battle is unsurprising, but looking more closely at Joker's reaction in relation to identity and ideology is crucial. He not only struggles with the realities of battle but does so as his own personal belief system evolves. Here, turning to Bakhtin is again informative. As Bakhtin explains,

> an individual's becoming, an ideological process, is characterized precisely by a sharp gap between these two categories: in one, the authoritative word (religious, political, moral; the word of the father, of adults and of teachers, etc.) that does not know internal persuasiveness, in the other internally persuasive word that is denied all privilege, backed up by no authority at all. . . . The struggle and dialogic interrelationship of these categories of ideological discourse are what usually determine the history of an individual ideological consciousness.[25]

From this perspective, Joker's behavior and thoughts are shaped not only by the simultaneous desires to fight and to seek peace, but by an internal struggle between competing belief systems: Hartman's authoritative discourse, representing the core of Marine masculinity, and Joker's own nascent internally persuasive discourse, rooted in his own personal history. With his understanding of the world coming into being, Joker struggles to reconcile these competing discourses.

Contrasting Joker with Animal Mother (Adam Baldwin), the epitome of Marine manhood, can help to explain this struggle. The tension between these characters illustrates a central conflict of the film. Animal Mother is the physical embodiment of the Marine Hartman hoped to create. Kubrick likely chose Adam Baldwin for the role in part because of his imposing physical presence. While Animal Mother is roughly the same size as Pyle, their bodies—Pyle's soft and flabby, Animal Mother's muscular and hard—represent very different masculine types.[26] In a sense, if the recruits were raw material to be shaped, the goal was to transform Pyle into an Animal Mother, a muscular and masculine killing machine. In contrast, Joker, a writer who wears glasses and who can often be seen jotting in a notebook, suggests a very different masculine type.

The conflict between these characters becomes evident when they first meet. While the scene can be read as Animal Mother's attempt to establish masculine dominance and Joker's attempt to resist, it also emphasizes the clash of masculine styles, with the characters' modes of understanding and engaging the world central to the conflict. By this point, viewers know that Joker responds to the world thoughtfully, attempting to observe and understand, often from an ironic perspective. In contrast, Animal Mother is a literalist engaging the world in the most basic terms: through sex, violence, and dominance. Their first meeting offers a clear visual contrast: Animal Mother is helmeted, draped with bullet bandoliers, and carrying an oversized weapon, while Joker's most prominent features are the camera he carries, his glasses, and the peace sign. While Animal Mother serves as the male warrior ideal, Joker's more nuanced and ironic disposition generally runs counter to the American project in Vietnam and specifically to Animal Mother's own sense of masculinity.

To dominate his world, Animal Mother is blunt and aggressive. We see this when a prostitute's services are offered to the full squad, and he claims the first turn in "the batting order," displaying masculine dominance at the most stereotypical and reductive level. His literal-mindedness also emerges when the squad stands over the bodies of two recently killed fellow Marines; as others offer sentiments such as "Semper fi," Animal Mother responds, "Better you than me," and when Rafterman naïvely suggests they died for "freedom," Animal Mother responds, "You think we waste gooks for freedom? This is a slaughter. If I'm going to get my balls blown off for a word, my word is 'poontang.'" This response not only confirms his literal approach but also reinforces the confused but consistent relationship between combat violence and sex that animates Marine masculinity.

The film's final scenes, with the sniper killing multiple Marines before being wounded by Rafterman and killed by Joker, resolves Joker's internal struggle, although unsurprisingly Kubrick does not make this resolution transparent. Joker's experience reflects what Bakhtin refers to as an individual's "ideological development."[27] By killing the sniper, particularly within this very specific context, Joker can incorporate elements of Hartman's teaching with his own developing understanding of the world and his role within it. Joker's voiceover at the end, despite its ambiguity, suggests as much.

The details of these scenes establish the meaning of Joker's resolution, as they emerge from and reference key elements from earlier in the film. The Marines argue about how to proceed, with Cowboy ordering that they pull back while Animal Mother demands that the wounded Marines be rescued. When Animal Mother takes action, Joker and the others follow his lead, and when Cowboy is killed, Joker and Animal Mother join forces to find the sniper for "payback." Navigating his way through the rubble of the devastated city, Joker discovers the sniper, a teenage girl not much older than a child, and attempts to shoot her. Instead of finally becoming a killer, however, his gun malfunctions, and as he struggles to unjam it, the sniper moves toward him while firing, seeking the best angle for the kill. When it seems certain that Joker will be shot, the sniper is riddled with bullets and collapses to the floor.

How is this scene to be interpreted? Joker's failure to shoot the sniper recalls one of Hartman's Parris Island lectures: "The deadliest weapon in the world is a Marine and his rifle.... Your rifle is only a tool.... If your killer instincts are not clean and strong you will hesitate at the moment of truth. You will not kill. You will become dead marines." Is Joker's weapon failure then a failure of character, an indication that he does not possess the "hard heart" or the "clean and strong instincts" required of a Marine? Or does it underscore Hartman's flawed worldview, particularly given the identity of the enemy? After all, the film's epitome of the killer instinct is not a Marine but a teenage Vietnamese girl, a character who destabilizes the foundations of Marine masculinity. Moreover, it is the naïve and immature Rafterman who saves Joker. The least experienced of the Marines, he childishly shouts, "I saved Joker's ass. I got the sniper, I fucking blew her away." Tellingly, he is ignored.

The film provides no clear answers to these questions. Instead, the focus—of both the Marines and the camera—turns to the young female sniper. In perhaps the film's most ironic twist, the merciless killer who decimated the Lusthog squad is a teenage girl. She exists outside of the conceptual framework established in basic training, where the production of masculine killing machines was all that mattered, and where the Marine was the ultimate hard-hearted killer. While this turn may shock viewers, it also stuns and confuses the Marines, who now, despite their desire for payback, cannot act. As they loom above her, uncertain about how to proceed, she quietly prays. Ultimately, Animal Mother, whose face communicates disbelief, decides they should leave her to die, and when Joker asks, "What about her?" Animal Mother responds, "Fuck her. Let her rot." Here, another brief confrontation between Joker and Animal Mother occurs, and while Animal Mother is clearly in charge of the squad, it is Joker who acts. In this moment of choice, Joker chooses to end her misery by shooting her, a decision influenced by her repeatedly whispering "shoot me." In a scene recalling his capitulation in beating Pyle, Joker again faces a moral challenge, again he is urged on by another, and again he hesitates. This time, however, he chooses the action he believes morally correct, resisting the expectation of others. Significantly, despite the scene's ironies, Joker cannot approach this moment ironically and must choose to meaningfully and morally engage.[28]

This act of mercy, which the other Marines cannot offer, also includes other resonances. From the Marine's perspective, Joker not only conforms to Marine ideology but exceeds it. Donlon's response, "Hard core, man. Fucking hard core," indicates as much, with the suggestion of "hard *corps*" apparent. The others cannot act because the teenage-girl killing machine they face subverts the gendered understanding of war taught on Parris Island. Unlike the Vietnamese prostitutes and the Mary-Jane Rottencrotches back home, they cannot fuck her, and unlike the Virgin Mary, they cannot worship her. As a result, they do nothing, behaving as if she no longer exists, and that their need for payback no longer exists, as well, because she has no place within their understanding of the world. In choosing to act, Joker confirms his masculinity for the others and for himself in a way that Hartman would understand, but he does so outside of the narrow context of Marine masculinity that Hartman taught.

Marching into the night against the backdrop of flames while singing the Mickey Mouse Club theme, Joker is content, much like someone who has experienced a religious conversion or epiphany, a instantiation of what Bakhtin called "the history of an individual ideological consciousness."[29] Here, Joker's voiceover invokes Hartman and recalls Pyle: "My thoughts drift back to erect nipple wet dreams about Mary Jane Rottencrotch and the Great Homecoming Fuck Fantasy. I am so happy that I am alive, in one piece and short. I'm in a world of shit, yes. But I'm alive, and I'm not afraid." Joker's words mark a moment of ideological resolution, as he has carved out a place for himself, a way to maintain a sense of self within the larger system that he has resisted.

NOTES

1. Critics have identified a lack of clarity in Joker's role. See James Naremore, *On Kubrick* (London: British Film Institute, 2002), 211, and Brad Stevens, "'Is That You John Wayne? Is This Me?'—Problems of Identity in Stanley Kubrick's *Full Metal Jacket*," *Senses of Cinema* no. 21 (July 2002), 2/5. Patricia Gruben observes that Kubrick's use of Joker is "radical in that his Joker is defined primarily through his self-consciousness, via irony and other devices, until almost the very end of the film." Patricia Gruben, "Practical Joker: The Invention of a Protagonist in *Full Metal Jacket*," *Literature Film Quarterly* 33, no. 4 (2005): 271.

2. Paula Willoquet-Maricondi explains, "By revealing the profound analogies between the making of the marine and the making of masculinity in general, Kubrick unmasks the true meaning of patriarchy and its motivation." Paula Willoquet-Maricondi, "Full-Metal-Jacketing, or Masculinity in the Making," *Cinema Journal* 33, no. 2 (Winter 1994): 5.

3. Linda Hutcheon, *Irony's Edge: The Theory and Politics of Irony* (New York: Routledge, 1995), 18.

4. Ibid., 12–13.

5. Naremore explains Joker's references to Wayne as "short-hand for the super-patriotic myths of cowboy masculinity and American triumphalism that were often purveyed by Hollywood in the years leading up to the US involvement in Vietnam." Naremore, *On Kubrick*, 220. Susan White observes that the "reference to John Wayne is hardly a casual one in a movie set during the days when *The Green Berets* was a gung-ho promotion for the U.S. Marine Corps." Susan White, "Male Bonding, Hollywood Orientalism, and the Repression of the Feminine in Kubrick's *Full Metal Jacket*," *Arizona Quarterly* 44, no. 3 (Autumn 1988): 121.

6. Paul Simpson, *On the Discourse of Satire: Towards a Stylistic Model of Satirical Humor* (Philadelphia, PA: John Benjamins Publishing Company, 2003), 72.

7. Robert Phiddian's claim that "Satires moralise and they also simplify. The two processes are linked though not identical" highlights another significant difference. Robert Phiddian, "Satire and the Limits of Literary Theories," *Critical Quarterly* 55, no. 3 (2013): 52. Though not a simple film, *Dr. Strangelove*'s satire simplifies Cold War politics while establishing the moral insanity of U.S. and Soviet policy. In contrast, *Full Metal Jacket* neither moralizes nor simplifies in depicting the disturbing realities of the Marines'war experience.

8. Thomas Doherty notes that Hartman is "such a virtuoso of vile invective that the main response to his torrents of abuse is delight in a master at work." Thomas Doherty, "Full Metal Genre: Stanley Kubrick's Vietnam Combat Movie," *Film Quarterly* 42, no. 2 (Winter 1988–1989): 26–27. With characteristic insight, Naremore writes, "it is not clear how we are supposed to take him. . . . Everything [he] says is outrageously offensive but delivered with such theatrical flair and poetic talent for disgusting metaphors that it invites laughter. . . . Hartman throws us off balance because he is revolting, scary and funny at the same time." Naremore, *On Kubrick*, 36.

9. For a nuanced analysis of the reconstruction of identity in relation to technology and weapons, see Richard Rambuss, "Machinehead," *Camera Obscura* 14, no. 3 (1999).

10. Mikhail M. Bakhtin, *The Dialogic Imagination* (Austin, TX: University of Texas Press, 1981), 259–422.

11. Ibid., 343.

12. Ibid.

13. Ibid., 342.

14. Ibid.

15. Ibid., 345–46.

16. White, "Male Bonding," 124–25.

17. Michele Pavan Deana, "Epicentre of an Earthquake: The Literary Sources of *Full Metal Jacket* (1987)," *Historical Journal of Film, Radio, and Television* 37, no. 3 (2017), 404.

18. Richard Rambuss, "After Male Sex." *South Atlantic Quarterly* 106, no. 3 (2007): 580.

19. Gruben, "Practical Joker," 274.

20. Nancy Sinatra, "These Boots are Made for Walkin'," Track 5 on *Boots*, Reprise Records, 1966, album.

21. Ibid.

22. Gene Siskel, "Candidly Kubrick," in *Stanley Kubrick: Interviews*, ed. Gene D. Phillips, 177–88. (Jackson, MS: University Press of Mississippi, 2001), 181.

23. Hutcheon, *Irony's Edge*, 13.

24. Ibid., 66.

25. Bakhtin, *Dialogic Imagination*, 342.

26. White notes that Animal Mother is like "the reincarnation of Pyle in the form of a fighting man, as though that repository of infantile or animal instincts could not be entirely repressed, but may in fact be necessary for the group's survival." White, "Male Bonding," 126.

27. Bakhtin, *Dialogic Imagination*, 346.

28. For varied interpretations of this scene, see Claude J. Smith Jr., "*Full Metal Jacket* and the Beast Within," *Literature/Film Quarterly* 16, no. 4 (1988): 230; White, "Male Bonding," 128; Rambuss, "Machinehead," 110; Zivah Perel, "Pyle and Joker's Dual Narratives: Individu-

ality and Group Identity in Stanley Kubrick's Marine Corps," *Literature-Film Quarterly* 36, no. 3 (2008): 229–30; and Naremore, *On Kubrick*, 215.

29. Bakhtin, *Dialogic Imagination*, 342.

REFERENCES

Bakhtin, Mikhail M. *The Dialogic Imagination: Four Essays*. Edited by Michael Holquist. Austin, TX: University of Texas Press, 1981.

Doherty, Thomas. "Full Metal Genre: Stanley Kubrick's Vietnam Combat Movie." *Film Quarterly* 42, no. 2 (Winter 1988–1989): 24–30.

Dr. Strangelove or: How I Learned to Stop Worrying and Love the Bomb. Directed by Stanley Kubrick, 1964. Culver City, CA: Columbia Tristar Home Entertainment, 2004, DVD.

Full Metal Jacket. Directed by Stanley Kubrick, 1987. Burbank, CA: Warner Brothers, 2001, DVD.

Gruben, Patricia. "Practical Joker: The Invention of a Protagonist in *Full Metal Jacket*." *Literature Film Quarterly* 33, no. 4 (2005): 270–79.

Hutcheon, Linda. *Irony's Edge: The Theory and Politics of Irony*. New York: Routledge, 1995.

Naremore, James. *On Kubrick*. London: British Film Institute, 2002.

Perel, Zivah. "Pyle and Joker's Dual Narratives: Individuality and Group Identity in Stanley Kubrick's Marine Corps." *Literature-Film Quarterly* 36, no. 3 (2008): 223–32.

Rambuss, Richard. "After Male Sex." *South Atlantic Quarterly* 106, no. 3 (2007): 577–88.

———. "Machinehead." *Camera Obscura* 14, no. 3 (1999): 97–122.

Pavan Deana, Michele. "Epicentre of an Earthquake: The Literary Sources of *Full Metal Jacket* (1987)." *Historical Journal of Film, Radio, and Television* 37, no. 3 (2017), 396–415.

Phiddian, Robert. "Satire and the Limits of Literary Theories." *Critical Quarterly* 55, no. 3 (2013): 45–58.

Simpson, Paul. *On the Discourse of Satire: Towards a Stylistic Model of Satirical Humor*. Philadelphia, PA: John Benjamins Publishing Company, 2003.

Sinatra, Nancy. "These Boots are Made for Walkin'," Track 5 on *Boots*, Reprise Records 1966, album.

Siskel, Gene. "Candidly Kubrick." In *Stanley Kubrick: Interviews*, edited by Gene D. Phillips, 177–88. Jackson, MS: University Press of Mississippi, 2001.

Smith, Claude J. Jr. "Full Metal Jacket and the Beast Within." *Literature/Film Quarterly* 16, no. 4 (1988): 226–31.

Stevens, Brad. "'Is That You John Wayne? Is This Me?'—Problems of Identity in Stanley Kubrick's *Full Metal Jacket*." *Senses of Cinema*, no. 21 (July 2002). http://sensesofcinema.com/2002/feature-articles/full_metal/

White, Susan. "Male Bonding, Hollywood Orientalism, and the Repression of the Feminine in Kubrick's *Full Metal Jacket*." *Arizona Quarterly* 44, no. 3 (Autumn 1988): 120–44.

Willoquet-Maricondi, Paula. "Full-Metal-Jacketing, or Masculinity in the Making." *Cinema Journal* 33, no. 2 (Winter 1994): 5–21.

Chapter Ten

"Violence Is a Very Horrible Thing"

Brechtian Alienation Effect in Kubrick's
A Clockwork Orange

Madison Mae Williams

In his key essay, "Theatre for Pleasure or Theatre for Instruction," theater practitioner and theorist Bertolt Brecht writes that the ideal spectator of epic theater responds to performance with reactions such as, "I'd never have thought it—That's not the way—That's extraordinary, hardly believable—It's got to stop—The sufferings of this man appall me, because they are unnecessary—That's great art; nothing obvious in it—I laugh when they weep, I weep when they laugh."[1] Coined by director and producer Erwin Piscator, epic theater refers to a twentieth-century political theater movement that privileged the relationship between drama's political content and form over audience emotional reaction and aesthetic value. Brecht's definition and popularization of epic theater was marked by his development of theatrical techniques such as breaking the fourth wall, fragmented narratives, flashes backward and forward in time, use of narration, and exaggerated acting; use of these techniques position epic theater as a practice that, like the real world, is "in disharmony with itself"[2] and calls for the audience to engage with it critically. These techniques have evolved and transformed over the years to be applied to art forms beyond that of stage performance, and are commonly translated in the cinema; Stanley Kubrick's 1971 film *A Clockwork Orange* is a key example of "epic film," achieved through Kubrick's utilization of the *verfremdungseffekt*, a term coined by Brecht usually translated as the alienation, distancing, or defamiliarization effect.[3] "Epic" is used here not as a reference to large-scale heroic films a la *The Lord of the Rings* series (Peter Jackson, 2001–2003), or Kubrick's own *Spartacus* (1960) and *2001: A Space*

Odyssey (1968), but instead refers to films that feature techniques commonly utilized in epic theater practice. This chapter examines Brechtian influence and practice in *A Clockwork Orange*. While Kubrick was no stranger to exploring questions regarding politics and violence in previous films such as *The Killing* (1956), *Paths of Glory* (1957), and *Dr. Strangelove* (1964), *Clockwork* marks a departure in terms of Kubrick's manipulation of cinematic form and technique to explore these topics. Examining *Clockwork* through the lens of epic theory allows for a critical reframing of the film as a work that engages with interdisciplinary performance technique. Through a combination of heavily stylized acting, dramatic sound design, and use of montage and narration, Kubrick showcases an aesthetic of alienation that provokes the audience to think critically about their affective and political relationships to violence.

Bertolt Brecht's works, both theoretical and creative, were driven by his desire to create performances that inspire audiences to think critically about the enactment of the world before them, and use the drama to critique their own societies. Brecht viewed performances based in realism and naturalism as dreamlike and inalterable, void of any critique that examines an unequal, bizarre world. In order for audiences to see the world as alterable, Brecht theorized that epic performances should depict the familiar as unusual, unfamiliar, and worth interrogating. This is realized in practice through deployment of the *verfremdungseffekt*, or alienation effect. The term refers to an ambivalent "making strange"; the alienation effect creates a representation that is recognizable to the audience, but is also made unfamiliar. Brecht utilized a lens of dialectical materialism as framework for his techniques; by "treat[ing] social situations as processes, and trac[ing] out all their inconsistencies,"[4] he constructed a performance practice that uses strange and conflicting elements to push the audience to a place of "understanding things so that we can interfere."[5] A representation of a final, definitive "truth" is not the point of epic media; for Brecht, it is about "whether it manages to interest [the spectator] in the world."[6] Rather than the work providing a tidy conclusion, it is up to the spectator to interpret the images presented from an analytical perspective, one that focuses on the world outside of the performance. Kubrick effectively manifests an aesthetic of alienation in *Clockwork* that pushes viewers to critique violence in contemporary society.

At the time of its release, *Clockwork* was criticized for its depictions of violent acts, with many critics suggesting that Kubrick included exploitative violence to desensitize audience members to the horrors of the acts themselves. One of many writers who shared this limited critique was film critic Pauline Kael, who argued in her 1972 review of the film that

> at the movies, we are gradually being conditioned to accept violence as a sensual pleasure. The directors used to say they were showing us its real face

and how ugly it was in order to sensitize us to its horrors. You don't have to be very keen to see that they are now in fact desensitizing us. . . . How can people go on talking about the dazzling brilliance of movies and not notice that the directors are sucking up to the thugs in the audience?[7]

However, Kael's argument is weak in that it does not engage with even the *possibility* that critical thought may occur, and treats the average spectator as too easily taken in by the spectacle of violence. This chapter argues that Kubrick's presentation of violence, distanced and "made strange," does not emotionally numb the spectator, but specifically *prevents* them from becoming desensitized to it. *Clockwork* is not an exploitation film in the sense that it is not "sucking up to thugs"[8] who celebrate or glorify violence outside the world of performance. The "gloating close-ups, bright, hard-edge, third-degree lighting, and abnormally loud voices"[9] that Kael finds disturbing in Kubrick's mise en scène are meant to remain disturbing for the length of the film. Framing depictions of violence through alienating aesthetic and technique conceptualizes *Clockwork* as a space for the audience's critical thinking to develop.

In a 1973 interview, Malcolm McDowell, who starred in *A Clockwork Orange* as protagonist and antihero Alex Delarge, described the film as not sensationally violent, but instead, a film that evokes a "violence of the mind"[10] in the viewer. By this, McDowell acknowledges an affective response to the violence, but it is not one of either glory or desensitization. Instead, the "violence of the mind" functions as the site for criticism to begin. McDowell emphasized that the film "is very important because the statement it makes is about the freedom of human beings to choose, and that's more important than any of these sensational elements that the press and people have been talking about."[11] That is not to say that there are no sensational elements, or elements meant solely for entertainment in *Clockwork*. If the film functioned solely on the didactic level, it would read as Brecht writes, "a highly disagreeable, humourless, indeed strenuous affair."[12] Likewise, it is a common misinterpretation that Brechtian works are devoid of emotional engagement; in fact, Brecht himself emphasizes in "The Modern Theatre is the Epic Theatre" that the differences between the dramatic and epic are not total dichotomies, but suggests that the epic performer or director may "choose to stress the element of emotional suggestion or that of plain rational argument"[13] depending on what is needed for a scene to function. These moments are exemplified in *Clockwork* through stylized acting; emotional suggestions and exploration of creating an abstracted "picture of the world"[14] through the actors' performances are a reflection of Kubrick's vision of the film as a tool meant for audiences to critique their own affective and sociopolitical positionality related to violence.

The opening two minutes of *Clockwork* are an introduction of the human being as "the object of inquiry"[15] through which spectators can begin their critique. From the opening image of the film, we begin to observe the dystopian world of the film via a kind of dis-identification with Alex's gaze. In a dolly shot that lasts over a minute and a half, the focus starts on Alex's smirking, staring face, with the shot remaining focused on the "Kubrick stare"—a term coined by Kubrick's director of photography Doug Milsome[16] describing the detached, unsettling gaze that signals that a character is "piercing through the illusion of conscious life to spy the deep archetypal forces that shape reality"[17]—before pulling back until the entire Korova milk bar is revealed. McDowell barely blinks during the entire shot, the stare invoking in the viewer a sense of unease, a threat, a feeling of being witnessed.[18] The shot pulls the viewer away from Alex into a world where explicit, hypersexualized decor—consisting of mannequin women that dispense drugged milk through their breasts and function as tables and chairs—is treated as normal. Equal parts Rococo and S&M aesthetically, the Korova is framed by harsh white light reminiscent of that produced by theatrical footlights. Although the viewer is signaled by the mise en scène that distance from the characters is key, Kubrick has set the stage, and Alex is all ready to perform; the audience is positioned as silent voyeurs to the chaos that is to come. As the camera pulls back, Alex subtly toasts the audience with his glass of milk plus, a moment of improvisation by McDowell. The actor later said of his dramatic choice, "[it lets] the audience know they were in for one hell of a ride."[19]

Alex, our self-described humble narrator, not only acts as the audience's lens into the "horrorshow" that is dystopian England, but also repositions the audience's gaze as acknowledged and observed subjects. Alienating acting technique emphasizes spectatorial distance through a subversion of the traditional audience gaze. As detailed by Brecht in "Alienation Effects in Chinese Acting," the actor "never acts as if there were a fourth wall besides the three surrounding him. He expresses his awareness of being watched. This immediately removes one of the European stage's characteristic illusions. The audience can no longer have the illusion of being the unseen spectator at an event which is really taking place."[20] Rather than identifying or empathizing with the character/actor, the viewer identifies with spectating itself. In *Clockwork*, McDowell's performative, self-reflective acting positions Alex as a character who is well aware that he is being observed, and seems to relish the uncomfortability of the spectator. This is established from the first time we see the character, which prevents the viewer from viewing Alex with an identificatory or empathetic gaze; instead, McDowell's alienating performance creates a space where focus is given for critical thought to occur.

One key moment of distancing in McDowell's performance came from a moment of improvising, prompted by Kubrick. After five days of experimenting with the scene where Alex and his droogs attack the Alexanders, the director, finding the scene too dull, asked McDowell if he could sing and dance to liven up the scene. McDowell famously went "into sort of a softshoe number . . . and then started to sing 'Singin' in the Rain,' because, subconsciously, [he] remembered that scene in the Gene Kelly film as being one of the happiest scenes [he'd] ever seen on film, and it was right for the moment."[21] "Singin' in the Rain," most famously performed in the 1952 movie *Singin' in the Rain* (Gene Kelly and Stanley Donen) by Kelly himself, is associated with charm and joy; Alex distorts the innocent song into one of perversion, gleefully warping the anthem of love into an abject nightmare. This scene is one of the most controversial in *Clockwork*, and has inspired much critical response; writer Susan Rice asks of this scene, "Has it occurred to anyone that, after having our eyes metaphorically clamped open to witness the horrors that Kubrick parades across the screen, like Alex and his adored 9th, none of us will ever again be able to hear 'Singin' in the Rain' without a vague feeling of nausea?"[22] However, it is important that this visceral response is not evoked simply for the sake of disgusting the viewer, but is purposeful in creating a site of critical potential. Brecht writes that in epic performance, the alienation effect "intervenes, not in the form of absence of emotion, but in the form of emotions which need not correspond to those of the character portrayed. On seeing worry the spectator may feel a sensation of joy; on seeing anger, disgust."[23] This prevents audience members from solely identifying or empathizing with characters, and instead challenges them to think critically about the actions and choices the characters make. The viewer is meant to find Alex's joy in viciously beating the writer and raping the writer's wife appalling enough; adding the perversion of the "Singin' in the Rain" song and dance makes identifying with Alex and with the violence shown near impossible, leading to a space where conscious critique and rejection of Alex's actions can take place in the mind of the viewer.

It would also be remiss to discuss acting in *A Clockwork Orange* that is effective in evoking the alienation effect without emphasizing Patrick Magee's performance as the writer of "subversive materials" Frank Alexander. After being brutally assaulted by Alex and his droogs in the beginning of the film, the writer takes Alex in after he is nearly drowned by his former friends. Not recognizing Alex at first, the writer only realizes that Alex is the one who assaulted him when he hears Alex singing "Singin' in the Rain" while bathing. Kubrick cuts immediately from a shot of Alex relaxing in the bathtub to the writer, overwrought with emotion, frozen in a scream reminiscent of Helene Weigel's in Brecht's own 1939 play *Mother Courage and Her Children*. Kubrick uses this shot as the fulcrum of the third act of the film; the writer's realization of Alex's identity as the boy who crippled him and raped his wife sets in motion the rest of the plot. During filming, Magee had feared his performance was too over the top, but was reassured that this was precisely the performance Kubrick was looking for.[24] The harrowing intensity of his silent scream is what makes this scene alienating. The writer's desperation, fear, and rage manifest in a *gestus* of pain; Magee's expression is alien and frightening, startling the viewer out of the relative calm of Alex's initial rescue. Kubrick and Magee choose here to highlight emotion over rational argument, and this visual representation of the writer's suffering is a heuristic symbol of the impact of violence enacted for the sake of violence.

Kubrick's works are well known for their distinctive scores, and *A Clockwork Orange* is no exception. In an interview with Michel Ciment, Kubrick shared his belief that "the most memorable scenes in the best films are those which are built predominantly of images and music."[25] Thus, it is fitting that Kubrick's collaboration with electronic musician and composer Wendy Carlos on the *Clockwork* score is key in understanding the film's Brechtian influence.[26] Known at the time for her Grammy award–winning album *Switched-On Bach* (1968)—one of the first to feature use of the Moog synthesizer—Carlos was invited to London to work with Kubrick on the project. In a 1979 interview in *Playboy*, Carlos noted that the use of a vocoder in some her *Clockwork* arrangements caused "uncomfortable reactions. People looked at us and said, 'Oh, my goodness, what is this?' They were scared by it. They were scared hearing a chorus of artificial voices."[27] Carlos and Kubrick's soundtrack uses discomfort and defamiliarization not simply to evoke emotion, but to tie audience response to critical thought. The distinctive combination of classical pieces, both performed on electronic instruments like the Moog and vocoder and in full orchestral arrangements, creates a sonic space that is simultaneously familiar and made strange. This resonates with Brecht's suggestion that music in epic performance communicates positionality and functions as a mode of communication within itself;[28] by creating a space in which the contrast between music and action alienates the viewer, Carlos and Kubrick use counterpoint to spur the audience to interrogate their relationship to violence.

The film opens with Carlos's take on the march from Henry Purcell's *Music for the Funeral of Queen Mary* (1695), a haunting and odd-sounding synthesized interpretation of a piece usually intended for a quartet of slide trumpets. Paired with Alex's previously discussed unblinking stare, the distorted but nonetheless unmistakable dirge evokes, if not an explicit threat of violence, certainly a distinct sense of unease and discomfort in the viewer. Each time that this theme recurs in the film, it functions as a signal that a shift in power—often catalyzed by an act of violence—is about to occur. Its use during the demonstration of the effects of the Ludovico treatment and scoring the attack Alex suffers at the hands of former-droogs-turned-cops Georgie (James Marcus) and Dim (Warren Clarke), both mark Alex's lack of control and loss of free will at the hands of the government. Later, when Alex is in the hospital after his suicide attempt, the final use of Purcell as a leitmotif (this time in a lighter, slightly happier-sounding synth arrangement) prefaces Alex's return to his pre-Ludovico demeanor where he relishes his thoughts of sex and violence again. For Kubrick, Purcell becomes a signal to the audience; pay attention, because the dynamics of power are about to shift again.

The first use of the overture to Gioachino Rossini's 1817 opera *The Thieving Magpie* happens while rival gang leader Billyboy and his four droogs are attempting to rape a young woman on stage (or, as Alex puts it, "getting ready to perform a little of the old in-out, in-out on a weepy young devotchka they had there"). When Alex and company arrive, a fight breaks out between the two groups. The fight is heavily stylized; while Rossini's overture underscores the action, the two rival gangs go at it with weapons as diverse as window panes and chains. Their theatricalized brawl reads as equal parts slapstick and ballet, ending with Alex and company emerging triumphant. This counterpoint is continued in a later scene, in which the "lovely music" of the overture again "[comes] to [Alex's] aid" while the droogs are walking along the Flat Block Marina. In a slow-motion fight scene, Alex demonstrates his authority over his underlings by beating Georgie and Dim with his cane and slicing open Dim's hand with a hidden stiletto. Christine Lee Gengaro suggests in *Listening to Stanley Kubrick: The Music in His Films* that the liveliness of Rossini's overture may bring us closer to the actions and sentiments of the characters; by framing the scenes that are violent as "dance-like, they are easier to accept."[29] While Gengaro's marking of these scenes as choreographic seems appropriate, we could argue that rather than making the violence acceptable, Carlos's score makes them "strange"; the lightness of Rossini counterpointed with the theatricalized violence reads as more grotesque than beautiful. The fight between Billyboy and Alex's droogs is not like the work of Jerome Robbins in *West Side Story* (1961), for example, which reads as more stylized dance than savage beatdown. The droogs' grapple in the theater is brutal, with furniture destroyed, bodies flying, and bottles and windows smashed into faces. Similarly, Alex's attack of his "brothers" is perhaps the most unhinged the audience has seen him thus far; he will just as enthusiastically and brutally attack his peers as he will strangers, grinning maniacally all the while. Even if there is a kind of playfulness to Kubrick's depiction of these brawls, the music, combined with Alex's deranged glee and the intensity of the acts performed, evokes a space of uncomfortability that distances the audience from being taken in by the style of the choreographed fights.

It is also important to note when tracks from Carlos's score play under scenes unmarked by violence, given they are few and far between. One moment of levity and purposeful humor is scored by an electronic version of the overture to Rossini's 1829 opera *Guillaume Tell*. Under a scene in which Alex has sex with two young women he met in a record shop, Carlos speeds up the already rapid-fire overture to match the accelerated film of the ménage à trois. The only consensual sex scene in the film is played as comic. As well as giving the audience a moment of humour—which, in combination with didacticism, Brecht deemed necessary for epic performance to function[30]—this sets the audience up for greater distancing when the violence continues. The viewer is *almost* distracted into forgetting about the violence of the first twenty-eight minutes of the film; however, this levity is abandoned after forty seconds as we are brought back into the tense, violent world of the droogs with the ending notes of the overture. Kubrick and Carlos contrast the mirth of the threesome scene with the seemingly unending violence that marks the rest of the film, increasing its impact by setting the audience up with its complete opposite.

Although the *Clockwork* score actually features more music by other composers, Beethoven's essentiality to both the plot and soundtrack should not be underestimated. The film uses the second and fourth movements from one of Beethoven's most famous works, Symphony No. 9, Op. 125. The first use of the second movement occurs simultaneously diegetically and in Alex's head as he masturbates to the symphony after a day of depravity with his droogs.[31] As he fantasizes, the music paints Alex's masturbation as a depraved ritual, a movement of idolatry and ecstasy scored by his greatest love. Once Alex undergoes the Ludovico treatment, the music of Beethoven becomes dangerous and sickening (as much of Carlos's score may well be for audience members), and is later used as a weapon against him. When he awakens with "the pain and sickness all over me like an animal," Alex names a more extreme, emotional sentiment of what violence in *Clockwork* does. The audience is unlikely to react as strongly as Alex does—to the point of wanting to kill themselves—but the visceral discomfort and need to find a solution to stop the feeling, and really, to stop violence, is key. Carlos and Kubrick present extremes in *Clockwork* of the right-wing totalitarian government's Ludovico treatment, which denies Alex free will, and the depiction of counterattack that the "subversive" Alexander and friends mount to make the incumbent government lose popularity before the upcoming election, and cite their opposing methodologies in their use of music. However, there is no clear didactic moment that offers "the answer" to the audience; while a starting point might be Doctor Branom's declaration that "violence is a very horrible thing," there is no explicit answer to the problem of interrogating violence in either the world of *Clockwork* or the real world. It is up to the viewer to parse out a solution for themselves, using that which they "viddy" and "slooshy" in the film to grapple with these issues.

After Alex's suicide attempt, it is implied that he has returned to his old self and way of thinking, but Kubrick and Carlos prove it with the grand finale. In a show of goodwill and, as the Minister of the Interior puts it, "as a symbol of our new understanding, an understanding between two friends," a set of comically large speakers is wheeled into the hospital room. In a moment of inverted poetic justice, Alex's depravity comes back full force—powerful to the point of his eyes rolling back into his head—with an orchestral version of the symphony's fourth movement. The "perfect ending" that he imagines—having sex in the snow with a young woman while men and women in Victorian dress applaud their action—does indeed end up involving "a bit of the old Ludwig Van," calling back to Alex's earlier narration. However, the film's credits deflate the triumphal sonic space of Alex's "cure" with Gene Kelly's version of "Singin' in the Rain." The lighthearted, performative recording feels out of place and takes us back to the harsh strangeness of Alex's own performance, reminding the audience of what Alex, now "cured, all right,'" is certain to return to.

Kubrick's use of montage and narration in *A Clockwork Orange* was inspired by his goal to "find something like a cinematic equivalent of Burgess's literary style and Alex's highly subjective view of things."[32] The original novel presents Alex as an unreliable narrator with whom the reader engages as he recounts the events of the novel. Kubrick translates this to the screen through the use of Alex's isolated narration combined with images of extreme violence; this emphasizes Alex as one of the aforementioned objects of inquiry, forcing the audience to bear witness to Alex's point of view without centering empathy for the character. Alex's obsession with sex and violence is highlighted from the beginning of the film, but made explicitly clear during the montage of "lovely pictures" that Alex imagines while masturbating to Beethoven. As Alex's fantasies progress, we see a montage of a woman being hanged, buildings exploding, and people being crushed by an avalanche, intercut with Alex grinning, fangs dripping with blood. Reminiscent of Christopher Lee's Dracula from the Hammer Films series, Alex the vampire is equally as monstrous, bloodthirsty, and sexually driven; Kubrick gives us flashes of Alex as abhuman, further alienating the audience from identifying with him. Culminating in another variation on the Kubrick stare, the gaze Alex gives the camera is reminiscent of the opening shot: grotesque, dirty, and uncomfortable. The delight Alex finds in his ritualistic sexual explorations of violent acts are meant to alienate the viewer from finding personal resonance with him as a character; where Alex feels perverse excitement and joy, the audience feels disgust and horror.

Alex's obsession is also referred to in montage during his incarceration in the second act of the film. While Alex is in prison, we see a series of images in which he imagines himself as a Roman whipping Jesus on his way to the cross, slitting the throat of a soldier in combat, and being fed grapes by naked women. Biblical sex and violence are what sustain Alex in his incarceration; it is his depraved fantasies that keep him going. Kubrick highlights Alex's obsession with sex and violence through montage in order to show the depravity of the ideas that fuel his actions. To Alex, rape, assault, and murder are normalized.

The audience cannot break away from Alex's point of view, and is made to endure uncomfortable, startling images of violence. Despite being bombarded with these images, the viewer is not meant to identify with Alex and his fantasies. Regarding audience identification with Alex, Stephen Mamber suggests in his 1973 analysis of the film that "audience identification (rather than just interest) depends upon two factors—a realistic context and a character one either agrees with or aspires to be."[33] From the beginning, Kubrick presents Alex as a morally corrupt and manipulative sociopath, indiscriminate in choosing his victims of violence and disgustingly self-involved in his own perverse fantasies. McDowell's handsomeness and stylized charm alone are not enough to move audience engagement to empathy. Brecht writes that the spectator "must not start *with* man [as the object of inquiry], we must start *on* him. This means, however, that [the viewer] must not simply set [themselves] in his place, but set [themselves] facing him."[34] Alex is framed as the observed and observant cite of criticism; he is not the redeemable antihero that many critics suggest him to be, but the subject of examination, meant to be kept at arm's length from sympathetic identification.

Even in the situation that we somehow, as Mamber suggests, "do find Alex to be the most sympathetic character . . . there are just too many factors at work throughout the film to let this identification continue."[35] One of these factors is the introduction of the Ludovico technique at the end of the second act. Alex agrees to submit to this treatment in order to be released from prison earlier.[36] The technique involves exposure to images of violence and sexual assault, which combined with drugs, leads to physical sickness and aversion to any related act. Like the audience itself, Alex is forced to endure these unwanted images of violence, made worse to the extent that his eyes are forced open by the scientists running the treatment. Alex's reactions to the montage of violence are a metacinematic commentary included to make the audience examine their own role as voyeurs. However, the stakes are different for Alex; he is physically restrained, eyes held open by clamps, and drugged to induce the feeling of sickness. Audience members still retain the free will to look away, to stop watching the film and walk out of the theater or turn off the television. Alex cannot escape the violence, and this key difference marks Kubrick's ultimate "film-within-film abstraction of violence"[37] through the Ludovico technique. This functions as the most deliberate way of distancing the viewer; unlike Alex, from whom we have been distanced from the opening scene, the viewer can begin to move beyond the "violence of the mind" toward an interrogation of violence beyond the world of the film.

In his narration over the first film shown as part of the Ludovico technique, during which a man is assaulted by four droogs, Alex ironically comments that "it's funny how the colors of the real world only seem really real when you viddy them on a screen." It is only when Alex views a heavily stylized, edited, and exaggerated presentation of violence that he is able to grasp its horror. Both Brecht and Kubrick seem to take Alex's argument as their modus operandi; *A Clockwork Orange* becomes a space of examining the real world—and the real person—through a focused defamiliarization and abstraction through the mode of film. It is interesting that Anthony Burgess writes in his introduction to *A Clockwork Orange* that he tends to "disparage [his novel] as a work too didactic to be artistic," naming the job of the novelist as one who shows rather than preaches.[38] While the *Clockwork* film adaptation functions as an equally didactic piece, it does not feel "preachy" or lacking in artistic value; in fact, it is its narrow framing and hyperdeveloped aesthetic that transforms the viewer's perception of the purpose of the art itself from solely entertainment or surface-level commentary to a space of criticism. It is important to note that film differs from both literature and theater in the way that it is edited. Film directors and editors have a much tighter control over what is seen and experienced by audiences when the improbability of the live theater is removed, and audience response to visual and sonic performance differs from that evoked by the written word. The locus for inciting reaction in an audience member is transformed when there are no bodies on stage; Kubrick's utilization of epic techniques translated for film emphasizes the didacticism that forces audience members to critique both their own perception of art and how violence manifests itself in the world around them. When watching *Clockwork*—and especially when watching the film alone—it is extremely difficult to be drawn into the world that Kubrick creates. Without live performance and the dynamic of sharing space with a group while watching theater, the *Clockwork* audience member can never completely forget that they are watching a film and are being purposefully unsettled. The spectator as a site for change is key in Kubrick's methodology as a filmmaker, and is reflected in the plot itself through Alex's journey. By rooting its aesthetic, mise en scène, and acting in epic techniques, Kubrick's *A Clockwork Orange* is a vehicle for the individual viewer to critique their own relationship to contemporary violence.

NOTES

1. Bertolt Brecht, *Brecht on Theatre: The Development of an Aesthetic*, ed. and trans. John Willett (London: Bloomsbury, 2015), 71.
2. Ibid., 193.
3. All three are used interchangeably in this chapter.
4. Brecht, *Brecht on Theatre*, 193.
5. Ibid.
6. Ibid., 161.
7. Pauline Kael, "Stanley Strangelove," *The New Yorker*, January 1, 1972, http://www.archiviokubrick.it/english/works/reviews/aco/1972NYkael.html (accessed June 30, 2019).
8. Ibid.

9. Ibid.
10. Malcolm McDowell, "Interview with Malcolm McDowell," interview, 1973, https://www.youtube.com/watch?v=-RMrv4nanxc (accessed May 15, 2019).
11. Ibid.
12. Brecht, *Brecht on Theatre*, 72.
13. Ibid., 36.
14. Ibid., 37.
15. Ibid.
16. Vincent LoBrutto, *Stanley Kubrick: A Biography* (New York: Da Capo Press, 1999), 466.
17. J. F. Martel, "The Kubrick Gaze," *Reality Sandwich*, June 5, 2014, https://realitysandwich.com/149960/the-kubrick-gaze/ (accessed November 19, 2019). Also, see Keir Dullea in *2001: A Space Odyssey* (1968), Jack Nicholson in *The Shining* (1980), Vincent D'Onofrio in *Full Metal Jacket* (1987), Tom Cruise in *Eyes Wide Shut* (1999), etc.
18. This could also be foreshadowing how Alex's eyes are forced open during the Ludovico treatment.
19. Malcolm McDowell and Nick Redman, "Audio Commentary." On *A Clockwork Orange*, DVD, directed by Stanley Kubrick (Burbank: Warner Home Video, 2007).
20. Brecht, *Brecht on Theatre*, 92.
21. "Examination of Kubrick's A Clockwork Orange," *Camera Three*. CBS. February 1972.
22. Susan Rice, "Stanley Klockwork's Cubrick Orange," *Media and Methods* 8, no. 7 (March 1972): 39–43.
23. Brecht, *Brecht on Theatre*, 94.
24. McDowell, "Audio Commentary."
25. Michel Ciment, *Kubrick* (London: Collins, 1983), 156.
26. This section is not meant to be a comprehensive examination of *Clockwork*'s score, as much critical writing has been dedicated to this subject, but instead highlights the tracks that most exemplify Kubrick's goal of realizing a defamiliarizing aesthetic.
27. L. Vernon Smith, "Playboy Interview: Wendy/Walter Carlos," *Playboy Magazine*, July 1979.
28. Brecht, *Brecht on Theatre*, 38.
29. Christine Lee Gengaro, *Listening to Stanley Kubrick: The Music in His Films* (Lanham, MD: Rowman & Littlefield, 2014), 114.
30. Brecht, *Brecht on Theatre*, 72.
31. "Oh, bliss, bliss and heaven," Alex tells the audience during this scene. "Oh, it was gorgeousness and gorgeosity made flesh. It was like a bird of rarest spun heaven metal, or like silvery wine flowing in a spaceship, gravity all nonsense now, as I slooshied . . ." "Slooshied" in Nadsat, the language created by Burgess in the novel and utilized by Kubrick in the film, refers to listening (from the Russian slušat′, "listen"), but is clearly meant to also refer to masturbation (and ejaculation) in context.
32. Ciment, *Kubrick, The Definitive Edition* (New York: Faber & Faber, 2001), 151.
33. Stephen Mamber, "A Clockwork Orange," *Cinema* 7, no. 3 (Winter 1973): 56.
34. Brecht, *Brecht on Theatre*, 193 (emphasis added).
35. Mamber, "A Clockwork Orange," 56.
36. When Alex first arrives at the prison, he does not hesitate to let the viewers know, "This is the real weepy and like tragic part of the story beginning, O my brothers and only friends."
37. Mamber, "A Clockwork Orange," 56.
38. Anthony Burgess, *A Clockwork Orange* (New York: W.W. Norton & Company), xiv.

REFERENCES

Brecht, Bertolt. *Brecht on Theatre: The Development of an Aesthetic*. Edited and translated by John Willett. London: Bloomsbury, 2015.
Burgess, Anthony. *A Clockwork Orange*. New York: W. W. Norton & Company, 2011.
Ciment, Michel. *Kubrick*. London: Collins, 1983.

———. *Kubrick, The Definitive Edition*. New York: Faber & Faber, 2001.
A Clockwork Orange. Directed by Stanley Kubrick, 1971. Burbank: Warner Home Video, 2007, DVD.
"Examination of Kubrick's A Clockwork Orange." *Camera Three*. CBS. February 1972.
Gengaro, Christine Lee. *Listening to Stanley Kubrick: the Music in His Films*. Lanham, MD: Rowman & Littlefield, 2014.
Kael, Pauline. "Stanley Strangelove." *The New Yorker*, January 1, 1972. http://www.archiviokubrick.it/english/works/reviews/aco/1972NYkael.html.
LoBrutto, Vincent. *Stanley Kubrick: A Biography*. New York: Da Capo Press, 1999.
Mamber, Stephen. "A Clockwork Orange." *Cinema* 7, no. 3 (Winter 1973): 48–57.
Martel, J. F. "The Kubrick Gaze." *Reality Sandwich*, June 5, 2014. https://realitysandwich.com/149960/the-kubrick-gaze/.
McDowell, Malcolm. "Interview with Malcolm McDowell." Interview. 1973. https://www.youtube.com/watch?v=-RMrv4nanxc.
McDowell, Malcolm, and Nick Redman. "Audio Commentary." On *A Clockwork Orange*. Directed by Stanley Kubrick, 1971. Burbank: Warner Home Video, 2007, DVD.
Smith, L. Vernon. "Playboy Interview: Wendy/Walter Carlos." *Playboy Magazine*, July 1979.

Chapter Eleven

Reading Reality in *A Clockwork Orange*

Film Censorship, Metalepsis, and "Media Effects"

Rachel Cole

Alfred Hitchcock's *Psycho* (1960) had a wider impact than merely changing the conventions of the thriller genre. For Rick Worland, the film also affected how characters signify as "good" or "bad" in film more generally.[1] A decade later in the film *A Clockwork Orange* (1971), Stanley Kubrick drew attention to film's capacity to reorder signifiers of "good" and "bad," illustrating how these concepts operate within cinematic language in ways that fascinate cult audiences and film experts around the world. *A Clockwork Orange* received an extraordinary level of media and critical attention on release, at a time when accepted levels of violence on screen were being tested. Representations of sex and violence became more explicit in both popular and art film, as many directors drew on these to address potent social questions. Theories abounded regarding the film's "message," coalescing into a tight-knit set of debates around the consumption of film that subsequently also veered toward commentary about the "effects" of film in general.

Although Kubrick was cautious about releasing the film due to its influence on audiences, *A Clockwork Orange* clearly took aim at the stale logic of juvenile delinquency as caused by the consumption of media violence alone. As the difficult subject of *A Clockwork Orange*, adolescent boys are also restricted from watching this film under a range of media governance systems, on first release and subsequently. This indicates the extent to which age restriction was already a *sine qua non* for the circulation of film in 1971, at least in Anglo-Western countries such as the United Kingdom, United States, and Australia.[2] In noting the significant change from "censorship" to "classification" occurring transnationally in this period, this chapter will consider the metalepsis, or slippage between layers of narrative, that besieged the film's commercial release in these regions.

Classification involves the examination of cultural products by a group of censorship/classification officers to decide what types of content should be accessible to viewing publics through the prism of an existing schema of age-rating categories. *A Clockwork Orange*, however, has difficulty fitting within the usual realm of censorship and classification discussions because of the extremely rare event of a self-imposed ban undertaken by Kubrick himself and his reluctant production company Warner Bros. in 1972. Their withdrawal of the film from circulation made it legally unavailable for viewing by U.K. audiences until after Kubrick's death in 1999.[3] Rather than providing an "end" to an extra-diegetic layer of the film's meaning, this censorship seemed to further promote the film's formative place in this period's new debates about violence and media. This chapter will use metalepsis to contend part of Kubrick's genius as a filmmaker lay in his ability to render sensible the meaning-making that occurs around film. Part of his unique legacy is apparent in the media cultures that assemble around filmmaking, including structures of film appreciation and governance.

A phenomenon widely identified in rhetoric until repurposed for literary analysis and beyond by Gérard Genette,[4] metalepsis involves the slippage of textual detail between layers of diegetic narrative. While ontological separation between these layers makes such slippage paradoxical,[5] each transgression highlights the very nature of the boundaries that are overstepped.[6] Although metalepsis occurs frequently within cinema, it is not often discussed with reference to how it can occur across media.[7] This is perhaps unsurprising given the great variety of ways in which metalepsis could be identified in film, made even more vast by Erwin Feyersinger's (2010) discussion of metalepsis in animated films. He suggested films such as *Who Framed Roger Rabbit* (Robert Zemeckis, 1988) utilize metalepsis to represent one coherent narrative or "hybrid" world that relies upon conflict between two domains separated in physical, social, moral, and perceptual senses.[8] Another example of such a hybrid appears in *Isn't It Romantic* (Todd Strauss-Schulson, 2019). This film illustrates knowledge about the everyday place of classification and generic codes of romantic comedy in contemporary film through metalepsis. At the point where the main character, Natalie (Rebel Wilson), recognizes she has entered an alternative reality, she exclaims "My life has become a mother#$%ing romantic comedy . . . and it's PG-13!"

Metalepsis is not to be confused with the way film is metareferential, where stories are told over different films, particularly in popular film franchises in genres such as horror, action, and comedy. Furthermore, adding film regulation to the scholarly discussion of metalepsis should not be seen as a substitute for ascertaining iterability or banal forms of "slippage" as potential objects of regulation that dictate certain pressure points around sex, violence, drug use, and so forth. While decision-making processes in classification systems are partly concerned with how audiences will "read" a film, such discussion does not do justice to the complex processes of film governance that occur at the hands of vast and varied parties. Instead, this chapter uses metalepsis to describe the extra-diegetic layers at play in the transnational processes of film classification and film controversy. This intensifies the way metalepsis can act as a functional reminder to consider fictional content in relation to the world that interprets it as comic, satire, or in the case of *A Clockwork Orange*, as "dangerous" or "fascist" in terms embraced by the British and U.S. press at the time of its release.[9] This chapter makes a case for a form of transmedia metalepsis that acknowledges how film circulates as a discursive object.

Considering *A Clockwork Orange* as a discursive object, and importantly as an object of restriction for young audiences, allows a number of ideas to surface regarding both Kubrick's work itself and the operation of metalepsis. This chapter will discuss three narrative slippages as metalepsis, occurring when: (1) the film's narrator, Alex DeLarge (Malcolm McDowell), explicitly addresses the film audience; (2) the moral panic and film criticism position the film as an attempt by Kubrick to desensitize audiences; and (3) the censorship of the film in the United Kingdom by Kubrick himself. These "leaks" suggest how film governance, and the social context it explicitly aims to represent, accounts for media's "effects," making decisions and garnering opinions based upon interrelated factors of content, tone, artistry, and consistency.

Metalepsis number one represents a type of "ascending" and "ontological" infringement, initiated by Alex and entirely rhetorical.[10] Number two, however, refers to a conceptual interference introduced by commentators on *A Clockwork Orange*, who sensed the potential for audiences to be desensitized. Such commentary assumed a particular model of audience reception, stoking fears that culminated in a moral panic regarding *A Clockwork Orange* and films of a similar ilk. This panic included media framing in both Britain and the United States, echoed by the Motion Picture Association of America (MPAA) and the newly formed classification procedures of the Australian Film Censorship Board (FCB). Although more rare, the third metalepsis challenges the idea that film censorship and classification are simply the domain of formal (or top-down) systems of governance. The "descending" and authorial metalepsis of Kubrick playing censor to his own film seemed to further animate discussion of the effects of media, despite being entirely extra-diegetic. As these incidents are significant to understanding the mystique of Kubrick as director, they also signal how filmic metalepsis is different from the literary device. Whereas metalepsis in fictional literature often stirs the audience's critical thinking about reality, the same terms do not always apply to cinematic metalepsis for a number of reasons that also cipher differences between the occurrence of "actual" and "metaphorical" metalepsis. While Eric Thoss posits that metalepses between reality and fiction cannot occur,[11] the historical censorship and classification treatments of film suggest that differentiating between "actual" and "fictional" transgression is not only "difficult" but impossible. The moment a transgression is perceived to have occurred, in one sense, it has, and this does not always proceed in ways that could be foreseen by a film director.

A Clockwork Orange is set in a not-too-distant future, a dystopia that lacks key infrastructure to protect citizens, particularly the modern structures that seek to govern young people for their own protection. A number of narrative elements perpetuate a cycle of violence and apathy, including a cold and uncaring state that exercises heightened powers over life, and bars where drugged "milk-plus" is freely consumable and violent videos can be watched by the young as part of a night out. One such place, the Korova Milkbar, is where we first encounter Alex, the main character and young narrator. Surrounded by white, placid female mannequins that present as furniture, serving milk-plus from their plastic nipples, Alex and his gang the "droogs" contemplate a night on the town to take delight in fighting and breaking the law.

These young men converse with each other in "nadsat," a language originally created by Anthony Burgess for the 1962 novel from which the film was adapted. The droogs' white outfits add to the futuristic milieu, where their oversized codpieces are offset by their larger-than-life black accents of eyeliner, bowler hats, and army boots. Alex appreciates classical music, especially Ludwig van Beethoven and his 9th Symphony. For the audience, this represents something of a contradiction to his appearance and status as violent gang leader for it strongly subverts conceptions of "high" culture as "civilizing" and enriching to the individual that featured in media consumption debates surrounding the British release of the D. H. Lawrence novel *Lady Chatterley's Lover* in 1960, for example. The droogs' first victim, an elderly inebriated tramp, relates to Alex that there's "no law and order anymore. . . . It's a stinking world because it lets the young get onto the old" before he succumbs to a kicking from the gang. In this world, not only do the young disrespect their elders but seemingly all forms positioned as moral decency or authority. The droogs take on a rival gang before talking their way into an unsuspecting home where Alex rapes a woman, forcing her husband to watch, followed by more murder at another location. These violent scenes are accompanied by classical music or Alex's rendition of "Singin' in the Rain." Reading the film in 2020, the droogs' behavior appears to be directly related to the videos they watch at Korova. Links between vision and knowledge, media and violence are referenced by the ongoing replacement of the term "see" with "viddy" in their diegetic language, preemptive of the video formats still in commercial development in the early 1970s. Kubrick's interest in the entanglement of human use of technology and desensitization was already nuanced in *2001: A Space Odyssey* (1968), released three years prior to *A Clockwork Orange*. In *A Space Odyssey*, astronaut Dave Bowman (Keir Dullea) mechanically completes his daily tasks before his life is calculatingly endangered by HAL 9000, a self-aware spaceship computer with the manner of an English gentleman. In the end, HAL 9000 expresses the entirely human capacity of being unable to observe his own flaws at the same time as he apparently gains the ability to "feel."[12]

In *A Clockwork Orange*, Alex is the sole character given any semblance of depth as well as maintaining credentials as "cool" or desirable.[13] Although willfully violent, he can never quite catch a break and even elicits sympathy. His parents are seemingly unaware of and unable to deal with his antisocial behavior. Alex's correctional officer makes a pass at him, heightening the vulnerability existing alongside his heinous nature. Post-rampage, the droogs are weary of being bullied by their hyper-masculine leader, and they wound and abandon Alex at the scene where he has just used an oversized sculpture of a phallus to bash a woman. The audience later learns that she died of her injuries. As Alex is carted off to face a jail sentence, he addresses the audience as "friends," announcing "This is the real weepy and like tragic part of the story beginning, O my brothers and only friends." This represents the first metalepsis of *A Clockwork Orange*, fulfilling one of the more obvious anxieties regarding film and metaleptic transgression—the shock that this physical transgression is possible, even if only in representation.[14] Alex attempts to endear himself to the audience, when he continues "After a trial with judges and a jury, and some very hard words spoken against your friend and humble narrator, he was sentenced."

Thus begins a sequence in which, instead of being disgusted by or fearing Alex, the audience is invited to sympathize. In prison, some of Alex's violent behaviors persist until he pretends to the judge that he "just wants to be good" and is allowed into a "rehabilitation" program of aversion therapy called the Ludovico treatment. This treatment involves the involuntary viewing of cinematic sex and violence, while listening to music such as Beethoven's 9th, and the simultaneous forced consumption of drugs that make him physically ill. Although this treatment can be viewed as another form of violence perpetrated by the state aimed at curbing his free will and choice, it also seems to quell his violent tendencies. Alex is released, but this is not a redemption story. The other droogs reappear with jobs that normalize their masculine bullying as policemen, and they attack him. Alex again becomes a victim of the violent society to which he had contributed. By the time he survives another attack from a former victim, which in turn resurrects his own violent tendencies, a typical understanding of cause and effect in which the media shapes behavior has become ultimately chaotic and confused.

Alex's final acts of violence are made all the more distasteful through the representative stamp of approval he receives, in the film, from the British Home Office.

A number of film and cultural theorists have noted how *A Clockwork Orange* reignited the tension of many debates present in discourses surrounding film regulation long before the film's commercial release. Determinations between im/morality and art/obscenity gave parameters to much discussion around the film but have since ostensibly declined in relevance to considerations of film classification. Other arguments evolved to discuss the film in relation to exploitation and the theme of juvenile delinquency (JD), and these concerns are still present today in film classification more generally. JD films famously capitalize on the figure of the rebel adolescent in films like *The Wild One* (Laslo Benedek, 1953), *Blackboard Jungle* (Richard Brooks, 1955) and *Rebel without a Cause* (Nicholas Ray, 1955). The difficulty of classifying the content of *A Clockwork Orange* and other JD films, and their determination as "for adults" in Britain and Australia clearly demarcated this content as different from the mainstream. Alex's status as adolescent is depicted ambivalently; it is displayed as Alex's *choice* to repeatedly act violently as well as incite others to.[15] His free will (or lack thereof) is a deliberate part of the narrative, challenging traditional thought about restriction as protection of the innocent, as well as other cinematic examples of risky yet misunderstood teenagers. The JD narrative in *A Clockwork Orange* also highlights a failure of institutional provisions to provide support and care.[16] Positioning the film within available genres such as teen, JD, artistic, child exploitation, and/or part of the "violent new wave" proves difficult and controversial. Although generic conventions are certainly significant to the regulatory context in which the film was released, without governmental programs that prominently figured segregation by age, the film might not have been released at all.

In 1967, a screenplay of *A Clockwork Orange* was initially rejected by John Trevelyan, the secretary of the British Board of Film Censors (BBFC). Written by Michael Cooper and Terry Southern, the film was set to be produced by Paramount.[17] This rejection was not without reference to concerns about juvenile delinquency, evident in the BBFC's delayed release of *The Wild One* in Britain from 1953 until fourteen years later in 1967.[18] On initially reading the Cooper-Southern screenplay, examiner Audrey Field stated "the visuals, however restrained, could not possibly get into even the 'X' category [for adults] unless we are willing to turn our existing standards upside down for the sake of this one film. In my opinion, this would be ill-advised."[19] Surprisingly in 1972, however, Kubrick's screenplay due to be produced in Britain was passed without cuts and given an "X" classification for adults over eighteen. This was allegedly due to social and political pressure surrounding other films featuring violence that preceded Kubrick's, notably *Straw Dogs* (Sam Peckinpah, 1971) and *The Devils* (Ken Russell, 1971).[20] When released with cuts, these films caused controversy and bad press for the BBFC that manifested as an impartiality crisis that ran from 1971 to 1972, centered on Stephen Murphy's short leadership.[21] One account, by James Robertson, argues that to release these films but not *A Clockwork Orange* would have appeared inconsistent and unjustified. Under Kubrick's own instruction, the film received a limited commercial release in London.[22] But before the film could be released in the County Councils it became the object of a campaign by the Festival of Light and persistent attacks by the press that delayed general release until 1973.[23]

Rather than simply representing fears about juvenile delinquency, this delay ensured another notable controversy surrounding *A Clockwork Orange* while still speaking to debates about screen violence and antisocial behavior in real life. *A Clockwork Orange* brought to fever pitch fears of media influence that have been more or less continuous since of the invention of cinema, particularly regarding vulnerable audiences, because of an artistic style that subverted social and cultural cues. Subsequently, *A Clockwork Orange* became the film most consistently associated with "moral panic."[24]

This term was coined by Stanley Cohen in 1972 to describe social anxieties often directed at youth with a formula that revisits concerns already present, such as the influence of film on children, and transforms them into a seemingly "new" problem. In *Folk Devils and Moral Panics*, Cohen states the objects of moral panics "are damaging *in themselves*—but also merely *warning signs* of the real, much deeper and more prevalent condition."[25] With reference to *A Clockwork Orange*, this statement speaks to the way cinematic language had become so developed, and Kubrick's use of it so revered, that purposely not following certain codes and narrative traditions could be read as evident of a greater social problem. This went beyond concern over the sympathetic depiction of a violent character. Openly claiming the detrimental effects of the film, the British *Mail* claimed: "The film could start off an 'Orange' cult that would eventually lead to Fascism. So, although the film is very well made, it's a very dangerous bit of work. The sex and violence can be seen in the wrong light and the next thing you know people are off on a new crusade that makes rapes and beatings an acceptable part of everyday living."[26] Part of this panic also coincided with a number of crimes that media outlets connected to the film. One incident involved the murder of a homeless man in 1973, which the prosecution argued "may have been carried out for excitement as a result of the film."[27] After reviewing the film himself, the Home Secretary found such concerns to be unfounded. In consequence, however, Joseph Darlington argues *A Clockwork Orange* became "shorthand for the dangers of unrestricted popular culture"[28] as well as acting as both signifier and signified for a world where youth and violence rules.

Although not enamored with Kubrick's approach, film reviewers, critics, and even censorship agencies made more serious attempts to critically engage with the film's content. The United States had moved to a system of classification in 1968, and the film received an "X" rating that restricted viewing to over eighteen. Kubrick, however, edited the film to resubmit for a more commercial "R,"[29] as films with this rating can be viewed by children when accompanied by an adult. Public relations official from the MPAA, Susan Rice, stated the film came close to Kubrick's own version of the Ludovico treatment for the audience.[30] American film critics Pauline Kael (*The New Yorker*) and Richard Schickel (*Time*) also warned that the violence of the film may have a desensitizing effect on audiences.[31] Film reviewer Fred Hechinger wrote an op-ed in the *New York Times* that warned liberal viewers should be able to recognize "the voice of fascism" illuminated by this pessimistic and violent view of the nature of man.[32] Both Hechinger and Kael were much more sympathetic to even director Sam Peckinpah's realistic treatment of violence.[33] These statements held concerns that Kubrick's use of violence broke with normative contextual boundaries; when accompanied by classical music, for example, the horror had the potential to be decreased. As commentators identified this aspect of *A Clockwork Orange* to be desensitizing, they also made an argument regarding desensitization and how it occurs. Contrary to popular media concerns, it was not Alex himself jumping out of cinema screens to push at the boundaries of community standards like Sadako (Rie Ino'o) crawling out of the television to get revenge in the horror film *Ring* (Hideo Nakata, 1998). By recognizing a simplified version of the Ludovico treatment in Kubrick's disturbing mismatch between content and form, the second metalepsis represented the discursive production of a particular model of human capacities after media use.

Metalepsis number two highlights *A Clockwork Orange* brought into the mainstream conversations occurring prior and since the film regarding torture tactics that had been rationalized in the name of Western democracy. The not-so-distant past of Cold War interrogation techniques created a basis for understanding the scenes of the Ludovico treatment as offering a form of "realism." Alex's torture in the film added to arguments against the use of science to "brainwash" and control citizens.[34] However, although providing a realistic backdrop for Alex's treatment by the state to be received as totalitarianism, this does not necessarily denote *A Clockwork Orange* as a piece of social realism, particularly in relation to how such mind control might work through command of film content and tone. The second metaleptic transgression is actually more subtle, a product of the assumption that there should be reciprocity between content and form.

Discourses around film consistently draw attention to the proximity between the ontological levels of the film narrative (a scene that offers possible outcomes) and "real life," finding them too close for comfort. This has been one of the crucial arguments for both censorship and its modified form in classification. Regulatory changes occurring around the release of *A Clockwork Orange* nonetheless clearly related the problem of screen violence to forms of age-restriction for audiences. By 1969, tighter policy on sexual material was deemed necessary in Britain to respond to growing permissiveness.[35] In 1970, Trevelyan changed the age restriction of "X" rating from sixteen to eighteen, just before retirement from the BBFC.[36] His intention had been to make the censorship and cutting of films for this category "virtually unnecessary."[37] At the same time, a new category "AA" was introduced to restrict films available to audiences under the age of fourteen, producing a system of progression from the age of fourteen to eighteen. In 1971, these changes ensured the new BBFC secretary, Stephen Murphy, inherited a system in a period of considerable adjustment. The new "AA" category was criticized as "confusing" by exhibitors and audiences, and met with resistance in Glasgow, where the category was introduced as advisory only.[38]

On *A Clockwork Orange*'s Australian release, legal age restriction was finally in place. The "R" category for over-eighteens had been introduced in 1971, and the film's self-awareness and reflexivity about whether media violence caused social violence were balanced with an appreciation for the integrity of film. The violence was recognized as artistically portrayed in order to make social commentary and invite further contemplation. The notoriety of *A Clockwork Orange* overseas ensured it was viewed by a full panel at the Australian FCB, which labeled the film a "futuristic drama" and gave it an "R" classification. One censorship officer stated that despite feeling that the film was of "little genuine worth," they recognized it should be passed rather than refused registration.[39] Illustrating the extra labor that goes into difficult and controversial decisions, this same board member wrote a report addendum after reading an article by the author Burgess, stating they understood the meaning of the film: "to warn against encroachments on personal liberty by the State and to demonstrate through the character of Alex that it may deprive us through brainwashing techniques of the free will which allows us to choose between good and evil."[40] For yet another censorship officer, the use of spectacle actually diminished the impact of the violence, giving reason to advise against cuts: "Some may consider its message arousal, I think it poses a number of questions [about] the effects of violence on film and the effects of violence on its perpetrators—and I think it should be released in its entirety."[41]

Some censorship officers were clearly aware that to comment on this film required addressing the model of viewer consumption and violent behavior discussed in popular commentary of the film. One censorship officer cited a review by Kael in *The New Yorker* claiming the film "grooves" on violence, as it asks the audience to revel in the violent scenes even when identifying them as repulsive. While recommending an "R" rating, another censorship officer claimed: "If Stanley Kubrick intended this film to have a message my interpretation is as follows: Society should consider the long term implications of permissive behavior and violence and think very seriously in terms of PREVENTION rather than CURE."[42] These comments in the classification file were clearly not commenting on the film's content or denigrating the film as "obscenity," but referring to the way content now had to be considered in tandem with a broader field of extra-diegetic meaning overshadowing the presence of violent content itself.

Such varied interpretations cast a long shadow over Kubrick's professional and personal life, and a year after the film's release Kubrick exposed his deeply personal affront concerning much of the film's critical reception. Writing a letter to the *New York Times*, he rebuffed comments that the film was the work of fascism: "Mr. Hechinger is no doubt a well educated man but the tone of his piece strikes me as also that of a well-conditioned man who responds to what he expects to find, or has been told, or has read about, rather than to what he actually perceives 'A Clockwork Orange' to be."[43] Kubrick argued critics were simply responding to what they *thought* they knew about the film, not the actual content. Further still, two years after its British release, Kubrick pulled *A Clockwork Orange* from any kind of release in the United Kingdom. The death threats and accusations of incitement to violence received by Kubrick and his family are cited as reasons for the withdrawal.[44] While the narrative of the film remains unchanged, this form of extra-diegetic intervention involves slippage between ontological worlds. Historically, the intervention of the animator's hand into the fictional worlds of their creation has been repeated so often as to almost become cliché.[45] Kubrick's similar act represents something of the personal responsibility he took for *A Clockwork Orange*, even as it seemingly took on a life of its own that threatened his. Understanding the policy of censorship and classification does not make the film's censorship in the United Kingdom clear. One must understand film as a discursive object to make sense of the film's censorship, representing something of the autonomy of this fiction that Kubrick attempted to recover from British audiences and critics.

This also tells us something about the potential "danger" of narrative slippage in cinema in comparison to literature. The debates outlined above have roughly similar stakes in suggesting that attempts to rearrange the boundaries of "good" and "bad" representations, or replacing "romantic" or "happy" visual scenes with "violent" ones, offer a particular version of societal decay. Metalepsis appears to prompt questions about what is "real," often asking "what world are we in now?"[46] In film, however, this is a living, breathing question. Some films draw attention to the boundary between worlds for dramatic effect, as when *Isn't It Romantic* depicts the boundary between filmic worlds as partly a product of age-rating and classification. That boundary can then be expressed through bleeped expletives or missing sex scenes. Many live action films, however, naturalize or conceal the boundary of different narrative layers, using computer-generated imagery (CGI) and visual effects to create the illusion of profilmic homogeneity.[47] Thus, the "paradox" of fiction-to-reality metalepsis and whether it occurs in cinema should be reconsidered as inbuilt into cinema and its discursive formations; it is often assumed inherent to the medium by audiences, critics, and regulators alike. What such discourses often do not take into account is the uncontrollable nature of *discursive metalepsis* that involves wider social processes than simply film content.

Film and its meaning emerge from a wide variety of social and cultural processes within which viewer consumption is only one source or method. This chapter demonstrates cinematic meaning can also explicitly involve film appreciation, cultural criticism, classification, and so on. While boundaries between fiction and reality are often extremely difficult to identify in relation to film, it is important to note this is not only because of cinema's symbiotic relationship and potent representation of reality, or "realism." Aspects of this realism involve upholding generic values that suggest content has an obvious and unitary relationship to form that are important to "safe" representations and reading. If film critics are to be believed, these are not just generic codes; positing a coherent relationship between film content and tone is important to maintaining the status quo in many senses, classed as more or less overtly ideological and political. Whereas in literary studies, the fantastical use of metalepsis might promote critical thinking,[48] in contrast, examining metalepsis in *A Clockwork Orange* identifies the way film audiences and their critical faculties are overwhelmingly thought to be decreased by cinematic and interactive media. The term "desensitization" would further feature in discussions around film and video games in the decades that followed, specifically in regard to media's relationship to violence and based on research from the human sciences. Media classification systems systematically engage with some of the wider themes explored in *A Clockwork Orange* that still circulate as open questions in contemporary society: media consumption and its influence over audiences (highly relevant to recent debates around *The Hunt* [Craig Zobel, 2020] and *Joker* [Todd Phillips, 2019], for example);[49] how to account for multiple film readings; and the role of classification and the state in administering "freedom." These questions require further examination.

NOTES

1. Rick Worland, *The Horror Film: An Introduction* (Malden, MA: Blackwell, 2007), 86–87.

2. This research received funding from the Australian Research Council as part of an international comparative study into media classification systems by Catherine Driscoll and Liam Grealy (DP150101226). The author would like to thank her supervisors, the Australian

Classification Board and Classification Branch, and the Department of Gender and Cultural Studies at the University of Sydney who also supported this research.

3. Stuart Y. McDougal, "'What's It Gonna Be Then, eh?' Questioning Kubrick's *Clockwork*," in *Stanley Kubrick's A Clockwork Orange*, Cambridge Film Handbook, ed. Stuart Y. McDougal, 1–18 (Cambridge: Cambridge University Press, 2003), 1.

4. Gérard Genette, *Narrative Discourse: An Essay in Method*, tr. Jane E. Lewin (Ithaca, N.Y: Cornell University Press, 1980), 235–36.

5. Erwin Feyersinger, "Diegetic Short Circuits: Metalepsis in Animation," *Animation: An Interdisciplinary Journal* 5, no. 3 (2010): 279.

6. Genette, *Narrative Discourse*, 236.

7. Feyersinger, "Diegetic Short Circuits," 279.

8. Ibid., 289. Feyersinger states films with hybrid worlds do not constitute "proper" metalepses.

9. The British *Daily Mail* quoted in Joseph Darlington, "*A Clockwork Orange*: The Art of Moral Panic?" *The Cambridge Quarterly* 45, no. 2 (2016): 121; Fred M. Hechinger, "A Liberal Fights Back," *The New York Times*, February 13, 1972. https://www.nytimes.com/1972/02/13/archives/a-liberal-fights-back-a-liberal-fights-back.html (accessed January 26, 2020).

10. Karin Kukkonen, "Introduction," in *Metalepsis in Popular Culture*, ed. Karin Kukkonen and Sonja Klimek, 1–21 (Berlin: De Gruyter, 2011), 9.

11. Jeff Thoss, *When Storyworlds Collide: Metalepsis in Popular Fiction, Film and Comics* (Leiden: Brill Rodopi, 2015), 11.

12. Although not technically metalepsis, a popular conspiracy theory accompanied *A Space Odyssey* that the U.S. moon landing of 1969 was a hoax directed by Kubrick. This highlights the very unpredictability of "slippage" between fiction and reality, and can be noted as a sort of "Kubrick effect."

13. Janet Steiger, "The Cultural Productions of *A Clockwork Orange*," in *Stanley Kubrick's A Clockwork Orange*, ed. Stuart Y. McDougal, 37–60 (Cambridge: Cambridge University Press, 2003); Catherine Driscoll, *Teen Film: A Critical Introduction* (Oxford: Berg, 2011), 103.

14. Feyersinger, "Diegetic Short Circuits," 281.

15. Driscoll, *Teen Film*, 102.

16. Ibid., 104.

17. James C. Robertson, *The Hidden Cinema: British Film Censorship in Action, 1913–1975* (London: Routledge, 1993), 143.

18. Ibid., 110.

19. Audrey Field quoted in ibid., 143.

20. Ibid., 146.

21. Guy Phelps, *Film Censorship in Britain* (London: Victor Gollancz, 1975), 65; Robertson, *The Hidden Cinema*, 148; Julian Upton, "Innocence Unprotected? Permissiveness and the AA Certificate 1970–82," *Journal of British Cinema and Television* 14, no. 1 (2017): 68.

22. Steiger, "Cultural Productions."

23. In 1970, the British faction of the Nationwide Festival of Light were an evangelical "moral reform movement" against permissiveness in mass media and community standards. (Amy C. Whipple, "Speaking for Whom? The 1971 Festival of Light and the Search for the 'Silent Majority,'" *Contemporary British History* 24, no. 3 [2010]: 322, 325).

24. Darlington, "*A Clockwork Orange*," 119–34.

25. Stanley Cohen, *Folk Devils and Moral Panics*, 3rd ed (New York: Routledge Classics, 2011), original emphasis.

26. Ibid., 121.

27. Ibid., 122.

28. Ibid., 121.

29. McDougal, "Questioning Kubrick," 3–4.

30. Susan Rice quoted in Steiger, "Cultural Productions," 37.

31. Steiger, "Cultural Productions," 39.

32. Hechinger, "A Liberal Fights Back."

33. Steiger, "Cultural Productions," 39.

34. Psychiatrist Peter R. Breggin quoted in Carolyn Strange, "Stanley Kubrick's A Clockwork Orange as Art against Torture," *Crime, Media, Culture: An International Journal*, 6, no. 3 (2010): 279.
35. Ibid., 65.
36. Upton, "Innocence Unprotected?" 64.
37. John Trevelyan quoted in ibid., 66.
38. Although these changes initially stemmed the flow of "X" rated films into Britain, the "AA" rating was eventually changed in name and age restriction to "15" in 1982. (Upton, "Innocence Unprotected?" 66, 75).
39. Censorship officer report, March 2, 1972.
40. Addendum to censorship officer report, March 2, 1972.
41. Censorship officer report, February 18, 1972.
42. Censorship officer report, February 16, 1972, original emphasis.
43. Stanley Kubrick, "Now Kubrick Fights Back," *The New York Times*, February 27, 1972, https://www.nytimes.com/1972/02/27/archives/now-kubrick-fights-back-movies-now-kubrick-fights-back.html (accessed January 26, 2020).
44. *Stanley Kubrick: A Life in Pictures*, dir. Jan Harlan, 2001, Burbank, CA: Warner Bros. & Warner Home Video, DVD.
45. Feyersinger, "Diegetic Short Circuits," 283–84.
46. Thoss, *When Storyworlds Collide*, 87.
47. Feyersinger, "Diegetic Short Circuits," 289.
48. Rebecca Suter, "Critical Engagement through Fantasy in Hard-Boiled Wonderland and the End of the World," in *Haruki Murakami Challenging Authors*, ed. Matthew C. Strecher and Paul L. Thomas, 59–71 (Rotterdam: Sense Publishers, 2016), 70.
49. Satirical social thriller *The Hunt* depicts hunting humans for sport. Universal Studios first canceled the release after comments from President Donald Trump on Twitter and in the aftermath of extremist shootings involving over 30 deaths. The film was finally released in March 2020. (Edward Helmore, "Universal Cancels Release of Violent Satire *The Hunt* after Trump Criticism." *The Guardian*, August 10, 2019, https://www.theguardian.com/film/2019/aug/10/the-hunt-release-cancelled-gun-violence-trump-criticism, accessed 26 January 2020). In 2019, the Warner Bros. blockbuster *Joker* is the origin story of the "evil" Marvel comic character who could be read as a misunderstood hero. Criticized for inciting gun violence, references were made to a shocking gun massacre in a cinema theater in Colorado in 2012 (Chris Lee, "How *Joker* Became the Most Hated, Loved, Obsessed-over Movie of 2019," *Vulture*, October 9, 2019, https://www.vulture.com/2019/10/all-the-joker-controversy-and-threats-explained.html, accessed 26 January 2020).

REFERENCES

Australian Classification Board & Classification Branch. Censorship reports: *A Clockwork Orange*, ACB, Sydney.
Capshaw, Ron. "The Age of Movies: Selected Writings of Pauline Kael/Pauline Kael: A Life in the Dark." *The Humanist*, 44–45. Washington, DC: American Humanist Association, 2012.
Cohen, Stanley. *Folk Devils and Moral Panics*, 3rd edition. New York: Routledge Classics, 2011.
Darlington, Joseph. "*A Clockwork Orange*: The Art of Moral Panic?" *The Cambridge Quarterly* 45, no. 2 (2016): 119–34.
Driscoll, Catherine. *Teen Film: A Critical Introduction*. Oxford: Berg, 2011.
Feyersinger, Erwin. "Diegetic Short Circuits: Metalepsis in Animation." *Animation: An Interdisciplinary Journal* 5, no. 3 (2010): 279–94.
Genette, Gérard. *Narrative Discourse: An Essay in Method*. Translated by Jane E. Lewin. Ithaca, NY: Cornell University Press, 1980.
Hechinger, Fred M. "A Liberal Fights Back." *The New York Times*, February 13, 1972. https://www.nytimes.com/1972/02/13/archives/a-liberal-fights-back-a-liberal-fights-back.html.

Helmore, Edward. "Universal Cancels Release of Violent Satire *The Hunt* after Trump Criticism." *The Guardian*, August 10, 2019. https://www.theguardian.com/film/2019/aug/10/the-hunt-release-cancelled-gun-violence-trump-criticism.

Kubrick, Stanley. "Now Kubrick Fights Back." *The New York Times*, February 27, 1972. https://www.nytimes.com/1972/02/27/archives/now-kubrick-fights-back-movies-now-kubrick-fights-back.html.

Kukkonen, Karin. "Introduction." In *Metalepsis in Popular Culture*, edited by Karin Kukkonen and Sonja Klimek, 1–21. Berlin: De Gruyter, 2011.

Lee, Chris. "How *Joker* Became the Most Hated, Loved, Obsessed-over Movie of 2019." *Vulture*, October 9, 2019. https://www.vulture.com/2019/10/all-the-joker-controversy-and-threats-explained.html.

McDougal, Stuart. "'What's It Gonna Be Then, eh?' Questioning Kubrick's *Clockwork*." In *Stanley Kubrick's A Clockwork Orange*, Cambridge Film Handbook, edited by Stuart Y. McDougal, 1–18. Cambridge: Cambridge University Press, 2003.

Phelps, Guy. *Film Censorship in Britain*. London: Victor Gollancz, 1975.

Robertson, James C. *The Hidden Cinema: British Film Censorship in Action, 1913–1975*. London: Routledge, 1993.

Stanley Kubrick: A Life in Pictures. Directed by Jan Harlan, 2001. Burbank, CA: Warner Bros. & Warner Home Video, DVD.

Steiger, Janet. "The Cultural Productions of *A Clockwork Orange*." In *Stanley Kubrick's A Clockwork Orange*, Cambridge Film Handbook, edited by Stuart Y. McDougal, 37–60. Cambridge: Cambridge University Press, 2003.

Strange, Carolyn. "Stanley Kubrick's A Clockwork Orange as Art against Torture." *Crime, Media, Culture: An International Journal* 6, no. 3 (2010): 267–84.

Suter, Rebecca. "Critical Engagement through Fantasy in Hard-Boiled Wonderland and the End of the World." In *Haruki Murakami Challenging Authors*, edited by Matthew C. Strecher and Paul L. Thomas, 59–71. Rotterdam: Sense Publishers, 2016.

Thoss, Jeff. *When Storyworlds Collide: Metalepsis in Popular Fiction, Film and Comics*. Leiden: Brill Rodopi, 2015.

Upton, Julian. "Innocence Unprotected? Permissiveness and the AA Certificate 1970–82." *Journal of British Cinema and Television* 14, no. 1 (2017): 64–76.

Whipple, Amy C. "Speaking for Whom? The 1971 Festival of Light and the Search for the 'Silent Majority.'" *Contemporary British History* 24, no. 3 (2010): 319–39.

Worland, Rick. *The Horror Film: An Introduction*. Malden, MA: Blackwell, 2007.

Chapter Twelve

Through a Glass, Darkly

The Slow Rise of Women in Barry Lyndon, The Shining, *and* Eyes Wide Shut

Elsa Colombani

In an interview, Stanley Kubrick considered his representation of the world as in a constant state of war, including in his domestic sphere narratives. "How many marriages are happy ones?"[1] he asks, albeit rhetorically. For in his world there are no happy marriages, only theaters of war where every move equates a power play, and every bedroom turns into a battlefield. Kubrick's focus, remarks James Naremore, has often been on "the American nuclear family,"[2] staging domestic wars between the three triangle tops that are father, mother, and child. If Kubrick is at his most satirical regarding the American families of *Lolita* (1962), *The Shining* (1980), and *Eyes Wide Shut* (1999), war within the household concerns all families, whatever the country, whatever the century. For instance, Barry Lyndon (Ryan O'Neal) is only just married when his growing disinterest for his spouse (Marisa Berenson) begins to show—although she gave him her name and fortune. Barry's contempt for Lady Lyndon strongly echoes that of Jack Torrance (Jack Nicholson) for his wife Wendy (Shelley Duvall), the two male protagonists also sharing a common trajectory of tragic defeat. Dr. Bill Harford (Tom Cruise) in *Eyes Wide Shut* follows this same downward slope. "A man so troubled by his wife's sexuality starts on a quest for his own sexual adventures and can consummate none of them"[3] sums up Robert Kolker, for whom the film deals with "the deadness of the male spirit."[4] *Barry Lyndon*, *The Shining*, and *Eyes Wide Shut* are undoubtedly films about the fall of man, told from a male perspective. In these three films about marriages shaken to their core, the white man as the "head of the family" takes center stage: we witness

Barry's rise and fall in English society, Jack's descent into madness, Bill's tormented wanderings and adventures in New York City. "His films are rarely concerned with women, except in a peripheral and usually unpleasant way,"[5] writes Kolker, while Hannah McGill adds that "cruelty, violence and abusive sex are played for laughs and sincerity mocked; ideology is of interest only as a manifestation of man's hopeless efforts to master the incomprehensible."[6] Kubrick's overbearing interest in male protagonists can hardly be denied, especially in his films on domesticity where the main focus remains on "the fascistic tendencies in male sexuality."[7]

But to discuss the male must necessarily bring forth a consideration of the female—must every husband not have a wife? If *Barry Lyndon*, *The Shining*, and *Eyes Wide Shut*'s focal point remains on the male characters, the women at their side emerge slowly but surely. Seen through the "male gaze" of Barry, Jack, and Bill, these women are more often than not fantasies, classified into categories: the silent beauty or the unattractive hysteric, the faithful wife or the prostitute. Objectified by their husbands, they are reduced to the function they fulfill beside the "man of the house" in a patriarchal society. However, inside these biased portraits of women, Kubrick gives us variable and growing insight into who these women are. If the paths of Lady Lyndon, Wendy Torrance, and Alice Harford (Nicole Kidman) seem very different, taking them into account as a whole speaks volumes: when each man's trajectory leads him inevitably downward, the women's map out an undeniable ascent. Tellingly, this evolution is chronological both in the epochs during which the films are set as well as in Kubrick's own filmography. Lady Lyndon, the crushed and dramatic figure of eighteenth-century England, evolves into the rebellious Wendy Torrance who decides to fight her husband's violence with a baseball bat in the 1980s, and paves the way for the victorious woman who is Alice Harford, on her way to sexual emancipation at the dawn of the twenty-first century. This chapter considers the evolution of these three female protagonists, shown by Kubrick through the lens of his male characters, as they emerge from silence to claim their right to finally speak their minds.

Lady Lyndon, Wendy, and Alice are first and foremost defined in society and their own household as wives and mothers. Once married to Redmond Barry, the Irish rogue who quickly adopts his wife's name as his own to assert his newfound status in English society, Lady Lyndon is forced by her husband to abandon the very social activities that led to their encounter and dedicates herself to the raising of their son. From the very moment she first appears, Barry considers Lady Lyndon for her higher status and her monetary value—calculating thoughts that the narrator (Michael Hordern) hastens to vocalize:

he began to have it in mind, as many gentlemen had done before him, to marry a woman of fortune and condition. And, as such things so often happen, these thoughts closely coincided with him setting first sight upon a lady who will henceforth play a considerable part in the drama of his life. The Countess of Lyndon . . . Viscountess Bullingdon of England . . . Baroness Castle Lyndon of the Kingdom of Ireland. A woman of vast wealth and great beauty.

The narrator's ironic underlining of Barry's not so "gentle" strategy reinforces Lady Lyndon's identity in the eyes of her future husband as a means to an end, a never-ending list of titles that only her beauty has the power to match. In today's words, Lady Lyndon could be qualified as a trophy wife, whom Barry can parade when needed. The mise en scène strongly supports this perception of the character who remains passive and silent, frozen into beautiful but bleak tableaux as she "passes time with her two children, plays cards with her ladies-in-waiting, polishes her skills with the harpsichord . . . dresses herself like an art object to be admired . . . and tirelessly signs bank drafts to pay for that extravagance."[8] These activities, all connected to her mothering functions, her social persona, and her financial value, remain entirely non-performed: writing down her signature, her gestures are mechanical and repetitive; a shot where she is surrounded by both her sons shows her lying completely inert. During a scene where she plays cards with her entourage, Kubrick focuses on her perfect stillness, diametrically opposed to the women around her who are actively playing, so much so that the impression given is that of a lifeless mannequin, a wax doll, a two-dimensional painting.

In *Eyes Wide Shut*, Alice holds a comparable function of display. In the film's opening shot, Kubrick places her at the center of the frame, alone and undressing. She turns her back to the camera, her naked body briefly exposed before the title card cuts in, as if embodying the blink of the caption's shut eyes. Thus "represented as a classical nude with a body that is complete and idealized,"[9] Alice appears from the get-go as an object of desire, exhibited like a work of art. Her perfect body kindles the admiration of everyone, from the couple's babysitter to the host of the Christmas party they attend, Victor Ziegler (Sydney Pollack). Her husband Bill, however, fails to notice her: "You're not even looking at it" is Alice's reproach when she asks him about her hair. "The presence of her body has become one of many beautiful objects that adorn their apartment,"[10] remark Miriam Jordan and Julian Jason Haladyn, echoing the words of *Barry Lyndon*'s narrator: "Lady Lyndon was soon to occupy a place in Barry's life not very much more important than the elegant carpets and pictures which would form the pleasant background of his existence." Bill's compliments—"It's beautiful. You always look beautiful"—reveal his inattention to his wife, how her presence is taken for granted in the background of his own activities. His carelessness at home turns into self-sufficiency at the Christmas party when Ziegler exclaims, "You're absolutely stunning!" upon seeing Alice. Bill, an arm around his wife's waist as if asserting his property, casually pats her back and flashes a proud smile. Tellingly, Bill's sexual interest is revived when they return from the party. During the couple's naked embrace in front of the mirror, Bill asserts his feeling of possession, once again, as his hand comes to place itself around her neck. His neglect of Alice and his carefully staged feeling of ownership bring to light his utter shock at discovering his wife's sexual fantasies of infidelity, the effect her revelation creates in him being the core subject of the film. His very confusion reveals his blindness and incapacity to acknowledge Alice as an individual in her own right, separated from her role as a wife and mother of their child. Kubrick illustrates this in a striking sequence that starts with Bill coming home to find Alice helping their daughter Helena (Madison Eginton) do her homework. Watching this picture of domestic bliss—the mother at the service of the child—Bill's face suddenly freezes, his gaze focusing on his wife. In a POV shot, Kubrick's camera zooms on Alice's face, innocently smiling at her husband, while the words of her sexually charged nightmare come to overwhelm Bill in voiceover. Here, the viewer is explicitly confronted to Bill's gaze, and his realization that Alice (the voice) and Helena's mother (the image on the screen) are dissociated. Bill's everyday behavior continuously betrays his inability to really see Alice, repeatedly perceived in her spousal and motherly duties.[11] Coming back from work, he enquires if anyone called for him, banally expecting Alice to fill in at home the role held by his office's secretaries. Kubrick's cross cutting of Bill's day at work with Alice and Helena's day at home clearly establishes him as the breadwinner and her as the housewife. At no point during the sequence is Alice shown without Helena by her side, as she gives her breakfast, brushes her hair, or helps her wrap Christmas presents for Bill.

The shot of mother and daughter having breakfast in the kitchen strongly echoes a scene from *The Shining* that sees Wendy and Danny sitting at the kitchen table, while Jack is away interviewing for a job at the Overlook Hotel. Both scenes depict the children busy eating while watching a cartoon on the television while the mothers' attention is focused on what they are reading. But whereas Wendy happily abandons her magazine to engage in a conversation with Danny, Alice stays focused on her newspaper, positioned in such a way that she seems to be turning away from her daughter—a hint at her resentment for being considered as the dutiful mother—while Wendy appears satisfied in her relationship with her son. Both women fulfill the role of housewives, dedicated to the well-being of their household and dependent on their husbands' financial gains. The precariousness of Alice's former employment—an art gallery that went broke—stands in stark contrast with Doctor Bill's dependable job. As she remains unemployed and spends her days in the apartment, his days are filled with incoming, and often influential, patients. As for Wendy, she follows her husband wherever his activities lead them. Jack, a former teacher, interviews successfully for the position of winter caretaker at the Overlook, an isolated hotel in the Rocky Mountains, seeing in this fairly undemanding job the opportunity to focus on his desire to write a novel. As the Torrance family discovers where they will live in the next few months, Jack is led away by the hotel manager while the workings of the kitchen are shown to Wendy and Danny by the head chef, Dick Hallorann (Scatman Crothers). In fact, throughout the film, Kubrick keeps connecting the female character to the act of feeding. On their way to the Overlook, for example, Danny informs his father that he is hungry. Whereas Jack answers with animosity that he should have eaten his breakfast,[12] Wendy resolves the issue with kindness, telling her son that they will tend to his needs once arrived at their destination. Later on, Jack ironically rebuffs his wife when she expresses some advice on his writing after she has just brought him breakfast in bed (a scene that contrasts with the aforementioned sequence with Danny in the kitchen). Jack's condescension makes it clear he does not consider her as his equal. And so Wendy must content herself with the role she was given, one that she is resolved to succeed in: taking care of her son.

In all three films, the characters' social imprisonment translates into a geographical captivity, which symbolizes their entrapment into toxic relationships. In *Barry Lyndon*, Kubrick explores a sadomasochistic marriage. As the director underlines in the scene where the couple meets, "what she feels for him is purely physical.... The masochist and tragic relationships I had the occasion to observe all rely essentially on physical attraction."[13] In this respect, the horse and carriage scene is probably one of the most explicit. Kubrick shows the couple sitting next to each other but looking on opposite sides. Indisposed by her husband's smoking, Lady Lyndon tries to manifest her ailment, glancing at him and trying to clear the smoke away with her hand. Her gestures ignored, she finally resolves to ask him to stop smoking, a request to which he replies by blowing smoke directly into her face. The deliberate humiliation effectively silences his wife, whose voice is scarcely heard throughout the 185-minutes-long film, the actress Marisa Berenson having only thirteen lines of dialogue: "She preferred quiet, or to say the truth, he preferred it for her," the narrator says later on. But the scene also depicts the pleasure Barry derives from his sadistic behavior: right after his demeaning gesture (the smoke identical to a spit in the face), he amusingly smiles and kisses his wife. She remains as passive as always but her stare conveys her bewilderment upon discovering her husband's true nature and her resignation to be thus vilified. The cruelty of the scene is further highlighted by its positioning directly after the marriage sequence.

Wendy shares some of Lady Lyndon's compliance. Indeed, in *The Shining*, the dynamic between the married couple revolves around Wendy trying to say something and Jack being irritated by her and/or trying to squelch her voice: "Whenever I'm in here and you hear me typing or whether you don't hear me typing or whatever the fuck you hear me doing in here, when I'm in here that means I am working. That means don't come in." The "new rule" established by Jack is thought up to keep Wendy out of his way, to prevent her from talking to him spontaneously without him having requested for her to speak. The Torrances' marriage, like the Lyndons,' functions on recurring abuse: "The danger, at the Overlook, . . . is the daily tragedy of domestic violence,"[14] Bill Krohn remarks. With the ghost of Grady (Philip Stone), Jack finds an incentive as well as a twin, the former caretaker's brutal murder of his wife and daughters both becoming and foreshadowing Jack's fantasy to do the same. There are strong echoes to the tale of Bluebeard as the lavish establishment hides blood in its walls and rooms where one should not enter. Jack embodies the abusive husband, gleefully menacing Wendy to "bash [her] brains right the fuck in," and admitting to having hurt Danny when he was barely three years old: "I did hurt him once, okay? . . . The little fucker had thrown all my papers over the floor. All I tried to do was pull him up." Jack's choice of words openly reveals the fierce animosity he feels toward his wife, regularly referring to her as "that bitch" and accusing her of having restrained his career and his life's desires. As Wendy becomes increasingly subjected to Jack's violence, Shelley Duvall's acting puts more and more emphasis on her facial expressions—her face deformed by tears, anguish, and screams—and her shaking, almost dislocated, body. Because of the abusive nature of the depicted marriage, the choice of the actress who would play Wendy was of primary importance for Kubrick. John Calley recalls: "He was interested in a person that was probably more in love with her partner than her partner was with her. And who was needy in the relationship. And would . . . be perceived as somebody that might tolerate the intolerable longer than one would think that someone might."[15] Someone who would not be conventionally attractive, not as sexy as in Stephen King's original novel, without, however, being bland: "What's wonderful with [Shelley] is that her eccentricity shows on her face."[16] Hence Wendy appears both as a woman with her own personality while reflecting how Jack perceives her, that is to say unattractive and bordering on hysteria.

Men, in Kubrick's films, have a heavy tendency to objectify women, who are placed into patriarchal pre-established categories. In *Barry Lyndon*, they are muted art objects; in *The Shining*, they "interfere" and need to be "corrected"; while in *Eyes Wide Shut*, "the women assume roles in which they are little more than sexual playthings for men."[17] Toward the end of the latter film, Ziegler's vulgar and sexist speech displays the inherent misogyny of society, which Kubrick manifests through the overwhelming presence of naked female bodies. To the men of *Eyes Wide Shut*, women are either wives (Alice) or prostitutes (Mandy [Julienne Davis], Domino [Vinessa Shaw], or Milich's Lolita-esque daughter [Leelee Sobieski]). More often than not, women appear undressed, from the film's opening shot of Alice to the dozens of nude bodies during the orgy sequence. When Bill enquires about the identity of the woman who helped him at Somerton House, Ziegler contemptuously replies "she was a hooker" before referring to her as "the one with the great tits" who almost overdosed in his bathroom during the Christmas party, where Bill first met her. At the moment of their first encounter, Mandy is lying stark naked and motionless before Bill helps her wake up, a grim Sleeping Beauty to Bill's wannabe Prince Charming. Diane Johnson analyzes: "The film is a kind of ground plan of the male psyche, mapping the fear, desire, omnipresence of sex, preoccupation with death, the connection of death and Eros, the anxiety in men generated by female sexuality."[18]

Mandy's numb and limp body in Ziegler's bathroom recalls the famous sequence that unfolds in room 237 in *The Shining*. As Jack walks into the mysterious room he observes with relish an unknown and fully naked woman coming out of her bath, her wet body slowly advancing toward him. Her movements seem unnatural, almost choreographed, thus emphasizing her chimeric nature. But when Jack kisses the ghostly apparition, what he sees in the reflection of the mirror is not the heavenly creature he thought but a laughing old hag. Once again, the fantasy of the perfect woman demands silence while the "real" woman not only has a decaying body but also the power to laugh, and to humiliate. The laughing woman of room 237 finds an echo in Alice's uncontrollable fit of laughter when Bill tells her he never once doubted her fidelity in *Eyes Wide Shut*. The hilarity of both women breaks the spell of the male illusion by way of embarrassment, and compels them to open their eyes: Jack to the ghost's lurid deceit, Bill to his wife's sexual thoughts. It is also worth noting that Kubrick first insists on Bill's blindness in the couple's bathroom where he turns away while she is urinating and is thus turned into "a grotesque body . . . in the process of excreting fluids."[19] In *The Shining*, the decomposing body's wetness, as if embalmed, adds to the morbidity of the whole scene, which, as Nelson comments, is "yet another Kubrickian bathroom that links masturbatory fantasy and death."[20] The sequence where Barry asks for Lady Lyndon's forgiveness for having cheated on her, while she is taking her bath, is similar. Sitting once again perfectly immobile, her emaciated body barely covered by a cloth, Lady Lyndon resembles a corpse, and Barry kissing her has a necrophiliac feel, similar to Bill almost kissing Mandy's cadaver at the morgue. Kolker ingeniously analyzes how the scene echoes Jacques-Louis David's "The Death of Marat" 1793 painting,[21] adding to its bleakness.

Sex and death inevitably go together, and in *Eyes Wide Shut*, they are two sides of the same coin: Marion's declaration of love is "done in full view of her father's lifeless corpse";[22] Domino turns out to be HIV positive; and Mandy, after almost dying at the start of the film, is definitely deceased by the film's end. During the orgy sequence, death erupts once again when Bill, unmasked and in trouble, is saved by a then-unidentified woman who offers to "redeem him." The Somerton women's naked bodies, all similar in their proportions with model figures (and resembling the fantasy woman of room 237), are substitutable, their identities removed and their faces hidden behind bird masks, all at the service and at the mercy of men's pleasures and desires. Karen D. Hoffman remarks:

> Interestingly, this orgy at Somerton, a gathering that seems to represent the ultimate marital transgression, contains important echoes of marriage. "Fidelity" is required for entrance. The sexual encounter one experiences after entry—into the marital institution or into the masked party—is publicly sanctioned. Individuals who have entered are capable of redeeming one another through the willingness to make personal sacrifices. Finally, promises that are made are permanent and cannot be taken back.[23]

The orgy is a fantasy of marriage as wished by the patriarchy, a ritual where men are in command (the orgy's high priest), can order punishment (the woman's sacrifice), and interchange women as they please, treating them as bodies and not individuals. Most importantly, they can remain fully clothed while women appear in their birthday suit, flesh ready to be consumed. The women at Somerton House replicate the lethargic, almost mechanical way of moving exhibited by the ghost in room 237, thus highlighting their dehumanization. The individuality of Kubrick's female characters truly becomes manifest when their bodies are freed from their constraints. As Elisa Pezzotta observes, Lady Lyndon's first and only authentic, unrestrained movements occur after the couple's young son's death: "When she tries to commit suicide, and writhes and groans for her pain, the handheld camera accentuates her grief. A character who has always been shown moving slowly, sumptuously, perfectly dressed and made up, is now in frame in her nightgown, with ruffled hair, and her uncontrolled acting is stressed by the handheld camera."[24] Paradoxically, Lady Lyndon is most alive when in the clutches of death. In *Eyes Wide Shut*, a hand-held shot shows Alice during her laughing fit replicating Lady Lyndon's contortions. However, in this case, the body spasms bring life to a new Alice, new in the eyes of her husband and the viewer's, as she delivers her first monologue and confesses her most intimate fantasies. In *The Shining*, Wendy bridges the gap between Lady Lyndon's deadly destiny and Alice's driving force of life. As the plot unfolds, Wendy is forced into continuous action. For in her case, movement means life: she is running away from her husband—death itself—and trying to save what Lady Lyndon could not, her son's life.

If one focuses on Wendy's character, *The Shining* is divided into two contradictory movements. At first, Wendy wants to get closer to Jack while he pushes her away, wishing to be alone to concentrate on his writing. In a second phase, she tries to get as far away from him as she can while he is chasing her, with verbal threats and an ax. The turning point occurs when Danny comes out of room 237 with bruises on his neck and barges in on his parents, catching them in a rare if awkward moment of closeness. Jack, stunned by the nightmare he just had of him killing his entire family, is consoled from his tearful anguish by a motherly Wendy, who strokes his hair and assures him that all will be all right. Her face, however, betrays her own confusion at the violence of her husband's subconscious, and his revelatory choice of words—"I had the most terrible *nightmare* I ever had. The most horrible *dream* I ever had." At the opposite side of the room, Danny enters, silent, staring into the void as if in a trance. Wendy's first instinct is to turn her son away. But as Danny seems not to hear his mother's request to leave them alone, she goes toward him and discovers the strangulation marks. The shift then occurs and the accusation falls: "You did this to him didn't you?" as she grabs her child and storms away in shock. Afterward, Danny's off-screen revelation of the evil ghost in room 237 leads to Wendy's return and plea for Jack's help. But this relapse is short-lived and the discovery of Jack's manuscript eventually pushes her further away. Wendy's confrontation with Jack in the staircase is also the first time she asserts her individuality, as she takes up arms to rebel against her sadistic husband. Naremore underlines how Wendy exceeds the viewer's expectations in the way she deftly takes the upper hand.[25] Kolker even compares her to Ripley in Ridley Scott's *Alien* (1979) in the way she assumes the manly function by taking hold of the phallic shaped baseball bat and knocking Jack down,[26] and later "stabs his hand with a large knife, an act of displaced castration that further reduces Jack's potency and threat."[27] One could also add that Wendy's household function helps her in fighting Jack since she manages to lock him up in the kitchen's pantry.

Watching *The Shining* through the eyes of Wendy, one sees the story of a woman finally opening her eyes to her husband's true nature, that of a violent man who has been tormenting their son: "If you examine the factual elements of the film, you must presume that this little boy has had a nightmarish childhood and that Jack has been a harsh and traumatizing father."[28] Although quick to dismiss Jack's past assault on Danny as an accident, the family's stay at the Overlook forces her to face the truth, which she literally sees when she finally shines. Her vision of two men having oral sex could be understood as Wendy's discovery of Jack's homosexuality, an interpretation thoroughly analyzed by Patrick Webster, who focuses on the character's homoerotic encounters with men, especially the barman Lloyd (Joe Turkel) and Grady.[29] Film scholar Rob Ager provides another possible and convincing interpretation, namely that Jack has been abusing his son.[30] Ager builds his argument on the fact that the man seen by Wendy performing fellatio is dressed in a bear costume. Throughout the film, he argues, teddy bears are constantly associated with Danny and can be most notably seen during the scene at the doctor's and in a framed picture above Danny's bed at the Overlook. Among other clues are the story title "Incest: Why Parents Sleep With Their Children" on the cover of the *Playgirl* magazine Jack is reading, the chilling fatherly love scene where Danny sits in Jack's lap, his small body limp and hunched while asking his father if he "would never hurt Mommy or me." Finally, there is Danny's imaginary friend Tony, "the boy that lives in [his] mouth," who surfaced after Jack snapped his son's shoulder, as Wendy tells the doctor in a conversation "full of innuendos about abuse."[31] As Nelson remarks, "Wendy fail[s] to make the psychological connection between 'Tony' and Jack's violence."[32] Following her shine, Wendy's eyes are finally wide open to the threat her husband represents.

The Shining's bear man scene strikingly forebodes the Somerton orgy with its characters engaged in sex and voyeurism, and the use of animal masks to expose the reality of a marriage, and, more precisely as far as *Eyes Wide Shut* is concerned, "an allegorical unmasking of masculinity itself."[33] Correlatively to his analysis of Jack's troubled sexuality, Webster evokes the possibility that Kubrick used the rumors surrounding Tom Cruise's supposed homosexuality to fuel the character of Bill.[34] The film undeniably depicts the story of a man who repeatedly fails to engage in sexual activities with sex-craved women, shows restraint and sometimes anguish at the very idea of having sex (the two models at the Christmas party, Domino), but exhibits confidence and tactility around his male friends, as his first encounter with Nick Nightingale (Todd Field) demonstrates. This interpretation could account for Alice's sexual frustration, which she expresses both in the scene where she and Bill are having sex—her gazing at herself in the mirror indicating a possible boredom and showing her more engaged in her own image than in her husband's—and most importantly during the confession sequence.

Michel Chion writes that Alice is "a storyteller," whose "two narratives structure the film."[35] One could go even further and claim that, even though *Eyes Wide Shut* plunges the viewer in the male psyche, the story unfolds like a play in three acts entirely structured by Alice's words and presence. She triggers Bill's uncovering of his own subconscious and shows a "willingness to face the presence of unconscious fears that occupy the same emotional space as her sexual desires,"[36] which her husband would rather not see. "Women generally have a dominance and assertiveness in the film"[37] writes Webster, who puts forward the idea that all the women of the film can be viewed as different versions of Alice as seen through her husband's psyche.[38] Bill's adventures essentially consist of him being told what to do by the women he encounters, while he passively listens and repeats what they say— "Alice, what do you think we should do?" Bill asks his wife in the final scene. Unlike Bill, always unsure of his words, Alice knows exactly what to say. So much is clear in the sequence where the couple argues, leading to Alice's revelation. Kubrick starts the scene with a dialogue but quickly turns it into Alice's soliloquy. The monologue begins with a long shot that summons the image of a theatric stage with Alice being framed, slightly off-center, by the window's red curtains. After she recalls the naval officer's "glance," Kubrick separates us from Bill's gaze by changing his angle and focuses in close shot on Alice's left profile, placing us closer to her as she is about to reveal her most intimate thoughts. Sitting on the bedroom floor, she stares directly at Bill as she speaks, and her physical attitude toward her husband stands in stark opposition with her past reaction to the naval officer: "I could hardly move" she says, while keeping her body in motion. During the entire sequence, Alice's small but tellingly sensual gestures—her hand caressing her knee, her leg slowly swinging—contrast with Bill's complete stillness. Kubrick's regular counter-shots show the character's bewilderment, he who has been reduced to a Lady Lyndon–like silence.

Alice's second monologue essentially follows the same pattern. The scene starts with a conversation between the couple as she wakes from her nightmare. At Bill's request, she starts to recount her awful dream and has the floor to herself once again, as he grows mum and listens. Alice's second narrative provides an insight into her subconscious of rare richness and complexity. If the details of her nightmare echo Bill's Somerton misadventures, her candid account stands worlds apart from the orchestrated orgiastic ceremony. Nelson remarks that Alice's dream both translates her desire to be freed from the male gaze—"I was lying in a beautiful garden stretched out naked in the sunlight"[39]—but also her fear that if she were to obtain her sexual freedom, she would then be regarded as promiscuous.[40] Her feeling of entrapment in her marriage and her ambivalent feelings toward her husband also transpire: "As soon as you were gone it was completely different. I felt wonderful." On the whole, her monologue also expresses her guilt at fantasizing on other men and for humiliating Bill by laughing at him during her first soliloquy, her hilarity resurfacing albeit negatively at the end of her nightmare. Once again, she triggers Bill's reaction, as he will later confess his own culpability after his experiences at Somerton.

Alice asserts her right to "fuck" on her own terms and her two monologues lead up to her blatant conquering of the word, which will be hers, the film's, and Kubrick's, last. In *The Shining*, the word belongs to Jack who essentially uses it as an expletive to demean Wendy. However, as Webster notes, Jack's story is "[a] loss of control over 'the word' . . . best exemplified in the film's 'All work and no play makes Jack a dull boy.'"[41] In *Eyes Wide Shut*, Alice actively uses the word, in all its meanings. In fact, an echo of *The Shining* can be found in the dialogue of the film's last scene:

> ALICE: The important thing is we're awake now and hopefully . . . for a long time to come.
> BILL: Forever.

ALICE: Forever?
BILL: Forever.
ALICE: Let's not use that word. You know? It frightens me. But I do love you and you know there is something very important that we need to do as soon as possible.
BILL: What's that?
ALICE: Fuck.

During the exchange, Alice firmly refuses to conform to the fairy tale myth that they will love each other "forever." Rightly so, Kubrick seems to suggest, if you consider his own take on the fairy tale, embodied by the frightening Grady girls inviting Danny to play "forever and ever" in the cursed Overlook Hotel's corridors. *Eyes Wide Shut*'s opening shot exposed Alice as a vision of male fantasy, but the closing shot is hers and hers only: "The last word," writes Naremore, "is significantly given to a woman."[42] At last, she stands an equal to her husband, fully dressed, her glasses on to make her vision sharper. But while Bill's uncertainty and confusion remain, her eyes are wide open, and her final word rings loud and clear.

If "Bill is Kubrick's last man"[43] as Kolker writes, Alice is perhaps most importantly Kubrick's last woman. A filmmaker who often relegated women to the background, Stanley Kubrick nonetheless proved he was capable of creating impactful women characters with Alice Harford. The gradual evolution of women in *Barry Lyndon*, *The Shining*, and *Eyes Wide Shut* exposes the subtlety of his multiply layered vision. In these three films, women are certainly objectified, vilified, and tormented. But far from being misogynistic representations, they embody two different versions of women at a time: what they appear to be through the male gaze that their husbands personify, but also who they really are as individuals. The silent resignation of an eighteenth-century woman's destiny to remain a man's property, an abused wife who rebels to save her son from a violent husband, and finally, a modern woman who stands up for herself thanks to her awareness of the twentieth-century patriarchal world, her readiness to understand her own self, and her claim to see her desires acknowledged and, at last, spoken out loud.

NOTES

1. Stanley Kubrick in Michel Ciment, *Kubrick* (Paris: Calmann-lévy, 2011), 171. My translation.
2. James Naremore, *On Kubrick* (London: British Film Institute, 2007), 4.
3. Robert Kolker, *A Cinema of Loneliness*, 3rd ed. (Oxford: Oxford University Press, 2000), 170.
4. Ibid.
5. Kolker, *A Cinema of Loneliness*, 106.
6. Hannah McGill, "Eyes of the Beholder," *Sight and Sound* 29, no. 12 (December 2019): 26.
7. Naremore, *On Kubrick*, 4.

8. Thomas Allen Nelson, *Kubrick: Inside a Film Artist's Maze* (Bloomington, IN: Indiana University Press, 2000), 186.
9. Miriam Jordan and Julian Jason Haladyn, "Carnivalesque and Grotesque Bodies in *Eyes Wide Shut*," in *Stanley Kubrick: Essays on his Films and Legacy*, ed. Gary D. Rhodes, 181–95 (Jefferson, NC: McFarland, 2008), 182.
10. Ibid., 183.
11. Spousal and motherly duties often seem to mix as revealed by Alice's maternal comforting in Bill's confession scene. She strokes his hair and face while he cries and huddles against her in a fetal position.
12. Jack's cruelty further continues when he tells his son about the "Donner party," a group of pioneers traveling the California Trail who had to resort to cannibalism to survive in 1847.
13. Kubrick in Ciment, *Kubrick*, 172. My translation.
14. Bill Krohn, *Masters of Cinema: Stanley Kubrick* (Paris: Cahiers du cinéma, 2007), 75.
15. John Calley in *View From the Overlook: Crafting "The Shining,"* dir. Gary Leva, 2007, in *The Shining*, dir. Stanley Kubrick (1980; Los Angeles: Warner Bros. Pictures, 2008), 2 DVD Special Edition.
16. Kubrick in Ciment, *Kubrick*, 189. My translation.
17. Patrick Webster, *Love and Death in Kubrick: A Critical Study of the Films from* Lolita *through* Eyes Wide Shut (Jefferson, NC: McFarland, 2011), 149.
18. Diane Johnson, "Writing *The Shining*," in *Stanley Kubrick: Film, and the Uses of History*, ed. Geoffrey Cocks, James Diedrick, and Glenn Perusek, 55–61 (Madison, WI: The University of Wisconsin Press, 2006), 61.
19. Jordan and Haladyn, "Carnivalesque and Grotesque Bodies in *Eyes Wide Shut*," 184.
20. Nelson, *Kubrick: Inside a Film Artist's Maze*, 220.
21. Kolker, *A Cinema of Loneliness*, 154.
22. Mario Falsetto, *Stanley Kubrick: A Narrative and Stylistic Analysis* (Westport, CT: Praeger, 2001), 75.
23. Karen D. Hoffman, "Where the Rainbow Ends: *Eyes Wide Shut*," in *The Philosophy of Stanley Kubrick*, ed. Jerold J. Abrams, 59–83 (Lexington, KY: University Press of Kentucky, 2007), 70.
24. Elisa Pezzotta, *Stanley Kubrick: Adapting the Sublime* (Jackson: University Press of Mississippi, 2013), 73.
25. Naremore, *On Kubrick*, 201.
26. Kolker, *A Cinema of Loneliness*, 166–67.
27. Ibid., 167.
28. Kubrick in Ciment, *Kubrick*, 193. My translation.
29. Webster, *Love and Death in Kubrick*, 101–5.
30. Rob Ager, "Mazes, Mirrors, Deception and Denial: An In-depth Analysis of Stanley Kubrick's *The Shining*," Collectivelearning.com, 2008, https://www.collativelearning.com/the%20shining%20-%20chap%2016.html (accessed December 31, 2019).
31. Ibid.
32. Nelson, *Kubrick: Inside a Film Artist's Maze*, 209.
33. Webster, *Love and Death in Kubrick*, 156.
34. Ibid.
35. Michel Chion, *Stanley Kubrick: l'humain, ni plus ni moins* (Paris: Cahiers du cinéma, 2005), 395. My translation.
36. Nelson, *Kubrick: Inside a Film Artist's Maze*, 283.
37. Webster, *Love and Death in Kubrick*, 150.
38. Ibid.
39. Lars Von Trier seems to have translated Alice's dream in his 2011 film *Melancholia*, in the scene where Justine (Kirsten Dunst) is lying naked and alone in a marvelous garden, reveling in the light produced by the Melancholia planet.
40. Nelson, *Kubrick: Inside a Film Artist's Maze*, 290.
41. Webster, *Love and Death in Kubrick*, 97.
42. Naremore, *On Kubrick*, 242.
43. Kolker, *A Cinema of Loneliness*, 173.

REFERENCES

Ager, Rob. "Mazes, Mirrors, Deception and Denial: An In-depth Analysis of Stanley Kubrick's *The Shining*." *Collectivelearning.com*, 2008. https://www.collativelearning.com/the%20shining%20-%20chap%2016.html.
Chion, Michel. *Stanley Kubrick: l'humain, ni plus ni moins*. Paris: Cahiers du cinéma, 2005.
Ciment, Michel. *Kubrick*. Paris: Calmann-lévy, 2011.
Falsetto, Mario. *Stanley Kubrick: A Narrative and Stylistic Analysis*. Westport, CT: Praeger, 2001.
Hoffman, Karen D. "Where the Rainbow Ends: *Eyes Wide Shut*." In *The Philosophy of Stanley Kubrick*, edited by Jerold J. Abrams, 59–83. Lexington, KY: University Press of Kentucky, 2007.
Johnson, Diane. "Writing *The Shining*." In *Stanley Kubrick: Film, and the Uses of History*, edited by Geoffrey Cocks, James Diedrick, and Glenn Perusek, 55–61. Madison, WI: University of Wisconsin Press, 2006.
Jordan, Miriam, and Julian Jason Haladyn. "Carnivalesque and Grotesque Bodies in *Eyes Wide Shut*." In *Stanley Kubrick: Essays on his Films and Legacy*, edited by Gary D. Rhodes, 181–95. Jefferson, NC: McFarland, 2008.
Kolker, Robert. *A Cinema of Loneliness*, 3rd edition. Oxford: Oxford University Press, 2000.
Krohn, Bill. *Masters of Cinema: Stanley Kubrick*. Paris: Cahiers du cinéma, 2007.
McGill, Hannah. "Eyes of the Beholder." *Sight and Sound* 29, no. 12 (December 2019): 24–33.
Naremore, James. *On Kubrick*. London: British Film Institute, 2007.
Nelson, Thomas Allen. *Kubrick: Inside a Film Artist's Maze*. Bloomington, IN: Indiana University Press, 2000.
Pezzotta, Elisa. *Stanley Kubrick: Adapting the Sublime*. Jackson, MS: University Press of Mississippi, 2013.
View From the Overlook: Crafting "The Shining." Directed by Gary Leva, 2007. In *The Shining*, directed by Stanley Kubrick, 1980. Los Angeles, CA: Warner Bros. Pictures, 2008. 2 DVD Special Edition.
Webster, Patrick. *Love and Death in Kubrick: A Critical Study of the Films from* Lolita *through* Eyes Wide Shut. Jefferson, NC: McFarland, 2011.

Part III

The Visionary Auteur

Chapter Thirteen

Kirk Douglas and Stanley Kubrick

Reconsidering a Creative and Business Partnership

James Fenwick

"Stanley Kubrick is a talented shit."[1] It has become somewhat of an infamous comment, perhaps written as an attempt at the last laugh, as it were, in a relationship that started with such promise and ended in acrimony over contractual obligations. Kirk Douglas, reflecting on his working relationship with Stanley Kubrick some three decades after it had ended, summed up his feelings about the director in his autobiography *The Ragman's Son* (1989). Of course, people only remember that one line, not helped by the fact that Douglas himself repeats it at any given chance, elaborating on the expletives. Most recently, in an interview with *Variety* to celebrate his 100th birthday, Douglas declared that Kubrick "was a bastard."[2] Amidst the sensational language, however, what often gets lost is the deep appreciation Douglas has consistently shown for Kubrick's ability as an artist. Indeed, that most infamous of comments is preceded by Douglas calling Kubrick "extremely talented" (though, conversely, a poor writer).[3]

This chapter will explore the creative and business relationship between Kubrick and Douglas, moving beyond the myth that has formed about the partnership between the two. Lasting only four years and resulting in only two films, *Paths of Glory* (1957) and *Spartacus* (1960), the relationship had the potential for many more productions, with a contract that had called for at least three films to be directed and produced by Harris-Kubrick Pictures for Bryna Productions. Only one of these had been a genuine Harris-Kubrick / Bryna collaboration (*Paths of Glory*), while the other had seen Kubrick hired as an employee from Harris-Kubrick by Bryna (*Spartacus*). The aim of the chapter will be to understand why so few pictures were produced, why the contract was ended, and the impact of the relationship on the careers of both

Douglas and Kubrick. The chapter will assess the contracts between the Harris-Kubrick Pictures Corporation and Douglas's Bryna Productions, the first of which was agreed in January 1957. However, the contract underwent a series of revisions until its termination in 1958, followed by a second release contract, which was dissolved in 1961, bringing a final, legal end to the partnership. The chapter will reconsider how the contractual negotiations and the creative collaborations were pivotal in Kubrick's own growth primarily as a film producer. Far from being a period in which Kubrick suffered from creative bondage due to the contractual obligations with Douglas and Bryna, it in fact was one of Kubrick's most creative periods, with scholarly evidence pointing toward numerous projects being developed, researched, and even worked into scripts (though ultimately abandoned). The chapter will conclude that the affiliation with Douglas served as a transformational point for Kubrick that allowed him to fully develop as an independent film producer working in mainstream Hollywood, while Douglas's career entered a period of gradual decline.

Both Kubrick and Douglas had underlying dynamics within their respective careers that led them to want power and control over the productions in which they were involved. These dynamics and how they influenced Douglas and Kubrick's subsequent working relationship differ given the trajectories their careers were on. Douglas was at his peak by the end of the 1950s; he was one of the biggest box office draws in Hollywood, a leading man, and one of the most successful independent producers in the industry. Kubrick's career was nascent, but fragile; he had had minor success in terms of critical praise—*The Killing* (1956) was regarded highly by much of the critical establishment—but he had achieved no commercial success. More important, Kubrick had alienated a key company at the time, United Artists (UA), which was at the forefront of the rapidly changing industrial contexts of Hollywood. Kubrick and his business partner, James B. Harris, had gone against the express wishes of the vice president of production, Max Youngstein, and published a one-page ad that publicized the Harris-Kubrick Pictures Corporation as the "new UA team."[4] Youngstein immediately rebuked the pair in a heated phone call exchange, bringing an effective end to what had been meant to be a multi-picture contract commencing with *The Killing*.[5]

Kubrick needed access to finance and influence in order to grow his own career. At the same time, Kirk Douglas was looking to acquire the services of a talented director who would strengthen the reputation of Bryna Productions in Hollywood. But the one thing that both Douglas and Kubrick wanted was autonomy in order to further develop their careers in their own ways and on their own terms. Sown within their respective motivations were the seeds of the eventual conflict that would impinge on their working relationship. The issue of motivation with regard to *Paths of Glory*, the first film that Douglas and Kubrick worked on together, is complicated. Douglas only agreed to appear in the film after securing a long-term contract for Harris-Kubrick Pictures to produce three further films for Bryna. One of the films would feature Douglas in a leading role, while the other two would be smaller-budgeted features. The deal, signed in January 1957, coincided with the rapid growth of Bryna Productions.[6] The company's contract with UA required it to produce several films that were labeled as "B" pictures, due to their low budgets and non-appearance of Douglas. It may have been that Douglas spotted an opportunity to ensnare a budding producing duo eager to work in Hollywood that could turn around such low-budget pictures for Bryna, allowing him to focus on the big-budget "A" pictures in which he would appear.

As for Harris-Kubrick Pictures, it was in vital need of a high-profile leading man in order to secure a package with a major Hollywood studio following the fallout with UA (and following the abrupt termination of a contract that had been signed with MGM in 1956 to produce *Burning Secret*, an adaptation of the Stefan Zweig 1913 novel of the same name). This contributed to an uneven power balance in the relationship with Bryna, with Kubrick needing Douglas more in these early years. The initial contract was agreed on January 9, 1957. Titled a "Memorandum of Understanding," it reflected the uneven power dynamic, clearly putting Bryna and Douglas in a position of ownership over the creative and business functions of Harris-Kubrick.[7] A number of clauses within this initial agreement would cause disagreements and friction throughout the duration of their working relationship.

First, despite the contract being nonexclusive—in other words, Harris-Kubrick was, in theory, allowed to produce its own pictures on its own terms and with whomever it chose—Harris-Kubrick was required to advise Bryna "of all commitments and pending negotiations so that mutually agreeable times can be worked out for the production of the pictures with Bryna."[8] This clause would cause tension in the coming months and years, particularly when Harris-Kubrick sought collaborations with among others, Melville Productions (Gregory Peck's production company) and Pennebaker Productions (Marlon Brando's production company).

Second, and potentially more problematic, was that Harris-Kubrick had to agree to sell any literary property for which it owned the rights to Bryna, should Bryna desire them. Again, this caused major concerns for Harris-Kubrick, particularly following the purchase of the option rights to Vladimir Nabokov's *Lolita* (1955) in 1958. The clause also extended to any original material that Harris-Kubrick had in development.

Third, and perhaps the most important of all, was the clause that stated, "Kubrick and Harris are employees of Bryna Productions."[9] This was antithetical to what Kubrick aimed to achieve in his career and would arguably lead to an absolute loss of autonomy. Indeed, in the coming months Kubrick would contend the point and fight over the wording of the contract to ensure he maintained a degree of creative autonomy.[10] But even so, why did Kubrick sign up to such an agreement in the first place if it was against everything he stood for? Perhaps it indicates the extent to which Harris-Kubrick needed influential and powerful contacts like Douglas and how it arguably faced an existential threat to its existence if the contract was not accepted. In short, if Harris and Kubrick did not sign up to the deal, their production company and their own careers in the film industry faced a premature end.

One cannot overstate the financial straits that Kubrick found himself in throughout the 1950s, consistently relying on friends and family—and even unemployment checks—after leaving the secure employment of *Look* magazine in 1950, where he had worked as a photographer for four years. He even allowed himself to be hired freelance to work on the dubbing of low-budget features, including the dubiously titled *Shark Safari* in early 1955, and working with his close friend Sig Shore in the 1950s to dub Russian films being exported for the burgeoning U.S. foreign film circuit.[11] Kubrick was aware of his precarious employment situation and it no doubt weighed on his mind. This is clear from ideas and scripts that he came up with between 1951 and 1956, many of which were autobiographical in nature, containing characters who, living bohemian lifestyles, had to regretfully fall back on the goodwill of close friends and family members to fund them.[12] The decision to agree to the contract with Kirk Douglas and Bryna has to be seen in this context. Not only did Harris-Kubrick need the influence and power network of Kirk Douglas, but Kubrick himself needed the financial security of the contract.

Douglas was extraordinarily keen to work on *Paths of Glory* and believed strongly in its liberal values and political message. We can gauge his level of enthusiasm from his correspondence with Kubrick and Harris in January and February 1957, when the script was undergoing rewrites. Indeed, at one point Douglas intervened in the writing process with a lengthy seven-page letter critiquing the script and making recommendations.[13] Douglas prefaced the letter by saying that his detailed comments were made in a constructive spirit because he believed the project was both worthwhile and interesting given its anti–military hierarchy stance. He emphasized that he would not have consented to appear in the film if he did not think so. This remark suggests that a key motivator for Douglas in working with Kubrick was to appear in a film that could amplify his own liberal credentials.

As for Douglas's intervention in the screenwriting process, it reflected his ongoing hands-on producing style, even if he was not technically a producer on *Paths of Glory*. He had spent January 1957 rereading Humphrey Cobb's book and researching ways to develop the screenplay and the main character of Colonel Dax, the role he was to play. He focused his initial criticism on Dax, stating that the character lacked "depth and dimension."[14] Repeatedly, Douglas stressed to Kubrick that Dax was presented as too much of a "Noble Joe"—an average soldier who came across as "sanctimonious" in his desire to do good.[15] Important in Douglas's analysis of *Paths of Glory* was his own role as an actor in the film. He wanted Dax to have both prominence and a complex characterization so that he could flex his acting abilities. Indeed, this is apparent from a further suggestion he made to Kubrick, asking, "Where is Dax during the attack?"[16] Douglas was referring to the only battle sequence in the film, in which the soldiers attack a German fortress, the Ant Hill. Douglas went on, "Remember, this is the only time in this picture where we may have a justifiable reason to use our star in some piece of action. We don't take advantage of it. Something very interesting must be created."[17]

Kubrick responded in good spirit to Douglas's intervention, saying, "I am very happy that you have such a deep interest in the project, above and beyond the mere earning of dollars."[18] However, Kubrick did not address any of Douglas's ideas, instead deferring any discussion to when they would meet in person in Germany. Somewhat diplomatically, he merely agreed with Douglas, saying that he too wanted to make a film that was both a commercial success but also one with "great artistic stature."[19] One must wonder what Kubrick's true reaction was to Douglas's memorandum and what discussions followed between the two. This first documented "intervention" by Douglas into the creative decisions being made by Kubrick also highlights the beginnings of a key source of tension: the sense that Douglas was exploiting Kubrick and Harris for Bryna's and his own promotional means. Whether or not Douglas's comments were being made out of sincerity for the quality of the picture, it generated a conflict for Kubrick and Harris, between genuine collaboration or producing a film to help further the star image of Douglas.

These tensions soon came to a head. Harris-Kubrick believed that Bryna was sidelining the contribution—the centrality—of both Harris and Kubrick on *Paths of Glory* in press releases issued during the production. It had been agreed that the film would be branded as a Bryna Production, due to Douglas's company having been the one to negotiate a deal with UA. But Bryna had no ownership interest in *Paths of Glory*. However, Harris-Kubrick was obliged to utilize the promotional services of Douglas's own publicity unit, Public Relations, headed by Stan Margulies. This took the autonomy of the publicity process out of the hands of Harris, the film's credited producer, and placed it within Douglas's sphere of influence. As a result, Harris and Kubrick came to assume that the publicity machine of Public Relations was geared toward one thing only: the Kirk Douglas celebrity image, at the expense of the film. Harris outlined his concerns in a letter to Margulies in March 1957, arguing "I definitely do not have the feeling that your office is working for Harris-Kubrick Pictures."[20] Whatever the truth of the matter, and whether Bryna was pushing its own image over that of Harris-Kubrick, is perhaps not the point. A feeling of mistrust had developed, only three months into the working relationship, with Harris-Kubrick assuming that Douglas was exploiting the company and getting the most out of their arrangement, when it was meant to be the other way around.

What emerged during those initial months that Kubrick and Douglas worked together was a clear difference in an understanding of their roles. For Kubrick, he would never accept being a mere "employee" of Douglas and Bryna, while Douglas wanted to recruit Kubrick to work for Bryna, potentially on a permanent, exclusive basis.[21] But Harris and Kubrick wanted to end the relationship with Douglas as soon as feasibly possible. To that end, when the pair floated the possibility of breaking up Harris-Kubrick Pictures in May 1957, it may have been partially as a means to end the contract with Bryna.[22] But there was only one problem: despite having secured Douglas in the leading role of *Paths of Glory*, Harris-Kubrick was still relatively unknown outside of Hollywood and reliant on the power network of Douglas and Bryna. If Kubrick had insisted on ending the contract in the short term, then the long-term future of Harris-Kubrick, and his own career in Hollywood, was in doubt.

This perhaps suggests why Harris and Kubrick continued to work with Bryna in the immediate aftermath of the post-production and release of *Paths of Glory*. But in doing so, they developed a creative approach to manage the relationship with Bryna. This involved, first, a process of persistent renegotiation of their contract, with Kubrick displaying clear levels of understanding that his own autonomy existed in the semantic wording of any agreement he had with producers and financiers. Second, they attempted to establish their own network of contacts and influence. James B. Harris was particularly useful in this regard, seeking out new options (including for *Lolita*) and utilizing the established contacts of his father, Joseph Harris, the influential co-owner of Essex Universal Corporation, a media group that financed, distributed, and imported American and foreign films. It was via his father that Harris initiated contact with Eliot Hyman, chief executive of Seven Arts, to negotiate a deal for the financing of *Lolita*. Third, they implemented an intensification of their overdevelopment strategy, in which they committed Harris-Kubrick Pictures to the development of more projects than could feasibly be produced. Kubrick was working on a number of adaptations and original projects during this period, including an American Civil War epic tentatively titled *Mosby's Rangers* and a World War II combat film initially titled *Nazi Paratroopers* and later renamed *The German Lieutenant*.[23] Meanwhile, Harris was instrumental in establishing potential deals with other independent producers as well as seeking out the rights to a variety of literary properties, ranging from Arthur C. Clarke's *The Deep Range* (1957) to Boris Pasternak's *Doctor Zhivago* (1957).[24] All of this overdevelopment may have been an attempt to frustrate and delay the contract with Bryna. And yet, they actively collaborated with Bryna.

It is to the latter we must briefly turn to understand how the creative and business partnership evolved following *Paths of Glory*, with a brief case study of a project Bryna and Harris-Kubrick agreed to develop together: *I Stole $16,000,000*. The film was to be an adaptation of Herbert Emerson Wilson's 1955 autobiography of the same name. Wilson had been a pastor who turned to a life of crime, becoming a notorious bank robber across the United States. When looking at the available archival documentation for the project, it becomes clear that, contrary to their belief that Douglas and Bryna were somehow trying to exploit and sideline their contributions in the working relationship, Harris and Kubrick were in fact being promoted heavily by Douglas's publicity unit, Public Relations. For example, Stan Margulies was contacting journalists and industry insiders about the new project in the winter of 1957. He explained how it had been Harris and Kubrick who had chosen the book due to their ongoing interest in crime as a genre.[25] Press releases issued by Margulies placed prominence on Harris and Kubrick as a team working for Bryna Productions and developing their own ideas, with Kirk Douglas only being mentioned in relation to having played the lead in *Paths of Glory*.

The aim was for Kubrick to finish the *I Stole $16,000,000* screenplay by the beginning of 1958 so the film could enter production by April of that year.[26] This was consistent with the original agreement, in which a second picture had to be produced for Bryna within fifteen months of the completion of production on *Paths of Glory*. Therefore, it indicates how Harris and Kubrick were, to some degree, contractually compliant. But more than that, it may have been a realization that they could use the agreement to their advantage, allowing their names to be further established via Douglas's power network and through the close association with the Douglas star brand.

So was *I Stole $16,000,000* ever a serious venture and did Harris-Kubrick actually intend for it to be produced at Bryna Productions? This is a difficult question to answer and one that needs to be placed in the wider contexts of Harris-Kubrick's activities and the fact that Harris has himself admitted that he and Kubrick were looking to extricate themselves from the deal with Bryna by whatever means necessary.[27] Certainly, by spring of 1958, the prospect of the project going ahead had become unclear. Press releases issued by Public Relations stated that Kirk Douglas would "probably" work on the film,[28] while Harris and Kubrick had apparently encountered creative differences with Bryna over the ending of the film.[29]

Further indication of Harris-Kubrick's lack of immediate commitment to *I Stole $16,000,000* came in the form of a collaboration with Gregory Peck for an original screenplay based on the life of Colonel John S. Mosby, *Mosby's Rangers*. Harris-Kubrick notified Bryna of the collaboration in March 1958, which seems to have initiated a process that led to the termination of the original contract with Bryna.[30] Presumably this was based on the perceived uncooperative behavior of Harris-Kubrick. By April 1958, Douglas's lawyer, Samuel Norton, was devising a termination release agreement, the terms of which were arguably even worse than those of the original contract. In order to be released from the contract, Harris-Kubrick had to hand over two-thirds of its share of *Mosby's Rangers* to Bryna. And if Harris-Kubrick did not produce *Mosby's Rangers*, this requirement would carry over to any subsequent feature it did produce.[31] The termination agreement also stated that Harris-Kubrick had to arrange a new deal with UA for *I Stole $16,000,000* to allow it to take ownership of the project from Bryna.

The effect of the termination agreement was to push Harris-Kubrick away from the production of immediate projects such as *Mosby's Rangers* and *I Stole $16,000,000* in an attempt to force it into producing a project with Bryna. But the long-term impact was that it actually persuaded Harris-Kubrick to pursue an adaptation of *Lolita*. Douglas did not want to be associated with such a project, believing that the book's notorious reputation—the story of a grown man's sexual obsession with a prepubescent teenager—and its publication by the Parisian-based Olympia Press—a proprietor of pornography—would not reflect well either on his own star image or the international standing of Bryna. A compromise was therefore reached: *Lolita* would be excluded from the terms and conditions of the termination agreement, in return Kubrick agreed to direct *Spartacus* on a temporary contract.[32]

In effect, a mutual agreement of sorts occurred, in which Kubrick favored Douglas with his directorial prowess for *Spartacus*, a production that was struggling following the firing of the original director, Anthony Mann. And in return, Douglas gave Harris-Kubrick the space to produce *Lolita* without any contractual obligation to Bryna. What resulted were the two most successful pictures of each company's respective histories, as well as two of the most commercially successful films in Hollywood history. Therefore, there was a further side-benefit to Kubrick directing *Spartacus*: it provided him with the necessary credentials to rightly claim that he had successfully directed a multimillion-dollar epic (the most expensive film ever financed by Universal up to that point) with a stellar cast of some of Hollywood's biggest names. The cultural capital that this brought him, and Harris-Kubrick, cannot be overstated.

The loan-out agreement between Harris-Kubrick and Bryna for the directorial services of Kubrick on *Spartacus* did not specify anything about creative control.[33] Instead, Kubrick was hired as an employee of Bryna with one task: to competently direct the film. In fact, Douglas seems to have welcomed Kubrick's creative interventions on the set of *Spartacus*, including suggestions on how to develop the script and its characters.[34] This approach played to Douglas's own preferences for lengthy deliberations about character, motivation, and theme, and he even acknowledged the extent to which Kubrick had influenced the production in correspondence and, later, in his autobiography.[35] The myth, if we can call it that, that Kubrick and Douglas were somehow in conflict on *Spartacus* and that Kubrick had no control is not entirely true. After all, the contract between Bryna and Harris-Kubrick continued for a further two years after the completion of shooting on *Spartacus*. Instead, the myth of a lack of control seems to have been developed by Kubrick himself in the months after the film's release. This was perhaps a means of distancing himself from the project, and *it* from his own authorial image. It must be remembered that for Harris-Kubrick the *Spartacus* venture was a means to an end: that being the production of *Lolita* free from the constraints of any agreement with Bryna. There was no overriding artistic motivation in directing *Spartacus*, only the business interests of Harris-Kubrick.

But before Kubrick put distance between himself and *Spartacus*, he first exploited the publicity that the film brough him and Harris-Kubrick. Following the film's release in October 1960, Kubrick gave an in-depth interview to the *New York Times*. It was a paper with which he had cultivated a relationship since his earliest days as a short documentary filmmaker in 1950, when he had first reached out to the paper in a bid to raise his profile.[36] He now did so again, talking to Eugene Archer for a story eventually headlined "Hailed in Farewell: 'Spartacus' Gets Praise of Pleased Director."[37] In it, Kubrick claimed to have been the only one in a position to "authentically impose his personality" onto the film in his role as director.[38] He also alleged that he had overruled the power of Douglas to take charge of elements of the script, ultimately making the film more visual. Douglas did concede in correspondence with producer Ed Lewis that he had been "weaned off" aspects of the script by Kubrick.[39] But Kubrick was most certainly overstating in the claim he made to the *Los Angeles Times*, telling film critic Philip Scheuer, "I was given complete freedom."[40] Kubrick even aligned *Spartacus* with his own filmography, claiming that it was "just as good as *Paths of Glory*" and contained "just as much of myself in it."[41] These claims of creative autonomy have to be viewed with caution—especially given how in later years he emphatically stated "*Spartacus* is the only film over which I did not have absolute control"[42]—and instead viewed in the light of the business interests of Harris-Kubrick. Kubrick appeared to be using the publicity of *Spartacus* to raise his own profile and the work of Harris-Kubrick, using interviews to promote the ongoing development of *Lolita*.

By 1961, when Kubrick began to dissociate himself from *Spartacus*, telling journalists he would prefer to be judged by the quality and reception of *Lolita* instead,[43] it became clear that the relationship between Douglas and Kubrick was not going to work. The sensational press surrounding the production of *Lolita* had propelled Harris and Kubrick into the limelight and clearly signaled that they no longer required the power network and influence of Douglas. Indeed, they had begun to establish their own network of contacts and power that would sustain them through the production and release of *Lolita*, through to the initial development of *Dr. Strangelove* (1964). Douglas, Kubrick, and Harris mutually agreed to part ways in December 1961. They severed all contractual and legal obligations, with the only penance being that Harris-Kubrick had to pay a $40,000 release fee by 1963.[44] The business and creative relationship that had commenced four years previous was over with no films actually produced in line with the contract (both *Paths of Glory* and *Spartacus* were produced outside of the three-picture deal).

The final release agreement allowed Harris-Kubrick to reclaim its total creative and business autonomy, at least from Bryna. Following the agreement, the company was established as one of the leading independent production outfits in the world, with the successful release of *Lolita* in 1962 by MGM. As for Douglas, arguably he had reached his peak with *Spartacus* and increasingly turned to more personal, lower-budget material, exemplified by *Lonely Are the Brave* (1962), a black-and-white Western. That is not to say he did not continue to appear in leading roles in big-budget spectacles; one only has to think of his appearances in the likes of *The Heroes of Telemark* (1965) and *Cast a Giant Shadow* (1966). And his presence on the cinema screen intensified, appearing in over forty pictures throughout the second half of the twentieth century. But the influence and power he had exuded in Hollywood in the 1950s, and which had brought Harris-Kubrick into his orbit, was waning. In contrast, Kubrick's power grew so that, by the end of the 1960s and the release of *2001: A Space Odyssey* (1968), he was one of the most influential and powerful film producers in Hollywood.

However, it could have been very different for Kubrick. While it is only hypothetical, without the assistance of Douglas and Bryna, Kubrick may never have become the producer that he did. After all, following the release of *The Killing*, Harris-Kubrick was struggling to find financing, with its initial contract with MGM in 1956 being canceled and its relationship with the most influential company for independent producers, UA, being nonexistent. What Harris-Kubrick needed more than anything was access to a network of power that it could then exploit to its own ends. Kirk Douglas and Bryna offered exactly that and while it is not to suggest that Kubrick and Harris were somehow acting with nefarious means in signing their contract with Bryna, they were certainly trying to use it to their advantage. The association with Douglas's star allowed them to grow. But at the same time, the desire to escape the perceived creative bondage in which they found themselves arguably pushed them toward a particularly controversial project, *Lolita*, as they knew Douglas wanted no part in its adaptation. What this also hints toward is fuller consideration of a wide range of industrial contexts to understand why some projects come to fruition and others remain unmade. After all, one must ask, was it Kirk Douglas who was responsible in the end for *Lolita*? What if that project had been included in the 1958 termination agreement, allowing Douglas considerable ownership of it? As Douglas himself later made clear, "In the nearly thirty years since *Spartacus*, Stanley has made only seven movies. If I had held him to his contract, half of his remaining movies would have been made for my company."[45] The history of Kubrick's career would certainly have been very different.

NOTES

1. Kirk Douglas, *The Ragman's Son: An Autobiography* (London: Pan Books, 1989), 333.
2. "Kirk Douglas on Stanley Kubrick: He was a bastard," *Variety*, December 8, 2016, https://variety.com/2016/biz/news/kirk-douglas-on-stanley-kubrick-1201937274/ (accessed January 7, 2020).
3. Douglas, *The Ragman's Son*, 332–33.
4. "The New UA Team," *Variety*, March 21, 1956, 17.
5. Letter from James B. Harris to David Stillman, June 1, 1956, private archive of James B. Harris, Los Angeles.
6. James Fenwick, "'Look, Ma, I'm A Corporation!'" in *United Artists: The Routledge Hollywood Centenary Series*, eds. Yannis Tzioumakis, Peter Krämer, Gary Needham, and Tino Balio (London: Routledge, 2020), 96–97.
7. Memorandum of Understanding between Bryna Productions, Kirk Douglas, James Harris and Stanley Kubrick, January 9, 1957, Box 11, Folder 21, KDP.
8. Ibid.
9. Ibid.
10. James Fenwick, *Stanley Kubrick Produces* (New Brunswick, NJ: Rutgers University Press, 2020).
11. *Shark Safari*, uncatalogued, Brown Wallet K, University of the Arts London, Stanley Kubrick Archives (SKA).
12. Take, for example, Kubrick's idea for a script titled *The Famished Monkey*, a story of a young intellectual in Greenwich Village who "lives off other people." Similarly, Kubrick devised an idea for a script called *New York Story*, in which an artist in Greenwich Village lives off the "kind issuances of money from a 50-year-old widow." "Early Work," Brown Wallet E, uncatalogued, SKA.
13. Letter from Kirk Douglas to Stanley Kubrick, February 13, 1957, Box 23, Folder 19, KDP.
14. Ibid.
15. Ibid.
16. Ibid.
17. Ibid.
18. Letter from Stanley Kubrick to Kirk Douglas, February 19, 1957, Box 23, Folder 19, KDP.
19. Ibid.
20. Letter from James B. Harris to Stan Margulies, March 28, 1957, Box 23, Folder 19, KDP.
21. Letter from Kirk Douglas to Sam Norton, May 25, 1957, Box 11, Folder 21, KDP.
22. James Fenwick, "Kubrick and Production," in *The Bloomsbury Companion to Stanley Kubrick*, eds. Nathan Abrams and I.Q. Hunter (New York: Bloomsbury, 2021).
23. Fenwick, *Stanley Kubrick Produces*.
24. Private archive of James B. Harris, Los Angeles.
25. Letter from Stan Margulies to Mac Reynolds, December 4, 1957, Box 56, Folder 11, KDP.
26. Ibid.
27. James B. Harris, interview with the author, February 16, 2017.

28. Public Relations press release, February 17, 1958, Box 56, Folder 11, KDP.
29. Public Relations press release, February 13, 1958, Box 56, Folder 11 KDP.
30. Telegram from Bryna Productions to Harris-Kubrick, March 18, 1958, Box 11, Folder 21, KDP.
31. Memo from Sam Norton to Edward Lewis, April 22, 1958, Box 11, Folder 21, KDP.
32. Letter of agreement between Bryna Productions and Harris-Kubrick Pictures, March 30, 1959, Box 11, Folder 21, KDP.
33. Harris-Kubrick Pictures Loan-Out Agreement, April 8, 1959, 35/4, KDP.
34. Memo from Kirk Douglas, April 29, 1959, 33/6, KDP.
35. Ibid.; Douglas, *Ragman's Son*, 332–33.
36. Thomas Pryor, "Young Man with Ideas and a Camera," *The New York Times*, January 14, 1951, X5.
37. Eugene Archer, "Hailed in Farewell: 'Spartacus' Gets Praise of Pleased Director," *The New York Times*, October 2, 1960, X9.
38. Ibid.
39. Memo from Kirk Douglas, April 5, 1959, 33/4, KDP.
40. Philip Scheuer, "$12 Million Risk Taken by Douglas," *Los Angeles Times*, September 29, 1960, C9.
41. Archer, "Hailed in Farewell," X9.
42. Kubrick in Gene D. Phillips, "Spartacus," in *The Stanley Kubrick Archives*, ed. Alison Castle, 184–214 (Cologne: Taschen, 2005), 186.
43. Filippo Ulivieri, "Dr. Mabuse No. 2: An Investigation into Stanley Kubrick's Promotional Strategies and the Building of a Mythological Image" (unpublished manuscript, August 1, 2019).
44. Release agreement, December 15, 1961, Box 11, Folder 21, KDP.
45. Douglas, *Ragman's Son*, 333.

REFERENCES

Archer, Eugene. "Hailed in Farewell: 'Spartacus' Gets Praise of Pleased Director." *The New York Times*, October 2, 1960, X9.

Douglas, Kirk. *The Ragman's Son: An Autobiography*. London: Pan Books, 1989.

Fenwick, James. "A Production Strategy of Overdevelopment: Kirk Douglas's Bryna Productions and the Unproduced *Viva Gringo*." In *Shadow Cinema: Industrial and Production Contexts*, edited by James Fenwick, David Eldridge, and Kieran Foster. New York: Bloomsbury, 2020, 17–37.

———. "'Look, Ma, I'm A Corporation!' United Artists and Kirk Douglas's Bryna Productions 1955–1959." In *United Artists: The Routledge Hollywood Centenary Series*, edited by Yannis Tzioumakis, Peter Krämer, Gary Needham, and Tino Balio. London: Routledge, 2020, 94–111.

———. "Kubrick and Production." In *The Bloomsbury Companion to Stanley Kubrick*, edited by Nathan Abrams and I.Q. Hunter. New York: Bloomsbury, 2021.

———. *Stanley Kubrick Produces*. New Brunswick, NJ: Rutgers University Press, 2020.

Phillips, Gene D. "Spartacus." In *The Stanley Kubrick Archives*, edited by Alison Castle, 184–214. Cologne: Taschen, 2005.

Pryor, Thomas. "Young Man with Ideas and a Camera." *The New York Times*, January 14, 1951.

Roshanian, Arya. "Kirk Douglas on Stanley Kubrick: He Was a Bastard." *Variety*, December 8, 2016. https://variety.com/2016/biz/news/kirk-douglas-on-stanley-kubrick-1201937274/.

Scheuer, Philip. "$12 Million Risk Taken by Douglas." *Los Angeles Times*, September 29, 1960, C9.

Chapter Fourteen

Auteur versus Author

Kubrick's Relationship with Literary Writers

Annie Nissen

The legacy of Stanley Kubrick (1928–1999) and the influence he had on filmmaking and filmmakers is well established. Yet his career has not been without criticism, often leveled at both his choice of subject matter and his directorial approach.[1] This criticism has arisen in part because of Kubrick's unusual position as a filmmaker: from the beginning of his career, he remained largely independent of contractual obligations to studios, giving him creative freedom in his choice of subject matter, and allowing little interference from others in his film direction. His early experience working as a stand-in director on *Spartacus* (1960) is often seen as confirming his decision to retain as much creative control as possible in his future endeavors; even so, he succeeded "in reconciling his own uncompromising requirements with those of the industry."[2] Critics and biographers often discuss his background as a photographer contributing to the precise vision that he brought to his filmmaking practices and, although he is widely hailed as a visionary filmmaker, negative terms, ranging from "perfectionist" to "control freak," are also attached to this.[3] His total control included rare directorial involvement with aspects such as translation, insistence on choosing his own dubbing director, and selecting the foreign voice actors.[4]

The control that Kubrick maintained throughout his career established him as an authorial figure, a film auteur. His progress as director coincided with the rise of the auteur theory in the 1950s and 1960s, and Kubrick was classed as such early in his career, displaying many of the elements that defined the film auteur as the main influence over film productions. Equally essential to the definition of a film auteur, Kubrick constructed himself as a director who was not afraid to deviate from mainstream filmmaking practices in subject matter, cinematic form, or in his overall approach to film production. As a result, as Greg Jenkins points out, he was both "celebrated and chided as an idiosyncratic artist."[5] Alexander Walker further describes Kubrick's auteurism as "conceptual," explaining that he possessed "a talent to crystallize every film . . . into a cinematic concept" that exhibited his auteur "vision in an unexpected way."[6] Although Kubrick's directing career spanned only thirteen feature films from the 1950s until his death in 1999, the diversity of his oeuvre is astounding, encompassing war films, period and contemporary dramas, and horror and science fiction epics, to name only a few of the many genres he tackled.

As diverse as his films are in terms of genre, they do have one thing in common that is far too often overlooked: they are literary adaptations.[7] Kubrick always relied on literary material for his films, with the exception of his first two. His work, nonetheless, never identifies itself primarily as adaptation, but rather detaches from it through cinematic originality. Literary film adaptation scholars have been more attuned to these dynamics: he has been nominated as an "adapter-auteur"[8] and, for Elisa Pezzotta, Kubrick's cinema has become "the example *par excellence* of the fruitful encounter between the two arts," despite his films "being among the furthest from the written medium" that they adapt.[9] Kubrick himself was aware of this distance, describing his approach to literary adaptation as "an accidental process, and never one which can be attacked head-on."[10]

And yet Kubrick was himself a writer, actively participating in writing all his films in one way or another, writing for which he was both credited and uncredited. Early in his career, Kubrick described his filmmaking as uniting the roles of "writer, director, and editor" in one, stating in a 1958 interview that "You should try to be one solid entity just like the art you are creating is an individual entity."[11] Not only does this statement highlight his plenary method of filmmaking, it also articulates his view that each film acts as an artistic entity within itself. Considering Kubrick's penchant for adapting material and the fact that his work is not widely treated as adaptation, his statement here suggests his view of his source material not as something to be translated to film, but one of seminal generation of film as an independent work of art. Yet, Kubrick's assertion that the director must be a writer, among other things, complicates simplistic views of binary oppositions between literature and film, word and image, writing and directing. That said, Kubrick did not consider himself a screenwriter, frequently refusing this role and hiring others to write screenplays for his films.

Beyond his writing and directing, Kubrick's passion for editing his films is widely documented. He identified editing as the most "unique" art form in film, equaling only writing and shooting in filmmaking.[12] His approach to editing was all-consuming, being fully involved and admitting to being merciless with cutting and editing the final product: "Nothing is cut without me.

I'm in there every second . . . and have everything done exactly the way I want it."[13] The control he displayed in the editing room is emblematic of the control that he tried to preserve over his films. His role as film editor can also be likened to his role when working with other writers. Kubrick excelled at revising and, arguably, improving what others had written before him.[14]

This chapter examines some ways in which Kubrick worked with writers, particularly with literary writers whose work he adapted. This discussion is not concerned with issues of fidelity or with levying judgments on the characters or aesthetics of literary authors and this film auteur. Instead, it analyzes some encounters that Kubrick, the film auteur, had with literary authors and asks whether and how his experiences with writers shaped his approach to filmmaking. Since each and every relationship Kubrick had with literary writers would fill many books, the main focus of this chapter is on Kubrick's working relationship with novelist Vladimir Nabokov during the production of the film *Lolita* (1962), adapted from the author's 1955 novel. This early instance of literary collaboration is formative and also representative of Kubrick's approach to working with literary authors whose work he adapted and indicative of their influence on his filmmaking. Throughout his career Kubrick experienced continuous conflicts and contests with literary writers, including attempts by authors to reassert their own authority, yet his films were nevertheless shaped by the spirit of their texts,[15] combining his vision with theirs.

First published in 1955 in Paris, Nabokov's novel *Lolita* was initially rejected by American publishers due to its controversial subject matter. When it was finally published in America in 1958, Kubrick and his producer, James B. Harris, obtained the film rights for it for $150,000, and, in July 1959, they approached Nabokov to write the screenplay for the adaptation. Although Nabokov was ultimately credited as the only screenwriter and even received an Academy Award nomination in 1963, his screenplay was not much utilized for the film. Nabokov himself has stated that there are "just enough borrowings" from his *Lolita* script in Kubrick's adaptation to justify his "legal position as author of the script," but that "the final product is only a blurred skimpy glimpse of the marvelous picture I imagined."[16]

The film encountered numerous obstacles during production, not least of which was Nabokov himself. When Kubrick initially asked Nabokov to write the screenplay he declined, with his refusal to accept only strengthened when he learned that changes would need to be made to appease the censors. Censorship concerns often plagued Kubrick's films, but seldom did they interfere with his vision. Seeking to extend his own creative freedom to Nabokov, Kubrick promised Nabokov "a freer hand," and renewed his offer half a year later. Nabokov, who by now had a vision of his own for the adaptation, accepted.[17]

Their two visions clashed. In a short essay written for *Sight and Sound* during the filming of *Lolita*, Kubrick propounds his theory of screenwriting: "the dramatizing has to find a style of its own." Advising the screenwriter against using "paper and ink and words," he recommends "working in flesh and feeling" as well as fully grasping the content of the source, so that something different to the novel can be brought out in the film. Addressing the question of how a novel like *Lolita*, whose quality depends so much on Nabokov's prose style, can be adapted to film, he argues that the quality of writing is merely one element, and that another factor is "the quality of the writer's obsession with his subject," including "an understanding of character" as well as "a theme . . . concept and a view of life." This approach to adaptation as capturing the feeling, structure, authorial passion, themes, concepts, world view, and characters of a novel governs Kubrick's film adaptations throughout his career. He suggests that the resulting film in some way could possibly be even better than the novel.[18] Not only does Kubrick here display his ambitious belief that an adaptation can be better than its source, even a celebrated one such as *Lolita*, but he also indicates that the writer's obsessive relationship to his work mirrors that which he himself increasingly displayed as a director.

In direct contrast to Kubrick's theory of adaptation, Nabokov describes his screenwriting process as granting "words primacy over action, thus limiting as much as possible the intrusion of management and cast" and that he "persevered in the task until [he] could tolerate the rhythm of the dialogue and properly control the flow of the film from motel to motel, mirage to mirage, nightmare to nightmare."[19] It is clear from this that he had little sympathy with film techniques and conventions or even spoken dialogue and that he saw his task as being one of writing and rewriting until he perceived that his words could control the flow of the film—the editing, as it were.

Nabokov initially had no idea that his views of adaptation were so diametrically opposed to Kubrick's. Having been given, as promised, the free hand with the screenplay, Nabokov recounts that Kubrick's "attitude had convinced me that he was willing to heed my whims more closely than those of the censor." Before starting work on the script, Nabokov met with Kubrick to discuss how to cinematize the novel, a meeting that Nabokov described as "an amiable battle of suggestion and counter-suggestion," in which Kubrick "accepted all my vital points, I accepted some of his less significant ones." However, the meetings became less frequent, as did any criticism of the script, so that Nabokov was not feeling "quite sure whether Kubrick was serenely accepting whatever I did or silently rejecting everything."[20] By June 1960, Nabokov nonetheless thought he had finished his screenplay, even though it was 400 pages. He recalls that Kubrick met with him to explain that the screenplay was unworkable as a film, it being "too unwieldy, contained too many unnecessary episodes, and would take about seven hours to run,"[21] asking him to change and delete several things, some of which he adhered to and others of which he did not. By September, he had sent Kubrick a revised and shortened script, including new sequences and situations, which the director then accepted.

After this, however, Nabokov's involvement in the film ceased completely.[22] He recalls that "nobody insisted on my coming to Elstree" and that "the shooting of the *Lolita* film in England was begun and concluded far beyond the veil of my vanities."[23] In addition, his unease with film conventions and attempts to overwrite them, as well as his disappointment that *Lolita* did not turn out to be the "marvelous picture [he] imagined,"[24] indicate a lack of familiarity with the realities of film production. His belief that his script was the final version, with no changes being necessary, further shows his inexperience with film production processes. At this early point in Kubrick's career, Nabokov's position as celebrated literary author might have contractually ensured him more power over the adaptation; at the very least he could have been privy to changes that were being made to his script.

Surprisingly, given how little of Nabokov's script he used in the film, Kubrick expresses directorial deference to literary writers in his essay published during the filming of *Lolita*: "it is his [the director's] duty to be one hundred per cent faithful to the author's meaning," making no sacrifices to this "for the sake of climax or effect." Perhaps responding to the recent rise of *la politique des auteurs*, he criticizes directors who disregard "the inner design" of the work, describing this as the point where "the cult of the director" is seen at its worst.[25] His respect for the author, however, did not extend to involving him in the production process or in fidelity to the words of the novel or its plot structures, or, more importantly, to the author's screenplay. Instead, Kubrick focuses on the "meaning" of the author's words and the "inner design" rather than the manifest signs of the literary text. Nabokov's continued involvement with the film production process could have proven problematic for Kubrick. Even if his screenplay was not satisfactory, in contrast to other writers with whom Kubrick had worked before, such a famous, outspoken author might have challenged Kubrick's interpretation of his "meaning" and the "inner design" of his book. In a theoretical climate where authorial intent still loomed large in literary criticism and the author was still very much alive, Kubrick was unlikely to win any battles over what the other meant or what his "inner design" was. However, by letting Nabokov write the screenplay with only minimal interference from himself and then directing and editing the film with no interference from Nabokov, Kubrick avoided these potential debates and problems. Kubrick could determine what Nabokov "meant" in the novel and ignore what he "meant" in the screenplay. In this way, his literary film adaptation processes prefigured the death of the author that Roland Barthes would proclaim a few years later in 1967.

Intriguingly, for all his attempts to dominate film conventions with words, Nabokov himself realized his limitations as a screenwriter, admitting that "by nature I am no dramatist; I am not even a hack scenarist."[26] Even more intriguingly, he implicitly supported Kubrick's total control of the film, qualifying that:

> if I had given as much of myself to the stage or the screen as I have to the kind of writing which serves a triumphant life sentence between the covers of a book, I would have advocated and applied a system of total tyranny, directing the play or the picture myself, choosing settings and costumes, terrorizing the actors, mingling with them in the bit part of guest, or ghost, prompting them, and, in a word, pervading the entire show with the will and art of one individual.[27]

This view of absolute control over a production reiterates Kubrick's own theory of himself as a director, even before *Lolita*, and his obsessive directorial practices. However, writing here in retrospect in 1974, Nabokov makes clear that mastery of one's art form is a prerequisite for tyrannical control. That said, Nabokov became, according to his own account and despite his initial reluctance, very dedicated and deeply involved in the screenwriting. Yet he did not believe he was cut out for film (writing), which offers a better explanation of why he did not engage further with the production process.

If Nabokov felt that he had failed as a dramatist and a screenwriter, Kubrick viewed "a writer-director" as "the perfect dramatic instrument," with the mastery of both practices, already done by a few, producing reliably good work.[28] Yet, at this point, he did not consider himself able to master writing without the support of literary writers. Prior to working with Nabokov on *Lolita*, Kubrick had shown that he had no objection to hiring novelists inexperienced in film writing to collaborate on his films. For *The Killing* (1956), he hired novelist Jim Thompson, whose style had impressed him, though he had never written a screenplay. Indeed, his admiration for a writer's style appears dominant in his choice of screenwriters, explaining his choice of Nabokov. The choice was not simply aesthetic. Kubrick understood that crediting Nabokov as the screenwriter would have given the film more prestige, both with critics and audiences. Indeed, although Nabokov lamented that "only ragged odds and ends of my script had been used,"[29] he was credited as sole writer for the film, even though Kubrick had written most of the script. Amidst Kubrick's protestations of fidelity to the author's meaning, Nabokov judged the film as certainly "unfaithful to the original script."[30] Thus he was credited for Kubrick's infidelities to his script.

David Hughes describes Kubrick's omission of crediting himself, as a "shrewd rather than generous move," allowing the author "to take either the credit or the blame."[31] Following the controversy that the book had courted, on which the film capitalized in its promotional tagline "How did they ever make a movie of *Lolita*?" crediting Nabokov as the writer of both meant that he would be held partly responsible for the film. It is likely that Kubrick declined any credit for the writing to compensate Nabokov financially for deviating from his script. In addition to the $40,000 (plus expenses) that Nabokov received for writing it, his contract stipulated that a further $35,000 would be paid if he received sole credit.[32] This clause was possibly inserted following Kubrick's legal troubles with author-screenwriter writing credits. After *The Killing*, Thompson considered legal action against Kubrick when he was merely credited for the dialogue, whereas Kubrick was credited for the screenplay. He was only placated when he was given another screenwriting position on *Paths of Glory* (1957). Here, however, Kubrick encountered further trouble, as novelist Calder Willingham, also a first-time screenwriter, was hired to rewrite Thompson's script. Realizing that Kubrick would receive most of the writing credit, Willingham took the case to the Writer's Guild of America, claiming to have written the majority of the screenplay. The WGA ruled in Willingham's favor, resulting in Kubrick's shared writing credit alongside Willingham and Thompson.[33] *Lolita* remains the last and one of his few films in which Kubrick did not receive writing credit at all. The sole credit given to Nabokov for *Lolita* is thus somewhat anomalous.

Until Nabokov saw the film, he was unaware of what had happened to his screenplay. A few days before the *Lolita* premiere in New York, on June 13, 1962, he sat through a private screening, describing his first reaction as a "mixture of aggravation, regret, and reluctant pleasure." He did not consider that Kubrick had improved his screenplay: "Most of the sequences were not really better than those I had so carefully composed for Kubrick."[34] Yet rather than press the aesthetic equality of his writing to Kubrick's further, he articulates what he imagines Kubrick's point of view on the collaboration to be, as well as his own response: "I keenly regretted the waste of my time while admiring Kubrick's fortitude in enduring for six months the evolution and infliction of a useless product."[35] Nabokov's chief disappointment is over his wasted time; rather than accusing Kubrick of toying with him, he presumes that Kubrick was hoping that the screenplay would develop into a useful product.

These statements were written years later. At the time the film was released, Nabokov kept his mixed emotions regarding the film largely private, with Kubrick confirming that he "went to a party with Nabokov after the premiere, and he was very jolly and flattering about the film in every respect."[36] Nabokov also hailed the film as "absolutely first-rate" in a *Playboy* interview in 1964. Two years on from the film's release, however, he was keen to point out that he was not involved with the "actual production" and that, if he had been, he "might have insisted on stressing certain things that were not stressed." Even as he stated, "All I did was write the screenplay," he claimed (somewhat inaccurately) that "a preponderating portion of [it] was used by Kubrick."[37]

Despite describing Kubrick's film as "first-rate," Nabokov unceasingly perceived his own screenplay as an ideal adaptation of his novel, later declaring that, "I shall never understand why he [Kubrick] did not follow my directions and dreams."[38] The faith and pride that Nabokov had in his screenplay, as well as the labor he put into it, came to a head when he decided to publish it over a decade later in 1974, even including some scenes from his first draft. He was keen to point out that this decision was made "not in a pettish refutation of a munificent film," as "aggravation and regret soon subsided," but that it was rather so as to not waste his work. He did not present it as a superior screenplay, but "purely as a vivacious variant of an old novel."[39] Repeating his admiration for the film *Lolita* "in its own right," he nevertheless maintained "but it's not what I wrote."[40] Nabokov appeared satisfied that his screenplay was now available to anyone wishing to see what he had written, concluding that it was ultimately able to exist *alongside* the film. Stressing that the publication of his screenplay was not a "belated grudge" or "high-pitched depreciation of Kubrick's creative approach," he explained: "he saw my novel in one way, I saw it in another—that's all," going further to admit that his screenplay would not have worked as a film: "infinite fidelity may be an author's ideal but can prove a producer's ruin."[41]

Kubrick continued to use existing literature to inspire his filmmaking, explaining that by not writing the story himself, which he was not certain he would be able to do, "you have this tremendous advantage of reading something for the first time," like a "falling-in-love reaction," which he sought to retain as long as possible while adapting it.[42] Kubrick's films, then, were both shaped and characterized by his passion for literature as a reader and adapter, maintained as long as possible from start to finish. His early experiences with literary writers such as Thompson, Willingham, and Nabokov had by no means dissuaded him from further adaptations and collaborations with writers, although over time he was more direct and undertook more "hands-on" writing himself. With *2001: A Space Odyssey* (1968), for example, Kubrick actively joined forces with a popular literary writer and worked with him to create his vision for the film. In this instance, he not only optioned several published stories by Arthur C. Clarke in 1964, he also hired him to write a *new* treatment for the film, incorporating ideas from the stories that interested Kubrick. Even though he describes their joint efforts as "one of the most fruitful and enjoyable collaborations,"[43] and Clarke too was largely positive about their relationship, working together also proved challenging for both. Particularly galling for Clarke, as Michael Benson points out, was his exclusion from the financial profits of the film, despite his significance in developing the project.[44] Joining Clarke's devaluation in the economics of film profits, his work was further rendered secondary in the release dates. Kubrick wanted the film to precede Clarke's novel, so as to appear as its source, whereas Clarke expected to publish it prior to the film, as they had originally planned.[45] When Clarke's eponymous novel was published shortly after the film was released, he dedicated it "To Stanley," but was solely credited as its author, allowing Clarke to reassert independent authority over that writing. Clarke nevertheless stated in retrospect that, as novel and screenplay were written simultaneously, the credit for the novel should have read: "'by Arthur Clarke and Stanley Kubrick: based on the screenplay by Stanley Kubrick and Arthur Clarke'—whereas the movie should have the credits reversed."[46] Throughout his career, Kubrick's collaborations with writers proved thus contradictory, as he respected and admired them, while simultaneously promoting his vision above theirs in various ways.

As Kubrick's control over his films developed, and as he gained experience writing for the screen, he decided to forgo collaborating with literary writers partway through his filmmaking career and was credited as the sole screenwriter of the two films he made during the 1970s, *A Clockwork Orange* (1971) and *Barry Lyndon* (1975). Asked subsequently whether he liked writing alone or would like to work with a scriptwriter, he replied that he enjoyed working with someone he found "stimulating."[47] While of course the nineteenth-century novel *Barry Lyndon* offered Kubrick no opportunity to collaborate with its author William Makepeace Thackeray, this was not so for *A Clockwork Orange*. In this case, several screenplays had already been written when Kubrick acquired the rights. Kubrick chose to disregard them all, including one by its author Anthony Burgess, writing an entirely new script alone. He proceeded similarly with the adaptation of *The Shining* (1980), ignoring a screenplay written by its author, Stephen King. Here, however, he chose to collaborate on the screenplay with novelist and first-time screenwriter Diane Johnson. Yet the author was not entirely dead in the Barthesean sense, birthed solely by the film-auteur. Although Kubrick did not want either "author to adapt his own novel"—that is, to write it for film—he still valued their input in interpreting the meaning of their novels and was in frequent contact with both, asking numerous questions of them while working on the scripts.[48]

Despite Kubrick's obsessive pre-production planning and insistence on having absolute authority over his films, his approach to writing film scripts shows adaptability and openness to change in the process of their development: "Any art form properly practiced involves a to and fro between conception and execution, the original intention being constantly modified as one tries to give it objective realization."[49] With *Barry Lyndon*, for instance, he recalls that the writing process never really stopped: "However carefully you think about a scene, and however clearly you believe you have visualized it, it's never the same when you finally see it played," requiring new ideas and ways to tell the story.[50] Moreover, in spite of his control of every aspect of the film, he was not closed to collaborative filmmaking, believing in developing the script continuously along with the actors.[51] The shooting stage and the process of directing actors therefore played an important part in developing Kubrick as a screenwriter.[52] Encouraged by Kubrick, Peter Sellers was known to improvise on set, not only during *Dr. Strangelove* (1964) but also while filming *Lolita*. This makes clear that not all of the changes made to Nabokov's script were Kubrick's, but were the product of collaborations between Kubrick and other filmmakers.

As both Nabokov and Clarke had pitted their authorship and authorial claims against Kubrick's, other writers also attempted to reaffirm authority over their work in different ways. King went further than either when he not only rewrote but also adapted and executive produced *The Shining* as a TV miniseries in 1997. The fact that Kubrick was in possession of the exclusive rights meant that the fate of King's adaptation lay in his hands. Rather than refuse King, Kubrick struck a bargain: in addition to a large pecuniary compensation, King had to refrain from publicly criticizing Kubrick's version and from making any comparisons between the two adaptations.[53] Prior to this agreement, King had criticized Kubrick's film, stating that his problems were not with the directing, but "mostly with the scripting"[54] by Kubrick and Johnson: it was "a film by a man who thinks too much and feels too little." Having had great expectations for the adaptation and having admired Kubrick for years, he "was deeply disappointed in the end result."[55] Despite not being allowed to continue criticizing Kubrick's version, the act of self-adapting his work was enough to convey the message. Furthermore, overwriting and re-filming Kubrick's work in a later adaptation could not stop others from comparing them, potentially to King's critical advantage, as these works pitted the author's adaptive vision against the auteur's.[56]

Intriguingly, Kubrick's reaction to King's adaptation and Nabokov's published screenplay are undocumented and neither has interfered with the reputation of his film versions. Jenkins's view is that, while Kubrick, as adapter, must be viewed as part of a "rhetorical community ... that unites most if not all adapters," his films are "unique and personal."[57] Yet his films remain imbued with the creativity of other authors. Discussing Kubrick's adaptation of *The Shining*, Jarrell D. Wright argues that Kubrick did "not merely" adapt the novel, but rather the "themes that King was also developing in the source text."[58] We have seen that this is what Kubrick himself claimed about his process of adaptation. Kubrick's films are composites of literary concepts developed by other writers, actor improvisation, and visual imagery developed by cinematographers and special effects departments, mixed with and overseen by his own cinematic vision. Although Kubrick asserted his control over all the writers he collaborated with, both directly and indirectly, he nevertheless gave recognition to the writers whose work imbued his films, albeit not always in the way they wanted. He clearly recognized their authorial abilities and claims over their work, just as they recognized Kubrick's abilities and claims over his as adapter-auteur.

NOTES

1. The impact Kubrick's work had, including his style and filmic themes, can be seen in the critical attention he received continuously throughout his career. See, for example, Alison Castle, ed., *The Stanley Kubrick Archives* (Köln: Taschen, 2016).
2. Alexander Walker, *Stanley Kubrick Directs* (London: Abacus, 1973), 8.
3. See, for example, Vincent LoBrutto, *Stanley Kubrick: A Biography* (London: Faber & Faber, 1998).
4. See Serenella Zanotti, "Auteur Dubbing: Translation, Performance and Authorial Control in the Dubbed Versions of Stanley Kubrick's Films," in *Reassessing Dubbing: Historical Approaches and Current Trends*, ed. Irene Ranzato and Serenella Zanotti, 79–102 (Amsterdam: John Benjamins Publishing, 2019).
5. Greg Jenkins, *Stanley Kubrick and the Art of Adaptation: Three Novels, Three Films* (Jefferson, NC: McFarland Press, 1997), 160.
6. Walker, *Kubrick Directs*, 7.
7. This lack of attention has been addressed by Kubrick adaptation scholars before, see Elisa Pezzotta, *Stanley Kubrick: Adapting the Sublime* (Jackson, MS: University of Mississippi Press, 2013). An MLA International Bibliography count reveals the total number of publications on "Kubrick" to be 720, whereas "Kubrick" and "Adaptation" reveals 244 results. Accessed August 26, 2019.
8. See Thomas Leitch, *Film Adaptation and its Discontents: From* Gone with the Wind *to* The Passion of the Christ (Baltimore, MD: Johns Hopkins University Press, 2009), 236–57.
9. Pezzotta, *Adapting the Sublime*, 3.
10. Quoted in Walker, *Kubrick Directs*, 20.
11. Interview by Jay Varela, 1958, reprinted in *The Stanley Kubrick Archives*, 171.
12. Interview by Tim Cahill, *Rolling Stone*, 1987, reprinted in *Stanley Kubrick: Interviews*, ed. Gene D. Phillips, 189–204 (Jackson, MS: University of Mississippi Press, 2001), 199.
13. Interview by Joseph Gelmis, 1970, reprinted in *Stanley Kubrick: Interviews*, 80–104, 94.
14. Kirk Douglas similarly remarked that Kubrick always functioned better if he "got a good writer and worked with him as an editor." Quoted in Walker, *Kubrick Directs*, 7.
15. See Kamilla Elliott, "The Psychic Model of Adaptation," in *Rethinking the Novel/Film Debate* (Cambridge: Cambridge University Press, 2003), 136–43.
16. Interview by Herbert Gold, *Paris Review*, 1967, reprinted in *Strong Opinions*, Vladimir Nabokov, 80–92 (New York: McGraw Hill, 1973), 91.
17. Vladimir Nabokov, *Lolita: A Screenplay*, (New York: Vintage Books, 1997), viii.
18. Stanley Kubrick, "Words and Movies," *Sight and Sound* 30, no. 1 (Winter 1960): 14.
19. Nabokov, *Screenplay*, x.
20. Ibid., ix.
21. Ibid., x–xi.
22. Kubrick included Nabokov in the casting of *Lolita*.
23. Nabokov, *Screenplay*, xii.
24. Interview by Herbert Gold, *Paris Review*, 1967, reprinted in *Strong Opinions*, 91.
25. Kubrick, "Words," 14.
26. Nabokov, *Screenplay*, ix.
27. Ibid., ix–x.
28. Kubrick, "Words," 14.
29. Nabokov, *Screenplay*, xii.
30. Ibid., xiii.
31. David Hughes, *The Complete Kubrick* (London: Virgin, 2000), 89.
32. Ibid., 90.
33. Similar trouble with writing credits continued throughout Kubrick's career: for example, with Gustav Hasford, whose book Kubrick adapted to the film *Full Metal Jacket* (1987). See LoBrutto, *Kubrick Biography*, 458–90.
34. Nabokov, *Screenplay*, xiii.
35. Ibid.
36. Hughes, *Complete Kubrick*, 90.

37. Interview by Alvin Toffler, *Playboy*, 1964, reprinted in *Conversations With Vladimir Nabokov*, ed. Robert Golla, 70–89 (Jackson, MS: University of Mississippi, 2017), 72.
38. Gold, interview, 91.
39. Nabokov, *Screenplay*, xiii.
40. Gold, interview, 91.
41. Nabokov, *Screenplay*, xiii.
42. Cahill, interview, 199.
43. Interview by Michel Ciment, 1976, reprinted in *Kubrick: The Definitive Edition* (London: Faber & Faber, 2001), 177.
44. Nor was Clarke the only writer who saw his pecuniary remuneration as insufficient: Anthony Burgess is another example. See LoBrutto, *Kubrick Biography*, 367.
45. See Michael Benson, *Space Odyssey: Stanley Kubrick, Arthur C. Clarke, and the Making of a Masterpiece* (New York: Simon & Schuster, 2018).
46. Arthur C. Clarke, *Lost Worlds of 2001* (New York: New American Library, 1972), 31.
47. Ciment, interview, *Kubrick: The Definitive Edition*, 177.
48. LoBrutto, *Kubrick Biography*, 414.
49. Kubrick, "Words," 14.
50. Ciment, interview, 177.
51. Kubrick, "Words," 14.
52. The development of visual imagery, such as in *2001: A Space Odyssey*, was also formative and adaptive of Kubrick's writing. See Walker, *Kubrick Directs*, 246–47.
53. See Tony Magistrale, *Hollywood's Stephen King* (Basingstoke: Palgrave Macmillan, 2003), 198. Magistrale believes that King's negative opinion was also "hardened" due to continued provocation from fans and interviewers.
54. Quoted in Magistrale, *Hollywood*, 197.
55. Interview by Eric Norden, *Playboy*, 1983, reprinted in *Bare Bones: Conversations on Terror with Stephen King*, ed. Tim Underwood and Chuck Miller, 24–56 (New York: McGraw-Hill, 1988), 29.
56. With permission from the Kubrick estate and King, Kubrick's film and King's literary text unite in the adaptation of *Doctor Sleep* (2019), based on King's sequel to *The Shining*.
57. Jenkins, *Kubrick Adaptation*, 161.
58. Jarrell D. Wright, "Shades of Horror: Fidelity and Genre in Stanley Kubrick's *The Shining*," in *True to the Spirit: Film Adaptation and the Question of Fidelity*, ed. Colin MacCabe, Rick Warner, and Kathleen Murray, 173–94 (Oxford: Oxford University Press, 2011), 186.

REFERENCES

Benson, Michael. *Space Odyssey: Stanley Kubrick, Arthur C. Clarke, and the Making of a Masterpiece*. New York: Simon & Schuster, 2018.
Cahill, Tim. "The *Rolling Stone* Interview: Stanley Kubrick." In *Stanley Kubrick: Interviews*, edited by Gene D. Phillips, 189–204. Jackson, MS: University of Mississippi Press, 2001.
Castle, Alison, ed. *The Stanley Kubrick Archives*. Köln: Taschen, 2016.
Ciment, Michel. *Kubrick: The Definitive Edition*. London: Faber & Faber, 2001.
Clarke, Arthur C. *Lost Worlds of 2001*. New York: New American Library, 1972.
Elliott, Kamilla. *Rethinking the Novel/Film Debate*. Cambridge: Cambridge University Press, 2003.
Gelmis, Joseph. "The Film Director as Superstar: Stanley Kubrick." In *Stanley Kubrick: Interviews*, edited by Gene D. Phillips, 80–104. Jackson, MS: University of Mississippi Press, 2001.
Gold, Herbert. "The Art of Fiction XL: Vladimir Nabokov, An Interview." In *Strong Opinions*, Vladimir Nabokov, 80–92. New York: McGraw Hill, 1973.
Hughes, David. *The Complete Kubrick*. London: Virgin, 2000.
Jenkins, Greg. *Stanley Kubrick and the Art of Adaptation: Three Novels, Three Films*. Jefferson, NC: McFarland Press, 1997.

Kubrick, Stanley. "Words and Movies." *Sight and Sound* 30, no. 1 (Winter 1960): 14.
Leitch, Thomas. *Film Adaptation and its Discontents: From* Gone with the Wind *to* The Passion of the Christ. Baltimore, MD: Johns Hopkins University Press, 2009.
LoBrutto, Vincent. *Stanley Kubrick: A Biography*. London: Faber & Faber, 1998.
Magistrale, Tony. *Hollywood's Stephen King*. Basingstoke: Palgrave Macmillan, 2003.
Nabokov, Vladimir. *Lolita: A Screenplay*. New York: Vintage Books, 1997.
Norden, Eric. "*Playboy* Interview: Stephen King." In *Bare Bones: Conversations on Terror with Stephen King*, edited by Tim Underwood and Chuck Miller, 24–56. New York: McGraw-Hill, 1988.
Pezzotta, Elisa. *Stanley Kubrick: Adapting the Sublime*. Jackson, MS: University of Mississippi Press, 2013.
Toffler, Alan. "*Playboy* Interview: Vladimir Nabokov." In *Conversations with Vladimir Nabokov*, edited by Robert Golla, 70–89. Jackson, MS: University of Mississippi Press, 2017.
Varela, Jay. "Conversation with Stanley Kubrick." In *The Stanley Kubrick Archives*, edited by Alison Castle, 166–71. Köln: Taschen, 2016.
Walker, Alexander. *Stanley Kubrick Directs*. London: Abacus, 1973.
Wright, Jarrell D. "Shades of Horror: Fidelity and Genre in Stanley Kubrick's *The Shining*." In *True to the Spirit: Film Adaptation and the Question of Fidelity*, edited by Colin MacCabe, Rick Warner, and Kathleen Murray, 173–94. Oxford: Oxford University Press, 2011.
Zanotti, Serenella. "Auteur Dubbing: Translation, Performance and Authorial Control in the Dubbed Versions of Stanley Kubrick's Films." In *Reassessing Dubbing: Historical Approaches and Current Trends*, edited by Irene Ranzato and Serenella Zanotti, 79–102. Amsterdam: John Benjamins Publishing, 2019.

Chapter Fifteen

"May I Have the Password?"

Heterotopic Space in Eyes Wide Shut

Carl Sweeney

The interplay between space and sexual activity is integral to Stanley Kubrick's *Eyes Wide Shut* (1999). Narratively, the film focuses on Dr. Bill Harford (Tom Cruise), who is deeply affected when his wife Alice (Nicole Kidman) reveals her erotic fantasies about committing adultery. Alice's confession prompts Bill to undertake a bizarre odyssey into the Manhattan night. Plagued by intrusive thoughts about his wife and another man, Bill indulges in uncharacteristic behavior that is underpinned by a key spatial dynamic. He departs from the settled routines of his everyday life to journey to unfamiliar locations that are closely associated with illicit sex, danger, and masculine control over women. Most notably, this includes a secluded country house where Bill attends a secretive masked orgy without permission, being fortunate to escape unscathed.

Kubrick's film relocates the narrative of Arthur Schnitzler's novella *Dream Story* (1926) from early-twentieth-century Vienna to 1990s New York. For Thorsten Botz-Bornstein, this change to the novella serves to subordinate real space to drama.[1] He states that whereas Vienna has a specific spatial quality that lets it appear as a dream culture, the film does not achieve the same effect, claiming that "[w]hat matters for Kubrick is not the artistic elaboration of space."[2] Despite this assertion, the utilization of key settings in *Eyes Wide Shut* is consistent with an existing consideration of practical measures of separation, namely Michel Foucault's conception of heterotopic space.[3] To a greater or lesser extent, important narrative settings align with this theory, their depiction forming a pivotal aspect of the associations the film draws between space and masculine sexual dominance.

Unsurprisingly, Kubrick's representation of sexuality has attracted substantial attention from critics and commentators, proving to be a polarizing element. On initial release, the film's handling of carnality was often said to be badly dated. For instance, Stephen Hunter observed that it "feels creaky, ancient, hopelessly out of touch, infatuated with the hot taboos of [Kubrick's] youth and unable to connect with that twisty thing contemporary sexuality has become."[4] Similarly, Rod Dreher described the film as "a sex-themed movie made by someone who hadn't left the house in 30 years."[5] The extent to which the film is outmoded remains a point of contention, with Lila Shapiro recently arguing that not only were contemporaneous reviewers wide of the mark, but that "it's timely now, and as sad as it is to say this about the world, it may well be timely forever."[6] Likewise, Hannah McGill observes that, in the aftermath of scandals including the exposure of abuse in the Catholic Church, "the suggestion that sex between individuals can be covert, ritualistic and linked to fiscal power has a certain renewed credibility."[7] Indeed, McGill's reference to the clandestine nature of sex in the film is pertinent, because excesses of male sexuality in *Eyes Wide Shut* are often cloaked by calculated spatial divisions.

If the film is alternately regarded by critics as old-fashioned, everlasting, or ahead of its time, then comparable differences are also reflected in scholarly approaches. For instance, where many reviewers found the film's treatment of sexuality antiquated, Celestino Deleyto argues that "the movie attempts to summarize a whole century of sexual discourses, narrativizing and highlighting the most important cultural developments in the field in the twentieth century."[8] Meanwhile, Sidney Eve Matrix discusses the film as an example of cinematic folklore with a distinct intertextual relationship to fairy tale storytelling. She describes the manner in which Kubrick, possibly unwittingly, reshapes classic structures and motifs to tell a story that is "modernized, yet timeless."[9] Specifically, Matrix notes that *Eyes Wide Shut* follows a common quest pattern involving "a separation (a call to adventure, a threshold crossing into an otherworldly realm), an initiation (a ritual or test, resulting in a behavioral transformation), and the hero's return (a reincorporation into society)."[10] In Matrix's reading of the film, Bill's nighttime expeditions represent "a journey that is both literal and psychological"[11] and "a crucial liminal and transitory experience."[12]

Whereas Matrix focuses on narrative details, this chapter foregrounds the territorial aspects of Bill's travels to demonstrate that Kubrick's methods of ordering the film's locations are significant. Because of its focus on the interrelationship of spatiality and human activity, Foucault's conception of heterotopic space is relevant to this argument. He contends that, while the nineteenth century was defined by an obsession with history, the twentieth became characterized by anxieties about space.[13] Foucault posits that, spatially, "our lives are still ruled by a certain number of unrelenting opposites,"[14] such as sites of work and of pleasure. He analyzes those locations "which are endowed with the curious property of being in relation with all the others, but in such a way as to suspend, neutralize or invert the set of relationships designed, reflected or mirrored by themselves,"[15] designating such sites as heterotopias. According to Foucault, whereas utopias are fictional sites representing "society itself brought to perfection,"[16] heterotopias function as practically realized utopias that challenge or replace arrangements found elsewhere. Foucault suggests a series of principles that govern such spaces. The first tenet relates to the ubiquity of such sites, as "there is probably not a single culture in the world that is not made up of heterotopias. It is a constant feature of all human groups."[17] The other rules he puts forward are applied in this chapter to pertinent locations in *Eyes Wide Shut*.

Robin Rymarczuk and Maarten Derksen suggest that Foucault's ideas can be employed too liberally, stating that heterotopic space "is a concept that is easily abused."[18] If this is so, it raises the question about the justification for utilizing this theory in connection with Kubrick's film. However, analyzing three locations in particular through Foucault's prism illuminates the extent to which the manipulation of spatial dynamics is an important component of Bill's experiences. These are, respectively, the lavish home where Victor Ziegler (Sydney Pollack) hosts a Christmas party, the apartment occupied by Domino (Vinessa Shaw) and the Somerton house where the masked orgy takes place.[19] In each of these places, contrasts with more regular locations can be observed that align with the patterns of separation Foucault describes, these differences augmenting the film's presentation of entrenched, yet often disguised, power structures.

Before turning to these sites, it is necessary to briefly discuss *Eyes Wide Shut*'s more regular settings. As noted, a division should exist between heterotopias and other spaces. Foucault states that such separations are taken for granted, including "the contrast between public and private space, family and social space, cultural and utilitarian space."[20] In the film, Kubrick's approach to the everyday interior spaces the Harfords inhabit is in keeping with this, as he emphasizes the typicality of their surroundings in a way that varies with the presentation of other locations. For instance, at various points the director presents aspects of their mundane daily routines, such as Bill attending to his patients at work and Alice taking care of their daughter Helena (Madison Eginton). Meanwhile, in the first sequence of the film, set in the couple's apartment as they prepare to attend a party, Michel Chion notes that everything "is done to ensure that a western audience will recognize elements of their own daily lives in what happens on screen; at least this applies to a European or American audience who are not too impoverished."[21] For instance, Bill cannot immediately find his wallet, and Helena wants to stay up late to watch television. An important spatial distinction is also evident here, as Bill walks into the bathroom at one point while Alice is sitting on the toilet. His presence during this moment suggests an unceremonious lack of boundaries between the pair, in a manner that contrasts starkly with the film's later emphasis on spatially determined rituals.

Also germane to the dichotomy between heterotopias and other spaces is Kubrick's broader presentation of Manhattan's public spaces. Whereas heterotopias, if maintained correctly, should remain stable, other spaces are typically "disordered, ill-conceived and in a sketchy state,"[22] the French philosopher affirms. In *Eyes Wide Shut*, the unruly nature of the streets of New York becomes apparent when Bill is verbally abused by a group of homophobic youths, with one of the group pushing him into a parked car. Notably, the appearance of New York's public spaces in the film represents a fusion of scenes shot on sets built in England with establishing shots of real locations. While Chion claims that the displays of genuine sites are significant because "they relocate everything that is happening in the continual flow of life,"[23] the studio-shot scenes may seem uncanny to the viewer because of a lack of verisimilitude. Taken together, then, the combination of artificially created New York streets with authentic locations contributes to a thematically productive tension in the film between reality and fantasy. Nevertheless, the demarcations between regular spaces and heterotopias remain in keeping with the spatial norms Foucault identifies.

An area of interest that is pertinent to most spaces featured is the narrative occurring in the period prior to Christmas. To an extent, this is revealing of the dichotomy between timelessness and cultural specificity at the heart of the film. On the one hand, an array of decorative lights is displayed throughout *Eyes Wide Shut*, in a manner that supplements the narrative's fantastical, fairy tale associations. On the other, Chion argues that the Advent setting has a particular late-twentieth-century resonance, as it "enables the film to reveal a society that has 'forgotten' or abandoned the meaning of the religious festivals that occur at regular intervals in its calendar. Christmas has become simply an opportunity to host magnificent parties and give presents to children."[24] In terms of the film's spatialities, Christmas displays are in evidence in both heterotopic spaces and everyday ones. The exception to this is the Somerton house, where the absence of decorations is one facet that contributes to the site's unique status within the film. Furthermore, the elaborate rituals conducted at that location throw the halfhearted adoption of religious practices elsewhere in the film into sharp relief.

The approach of Christmas provides the pretext for a party hosted by Ziegler, one of Bill's patients. Ziegler is a notable character, whom Chion describes as belonging to "the family of provocative, shocking and libidinous father figures"[25] found in Kubrick's filmography. Moreover, he is a figure with no equivalent in Schnitzler's novella. The depiction of the party also marks a significant departure from the source material, in which the corresponding event takes place before the narrative begins, being referred to in the past tense. By visualizing this extravagant setting, Kubrick therefore foregrounds a pivotal heterotopia in a manner that establishes spatial patterns the film will repeat.

This site can be considered a heterotopia for several reasons. For one, Rymarczuk and Derksen refer to the power of these sites to combine a variety of different spaces within a single place as "the defining character of heterotopias."[26] This is salient with regard to Ziegler's home, which comprises various arresting sites including a ballroom, a billiards room, and a sculpture gallery.[27] Here, the principle that heterotopias are in opposition to other aspects of society relates to social status, as Ziegler's lavish home is of a much higher order than the Harfords' living quarters. Furthermore, the obvious exclusivity of the black-tie occasion aligns with the notion that one can only enter certain heterotopias by invitation.[28] Notably, Bill and Alice do not seem fully part of this world, their comments revealing that they do not know the other guests and that their attendance is an uncommon perk associated with Bill's job.

The presentation of the film's heterotopias varies depending on the film's narrative concerns. In this sequence, the stylistic choices made strengthen the heterotopia's dazzling effect. Ziegler and his wife greet the couple in a vast hall, as elegant swing music, emanating from a band playing within, is heard on the soundtrack. The opulence of the room is striking, with an enormous Christmas tree and a large curved staircase visible at the back of the frame. The Harfords proceed into the house, with a slow dissolve leading to a scene in a ballroom. In fact, this type of transition, which connotes stylishness, is employed several times during the sequence. In a wide shot, the ballroom is revealed to be festooned with bright lights, while a large chandelier occupies the center of the frame and the prevailing sense of glamour is reinforced by the smart attire of all the partygoers. As the couple dances, the camera circles them, the gracefulness of this movement contributing to the production of a sense of marvel that is in keeping with the fairy tale aspects of the film described above.

A less attractive component of the heterotopia becomes apparent when Bill is summoned upstairs to attend to a woman, Mandy (Julienne Davis), who has fallen unconscious after taking an overdose of drugs while consorting with Ziegler. Ari Ofengenden alludes to a spatial dynamic to Ziegler's acts, for "his sexual practices, although partly hidden from society, are part of the status quo. His sexual actions do not destabilize or threaten society: they take place on a top floor but at the same time they are an essential part of the 'use and discard' character that is the essence of patriarchal capitalism."[29] Certainly, Ziegler's illicit activity, conducted during a busy party in his own home while his wife is on the premises, aligns with Foucault's notion that some heterotopias can "conceal curious exclusions,"[30] providing the first example of heterotopic space giving cover for secretive abuses of masculine power.

This sequence is illustrative of Kubrick's approach to space in *Eyes Wide Shut* in several ways. Significantly, the emphasis on Ziegler's infidelity establishes the link, seen elsewhere, between heterotopic spaces and illicit sex. Despite Mandy's overdose, Ziegler's party apparently passes without his behavior becoming public, this being the first instance in the film where excesses of patriarchal authority are associated with heterotopian locations, with the negative repercussions falling most heavily on female characters. Meanwhile, though *Eyes Wide Shut* has been discussed as a timeless film, disorder often intrudes on these spaces in a manner associated with the contemporary world. Here, for instance, Mandy's overdose is caused by a mix of drugs known as a speedball, a combination of cocaine and heroin that "didn't take off with full vigor until the late 1970s and early 1980s."[31] Bill's position is also brought into focus at Ziegler's home, this being the first site in which he assumes an outsider status in ways that relate to Foucault's principles. Foucault observes that types of heterotopia where "one thinks one has entered and, by the sole fact of entering, one is excluded"[32] have largely vanished from society. As an example, he cites South American farm buildings, where "the rooms were arranged in such a way that anyone who went in there could never reach to the heart of the family: more than ever a passing visitor, never a true guest."[33] This latter part describes Bill's predicament in these spaces well.

These patterns recur, albeit in a rather different context, when Bill meets a prostitute, Domino, who invites him into her home. In Foucault's description of the main types of heterotopia, he discusses the heterotopia of crisis, "reserved for the individual who finds himself in a state of crisis with respect to the society or the environment in which he lives."[34] Foucault cites boarding schools where adolescents first manifest signs of sexuality as an example, also noting that this type of site appears to be disappearing from Western society. Domino's apartment, though, can be considered as this type of heterotopia, as it is a place Bill goes to after his relationship is placed in difficulty by his wife's confession about her fantasies of adultery. However, the space proves imperfect and Bill's visit there does not resolve his state of crisis. Nevertheless, the unsatisfactory nature of the site does not preclude consideration of it as a heterotopia, because Foucault situates these locations as the product of human activity, as opposed to the perfection offered by unreal utopias. Therefore, the potential for unconvincing productions of such spaces exists. In the case of Domino's apartment, this manifests in a slippage whereby some of Foucault's principles are not fully maintained. Despite this, distinctions between this location and more regular ones are still evident.

This sequence occurs after the aforementioned scene when Bill is assaulted on the street, the contrast between the disorder outside and the stability offered in the apartment emphasized by Domino in remarks that suggest she can offer a more controlled space. "It's a lot nicer in there than it is out here," she tells him. She further emphasizes how secure Bill will be if he goes inside: "Listen, no one will bother us." Bill decides to enter with her. However, although a heterotopic site should be well arranged,[35] Domino's apartment instead appears cluttered and messy, with stains visible on the wall above the cooker. Compared to Ziegler's house, then, this setting represents a visually unappealing space.

Instead of effacing Bill's outsider status, though, the difference between the two spaces reframes it. Whereas the Harfords appeared as interlopers in the imposing surroundings at Ziegler's party, here the cramped living quarters contrast with the more spacious interiors found at their home. Despite enjoying a higher social status than Domino, Bill's inquiries about paying for sex are halting, which suggests he is unpracticed at such encounters and not used to being transgressive. This exchange is relevant because Foucault states that one can only pass through a heterotopia "by special permission and after one has completed a certain number of gestures."[36] Ordinarily, conducting the acts required to navigate a heterotopia would be straightforward, but this discussion in the apartment begins awkwardly. This contrasts markedly with the scenes at Ziegler's house, a difference further augmented by the scene's visual expression. Whereas the camera movement was fluid in the earlier heterotopia, here the camera is held in a static two-shot during Bill and Domino's negotiation, the inertness of the shot reflecting Bill's hesitancy.

Despite the apartment not being an alluring site for a heterotopia, Domino attempts to establish Foucauldian norms in a manner that temporarily remedies this. Having settled on a price, she assures Bill that she does not keep track of the time. This promise is in keeping with the manner in which heterotopias operate. For the most part, Foucault notes, such sites are linked "to bits and pieces of time,"[37] entering "fully into function when men find themselves in a sort of total breach of their traditional time."[38] When Domino and Bill kiss, the setting takes on a different visual quality, as an extended close-up of the pair on the bed conceals their broader surroundings. This, combined with the diegetic jazz music emanating from a stereo, serves to briefly imbue the setting with a tasteful feel. Before they can go any further, Bill's mobile phone rings, his wife calling to enquire how long it will be until he returns home. Following the interruption, Bill opts not to have sex with Domino. The disruption of the call represents another example of the contemporary world disrupting taboo sexual behavior in a heterotopia. Another such example occurs later in the film, when it is revealed that Domino has been diagnosed with HIV, a virus identified in the late twentieth century. She therefore represents another physically compromised female character to be closely associated with a space of covert masculine sexuality.

A central tenet of Foucault's concept is the otherness of heterotopic places that challenge other societal arrangements. He gives the example of a mirror, ostensibly a utopia because a reflection represents "a place without a place,"[39] but functioning as a heterotopia because "it really exists and has a kind of come-back effect on the place that [it occupies]."[40] Or, as Rymarczuk and Derksen put it, "other spaces enter into relationships with their surroundings to constitute peculiar spaces with attributes entirely their own."[41] Of all the settings in *Eyes Wide Shut*, this is most pertinent to the Somerton house, where Bill attends a masked gathering without permission, an act that has significant narrative repercussions. At first, the house is differentiated from the film's other settings in a fairly conventional way, as it is situated in a secluded wooded area outside the city. Heterotopias "always presuppose a system of opening and closing that isolates them and makes them penetrable at one and the same time,"[42] the Somerton house being not only found in a remote space, but also guarded by men who will only admit appropriately dressed guests who provide a password.

If the unusual codes of admittance immediately mark out this site as unconventional in comparison to wider society, the extent of the Somerton house's uncommonness becomes clearer when Bill enters a large hall where a ritual is under way. He witnesses a red-cloaked figure presiding over an elaborate ceremony while wielding a staff and an incense burner. During the service, a number of women disrobe, the camera circling them in a manner that recalls the ballroom dancing scenes earlier in the film. The similarity of the camera movements suggests a parallel between this location and Ziegler's house. Given the narrative details that subsequently emerge, and that both spaces are dedicated to ornate formalities, this correspondence is fitting. However, it is not exact. Whereas in the earlier setting the camera movement was one facet of a visual approach tailored to generate wonder, here it combines with the changed narrative circumstances and the unusual costumes to augment the strangeness of proceedings. So, too, does the ominous soundtrack, which features Romanian priests singing backward.[43]

The association between the Somerton house and aberrant sexuality, first apparent in the ritual, becomes plainer still when Bill passes through rooms where people have sex while being watched by others. Foucault refers to American motels as a heterotopia associated with illicit sex, where this type of activity "is totally protected and totally concealed at one and the same time, set apart and yet not under an open sky."[44] The Somerton house is another such location. Compared to Ziegler's house, this heterotopia stands as an unmistakable display of patriarchal power. Whereas in the earlier location, the taboo activity was effectively concealed from the other partygoers, here the male attendees appear united by a common purpose. Meanwhile, given the contextual information provided by the film, some or all of the women can be assumed to have been hired for the occasion.[45]

During the orgy scenes, Chion states, "we seem to be outside time, if not outside space, where anonymous and collective coitus, from which any notion of pleasure is strangely absent, seems to be creating new lives."[46] This in itself is a somewhat Foucauldian suggestion, because a heterotopia represents "a sort of place that lies outside all places and yet is actually localizable."[47] Although they really exist, heterotopias can also seem akin to "an unreal space that opens up potentially beyond its surface."[48] In relation to the ethereal qualities of the masked gathering, this is congruent with Foucault's statement that we live in a space "that may even be pervaded with a spectral aura."[49] Certainly, commentary about the Somerton house scenes often makes reference to their otherworldliness in a way that reflects this. For instance, Thomas Hobbs discusses the unsettling music, claiming that it transports the viewer "somewhere that sits between grandiose and hellish."[50]

Nonetheless, the site's transportive capacities are only figurative, because heterotopias are by definition rooted in reality. The Somerton house may appear as an otherworldly location in some respects, but Bill's passage through it is troubled by actual concerns, namely his incomplete knowledge about the house's customs. The first indication that Bill's outsider status has been noted comes during the ritual, when two people watching from a balcony stare directly at him. Later, a woman tells him he does not belong to this location, warning him he is in danger. Evidently, despite attempting to observe the customs of this heterotopia, something has marked Bill out as a trespasser. This is eventually exposed when he is led back to the hall where he witnessed the earlier ritual, where the red-cloaked figure summons him to the center of the room. Kubrick's arrangement of this scene generates a palpable sense that Bill is at risk, representing another example of his varied approach to depicting the unique characteristics of each heterotopia. Onlookers clad in black all turn toward him, the gravity of this occasion suggested by six closer shots of figures looking directly at the camera. The exaggerated expressions on their masks appear foreboding, while the sense of menace is heightened by the unsettling piano music.[51] Bill is asked for another password, which he does not know, finding himself in a situation where the limits of his knowledge about the heterotopia's system of access have been exposed. Though his falsified relationship to this space has put him in danger, Bill is released without physical harm after a woman offers to take his place in an apparent form of sacrifice. The woman, later revealed to be Mandy, subsequently dies in suspicious circumstances, these events providing the most potent example of the link between heterotopic space, patriarchal dominance, and imperiled femininity.

Foucault states, with regard to space, that "it remains to be seen whether we have achieved its desanctification in practice,"[52] yet the sacredness of each heterotopia in Kubrick's film is, to some extent, dispelled by modern factors. Admittedly, the ritualistic events inside the Somerton house are completely devoid of present-day trappings. As previously noted, for instance, this is the only setting in the film that does not exhibit any signs of a contemporary Christmas celebration. However, when Bill returns to the residence the following day he is unnerved by the surveillance system in operation at the gates, CCTV being a comparatively recent innovation. While admittedly limited to the exterior of the building, this weakens the sense that the Somerton house represents a space not bound to the contemporary world.

If the opposites inherent in Foucault's concept "are still actuated by a veiled sacredness,"[53] then a further intervention by Ziegler also seems intended to demystify some aspects of the events at the Somerton house, although this remains ambiguous. When Ziegler summons Bill to his home, he discloses that he was at the masked gathering, some aspects of Bill's passage through the heterotopia now taking on a new light. Earlier, it was unclear why Bill's presence was so alarming to the other guests, but Ziegler points out the discrepant factors that made him stand out, including his arriving in a taxi while the other guests mostly traveled by limousine. Furthermore, he reveals that Bill was tricked when he was asked for the second password, as there was no second password to give. Ziegler also claims that Mandy's intervention to save Bill was part of an act, and that her death was caused by her drug habit rather than murder. Taken at face value, Ziegler's remarks seem to reveal that events at the Somerton house were arranged, at least partly, to "perform the task of creating a space of illusion,"[54] as occurs in some heterotopias. Though the veracity of his account, and the extent to which Bill believes him, is impossible to establish, the overall impression that the Somerton house represents a threatening site of masculine supremacy remains unchallenged.

After Bill eventually tells Alice about what has happened to him, the couple takes Helena Christmas shopping in an attempt to maintain a sense of normality. In the film's final scene, they talk in a toy store, with Alice striking a hopeful tone at one point: "Maybe I think we should be grateful. Grateful . . . that we've managed to survive through all of our . . . adventures . . . whether they were real . . . or only a dream." Her remark is in keeping with the dichotomies identified in other readings of the film, which foreground its unreal tone. For instance, Chion describes *Eyes Wide Shut* as "a 'magical' film that transports us beyond time,"[55] while Stephanie Marriott states that "the primacy of dreams and fantasies in this text [puts] into question where reality is situated."[56] However, a consequence of the focus on the film's bizarre qualities is that its tangible spatial characteristics have been under-discussed.

Though the film exhibits a friction between realism and fantasy, the compatibility of important narrative settings with the concept of heterotopic space complicates Botz-Bornstein's suggestion that space in *Eyes Wide Shut* is deterritorialized. While a series of commonalities emerges between the sites, a significant difference can be noted. This is related to Foucault's description of the two main types of heterotopia. As noted, one of Foucault's categories is the heterotopia of crisis, which describes Domino's apartment. Foucault's other category is the heterotopia of deviance, which are sites "occupied by individuals whose behavior deviates from the current average or standard."[57] Ziegler's home and the Somerton house are examples of this. In the former case, this applies in a more limited context, as the trappings of polite society obscure the extent of Ziegler's aberrant behavior. However, the Somerton house, a site of ritualistic sex that stands apart from the conventions of normal civilization, is an unfettered case of this type of location. Bill manages to extricate himself from this site, but the full repercussions of his actions remain unclear at the film's end.

Heterotopias have, "in relation to the rest of space, a function that takes place between two opposite poles,"[58] this being reflected in the contrasts established between Bill's normal life and the odyssey he undertakes following Alice's confession. Although the narrative significance of the settings considered varies, the spatial principles of practically realized utopias are shown to be susceptible to disruption. The impression that emerges from Bill's passage through these sites is that heterotopic spaces contribute to a widespread, usually concealed, system of patriarchal injustice. Read in this way, the utilization of space becomes an important element of *Eyes Wide Shut*'s contemporary relevance.

NOTES

1. Thorsten Botz-Bornstein, "From 'Ethno-Dream' to Hollywood: Schnitzler's *Traumnovelle*, Kubrick's *Eyes Wide Shut* and the Problem of 'Deterritorialisation,'" *Consciousness, Literature and the Arts* 2, no. 2 (August 2007), http://www.dmd27.org/botz.html (accessed November 3, 2019).

2. Ibid.

3. Michel Foucault, "Of Other Spaces: Utopias and Heterotopias," in *Rethinking Architecture: A Reader in Cultural Theory*, ed. Neil Leach (London: Routledge, 1997), 350–56.

4. Stephen Hunter, "Kubrick's Sleepy 'Eyes Wide Shut,'" July 16, 1999, https://www.washingtonpost.com/wp-srv/style/longterm/movies/videos/eyeswideshuthunter.htm (accessed December 8, 2019).

5. Rod Dreher, "Eyes Glaze Over: Softcore Finale Gets Just **1/2," July 16, 1999, https://nypost.com/1999/07/16/eyes-glaze-over-softcore-finale-gets-just-12/ (accessed November 5, 2019).

6. Lila Shapiro, "What I Learned after Watching *Eyes Wide Shut* 100 Times," July 1, 2019, https://www.vulture.com/2019/07/what-i-learned-after-watching-eyes-wide-shut-100-times.html (accessed November 5, 2019).

7. Hannah McGill, "Eyes of the Beholder," *Sight and Sound* 29, no. 12 (December 2019): 30.

8. Celestino Deleyto, "1999, A Closet Odyssey: Sexual Discourses in *Eyes Wide Shut*," *Atlantis* 28, no. 1 (June 2006), 30.

9. Sidney Eve Matrix, "A Secret Midnight Ball and a Magic Cloak of Invisibility," in *Fairy Tale Films: Visions of Ambiguity*, ed. Pauline Greenhill and Sidney Eve Matrix, 178–97 (Logan, UT: Utah State University Press, 2010), 196.

10. Ibid., 194.
11. Ibid., 181.
12. Ibid., 194.
13. Foucault, "Of Other Spaces," 350.
14. Ibid., 351.
15. Ibid., 352.
16. Ibid.
17. Ibid., 353.
18. Robin Rymarczuk and Maarten Derksen, "Different Spaces: Exploring Facebook as Heterotopia," *First Monday* 19, no. 6 (June 2014), http://firstmonday.org/ojs/index.php/fm/article/view/5006/4091 (accessed December 8, 2019).
19. The Rainbow costume shop, where the owner appears to condone the abuse of his underage daughter, fits this paradigm too.
20. Foucault, "Of Other Spaces," 351.
21. Michel Chion, *Eyes Wide Shut* (London: BFI Publishing, 2002), 43.
22. Foucault, "Of Other Spaces," 356.
23. Chion, *Eyes Wide Shut*, 44.
24. Ibid., 58.
25. Ibid., 21.
26. Rymarczuk and Derksen, "Different Spaces: Exploring Facebook as Heterotopia."
27. This latter site is not seen onscreen, but is referred to in dialogue by Sandor Szavost (Sky Dumont).
28. Foucault, "Of Other Spaces," 355.
29. Ari Ofengenden, "Agency, Desire, and Power in Schnitzler's *Dream Novel* and Kubrick's Adaptation *Eyes Wide Shut*," *CLCWeb: Comparative Literature and Culture* 17, no. 2 (June 2015), https://doi.org/10.7771/1481-4374.2465 (accessed November 3, 2019).
30. Foucault, "Of Other Spaces," 355.
31. Katie Serena, "Speedball: The Deadly Drug Cocktail That's Claimed Too Many Lives," June 27, 2018, https://allthatsinteresting.com/speedball-drugs (accessed November 3, 2019).
32. Foucault, "Of Other Spaces," 355.
33. Ibid.
34. Ibid., 353.
35. Ibid., 356.
36. Ibid., 355.
37. Ibid., 354.
38. Ibid. Arguably, Bill finds himself in a breach of traditional time in a broader sense following Alice's confession, albeit not always in heterotopic locations. However, of direct relevance here are his interactions in the spaces corresponding to Foucault's theory.
39. Ibid., 352.
40. Ibid.
41. Rymarczuk and Derksen, "Different Spaces: Exploring Facebook as Heterotopia."
42. Foucault, "Of Other Spaces," 355.
43. Thomas Hobbs, "How *Eyes Wide Shut*'s Uniquely Unsettling Score Was Made," October 30, 2018, https://www.dazeddigital.com/music/article/41996/1/eyes-wide-shut-stanley-kubrick-soundtrack-jocelyn-pook-interview (accessed November 3, 2019).
44. Foucault, "Of Other Spaces," 356.
45. In a later scene, for instance, Ziegler states that Mandy was a prostitute, though we do not learn about the backgrounds of the other women.
46. Chion, *Eyes Wide Shut*, 59.
47. Foucault, "Of Other Spaces," 352.
48. Ibid.
49. Ibid., 351.
50. Hobbs, "How *Eyes Wide Shut*'s Uniquely Unsettling Score Was Made."
51. This piece, by György Ligeti, is heard on a number of occasions during the film, always at times when Bill is particularly vulnerable.
52. Foucault, "Of Other Spaces," 351.

53. Ibid.
54. Ibid., 356.
55. Chion, *Eyes Wide Shut*, 60.
56. Stephanie Marriott, "Desire and Crisis: The Operation of Cinematic Masks in Stanley Kubrick's *Eyes Wide Shut*," *Lectora: Revista de Donesi Textualitat*, 11 (2005), 95.
57. Foucault, "Of Other Spaces," 353.
58. Ibid., 356.

REFERENCES

Botz-Bornstein, Thorsten. "From 'Ethno-Dream' to Hollywood: Schnitzler's *Traumnovelle*, Kubrick's *Eyes Wide Shut* and the Problem of 'Deterritorialisation.'" *Consciousness, Literature and the Arts* 2, no. 2 (August 2007). http://www.dmd27.org/botz.html.
Chion, Michel. *Eyes Wide Shut*. London: BFI Publishing, 2002.
Deleyto, Celestino. "1999, A Closet Odyssey: Sexual Discourses In *Eyes Wide Shut*." *Atlantis* 28, no. 1 (June 2006): 29–43.
Dreher, Rod. "Eyes Glaze Over: Softcore Finale Gets Just **1/2." *New York Post*, July 16, 1999. https://nypost.com/1999/07/16/eyes-glaze-over-softcore-finale-gets-just-12/.
Eyes Wide Shut. Directed by Stanley Kubrick. Los Angeles, CA: Warner Bros. Pictures, 1999.
Foucault, Michel. "Of Other Spaces: Utopias and Heterotopias." In *Rethinking Architecture: A Reader in Cultural Theory*, edited by Neil Leach, 350–56. London: Routledge, 1997.
Hobbs, Thomas. "How *Eyes Wide Shut*'s Uniquely Unsettling Score Was Made." *Dazed & Confused Magazine*, October 30, 2018. https://www.dazeddigital.com/music/article/41996/1/eyes-wide-shut-stanley-kubrick-soundtrack-jocelyn-pook-interview.
Hunter, Stephen. "Kubrick's Sleepy 'Eyes Wide Shut.'" *The Washington Post*, July 16, 1999. https://www.washingtonpost.com/wpsrv/style/longterm/movies/videos/eyeswideshuthunter.htm??noredirect=on.
Marriott, Stephanie. "Desire and Crisis: The Operation of Cinematic Masks in Stanley Kubrick's *Eyes Wide Shut*." *Lectora: Revista de Donesi Textualitat* 11 (2005): 93–104.
Matrix, Sidney Eve. "A Secret Midnight Ball and a Magic Cloak of Invisibility." In *Fairy Tale Films: Visions of Ambiguity*, edited by Pauline Greenhill and Sidney Eve Matrix, 178–97. Logan, UT: Utah State University Press, 2010.
McGill, Hannah. "Eyes of the Beholder." *Sight and Sound* 29, no. 12 (December 2019): 24–33.
Ofengenden, Ari. "Agency, Desire, and Power in Schnitzler's *Dream Novel* and Kubrick's Adaptation *Eyes Wide Shut*." *CLCWeb: Comparative Literature and Culture* 17, no. 2 (June 2015). https://doi.org/10.7771/1481-4374.2465.
Raphael, Frederic. "Introduction." In *Dream Story*, Arthur Schnitzler, v–xvii. London: Penguin Books, 1999.
Rymarczuk, Robin, and Maarten Derksen. "Different Spaces: Exploring Facebook as Heterotopia." *First Monday* 19, no. 6 (June 2014). http://firstmonday.org/ojs/index.php/fm/article/view/5006/4091.
Schnitzler, Arthur. *Dream Story*, 1926. London: Penguin Books, 1999.
Serena, Katie. "Speedball: The Deadly Drug Cocktail That's Claimed Too Many Lives." *All That's Interesting*, June 27, 2018. https://allthatsinteresting.com/speedball-drugs.
Shapiro, Lila. "What I Learned after Watching *Eyes Wide Shut* 100 Times." *Vulture*, July 01, 2019. https://www.vulture.com/2019/07/what-i-learned-after-watching-eyes-wide-shut-100-times.html.

Chapter Sixteen

The Spectacle of Time, (Slow) Motion, and Stillness in the Films of Stanley Kubrick

Paul Johnson

Cinematic spectacle and attractions, particularly in the modern cinema, frequently make use of special and visual effects (VFX) in fast-paced action scenes. Tom Gunning defines his "Cinema of Attractions" theory as one "that displays its visibility, willing to rupture a self-enclosed fictional world for a chance to solicit the attention of the spectator."[1] To wit, the films of Georges Méliès often made use of early VFX techniques in genre films such as *Le Voyage dans la Lune/A Trip to the Moon* (1902), to show the passage of the rocket into the moon's "face," alongside (for its time) lavish sets and production values. But even Louis Lumière's *L'Arroseur arrosé* (1895), which features the simple gag of someone fooling with a gardener's hose and causing him to get splashed with a jet of water show concepts of energy and vibrancy as instrumental.

Initially Stanley Kubrick's output might not seem comparable with those of his contemporaries and certainly more recent Hollywood genre productions. There is an important and palpable inclusion of effects work within *2001: A Space Odyssey* (1968), and *Spartacus* (1960) has a scale akin to Biblical and historical epics like *Ben-Hur* (William Wyler, 1959) and *The Ten Commandments* (Cecil B. DeMille, 1956). But other films in Kubrick's seemingly narrative-based oeuvre made little use of VFX and special effects that theorists see as conducive to attractions and spectacle, such as *The Shining* (1980) or *A Clockwork Orange* (1971). Even the effects in *2001* are discrete to others in post-classical Hollywood cinema. Geoff King notes, the spectacle within *2001* is "slow, contemplative,"[2] reflecting the Kubrickian atmosphere. Furthermore, though Kubrick's films move in genre circles, they do not obviously use the same techniques, technology, or methodology in implementing and exploiting their mise en scène to produce spectacle.

Comparing *2001* to *Star Wars: A New Hope* (George Lucas, 1977), King highlights differences in the essence of speed and dynamism. He records *Star Wars* as offering a brand of spectacle that is "hyperkinetic, flashy and bright."[3] *Beneath the Planet of the Apes* (Ted Post, 1970) uses prosthetic make-up throughout to create its simians as key empathetic characters, whereas *A Clockwork Orange* delights in a stripped-back dystopian diegesis. However, central to Kubrick's concept of spectacle and attractions is the combination of mise en scène to time and its manipulation. By reforming cinematic time a unique evocation of spectacle can be achieved, focusing our attention. This reflects Steve Neale's statement on spectacle, wherein "the narrative starts to freeze."[4] Sean Cubitt similarly and persuasively argues how the medium is built out of so many discrete images (individual frames, shots, scenes, etc.) that to pursue conceptions of unity and wholeness is "a wrench."[5] How then can it be argued that time is stable in a medium constructed in such a way? Later, in examining *The Wild Bunch* (Sam Peckinpah, 1969) Cubitt notes: "The past exists simultaneously with the present because the present is in the process of becoming legend,"[6] which signifies how time is conceptually always ever-changing, which anticipates the theories to be discussed.

What follows will demonstrate how Kubrick marshals visual elements that concentrate attention upon time to develop a spectacle of time. This chapter will focus on how Kubrick exploits visual imagery via tracking shots, slow motion, and freeze frames. Tom Gunning's archetypal writing on attractions will be used, alongside other writers' evocations and explorations to emphasize spectacle's ability to produce images "at which we might wish to stop and stare,"[7] without consistent recourse to VFX. This consideration will be illustrated via *2001*, *A Clockwork Orange*, *Barry Lyndon* (1975), and *The Shining* and more deliberate use of formal conventions in *The Killing* (1956), highlighting how temporal spectacle is relevant to the director's work. Furthermore, reference will also be made to writers considering Kubrick's use of time, the sublime, and cinema, and how the director's training and employ as a photojournalist helped establish these concepts.

In *The Killing*, Kubrick already develops a thought-provoking play with time. Philip Kuberski notes "Kubrick's films can race through time or reveal it in all its leaden glory,"[8] sometimes simultaneously. Simply put, *The Killing* is a crime picture about a group of hoodlums led by Johnny Clay (Sterling Hayden) who choose to steal the takings of a racetrack's counting room. But Kubrick develops the narrative by showing the heist from multiple perspectives (à la *Rashomon* [Akira Kurosawa, 1950]) to create something far from generic. The film shows how Kubrick begins to hold, reverse, and manipulate the temporal duration of the environments of the films he directed. We see the gangs's preparation in a routine fashion, building to the day itself with meetings and characterization that will enable payoffs later. Even here however we move backward, as Derek Jacobs outlines in his essay. Jacobs notes indeed how Johnny explains the heist's motivations at 7:00 p.m., but we are then told by the narrator the next scene takes place at 6:30 p.m.[9] Though the film has technically moved onward, as viewers, we have moved backward.

On central race day the spectator's experience of time is constantly fluid. We see each scene unfold, progressing forward incrementally. But each subsequent sequence unfolds in ways that show the narrative temporally moving forward, backward, and sometimes apparently remaining stationary. One scene shows Johnny beginning his day, announced by the narrator as being 7:00 a.m. But, according to the narrator, we see him reaching the airport at apparently the same time.[10] As the heist itself gets closer we experience similar temporal actions. For example, the shooting of the front-running horse by Nikki Arane (Timothy Carey) is established by the narrator stating when Nikki leaves his farm *and* as he arrives at the track. The shooting then follows and triggers the chaos that will hide the heist, spatially taking place out on the far side of the track, with the narrator noting Nikki's time of death. Importantly this is viewed by audiences sequentially *after* we see a corresponding moment that takes place simultaneously, but spatially elsewhere as Maurice Oboukhoff (Kola Kwariani) creates a fight to distract onlookers inside the betting hall. We do not get a time check from the film's narrator here but see shots of the racehorses being led to the start and a race commentator is heard to aid us. These shots and the commentary are similar to earlier scenes featuring Nikki. But although Nikki's scene takes place at essentially the same time as Maurice's, one is viewed and occurs sequentially before the other.

The racetrack commentary and the narrator are providing us with details that can be seen as obfuscating at least and as unreliable at best. As Jacobs notes, "Brilliantly, Kubrick does not always give us 'the right' answers—some of the repetition is false, and most of the points-of-view only see a slim portion of the overall plan."[11] However, this daring approach was not liked by everyone. LoBrutto relates that Sterling Hayden's agent, Bill Shiffren, felt the film would harm the star. He quotes Shiffren: "This movie is all mixed up. . . . What is all this business of back and forth, back and forth? Just when you get to the crux of the robbery, you cut."[12] But this intensifies the brilliance of the film's impact on audiences, and more importantly demonstrates how Kubrick began to interrogate time to generate spectacle. The so-called "mixing-up" becomes essential not just to the narrative but indicates how Kubrick uses time in distinct and stimulating ways. It is arguably, as Philip Kuberski notes, the repetition of the scenes that allow an "escape from time,"[13] which sets up the creation of another element of Kubrick's auteurism: the activation and flexibility of time.

At this nascent stage of his career, Kubrick makes more palpable references to time (rather than the poetic uses that would come) by using narration, editing, and camera work more formally. At multiple points throughout the film, a narrator (Art Gilmore) announces times for us that temporally anchor the characters and key us into the structure of the story, so spectators can readily understand the film. Its formalities also allowed Kubrick to move forward into further studio work. Although intertitles and narration would continue, Kubrick soon used imagery in more poetic, experimental, and overtly spectacular ways, while demonstrating greater play and manipulation of time.

Spectacle is described by Sturken as "something impressive and unusual, which thrilled because it looked like things never seen before or which deployed immense scale to dwarf its spectators."[14] Additionally Sturken asserts spectacle also becomes a tool to stupefy society using awe and mystification.[15] But even when sociopolitical nuances are reined in, these core aspects are key; they allow spectators to become lost and meandering within the environs they experience, and their spatiotemporal disposition can become similarly unsettled. A film that uses visuals to achieve an awe-inspiring atmosphere will arguably impact the viewer most perceptibly, along with music and sound effects (with dialogue also potentially a factor). These often connect to conceptions of cinematic attractions, including Gunning's, wherein the core argument revolves about showing and "supplying pleasure through an exciting spectacle."[16] As Gunning maintains, images are fused with time in attractions to great effect: "a cinematic manipulation (slow motion, reverse motion, substitution, multiple exposure) [that] provides the film's novelty,"[17] albeit within trick films in this account. Nonetheless these ideas can be extrapolated within Kubrick's work, most especially those in which he had overarching control of production (post-*Spartacus*).

There is arguably a deliberate slow pace to many of Kubrick's films that allows us to soak up the imagery and atmosphere. As Lloyd Gross writes "For Kubrick . . . time is infinitely malleable,"[18] and watching his films it is possible to become awestruck with the situations within. This can be seen in instances quite early within Kubrick's work, with temporally longer shots in *Spartacus*. During a climactic battle sequence, we languorously watch the opposing sides scrutinizing each other as the Romans move into position. Kubrick uses wide shots to show the scale of the army and the grandeur of the fighting. But this is preempted by shots before the conflict itself: of Spartacus's men as they look out, with each shot holding on them that facilitates a glimmering sense of foreboding. Wide shots show distant troops moving slowly and their pace, diminutive scale, and the long takes combine to develop a sense of nascent spectacle. This scene creates suspense, but as with other shots and sequences in films that follow, there is also a strong focus on looking and soliciting our attention. The spectacle developed here enables "the production of images at which we might wish to stop and stare."[19] Kubrick shows speed as indelibly connected to images and scenes, starting—albeit gently at this stage—to infer how slowness, stasis, and stillness enable spectacle to be concentrated and empowered.

Similarly, the earlier *Paths of Glory* (1956) uses a series of tracking shots to develop the visuals as spectacular attractions to be enhanced through slowness. One set of shots shows Colonel Dax (Kirk Douglas) walking through the trenches as he and his men prepare to advance over the top. The sequence uses shots that are combined to demonstrate a series of gazes. These include a set of tracking shots with the camera positioned ahead of Dax and point of view (POV) shots that show the soldiers looking intently and gravely back at the lens. The POV itself, alongside other shots, is stately in travel, illustrating how Kubrick takes his time to show the situation of the men and the landscape they inhabit in a solemn and imposing way. There is almost a pause in the soldiers' reactions to the explosions on the landscape above their heads, and the plumes of dirt hurled up and falling from explosions linger in the air. They fall by design, but the temporal deliberateness allows viewers' concentration to be drawn out and crystalized. A later POV of Dax moving through the trench into a fog-like shroud of dust and smoke hanging imperiously, like a veil blocking the light, operates similarly. The visual obstruction momentarily reduces our ability to locate ourselves in the landscape, and infers the loss of time the soldiers felt as such assaults occurred. In this scene we see time becoming drawn out, through the pace of the tracking shot, the gazes of the performers, their motion, and the results of the explosions. Most especially as we slowly enter the foggy atmosphere a fugue-like ambience pervades that obfuscates the view and time in spectacular ways.

The use of tracking shots and longer takes remained central to sequences and scenes in other Kubrick films, with *The Shining* being the most redolent of showing spectacular events. *The Shining* allowed Kubrick to make use of the highly mobile Steadicam device, which enables the camera to smoothly move around sets and locations. Unlike traditional dolly and track systems the camera is considerably more mobile, allowing movement in various directions that would otherwise be difficult or impossible. Kubrick uses the system across many scenes, but most obviously when following Danny (Danny Lloyd) on his tricycle through the Overlook hotel's corridors, when Danny and his mother Wendy (Shelley Duvall) explore the hotel's vast maze, and in the climax as Jack (Jack Nicholson) chases his son. LoBrutto notes Steadicam operator Garrett Brown managed to navigate the lobby set "with the grace of a dancer and the precision of an Air Force bomber pilot,"[20] inferring fluidity, unceasing movement, and impact.

Kubrick uses the Steadicam for sequences that stretch for some length, captivating the spectators' attention by providing a consistent fixed gaze for the viewer. In reference to this, Daniel Morgan's analysis of camera movement and point of view in *The Shining* charts how time, spectacle, and attractions operate within the film. Morgan notes the shots that track behind Danny are

> deeply unsettling—not just because of what we see, and the increasing aura of fear and dread that surrounds the family, but because of the nature of the camera's movement. It moves smoothly behind Danny but is never quite in sync; it falls back and then catches up; it hesitates briefly as it turns corners and then accelerates across more open spaces. The absence of perfect following suggests the presence of some kind of agency—a spirit, the hotel, etc.—that inhabits the position of the camera . . . implicitly promising malevolent actions.[21]

Morgan's observation that the camera is out of sync, falls back, and catches up, hesitating and then accelerating, recognizes Kubrick's use of tracking shots are staged against time, and how instrumental temporality is in fashioning his spectacle with the tracking shot. The gliding camera that captures Danny is considered by Morgan as a preternatural, rather than technological capturer, but perhaps both these aspects are conjoined: malevolence technologized. And this assists Kubrick in expressing facets of cinematic attractions. Gunning recounts how early cinema saw performers break the fourth wall of the fictional space, an aspect undertaken with "brio," in order to "solicit the attention of the spectator," and make contact with the audience.[22] Kubrick here uses the camera itself to break the fictional diegesis, allowing the lengthy duration of shots alongside the changes in speed that Morgan references to suspend time and increase our attention to focus on the imagery.

Like earlier sequences showing Danny swooshing through the hotel, captured through a wide distorting lens that adds a sense of supernatural otherness, further shots break the narrative and create a sense of temporal exhibitionism. A scene where we finally enter room 237 exemplifies this via a faux POV shot, using altered moments already observed. The scenes in question show Danny entering the room, before cutting to shots of Wendy hearing Jack having a nightmare and rushing to comfort him in the lobby. Danny then appears, bruised and stupefied shortly after, which causes Wendy to accuse Jack of abuse. Afterward, a lone Jack starts talking to himself and gesticulating as he walks to the empty lounge. At the bar he looks directly at the camera, smiling, saying "Hello Lloyd. Little slow tonight isn't it?" Finally Lloyd (Joe Turkel) the bartender, a manifestation of Jack's imagination or a ghost, provides a drink and talks. Here we are housed amidst attractions, breaking the fourth wall, with Nicholson's performance often staged in close-up shots that use highly exaggerated gestures and overt physicalized facial movements to convey his state. This is much the same as a comedian might gurn, or perhaps in Jack's walk where he thrashes his arms in anger (again addressing the camera that moves ahead of him), like an aggressive version of the dancing woman seen in *Annabelle Butterfly Dance* (William K. Dickson, 1894).

Wendy now rushes into the lounge, finding Jack alone. She tells him about a woman in 237 who has attacked Danny. We cut to Hallorann (Scatman Crothers) watching television, but he quickly starts to "shine" and observe the entrance shot from earlier—discernible as Danny's perspective due to the door handle's height being in line to that of a child's eyeline. A quick cut to Danny convulsing and we cut to the room, slowly advancing inside, creating a tense atmosphere as we are unsure of what is around the corner, beyond the doorway, and what is behind the hazy shower curtain. Fundamentally we are seeing what Danny saw, and as the camera does not cut away we are enveloped in the sinister forces of the room via the shot (as suggested by Morgan's reading of the camera's use). However, cutting to a reverse shot reveals it is in fact Jack and his perspective, and the idea of temporality becomes part of the attraction's implementation. The editing, which moves quite rapidly and changes our perspective, means we are no longer truly sure of our situation in diegetic time, who owns the POV and the subsequent viewpoint. We discover a naked woman as the shower curtain is drawn, who steps up from the bath and approaches Jack. Although we see his reaction shots—which turns from fear to lust—the camera does not cut away and the male gaze is more overtly generated. Though somewhat troubling due to Danny sharing this perspective, there is an attraction style energy generated by the continued lack of speed as we hold upon the female form. But the soundtrack that envelops the scene both interrogates and intensifies the sexualized nature of the gaze. A slow pulsating sound effect throbs, inferring the pulse rate of someone or something alongside Wendy Carlos and Richard Elkind's sinister electronic and similarly slow-speed score signaling what we are experiencing is different to initial indications. Time has been manipulated and altered to produce a slowed-down sequence of spectacular display and attractions. This is not a narrative moment, but a classic use of the attraction to create a moment of excitement and closely follow the cinema of attractions core constituents. Gunning's writing on attractions is a useful support for this; within he surmises energy is expended outward in creating the attraction (of movement and therefore time) to produce the attraction. Moreover, it develops the Eisensteinian principle of attractions: producing "sensual or psychological impact," through the thrill of the camera capturing and freezing our attention through its lens.[23]

In these instances, tracking shots gloriously showcase the ability to break through the narrative to capture and significantly hold our attention and use time flexibly to do so. Yet the Steadicam's stylistic electrification of the long take though very obviously spectacular is nothing compared to the more languid and effective deployment of simple tracking shots and long takes in *Barry Lyndon*. During *Lyndon* Kubrick loads his film with scenes that use actors and their performances, costumes and makeup, and settings to produce highly static painterly moments that evoke the characters' lives and their predicaments. LoBrutto points out that paintings and artists were used to inform the film's aesthetic, and how the locations for the houses "were museumlike and contained extensive collections."[24] The inference here begins to position *Lyndon* as fixed—composed akin to a painting by fine artists and featuring curated objects. In furtherance of this, Pauline Kael notes in her review that "it becomes apparent that we are to sit and admire the lingering tableaux, we feel trapped," and additionally Kubrick, "sets up his shots peerlessly, and can't let go of them."[25] Kael is generally negative about much of *Barry Lyndon*, as filmmaking that looks magnificent but that "obliterates any emotion."[26] From Kael's remarks the film is rendered as a veritable *objet d'art*, but not something to engage with. However, in numerous shots, particularly interior shots lit by golden candlelight, captured with fast zoom lenses, the images produced are rapturous and spectacular. The shots, using long takes and/or slow zoom-ins such as Lady Lyndon's (Marisa Berenson) introduction, demonstrate the film is not a narrative film per se, so much as a series of vignettes Kubrick has constructed, arguably reveling as a cinematic attraction. The scene in question is effectively a series of long takes between Barry (Ryan O'Neal) and Lady Lyndon as they gaze back and forth, with the golden lighting of the candles (burnished by studio lights) creating a sense of embalming those within. As such, it is surely a trope André Bazin would have endorsed in his writing on cinema.[27] Tracking shots, when they do occur, are slow-paced, but often audiences are left to watch the almost immobile actors, which Kael saw as furniture.[28] But, as Tom Huddlestone asserts, the use of the photography to hold the characters in situ is the film's greatest feat. He states *Barry Lyndon* "is uniquely, heart-stoppingly gorgeous. But there's much more to it: this is a story of identity, and the lack of it."[29] Huddlestone's more positive remarks reinforce what is clear, that Kubrick works the imagery as spectacle, that he wants to hold the objects (actors and otherwise), as well as audiences, in thrall.

With *2001* there is an increase in recognizable uses of spectacle. Impressive visual imagery of both live action and visual effects are combined in ways that arguably provide audiences something new, using scale to create grand impressions, awe, and astonishment. Though some critics, such as Pauline Kael, found the film dull, it is difficult not to see the imagery as extraordinary. Today, on even a cursory viewing, the sequences involving the spacecraft, their solidity, evincing believability, the scale of the sets along with the Star Gate trip, recall how spectacle amazes and attractions seek to freeze our attention.

Moreover, the ways in which Kubrick uses the imagery in line with time cultivates the notion of how spectacle and attractions can operate more forcibly. Perhaps most brilliantly is the crystallization of spectacle occurring in the jump cut between the bone thrown into the air by Moonwatcher (Daniel Richter) and the space station millions of years in the future. The initial shot of the bone following Moonwatcher's throw is in slow-motion. It rises upward, spinning gently and out of frame, before cutting to a shot as it falls. The jump cut occurs to show the space station, but motion has been removed: it hangs in space, with the camera moving toward it. Visual slowness and then removal of speed for perceived objects have taken over.

The conception of slowness modeled by Kubrick is underscored by Martin Seel in his account of the cinematic medium, where he notes that like theater and other arts cinema is spectacle, but unlike these "film as such leaps around," and moreover demonstrates "space in motion."[30] This enables cinema perhaps a greater ability, for though Seel notes some media share uses of imagery and space, Seel sees film as obeying its own laws.[31] And perhaps this jump shot highlights cinema's ability to move, flex, leap, and use its own laws than any other cinematic spectacle within the medium, and, in terms of leaping around, who better than Kubrick to use such details. To a degree previous films in Kubrick's output had used spectacular temporal flexibility, but now Kubrick starts to genuinely break the images free, playing with them in ways that are unfettered. With this shot Kubrick demonstrates how imagery and slow-moving time coalesce to provide something truly spectacular: the demonstration of moving millions of years forward, showing ceaseless evolution of technology and ability, while simultaneously also removing motion.

The shots following this, set to Johann Strauss's *Blue Danube*, continue to house spectacle enhanced through slowness showing the space station and other craft. Shadows produced from the sun play across structures showing solidity, weight, and the spectacular scale of the object. But the spectacular sense is further sharpened by the slow speed and the duration of the shot, allowing greater focus upon its contents. It is continued in interior shots of a passenger shuttle, where we focus on a ballpoint pen that descends slowly in the low gravity, and in a subsequent shot hangs in space before the lens. In each shot the camera slowly racks to focus on and off of the pen, initially moving from the seat that houses Heywood Floyd (William Sylvester) and his arm and then, in a subsequent shot, from the pen in the foreground to a flight attendant entering the cabin in the background. Throughout the shot, the pen slowly holds position, or pirouettes idly, echoing the space station the shuttle approaches.

The use of deliberate slow speed may be seen as uninvolving. But, although removing speed may instill these reactions for some, it is possible to see examination of imagery over longer periods of time as thought-provoking, contemplative, and conceptual. Seel also signifies how cinematic images create specific spaces into which spectators move. This hinges upon using concepts of *"image space"* which Seel says form a virtual arena, "processing" the areas they are watching.[32] Further to this Seel also highlights cinema's ability to use the camera and mise en scène in sculptural ways, noting films probe objects optically. He thus urges: "This is a space that can be explored only by seeing, hearing, and otherwise sensing."[33] Many shots in *2001* emphasize this wondrous sensuality, following Gunning and others' considerations of cinematic display and showing.

Scott Bukatman also discusses wondrous sensuality, foregrounding cinema's visual conditions as engaging audiences to create "immersive, overwhelming, and apparently immediate sensory experiences."[34] Much of Kubrick's work conjures such affects, but more often without the need for obvious special and visual effects. Notably *2001* uses models and matte paintings to create awe, but significantly various Kubrick films mentioned here collectively promote a sense of the sublime without VFX. Bukatman notes the technological spectacle of effects used recalls antecedent media, such as the trompe l'oeil, panoramas, and the mimesis of the natural world.[35] Bukatman's theories focus on science fiction as the de facto genre in which the sublime can operate, and his notation is that the genre therein creates "the boundless and infinite stuff of sublime experience [that] produces a sense of transcendence beyond human finitudes."[36]

The boundless and infinite are easy to see in *2001*'s Star Gate sequence, wherein we become transfixed for almost nine minutes at Dave Bowman's subjective POV of the Gate as it transfixes the spectator. Initially kaleidoscopic and "trippy" colors are used that constantly and quickly stream from an indistinguishable space somewhere out there, beyond our field of view. This suggests an infinite void that, due to its positioning, we as spectators also seem to pass through. The combination of haunting soundtrack and apparently never-ending deploy of colors and their arrangement at this point posit a sense of wonderment. But this is strengthened further in the next series of shots that are altogether slower in motion. The imagery then switches to bright, nebulous bodies that hang before us, move vaguely, and dissipate. Interspersed with quick momentary still shots of Bowman's reactions—a frozen panicked face and eyes that become huge before us in close-up—time and its effects become actively played with. Just as when Kubrick "messed up" the narrative order in *The Killing*, so too does he jumble and remove temporal distinctions. But such concepts can be extrapolated beyond this genre.

Other instances in Kubrick's canon are perhaps not as overwhelming, but the painterly compositions in *Barry Lyndon* arguably operate like scenes of embalmed time, recalling the wide paintings and panoramas of traditional sublime arts. Similarly, slow tracking shots in *A Clockwork Orange* hold us in situ and use time to create a sense of transcendence. Examples include the opening shot of the droogs in the Korova bar, and when Alex (Malcolm McDowell) wanders the corridors of a store. Correspondingly the lengthy takes in *Paths of Glory*, and wide-angle lenses alongside the gliding surreal Steadicam shots in *The Shining* create enveloping scenes of duration and awe. During these scenes we are mesmerized, caught in time, frozen to the spot in our seats in wonder, terror, and disconcertion; we feel excited, scared, and amazed. Often, we lose track of time, in terms of how long we have been watching the film, alongside where we are within the diegetic world and its history.

This idea of how time operates is also present in Philippe Mather's analysis of Kubrick's photojournalism at *Look* magazine. He notes the congruence of still and moving imagery, and how image and words within photography established the foundation of his films. Mather states: "The use of series photography, in particular, may be viewed as the aesthetic equivalent to a long take or camera movement," and designates this as a precursor for his consistent use of long takes.[37] Of course, Kubrick was no stranger to using the latter cinematic techniques and his film work is a natural continuation and extension of the techniques used to capture subjects and tell their stories. As discussed here the long takes are often crucial in generating the Kubrickian spectacle. In addition, the ability to freeze a moment in time seen momentarily but crucially in the Star Gate sequence to show Bowman's reactions to his trip, demonstrates a further perhaps greater development of the photojournalistic practices.

Of the freeze frame, Mather notes the importance of twenty-four frames per second used to show the image, a constant repetition of the image "that does not interrupt the projection."[38] There is here a concentration of attention upon the image, perhaps more so than anything else that cinematic imagery could produce, and it is a high watermark in how spectacle and attractions make use of the formal characteristic in Kubrick's films. Indeed, Mather continues, "the freeze frame is a non-diegetic intervention, which stops the story [and is] the filmmakers explicit attempt to make a point."[39] Its use in the Star Gate sequence clearly stops the narrative, albeit momentarily, and therefore is of vital importance in creating an attraction. But Kubrick's background in photojournalism, where he created photographic moments that fixated attention, imbues not just the freeze frame, but all of the cinematic spectacle argued here. What is demonstrated here is that Kubrick's ability to capture, freeze, and display still images in photography is expanded throughout the films discussed to produce spectacle. Walter Benjamin states through film we "calmly and adventurously go travelling . . . space expands: with slow motion movement is extended,"[40] and although Kubrick reneges on the calm, we undertake adventure, simultaneously expanding space, using frozen imagery, slow motion, and long takes to extend movement.

Moreover, he extends the operation and methodology of spectacle and the cinema of attractions.

A final note from Benjamin concludes our exploration: "a different nature opens itself to the camera than opens to the naked eye—if only because an unconsciously penetrated space is substituted for a space consciously explored by man."[41] Stanley Kubrick's films allow us to enter worlds beyond what we can see, and what was initially captured or notionally seen on the screen. We break into arenas that are structured in different temporal ways, and Kubrick—though not alone in doing so—manages to structure moments and scenes that awaken the spectacularly impressive and unusual, and keep us mesmerized not just for their duration, but for long afterward.

NOTES

1. Tom Gunning, "The Cinema of Attraction[s]: Early Film, Its Spectator and the Avant-Garde," in *The Cinema of Attractions Reloaded*, ed. Wanda Strauven, 381–88 (Amsterdam: Amsterdam University Press, 2006), 382.
2. Geoff King, *Spectacular Narratives: Hollywood in the Age of the Blockbuster* (London: I.B Tauris, 2000), 70.
3. Ibid., 75.
4. Steve Neale, "Masculinity as Spectacle: Reflections on Men and Mainstream Cinema," *Screen* 24, no. 6 (1983): 12.
5. Sean Cubitt, *The Cinema Effect* (Cambridge, MA: The MIT Press, 2004), 5.
6. Ibid., 212.
7. King, *Spectacular Narratives*, 4.
8. Philip Kuberski, *Kubrick's Total Cinema: Philosophical Themes and Formal Qualities* (London: Continuum, 2012), 42.
9. Derek Jacobs, "Stanley Kubrick's 'The Killing' Disorients the Audience to Convey an Essential Truth: Dishonesty Doesn't Sell," *Plot & Theme*, https://plotandtheme.com/2017/01/30/stanley-kubricks-the-killing-disorients-the-audience-to-convey-an-essential-truth-dishonesty-doesnt-sell/ (accessed July 29, 2019).
10. Ibid.
11. Ibid.
12. Vincent LoBrutto, *Stanley Kubrick* (London: Faber and Faber, 1997), 122.
13. Kuberski, *Kubrick's Total Cinema*, 44.
14. Marita Sturken, "Spectacle," Wiley Online Library, last modified 5 June, 2008, https://onlinelibrary.wiley.com/doi/10.1002/9781405186407.wbiecs082 (accessed October 21, 2019).
15. Ibid.
16. Gunning, "The Cinema of Attraction[s]," 384.
17. Ibid.
18. Lloyd Grove, "Stanley Kubrick, At a Distance," *Archivio Kubrick*, last modified April 25, 2005, http://www.archiviokubrick.it/english/words/interviews/1987distance.html (accessed September 15, 2019).
19. King, *Spectacular Narratives*, 4.
20. LoBrutto, *Stanley Kubrick*, 422.
21. Daniel Morgan, "Where Are We?: Camera Movements and the Problem of Point of View," *New Review of Film and Television Studies* 14, no. 2 (2016): 222–23.
22. Gunning, "The Cinema of Attraction[s]," 382.
23. Ibid., 384.
24. LoBrutto, *Stanley Kubrick*, 382.

25. Pauline Kael, "Kubrick's Gilded Age," *When the Lights Go Down* (London: Marion Boyars, 1980), 102.
26. Ibid., 107.
27. André Bazin, *What is Cinema? Vol. 1*, trans. and ed. Hugh Gray (Los Angeles, CA: University of California Press, 1967), 14.
28. Kael, "Kubrick's Gilded Age," 103.
29. Tom Huddlestone, "Barry Lyndon," *Time Out*, https://www.timeout.com/london/film/barry-lyndon (accessed November 7, 2019).
30. Martin Seel, *The Arts of Cinema*, trans. Kizer S. Walker (Ithaca, NY: Cornell University Press), 52.
31. Ibid.
32. Ibid., 54.
33. Ibid.
34. Scott Bukatman, *Matters of Gravity: Special Effects and Supermen in the 20th Century* (Durham, NC: Duke University Press, 2003), 91.
35. Ibid., 81.
36. Ibid., 93.
37. Philippe Mather, *Stanley Kubrick at Look Magazine: Authorship and Genre in Photojournalism and Film* (Bristol: Intellect, 2013), 11.
38. Ibid., 230.
39. Ibid.
40. Walter Benjamin, "The Work of Art in the Age of Mechanical Reproduction," in *Illuminations*, ed. Hannah Arendt, trans. Harry Zohn, (London: Pimlico, 1999), 229.
41. Ibid., 230.

REFERENCES

Annabelle Butterfly Dance. Directed by William K. Dickson, William Heise, Thomas Dickson. New York: Edison Manufacturing Co., 1894.
L'Arroseur arrosé. Directed by Louis Lumière. Neuilly-sur-Seine: Société des Etablissements L. Gaumont, 1895.
Barry Lyndon. Directed by Stanley Kubrick. Burbank, CA: Warner Bros., 1975.
Bazin, André. *What Is Cinema? Vol. 1*. Translated and Edited by Hugh Gray. Los Angeles, CA: University of California Press, 1967.
Beneath the Planet of the Apes. Directed by Ted Post. Century City, CA: 20th Century Fox, 1970.
Ben-Hur. Directed by William Wyler. Beverley Hills, CA: MGM, 1959.
Benjamin, Walter. "The Work of Art in the Age of Mechanical Reproduction." In *Illuminations*, edited by Hannah Arendt, translated by Harry Zohn, 211–44. London: Pimlico, 1999.
Bukatman, Scott. *Matters of Gravity: Special Effects and Supermen in the 20th Century*. Durham, NC: Duke University Press, 2003.
A Clockwork Orange. Directed by Stanley Kubrick. Burbank, CA: Warner Bros., 1971.
Cubitt, Sean. *The Cinema Effect*. Cambridge, MA: The MIT Press, 2004.
Grove, Lloyd. "Stanley Kubrick, At a Distance." *ArchivioKubrick*. Last modified April 25, 2005. http://www.archiviokubrick.it/english/words/interviews/1987distance.html.
Gunning, Tom. "The Cinema of Attraction[s]: Early Film, Its Spectator and the Avant-Garde." In *The Cinema of Attractions Reloaded*, edited by Wanda Strauven, 381–88. Amsterdam: Amsterdam University Press, 2006.
Huddlestone, Tom. "Barry Lyndon." *Time Out*. https://www.timeout.com/london/film/barry-lyndon.
Jacobs, Derek. "Stanley Kubrick's 'The Killing' Disorients the Audience to Convey an Essential Truth: Dishonesty Doesn't Sell." *Plot & Theme*. https://plotandtheme.com/2017/01/30/stanley-kubricks-the-killing-disorients-the-audience-to-convey-an-essential-truth-dishonesty-doesnt-sell.

Kael, Pauline. "Kubrick's Gilded Age." *When the Lights Go Down*, 101–7. London: Marion Boyars, 1980.
The Killing. Directed by Stanley Kubrick. Century City, CA: United Artists, 1956.
King, Geoff. *Spectacular Narratives: Hollywood in the Age of the Blockbuster*. London: I.B Tauris, 2000.
Kuberski, Philip. *Kubrick's Total Cinema: Philosophical Themes and Formal Qualities*. London: Continuum, 2012.
LoBrutto, Vincent. *Stanley Kubrick*. London: Faber and Faber, 1997.
Mather, Philippe. *Stanley Kubrick at Look Magazine: Authorship and Genre in Photojournalism and Film*. Bristol: Intellect, 2013.
Morgan, Daniel. "Where Are We?: Camera Movements and the Problem of Point of View." *New Review of Film and Television Studies* 14, no. 2 (2016): 222–48.
Neale, Steve. "Masculinity as Spectacle: Reflections on Men and Mainstream Cinema." *Screen* 24, no. 6 (1983): 2–17.
Paths of Glory. Directed by Stanley Kubrick. Beverley Hills, CA: United Artists, 1957.
Rashomon. Directed by Akira Kurosawa. Tokyo: Daiei Film, 1950.
Seel, Martin. *The Arts of Cinema*. Translated by Kizer S. Walker. Ithaca, NY: Cornell University Press, 2018.
The Shining. Directed by Stanley Kubrick. Burbank, CA: Warner Bros, 1980.
Spartacus. Directed by Stanley Kubrick. Universal City, CA: Universal Pictures, 1960.
Star Wars: A New Hope. Directed by George Lucas. Century City, CA: 20th Century Fox, 1977.
Sturken, Marita. "Spectacle." Wiley Online Library. Last modified 5 June, 2008. https://onlinelibrary.wiley.com/doi/10.1002/9781405186407.wbiecs082.
The Ten Commandments. Directed by Cecil B. DeMille. Hollywood, CA: Paramount Pictures, 1956.
2001: A Space Odyssey. Directed by Stanley Kubrick. Beverly Hills, CA: MGM, 1968.
Le Voyage dans la Lune/A Trip to the Moon. Directed by Georges Méliès. France: Star Film Company, 1902.
The Wild Bunch. Directed by Sam Peckinpah. Burbank, CA: Warner Bros., 1969.

Chapter Seventeen

2001: A Space Odyssey

Kubrick's Allegory of Melancholia

Maurizia Natali

When three American astronauts reached the moon in 1969, TV live images of the event seemed like a pale imitation of Stanley Kubrick's *2001: A Space Odyssey*. Released just the year before, the film changed the history of science fiction with its hyper-realistic spaceships and metaphysical ending. Since *2001*'s big bang–like entry, this popular genre has become a vast hyper-text made of films, games, TV series, and websites, a complex iconological universe that belongs to the history of allegories, metaphors, and tales about our terrestrial condition, anthropological progress, techno-science, extra-planetary travels, aliens, and more. More than fifty years after its release, *2001* circulates as a ghost within this labyrinth, and viewers can still catch images or topics belonging to Kubrick's masterpiece in contemporary films. The director's symbolic strength and style are still without comparison in a genre that has produced countless blockbusters, spectacular special effects, and a number of subgenres. A blueprint for topics such as apes and humans, alien entities, and super-computers, the film is still a seminal *unicum* in the global visual culture. *2001* has stimulated countless interpretations, but it has also *resisted* them, as refractory as the monolith at the center of its story.

Kubrick consistently refused to give definitive explanations for the questions his film provokes; he always argued that cinema is about visual depth, emotion, and ambiguity, and should avoid intellectual verbalization in favor of a total visual and sound-based way of thinking.[1] *2001* is a philosophical tale in which Kubrick renews science fiction topics such as human evolution, artificial intelligence, and extraterrestrial travels. However, the film is no futurist utopia and by figuring the weird solitude of an all-male mission toward the unknown, it becomes the allegorical emblem of a post-human future.

For David Bordwell and Kristin Thompson, the film "violated several conventions of the science-fiction genre, beginning with a lengthy sequence set in prehistoric times, synchronizing classical music to outer-space action, and ending with an enigmatically symbolic fetus drifting through space."[2] In fact, what defies science fiction conventions also *defines* this film as an allegory to be interpreted, a tale made of exemplary characters, symbolic situations, and landscapes, in which editing, score, and special effects stress its enigmatic warning content.

This chapter compares *2001*'s iconic density and melancholic aura to an emblem of the humanist culture, Albrecht Dürer's *Melancholia I* (1514), a suspenseful allegory about the influence of the stars on human nature and creativity.[3] With the same iconological intent, we also evoke the ancient world of Wunderkammern, and reconnect *2001*'s exemplary science fiction characters and objects to these hermetic collections born at the dawn of modern science and exploratory travels. By arguing that Kubrick's *Odyssey* and its iconography belong to a much older tradition than that of Hollywood fantasies, I reframe the director's ambitious tale about human history and technology in a larger philosophical context. I particularly underline the role of the Star Child as Kubrick's strongest invention expressing his hope for human rebirth beyond any technological evolution, a hope that today may appear as a transhumanist act of faith. As David Wallace-Wells has recently written, what transhumanist thinkers wish for goes beyond a "technological escape velocity," in the hope that "technology may quickly carry us across a threshold into a new state of being," and "a true rupture in the evolutionary line"—what Christopher Hutton has defined as no less than a "transcendence of humanity."[4] In *2001*, ruptures of this kind happen each time the monolith's accelerationist interventions take place. However, with the advent of the Star Child at the end of the film, Kubrick opens a transcendent chapter in his own story of humanity.

From an art-historical point of view, *2001* is a cinematic installation of science fiction topics and characters, a polyptych of animated dioramas. As such, it belongs to the world of allegorical collections, the cabinets of curiosities, and Wunderkammern. At the dawn of modernity, erudite collectors accumulated rare stones and bones, exemplary scientific tools, or exotic animals, as well as anatomical reproductions and automatons, in order to emblematize—or even caricature—what natural scientists, alchemists, artists, and travelers were encountering in their adventures. As art historians have argued, these magic cabinets of curiosities were emblematic mises en scène of the encyclopedic model of knowledge dominant in early modernity.[5] Similarly, *2001* can be defined as an exemplary display of anthropological types, technological machines, and epistemic objects of Kubrick's time. The director stages his items starting with the primitive ape-men in their Darwinian dioramas, then displays a number of spaceships containing typical humans, such as the scientist Floyd (William Sylvester), the astronauts Frank (Gary Lockwood) and Dave, and finally HAL, the ultimate embodiment of artificial intelligence and the monocular avatar of ancient automatons.

Among these mirabilia, naturalia, and artificialia, the tunnel of fluid forms of the Star Gate sequence figures as a repertoire of wondrous life forms, while, at the end, the almost mummified Dave lying in his bed and the luminescent fetus represent the final items of Kubrick's cabinet of anthropology, astronomy, space-travel technology, and religious symbols. Dave playing chess with HAL, Frank running in the hamster wheel like a mouse in a cage, or the magic fetus suspended in the sky, all appear as both human and machine-like, alive and (almost) inanimate, weird and realistic, in a word, uncanny, like the eerie doll Sigmund Freud evokes in his homonymous essay.[6] And like the ancient Wunderkammern, Kubrick's uncanny display offers a number of different interpretive paths.

Within *2001*'s crystalline structure, we find a variety of heterogeneous mises en scène confirming the director's allegorical montage, such as the primitive landscapes of the "Dawn of Man," the elegant hyper-modern spaceships, and the French Salon with its antique aura. Such a contrast also appears between the cold environment of the Discovery spaceship and the psychedelic visuals of the Star Gate trip; or between the astronauts' everyday life and the Star Child's mystique. Two famous images particularly show what Kubrick's allegorical editing implies. First, the unexpected match cut between the ape-man's bone with the spaceship, which, by suddenly jumping years into the future, suggests both an anthropological rupture and a symbolic continuity among mankind's different technological ages. Secondly, the shortcut between the celestial fetus and the faraway earth produces, in a single frame, a mirroring effect between the child and the planet as well as the impression of an infinite and definitive distance.

Kubrick's anthropological and philosophical intentions are evident in the way he stages the interventions of the monolith as an alien entity interrupting the path of pre-humans, humans, and machines alike, and finally producing the mysterious advent of the fetus. Because of these breaking points, ape-men become intelligent but also murderous, scientists and astronauts progress but also fail, HAL mutates into a rebellious killer, and Dave undergoes a traumatic space-time travel. With these ruptures, Kubrick asserts his vision of the uncanny discontinuities and similarities he sees in the path of humankind and leaves their meaning open and undecided.

2001 offers cinematic moments of symbolic contact between characters and objects. These sequences are slow enough for the viewers to meditate on Kubrick's allegorical intention, such as when the ape-men (and later the astronauts) proceed to touch the monolith, or when the stewardess precariously walks in the zero-gravity spaceship. Lengthy minutes are repeatedly dedicated to Dave, when he manually disconnects HAL's brain cells while both his breathing and the computer's pathetic voice are heard, or when he steps into the Salon. The director invites us to read each of these moments beyond their narrative content, as emblematic compositions that possess an allegorical dimension and suspend the filmic flow. As Kubrick reaffirms the nonverbal, affective nature of cinema with the music score, the mournful adagio by Aram Khachaturian (from *Gayane*, 1939), used during Frank's jogging in the hamster wheel, fixes the film's deepest *Stimmung*.

While Mark Crispin Miller argues that the cold atmosphere of the story makes manifest "the negation of the myth of progress" as its "basic structural principle,"[7] Robert Kolker directly mentions *2001*'s characters as emotionless "automatons" living a "mournful journey."[8] In the artificial silence of the spaceship, everything is melancholy: HAL's soft voice; Frank watching the video of his parents singing happy birthday; Frank's dead body floating in the darkness, like a child cut from the umbilical cord; and finally the astonished Dave staring into the Star Gate corridor and fatally entering the Salon.

In tune with this dominant atmosphere, the cold mood of *2001*'s characters can be compared to the most famous allegory of enigmatic sadness, the engraving *Melancholia I* by the German artist Albrecht Dürer. Executed in 1514, this allegory of *acedia* is among the most famous iconological symbols of the Renaissance theory of temperaments, and represents the then prevalent idea of the creative mind as a melancholic nature under the influence of the planet Saturn. This symbolic alignment of Dürer and Kubrick leads us to define *2001* as a new and contemporary allegory of melancholia, and suggests that the science fiction genre can be included in a much larger iconosphere than that of modern cinema.

Dürer's age, the Renaissance, saw the dawn of modern science, the Protestant Reformation, the invention of print, and the explorations of the New World by European powers. In a similar way, the 1960s were dominated worldwide by accelerated cultural and scientific changes, taking place on the geopolitical background of the Cold War atomic fear and the American conquest of the moon. Although very distant in time, these two ages shared similar questions about knowledge or regression, evolution or entropy, tolerance or war, and Man's place on Earth and in the universe. While Dürer evokes the power of the planets by representing a bright Saturn in the night sky of his emblem of human freedom and creativity, Kubrick stages the alignments of the sun, the stars, and the planets as a product of his Saturnine monolith and directly affecting human history. While Dürer treated extraterrestrial powers with the astrological iconography of his age, Kubrick updated the influence of the stars using his own science-fictional imagery, but both the engraver and the filmmaker evoke a similar *ecological Stimmung*, a dysphoric, suspended atmosphere affected by what lays beyond the Earth.

With the pensive detachment of his main figure, Dürer intended to inspire a moral meditation, and even to produce a therapeutic effect on the viewer. Kubrick had similar ambitions for his films, which appear quite evidently in *Dr. Strangelove* (1964), for example, an ironic tale of atomic madness during the Cold War. Thus, in *2001* he transforms his astonishing imitation of NASA style into an unpredictable saga of astronauts lost deep in space, as if to design a prophetic *prequel* of dystopian enterprises to come.

Both Dürer's emblem of a troubled humanism and Kubrick's post-human astronauts are also self-portraits of the artist as a philosophical iconographer and *faber melancholicus* (melancholic craftsman). As Dürer represents himself through his speculative angel of acedia and the pensive baby artist, Kubrick transforms Dave's odyssey into an allegory of his own ambivalent feelings about the future of Man as a technophilic species. Art historians have interpreted Dürer's enigmatic woman and the little boy as figuring the weird environment of a creative being momentarily paralyzed by Saturn's influence. For Plato, Aristotle, and Albrecht Dürer, this mythological planet—the Discovery's first destination in *2001*—dominates the melancholic temperament and its accomplishments. Similarly, in Kubrick's Wunderkammer of science fiction, all characters and objects compose his own allegory of a Saturnine future in which alien powers determine the trajectory of humans, its progress or regress, and its open destiny.

In this sense, Kubrick's tale of a metaphysical fatality pending on terrestrial beings appears as an updated version of the Biblical dictum *"vanitas vanitatum, omnia vanitas"* (vanity of vanities, all is vanity). Indeed the director stages a series of *vanitas* and *memento mori*, such as the initial "apes and bones" sequence, the sarcophagi inside the Discovery, or Frank's dead body floating in space. The old Dave breaking his glass of wine, his agony in front of the monolith and the fetus, and the evocation of the Ages of Man through the various representations of the aging astronaut, are equally emblematic and baroque tableaux. Finally, the austere monolith itself, an ominous monument of alien powers, and the Star Child melancholically gazing at us, complete Kubrick's Wunderkammer of Saturnine times, a filmic panoply of *nature morte with technological tools*.

However, there is a significant difference between Dürer and Kubrick, precisely in their representation of women—a difference that actually deepens the meaning of both works. In Dürer's allegory, the little boy symbolizing the future artist is a secondary presence (it may correspond to *2001*'s fetus), but the main focus remains on the imposing and uncanny feminine angel. Conversely, the absence of women in Kubrick's film suggests that for the director this solitary adventure toward the unknown can only be an all-male enterprise. Following the long tradition in which figures of women embody a vast array of allegorical meanings, Dürer made a strong female creature impersonate the complex mood of human creativity. For, as Marina Warner has demonstrated,[9] the allegorical strength of feminine figures has lasted throughout the centuries in the Western culture, in significant contrast with patriarchal cultures. On the contrary, Kubrick confirmed the male-centered mythology of science fiction—a distinctive feature of the genre that began to change later, from the 1970s onward.[10] In *2001*, the few women characters—the marginal stewardesses, a Russian scientist who briefly appears alongside Floyd, and the latter's daughter (interpreted by Kubrick's own daughter Vivian)—are the pale equivalents to Dürer's powerful feminine angel. The choice of male protagonists, on the other hand, appears to project the symbolic absence of women onto the post-terrestrial space travels of the future.

In 1985, Vivian Sobchack wrote that the recurrent characteristic of the absent or subordinate woman in science fiction revealed the genre's trouble with sexuality, difference, and human birth. Sobchack later argued that "Kubrick's ambiguously spaced-out fetus . . . alters the semantic field of contemporary SF and provides the outer space in which to (re)produce a transformed patriarchy."[11] Moreover, in *2001*, the absence of women and particularly the *motherless* Star Child both allegorize what a future patriarchal techno-science might dismiss, that is a gendered humankind and even "natural" childbirth. This symbolic erasure is already encrypted in the melancholic solitude of the male characters well before the lonely fetus appears. For Freud, the pathological state of mind of the melancholic, solipsistic type is fixed on the neurotic mourning of a lost love object.[12] In Kubrick's allegory of melancholia, the Earth itself is the lost object mourned by the astronauts who are pushed toward a post-terrestrial destination. The director inscribes this detachment as part of the evolution of mankind, as the final shot of the fetus and the Earth may suggest. Once the technological environment dominated by HAL has become a deadly trap, the Odyssey morphs into an adventure with no possibility of returning home. While Kubrick first follows a Darwinian-like evolution of the human kind and represents scientists and astronauts as the descendants of ape-men ancestors, he then deviates toward a more radical version of the future by suggesting a post-terrestrial, alien-produced evolution of our species, which his motherless baby generated by a faceless alien totem well represents.

In *Planetary Dysphoria*, Emily Apter speaks of the dark melancholia that pervades some of the branches of contemporary philosophy that are inspired by gloomy feelings of extinction and ecological catastrophe, states of mind and topics she also finds in recent novels and films.[13] But in 1968, in contrast with NASA's optimistic mission, Kubrick gave his version of this technological dysphoria. With the interventions of the monolith (perhaps an alter-ego of the author), the director both accomplishes and interrupts the modern tale of progressive evolution and technological hubris. HAL's murderous turn and Dave's termination of its artificial brain manifestly break such a tale, but when Dave crosses the psychedelic Star Gate and lands into the Salon toward a wondrous death and rebirth, Kubrick further changes not only the modernist iconography of science fiction but its epistemic logic by literally suspending the viewers in a transhumanist dimension.

In the path from the Darwinian ancestors to the melancholic astronauts and the motherless super-baby, Kubrick has ambitiously directed the human species toward a post-human transcendence. At the end, viewers should have accepted the monolith's interventions as providential accelerationist intrusions in the slow history of humanity, and should have hailed the final mystic turn of the film as a daring allegory of transcendence.[14] For the phosphorescent fetus reinvents the ancient symbol of the male child, generated by a divine entity to restart human history. Thus, this hallucinatory rebirth both embodies transhumanist dreams of artificial generation, and paradoxically renews archaic patriarchal fantasies about woman-less creation and all male creators.

Framed in profile in a melancholic posture, his joined hands close to his face, the Star Child appears both near and lost in the "womb" of the universe. Then he slowly rotates and looks at us, while his large head and wide-open eyes make him similar to science fiction's typical alien creatures. However, this last item of Kubrick's Wunderkammer also belongs to an ancient iconographical tradition. While in the contemporary visual culture most images of embryos or fetuses belong to ultrasound scans, they figured for centuries in anatomical drawings and prints of pregnant bodies, and in wood or wax sculptures of little humans and their mothers.[15] Curiously, *2001*'s fiberglass baby, made by the sculptress Liz Moore, appears too as made of wax, like the carvings of those of ancient scientific museums.[16] Among these representations, Leonardo da Vinci's famous drawing of a fetus (1511)—crouched inside a shell-like open uterus while the mother's body remains absent—uncannily resembles Kubrick's solitary child in his symbolic separation from the mother as well as from the Earth.

Emerging from the monolith as in a mystic epiphany, the reborn-from-no-(woman's)-body super-Dave poetically sublimates and epitomizes contemporary experiments in reproductive engineering, which claim to act in the name of scientific progress and wish to "improve" on nature by trying to harness the *power* women have to decide about human life. In *2001*, while the absence of women and the cold melancholia of male characters run parallel, the super-fetus is the final symbol of a potential patriarchal transhumanism to come, where artificial childbearing may become the solution for a post-nature future.

Thus, Kubrick's dystopian odyssey has, in the Star Child, its final *coup de théâtre* still open to a number of speculative fantasies. *2001* has, for example, also been interpreted as a story based on ancient alchemical topics, in which the monolith evokes the philosophical stone of alchemists, here sent by unknown aliens to guide human history toward its rebirth. In Jean-Marc Elsholz's reading, the Star Gate sequence, with its geometric and biomorphic shapes and iridized landscapes, suggests the metamorphic chaos of an alchemic universe in progress, where each intervention of the monolith signals that the aliens' experiment with humanity is still taking place.[17] From ape-men to scientists and astronauts, from human to artificial intelligence, Man will be finally regenerated in a bluish, alchemical athanor of rebirth.

Interested in Carl Jung's ideas on myths, religions, and alchemical symbols, Kubrick combined NASA plans, 1960s psychedelic fantasies, and the alchemical imaginary of rebirth to create his own melancholic transhumanist version of the future. The director himself believed in the possible existence of non-terrestrial, superior, perhaps providential intelligences, and nourished a (very science fiction-like) hope that they could save terrestrials from nuclear folly and other forms of madness. Thus, what in 1968 first appeared as a modernist fabric of futuristic topics, could actually be the encrypted work of a mystic visionary transferring alchemical symbols into the transhumanist rhetoric of science fiction's space travels. Indeed, as Annette Michelson and Peter Kramer both recalled,[18] a number of viewers appreciated precisely this spiritualist aura of *2001* by reading the film as a psychodynamic path toward metamorphosis and rebirth.

However, while those euphoric interpreters found in *2001* what initiated adepts were searching in alchemy long time ago, the film's mystic "new age" aura can now be interpreted in terms of the transhumanist cult for artificial intelligence, bio-genetics, geo-engineering, and so on. Desires of rebirth, present in all civilizations and religions, now become a semi-religious submission to science and technology, intended as absolute powers capable of correcting or defeating imperfections such as sickness and death, climate change, birth, gender, and more. Like alchemists, transhumanists wait for trans-corporeal metamorphoses and plan to travel in cryogenic sleep toward eternal life on more fortunate planets—precisely like *2001*'s unlucky crew—but while alchemists had a humanist, earth-bound vision, transhumanists consider the human body and brain, the human species, and the entire planet as mere frontiers to be surpassed. However, even though *2001*'s ending allegorizes such a mystic faith, Kubrick's film has no triumphalist tone, for his alienated characters show that a post-terrestrial life is not a path to a heavenly eternity, but an Odyssey toward the Unknown under the sign of Saturn.

During the Cold War, NASA's plans to send men to the moon were staples of propaganda about American techno-ideological superiority to the Soviet Union. For Regina Peldszus, *2001* was a big advertising event for NASA projects, such as the Skylab with humans in space achieved a few years after.[19] NASA principally saw in *2001* the opportunity of exalting its own projects as well as their implicit ideology.[20] As Peldszus recalls, *2001* had for its excellent design the approval of NASA's guru Werner von Braun, a fact that signals how Kubrick and Clarke might have appeared as the ideal interpreters of NASA's transhumanist mission.

However, if the filmmaker profited from such an enthusiasm, he did not fully embrace NASA's optimistic mission. In *2001*, extraterrestrial travels are presented as a routine in which the U.S.S.R. and the United States collaborate, and Earth is just a base planet for new frontiers, but Kubrick's allegorical clues and strongest symbols are not about space travel accomplishments. Rather, the director offers us an undecipherable monolith behaving like an alien power, and a mystic fetus staring at us. As the film's cold melancholia betrays the author's mixed feelings about a technological future, HAL represents the evil turn of artificial intelligence, while the intrusions of the monolith suggest that any control the human species may have on its exploratory missions is an illusion.

In 1968, Kubrick declared that men "may have progressed from biological species . . . into immortal machine entities—and then, over innumerable eons, they could emerge from the *chrysalis of matter* transformed into beings of pure energy and spirit."[21] Thus *2001* became famous for its shining baby, the very *chrysalis* of a future transhuman(ist) butterfly. But at present, the uncanny frailty of this post-mother creature rather symbolizes what Timothy Morton calls the trauma of the "severing,"[22] the separation of the human species from nature already initiated with patriarchal agriculture during the most ancient civilizations, and greatly accelerated in our age of technological domination. Significantly for Morton the long-lasting symptom of this severing is the diffused melancholia of our "dark ecology."[23] Thus, fifty years later, the melancholic Star Child reaches us exactly where we are, more severed from nature than before, and fully immersed within the techno-capitalist age of the Anthropocene—an overwhelming, weird *"hyper-object"* as Morton calls it[24]—during which Man has definitely altered nature, Earth, and its species. However, similarly to Dürer's philosophical warning, Morton argues that we should cultivate the regenerative power of our dysphoric melancholia, a mood that no bio-engineered plan or cryogenic trips for the happy few can tolerate or cure.

For Gilles Deleuze, Kubrick makes a "cinema of the brain"[25] and in *2001* he conjoins planets, humans, machines, and the monolith to form a new intellectual plane of consistency, or what we can call a trans-ecological alignment of terrestrial and extraterrestrial beings, in which the fetus appears to be the weird angel, the messenger of a post-terrestrial future. For the end of the film, the director first imagined his Star Child watching the Earth ruined by nuclear wars, like in the early version of Clarke's novel, but then decided that the baby should rather stare enigmatically at the viewers.[26] Both versions remind us of Walter Benjamin's proverbial *angel of history* facing a catastrophic past of ruins while pushed away by the violent wind of History.[27] For under the fetus's gaze, we, as viewers, become those living ruins of history and the last humans to whom the fetus appeals, even though an enigmatic doubt can be read in his melancholic eyes.

In Dürer's humanist allegory, a feminine Melancholia embodies suspension and meditation among symbols of artistic work, while in Kubrick's post-humanist tale, solitary and melancholic men live the post-terrestrial routine of techno-civilization. But in Dürer, neither the winged creature nor the pensive child look at us, while in *2001* the fetus staring at the viewers uncannily makes us feel the director's strong intentional address. We may still recall the dark eyes of the ape-men, HAL's red eye, or Dave's blue eyes, but we do not expect this final eye contact that suddenly makes us feel the fascinating fragility of birth, the human body, and all terrestrial matters.

2001: A Space Odyssey still shines in its allegorical brightness as a Saturnine comet traversing our present skies, environmental troubles, and futuristic horizons. Immersed in its auratic halo, the film has become even more enigmatic than it was in 1968. *2001* still defies our expanded science fiction culture, and its resistance to time is the same that only grand allegories manifest. As an enigmatic, wondrous Wunderkammer, Kubrick's melancholic masterpiece still magnetically attracts in its orbit new and distant viewers.

NOTES

1. "Stanley Kubrick Explains the Ending of *2001: A Space Odyssey* in Newly Discovered Interview," *The Telegraph*, July 9, 2018. https://telegraph.co.uk/films/2018/07/09/stanley-kubrick-finally-explains-ending-of-2001-space-odyssey-unearthed/ (accessed May 1, 2019). For Kubrick on cinema, see Gene D. Phillips, ed., *Stanley Kubrick: Interviews* (Jackson, MS: University Press of Mississippi, 2001), 106. For allegory as "cosmic truth," see Kubrick's interview with William Kloman, "On 2001, Will Love be a Seven-Letter Word?" *The New York Times*, April 14, 1968. https://archive.nytimes.com/www.nytimes.com/library/film/041468kubrick-2001.html (accessed November 16 2019).

2. David Bordwell and Kristin Thompson, *Film Art: An Introduction*, 6th edition (New York: McGraw-Hill Education, 2001), 97.

3. For Dürer's allegory, see Elena Filippi, *Inesauribile Melancholia* (Venezia: Marsilio, 2018); and Raymond Klibansky, Erwin Panofsky, and Fritz Saxl, *Saturn and Melancholy; Studies in the History of Natural Philosophy, Religion, and Art* (London: Nelson,1964).

4. David Wallace-Wells, *The Uninhabitable Earth* (New York: The Duggan Books, 2019), 174. Christopher Hutton mentions Clarke's novel *2001* and its belief in the transcendence of humanity as a transhumanist idea, in "Google's Glass Castle: The Rise and Fear of a Transhuman Future," *Popmatters*, November 4, 2012, https://www.popmatters.com/163072-googles-glass-castle-the-rise-and-fear-of-a-transhuman-future-2495816530.html (accessed September 20, 2019). On transhumanism, see Max More and Natasha Vita-More, ed., *The Transhumanist Reader: Classical and Contemporary Essays on the Science, Technology, and Philosophy of the Human Future* (Chichester: Wiley Blackwell, 2013); Mark O'Connell, *To Be a Machine. Adventures among Cyborgs, Utopians, Hackers and the Futurists Solving the Modest Problem of Death* (New York: Doubleday, 2017).

5. Horst Bredekamp, *The Lure of Antiquity and the Cult of the Machine: The Kunstkammer and the Evolution of Nature, Art, and Technology*, trans. Allison Brown (Princeton, NJ: Markus Wiener Publishers, 1995).

6. Sigmund Freud, "The Uncanny," 1919, in *Sigmund Freud: On Creativity and the Unconscious. Papers in the Psychology of Art, Literature, Love, Religion*, ed. Benjamin Nelson, 122–61 (New York: Harper Colophon Books, 1958).

7. Mark Crispin Miller, "2001 A Cold Descent," in *Depth of Field: Stanley Kubrick, Film, and the Uses of History*, ed. Geoffrey Cocks, James Diedrick, and Glenn Perusek, 122–45 (Madison, WI: University of Wisconsin Press, 2006), 123.

8. Robert Kolker, "I'm Afraid . . . I Can Feel It," in *Film Analysis: a Norton Reader*, ed. Jeffrey Geiger and R. L. Rutsky, 613–21 (New York: W. W. Norton & Company, 2013), 620.

9. Marina Warner, *Monuments & Maidens: The Allegory of the Female Form* (New York: Athenaeum, 1985). Within patriarchal cultures, Warner argues, the female body has been a privileged signifier of allegorical contents in mythology, literature, and the arts, as well as in monuments and advertising.

10. Women have become central characters in science fiction films, most notably in *Alien* (1979) and *Blade Runner* (1982), and in recent years in films such as *Gravity* (Alfonso Cuarón, 2013), *Mad Max: Fury Road* (George Miller, 2015), *Arrival* (Denis Villeneuve, 2016), *Wonder Woman* (Patty Jenkins, 2018) and *Blade Runner 2049* (Denis Villeneuve, 2018).

11. Vivian Sobchack deals with women in science fiction in "The Virginity of Astronauts: Sex and SF Film," in *Alien Zone, Cultural Theory and Contemporary SF cinema*, ed. Annette Khun, 103–14 (New York: Verso, 1996); on the fetus in *2001*, see her article "Child/Alien/Father: Patriarchal Crisis and Generic Exchange," *Camera Obscura*, Fall 1986, 17.

12. Sigmund Freud, "Mourning and Melancholia," 1917, in *The Freud Reader*, ed. Peter Gay, 584–89 (New York: Norton & Company, 1989).

13. Emily Apter, "Planetary Dysphoria," *Third Text* 27, no. 1 (January 2013): 131–40. Apter considers the film *Melancholia* (Lars von Trier, 2011) as an example of "catastrophism, always a staple of sci-fi" (137). For this issue, see my article "Empire of Catalandia: Science Fiction as the Cinematic Space of the Anthropocene," in *New Approaches to Cinematic Space*, ed. Felipa Rosário and Ivan Villarmea Álvarez, 69–83 (New York: Routledge, 2019).

14. A redemptive child, son of a patriarchal God, is common to many religious tales. In science fiction, maternity is either absent or monstrous like in *Alien*; recently in *Blade Runner 2049*, Villeneuve deals with the reproduction of "replicants." Since the 1970s, the eco-feminist movement reframes environmental issues within male capitalist "His-tory" and denounces the patriarchal power exerted on nature, earth, and women. See Carolyn Merchant, *The Death of Nature: Women, Ecology, and the Scientific Revolution* (San Francisco, CA: Harper & Row, 1980). For reproductive engineering in a feminist perspective see Renate Klein, "From Test-Tube Women to Bodies Without Women," *Women Studies International Forum* 31, June 5, 2008, 157–75. https://www.researchgate.net/publication/222981245_From_test-tube_women_to_bodies_without_women (accessed December 18, 2019).

15. Karen Newman, *Fetal Positions: Individualism, Science, Visuality* (Stanford, CA: Stanford University Press, 1996), 41 (Leonardo's fetus) and 26 (Kubrick's *2001* baby).

16. Simone Odino, "Making the Starchild in '2001': A Tribute to Liz Moore," *2001Italia.it*, May 27, 2013, http://www.2001italia.it/2013/05/making-starchild-in-2001-tribute-to-liz.html (accessed February 19, 2019).

17. Jean-Marc Elsholz, "2001: L'Odyssée de l'espace: Le Grand Oeuvre," *Positif*, no. 439 (September 1997): 87–92.

18. Annette Michelson, "Bodies in Space: Film as Carnal Knowledge," *Artforum* 7, no. 6 (February 1969): 54–63; and Peter D. Kramer, *2001: A Space Odyssey* (London: British Film Institute, 2010), 20 and 99–103.

19. Regina Peldszus, "Kubrick's Interaction with Aerospace Industry during the Production of *2001*," in *Stanley Kubrick. New Perspectives*, ed. Tatiana Ljujic, Peter Kramer, and Richard Daniels (London: Black Dog Publishing, 2015), 200–217.

20. For Clarke's novel *2001* as a transhumanist tale see Hutton, "Google's Glass Castle: The Rise and Fear of a Transhuman Future."

21. Kubrick in Eric Norden, "A Candid Conversation with the Pioneering Creator of *2001: A Space Odyssey*, *Dr. Strangelove* and *Lolita*," *Playboy*, September 1968, https://scrapsfromtheloft.com/2016/10/02/playboy-interviewstanley-kubrick (accessed December 18, 2019). Italics are mine.

22. Timothy Morton, *Humankind: Solidarity with Nonhuman People* (London: Verso, 2017), 13–19.

23. Timothy Morton, *Dark Ecology: For a Logic of Future Coexistence* (New York: Columbia University Press, 2016).

24. Timothy Morton, *Hyperobject: Philosophy and Ecology after the End of the World* (Minneapolis, MN: University of Minnesota Press, 2013). For the debate on the Anthropocene, see Chris Hamilton, Charles Bonneuil, and François Gemenne, ed. *The Anthropocene and the Global Environmental Crisis, Rethinking Modernity in a New Epoch* (London: Routledge, 2015); and Wallace-Wells, *The Uninhabitable Earth*.

25. Gilles Deleuze, *The Time-Image*, trans. H. Tomlinson and R. Caleta (Minneapolis, MN: University of Minnesota Press, 2016), 266.

26. Arthur C. Clarke, *2001: A Space Odyssey* (New York: The New American Library, 1968). The Star Child's gaze anticipates the "I see you" formula by which the Na'vi express love in *Avatar* (2009) by James Cameron, a fan of *2001*.

27. Walter Benjamin, "Theses on the Philosophy of History," in *Illuminations*, ed. Hannah Arendt, 257–64 (New York: Shocken Books); for the Angelus Novus by Paul Klee as "angel of history" see 257–58, IX.

REFERENCES

Apter, Emily. "Planetary Dysphoria." *Third Text* 27, no. 1 (January 2013): 131–40.

Benjamin, Walter. "Theses on the Philosophy of History." In *Illuminations*, edited by Hannah Arendt, 257–58. New York: Shocken Books, 1968.

Blas Gonzalez, Pedro. "Stanley Kubrick's 2001: An Existential Odyssey." *Sense of Cinema* 52 (September 2009). http://sensesofcinema.com/2009/feature-articles/stanley-kubricks-2001-an-existential-odyssey/.

Bordwell, David, and Kristin Thompson. *Film Art: An Introduction*, 6th edition. New York: McGraw-Hill Education, 2001.

Bredekamp, Horst. *The Lure of Antiquity and the Cult of the Machine: The Kunstkammer and the Evolution of Nature, Art, and Technology*. Translated by Allison Brown. Princeton, NJ: Markus Wiener Publishers, 1995.

Clarke, Arthur C. *2001: A Space Odyssey*. New York: The New American Library, 1968.

Deleuze, Gilles. *The Time-Image*. Translated by Hugh Tomlinson and Robert Caleta. Minneapolis: University of Minnesota Press, 2016.

Elsholz, Jean-Marc. "2001: L'Odyssée de l'espace: Le Grand Oeuvre." *Positif*, no. 439 (September 1997): 87–92.

Filippi, Elena. *Inesauribile Melencolia. Chiavi e Ricchezza del Capolavoro Dureriano*. Venezia: Marsilio, 2018.

Freud, Sigmund. "Mourning and Melancholia," 1917. In *The Freud Reader*, edited by Peter Gay, 584–89. New York: Norton & Company, 1989.

———. "The Uncanny," 1919. In *Sigmund Freud: On Creativity and the Unconscious Papers in the Psychology of Art, Literature, Love, Religion*, edited by Benjamin Nelson, 122–61. New York: Harper Colophon Books, 1958.

Grundhauser, Eric. "The Cosmic Fetus of '2001: A Space Odyssey' Hasn't Aged a Day." *Atlas Obscura*, May 23, 2018. https://www.atlasobscura.com/articles/kubrick-2001-star-child-prop.

Hamilton, Chris, Charles Bonneuil, and François Gemenne, eds. *The Anthropocene and the Global Environmental Crisis, Rethinking Modernity in a New Epoch*. London: Routledge, 2015.

Hutton, Christopher. "Google's Glass Castle: The Rise and Fear of a Transhuman Future." *Popmatters*, November 4, 2012. https://www.popmatters.com/163072-googles-glass-castle-the-rise-and-fear-of-a-transhuman-future-2495816530.html.
Kara, Selmin. "Anthropocenema: Cinema in the Age of Mass Extinction." In *Post-cinema: Theorizing 21st Century Film*, edited by Shane Denson and Julia Leyda, 750–84. Falmer: REFRAME Books, 2016. https://reframe.sussex.ac.uk/post-cinema.
Klein, Renate. "From Test-Tube Women to Bodies without Women." *Women Studies International Forum* 31, June 5, 2008, 157–75. https://www.researchgate.net/publication/222981245_From_test-tube_women_to_bodies_without_women.
Klibansky, Raymond, Erwin Panofsky, and Fritz Saxl, eds. *Saturn and Melancholy; Studies in the History of Natural Philosophy, Religion, and Art*. London: Nelson, 1964.
Kloman, William. "In 2001, Will Love Be a Seven-Letter Word?" *The New York Times*, April 14, 1968. https://archive.nytimes.com/www.nytimes.com/library/film/041468kubrick-2001.html.
Kolker, Robert. "I'm Afraid . . . I Can Feel It." In *Film Analysis: a Norton Reader*, edited by Jeffrey Geiger and R. L. Rutsky, 613–21. New York: W.W. Norton & Company, 2013.
Kramer, Peter D. *2001: A Space Odyssey*. London: British Film Institute, 2010.
Kubrick, Stanley. "Stanley Kubrick Explains the Ending of *2001: A Space Odyssey* in Newly Discovered Interview." *The Telegraph*, July 9, 2018 . https://www.telegraph.co.uk/films/2018/07/09/stanley-kubrick-finally-explains-ending-2001-space-odyssey-unearthed/.
Merchant, Carolyn. *The Death of Nature: Women, Ecology, and the Scientific Revolution*. San Francisco, CA: Harper & Row, 1980.
Michelson, Annette. "Bodies in Space: Film as Carnal Knowledge." *Artforum* 7, no. 6 (February 1969): 54–63.
Miller, Mark Crispin. "2001 A Cold Descent." In *Depth of Field: Stanley Kubrick, Film, and the Uses of History*, edited by Geoffrey Cocks, James Diedrick, and Glenn Peruseck, 122–45. Madison, WI: University of Wisconsin Press, 2006.
More, Max, and Natasha Vita-More, eds. *The Transhumanist Reader: Classical and Contemporary Essays on the Science, Technology, and Philosophy of the Human Future*. Chichester: Wiley Blackwell, 2013.
Morton, Timothy. *Dark Ecology: For a Logic of Future Coexistence*. New York: Columbia University Press, 2016.
———. *Hyperobject: Philosophy and Ecology after the End of the World*. Minneapolis: University of Minnesota Press, 2013.
———. *Humankind: Solidarity with Nonhuman People*. London: Verso, 2017.
Natali, Maurizia. "Avatar, SF Mannerism and the Anthropocene." In *A Critical Companion to James Cameron*, edited by Adam Barkman and Antonio Sanna, 43–55. Lanham, MD: Lexington Books, 2019.
———."Empire of Catalandia: Science Fiction as the Cinematic Space of the Anthropocene." In *New Approaches to Cinematic Space*, edited by Felipa Rosário and Ivan Villarmea Álvarez, 69–83. New York: Routledge, 2019.
Newman, Karen. *Fetal Positions: Individualism, Science, Visuality*. Stanford, CA: Stanford University Press, 1996.
Norden, Eric. "A Candid Conversation with the Pioneering Creator of *2001: A Space Odyssey*, *Dr. Strangelove* and *Lolita*." *Playboy*, September 1968, https://scrapsfromtheloft.com/2016/10/02/playboy-interview-stanley-kubrick/.
O'Connell, Mark. *To Be a Machine: Adventures among Cyborgs, Utopians, Hackers and the Futurists Solving the Modest Problem of Death*. New York: Doubleday, 2017.
Odino, Simone. "Making the Starchild in '2001': A Tribute to Liz Moore." *2001Italia.it*, May 27, 2013. http://www.2001italia.it/2013/05/making-starchild-in-2001-tribute-to-liz.html.
Peldszus, Regina. "Kubrick's Interaction with Aerospace Industry during the Production of *2001*." In *Stanley Kubrick: New Perspectives*, edited by Tatian Ljujic, Peter Kramer, and Richard Daniels, 200–217. London: Black Dog Publishing, 2015.
Phillips, Gene D., ed. *Stanley Kubrick: Interviews*. Jackson, MS: University Press of Mississippi, 2001.

Sobchack, Vivian. "The Virginity of Astronauts: Sex and SF Film." In *Alien Zone, Cultural Theory and Contemporary SF cinema*, edited by Annette Khun, 103–14. New York: Verso, 1996.
———. "Child/Alien/Father: Patriarchal Crisis and Generic Exchange." *Camera Obscura*, Fall 1986, 7–34.
Wallace-Wells, David. *The Uninhabitable Earth: Life after Warming*. New York: The Duggan Books, 2019.
Warner, Marina. *Monuments & Maidens: The Allegory of the Female Form*. New York: Athenaeum, 1985.

Chapter Eighteen

The Everlasting Moment

Enchantment and Myth in A.I. *and* 2001: A Space Odyssey

Joshua Sikora

As two of Stanley Kubrick's most significant science fiction projects, *2001: A Space Odyssey* (1968) and *A.I. Artificial Intelligence* (2001) share a great kinship, both offering harrowing visions of technological futures marked by powerfully intelligent machines that seem to supplant and surpass humanity itself. Emerging from Kubrick's long-standing fascination with (and fear of) artificial intelligence, both films are drawn from exhaustive research, born out of collaborations with respected science fiction authors, and focus paradoxically on technology as humanity's greatest threat and potential salvation.

Buried underneath these twin prophecies of the future are deep roots that the films share in mythology and fairy tales. Kubrick strongly believed that these structural foundations would create a kind of universal resonance, playing timeless notes that harmonize with our human emotional core. In his youth, he had personally been shaped by these kinds of meaningful narratives, avidly devouring his father's collection of Grimm's folk tales and Greco-Roman mythology. In *Stanley Kubrick, Director*, biographer Alexander Walker suggests that, "Because he read them at a formative age, [fairy stories, folk tales, and mythology] had, Kubrick acknowledged, a considerable effect on his filmmaking. They showed the inadequacy of naturalism as the mainspring of a plot."[1] Kubrick would in fact argue that naturalism "does not elicit the more mysterious echoes contained in myths and fables; these resonances are far better suited to film than any other art form."[2]

Walker's study of Kubrick's oeuvre, published six months after the director's death in 1999, reveals an ever-present interest in "the energizing power of myth to work on our unconscious or touch the memory trace of our race" from the very concept of *2001*, to earlier films such as *Killer's Kiss* (1955) and *Lolita* (1962).[3] It should be no surprise then that mythology and fairy tales form the central foundation of *A.I. Artificial Intelligence*, a posthumous film that Kubrick developed for nearly two decades before passing a detailed story treatment to Steven Spielberg, who would go on to write and direct the film after Kubrick's death.

Although Spielberg brought many of his own sensibilities to the finished film, this was in itself by design, with Kubrick feeling that ultimately the story better fit Spielberg's directorial voice. Nevertheless, the completed film faithfully captures the narrative arc and thematic underpinnings that Kubrick and his writing partners had so tirelessly worked to craft over the preceding twenty years. Jane M. Struthers, of London's University of the Arts, where the Stanley Kubrick Archive is housed, writes, "It is almost impossible to separate out what was Stanley's and what was Steven's in the finished film, so seamlessly did the collaboration work and so profoundly did Steven understand what Stanley had been trying to achieve."[4]

To get at this core—at the thematic heart of *A.I. Artificial Intelligence*—requires a closer examination of Kubrick's story process and the key role that mythology and fairy tales played in the development of films like *2001: A Space Odyssey*. By examining their shared origins and parallel themes, both films take on a greater resonance and deeper meaning. Although Kubrick passed away before seeing his vision for *A.I.* brought to life, the finished film remains as a testament to his beliefs about the future of humanity—a poetic elegy on technology and mortality, which in its very existence may prove its underlying significance.

Stanley Kubrick is famous for his meticulous attention to detail at every stage of a film, known for lengthy productions and a tendency to repeatedly shoot a scene dozens of times before settling for something close to perfection. This intense process did not just begin when the cameras started to roll—Kubrick brought this same laser focus to pre-production and the extensive story development process, which often stretched out over many years. The director would spend a great deal of time exploring the possibilities of a particular story, hit a wall, shift to a different project for a while, and then return to the previous concept with a new breakthrough. *2001* went through countless permutations over its seven-year gestation, while *A.I.*'s story process stretched endlessly from the mid-seventies through Kubrick's death in 1999.

Research was at the heart of Kubrick's story development process for each of his films, whether it was exhaustive historical research for one of his sweeping epics, an examination of sociopolitical and psychological conditions to inform a film like *A Clockwork Orange* (1971), or the groundbreaking science that served as the foundation for *2001* and *A.I.* In his comprehensive behind-the-scenes book, *Space Odyssey*, Michael Benson noted, "Kubrick treated every film as a grand investigation, drilling down into his subject with a relentless perfectionist's tenacity as he forced it to yield every secret and possibility. Once he'd decided on a theme, he subjected it to years of interrogation, reading everything and exploring all aspects before finally jump-starting the cumbersome filmmaking machinery."[5]

For *2001*, this process began as early as 1961, when Kubrick heard a science fiction BBC radio drama, *Shadow on the Sun*, which told the bizarre story of a meteorite crashing on Earth, letting loose an alien virus, which then prompts humanity to lose its sexual inhibitions. While the premise was hard to take seriously, Kubrick was drawn to its cinematic potential, seeing an opportunity—as he often did—to improve upon the source material, using it as a springboard for a more serious interrogation into science, psychology, and sexuality. However, he was met with a great deal of skepticism, due to how poorly respected science fiction was as a genre in the early sixties (it did not help that his initial inspiration was a prime example of the more ridiculous, hackneyed plots that had come to define the genre).[6]

After several false starts, Kubrick came across Arthur C. Clarke's 1953 novel, *Childhood's End*, which chronicled an invasion of Earth by alien overlords. In Clarke's writing, he immediately found the science fiction voice he had been looking for—thoughtful, epic, with hints of the mythic. In 1964, he summoned Clarke to New York for a meeting that would kick off what Benson described as "the most balanced and productive creative partnership" of Kubrick's career.[7] Clarke would recall:

> Even from the beginning, [Kubrick] had a very clear idea of his ultimate goal. He wanted to make a movie about man's relation to the universe—something which had never been attempted, much less achieved, in the history of motion pictures. Stanley was determined to create a work of art which would arouse the emotions of wonder, awe, even, if appropriate, terror.[8]

While Kubrick and Clarke immersed themselves in the latest theories about space and extraterrestrials to ground their epic in as much fact-based science as possible, it was this central goal of crafting an emotionally impactful and universal experience that drew the two storytellers back to mythology. In *Space Odyssey*, Benson explains, "When they began work in 1964, one initial motivation was to study the universal structures of all human myths. They were aided by Joseph Campbell's magisterial study *The Hero with a Thousand Faces*, which provided them with a template for the conscious creation of a new work of mythology."[9] Fundamental to their project was Campbell's core thesis of the monomyth—an overarching theory that synergizes the most commonly repeated motifs in mythology into a single, cohesive journey taken by an archetypal hero. Campbell summarizes this arc as,

"*A hero ventures forth from the world of common day into a region of supernatural wonder: fabulous forces are there encountered and a decisive victory is won: the hero comes back from this mysterious adventure with the power to bestow boons on his fellow man.*"[10] In simpler terms, he suggests the pattern is "represented in the rites of passage: *separation—initiation—return*: which might be named the nuclear unit of the monomyth."[11]

Benson explains that this framework "helped Kubrick and Clarke delve into the archetypal workings of human mythological yearnings, expanding that template to encompass not just one story and hero, and not even just one species, but rather the entire trajectory of humanity—'from ape to angel,' as Kubrick put it."[12] The film's extended prologue, where primitive apes learn how to use tools after first contact with the mysterious monolith, poetically captures Campbell's first stage of *Separation* (or Departure, as he terms it elsewhere). In this stage, the hero receives a call to adventure, is provided supernatural aid, and ultimately crosses a threshold into a new reality—events mirrored in the unearthly monolith's piercing "call" to the apes and the emergence of a new reality in which early man masters tools and weapons. In Campbell's mythological examples, he recounts a Buddhist parable in which the hero learns to wield the "Weapon of Knowledge,"[13] which aptly describes the Edenic scenario that plays out in *2001*'s opening act. More succinctly, the crossing of the first threshold is powerfully depicted in one of the most effective editorial time jumps in cinema history, when an ape throws his primitive weapon into the air and Kubrick match cuts forward millions of years from the spinning prehistoric bone to a futuristic nuclear weapons satellite orbiting Earth.[14]

The second stage of the monomyth, *Initiation*, focuses on "the testings of the hero, which were preliminary to his ultimate experience."[15]—a road of trials in which Campbell describes, "the hero moves in a dream landscape of curiously fluid, ambiguous forms,"[16] culminating in a meeting with the supernatural "at the central point of the cosmos."[17] In *2001*'s second act, Kubrick and Clarke shifted from primitive man to modern man, with astronaut Dave Bowman (Keir Dullea) as the central heroic figure in the struggle against humanity's technological offspring, the supercomputer HAL 9000.

This seemingly inevitable clash with manmade artificial intelligence was a frequent preoccupation of Kubrick's, generating not just the central conflict of *2001*, but also obviously the whole premise of *A.I.*'s story. Kubrick feared that in humanity's pursuit of an evolved rationality, we would eventually lose our emotional capacity—a psychological fragmentation brought about by our efforts to master technology and science. This fragmentation is evident in the dispassionate calm with which Bowman and the other humans of *2001* carry themselves, as well as the drug-induced emotional suppression Kubrick examined in his next film, *A Clockwork Orange*.

In the 1960s, the fear of manmade technology ultimately destroying the entire human species was of course typified by the fear of nuclear annihilation, which Kubrick tackled head on in *Dr. Strangelove* (1964). In an interview with the *New York Times*, Kubrick suggested, "Since the means to obliterate life on earth exist, it will take more than just careful planning and reasonable cooperation to avoid some eventual catastrophe."[18] While *Dr. Strangelove* and *A Clockwork Orange* both serve as tragic, cautionary tales, *2001: A Space Odyssey* presented Kubrick the opportunity to explore a more optimistic alternative. "The problem exists as long as the potential exists, and the problem is essentially a moral and spiritual one," he explained in the same interview. "Somebody said that man is the missing link between primitive apes and civilized human beings. . . . We are semicivilized, capable of cooperation and affection, but needing some sort of transfiguration into a higher form of life."[19]

In *2001*, this transfiguration occurs in the final act, when Bowman is miraculously reborn as the Star Child. This supernatural transformation seems to be prompted when, like Michelangelo's Adam, an aged Bowman reaches out to touch the iconic monolith, the film's embodiment of the Divine. In a 1968 interview with *Playboy*, Kubrick explains that "the God concept is at the heart of *2001*"[20] —referencing a term employed by Carl Jung, whose study of human psychology was deeply influential on Campbell's theories on myth.[21] In Bowman's final godlike rebirth, Kubrick compellingly captures Campbell's image of this transfiguration:

> The disciple has been blessed with a vision transcending the scope of normal human destiny, and amounting to a glimpse of the essential nature of the cosmos. Not his personal fate, but the fate of mankind, of life as a whole, the atom and all the solar systems, has been opened to him; and this in terms befitting his human understanding, that is to say, in terms of an anthropomorphic vision: the Cosmic Man.[22]

The film concludes with this "cosmic man" returning to Earth—the *Return* being Campbell's final stage of the monomyth and the completion of Bowman's intergalactic journey. Benson notes that, "A *nostos*, or homecoming, was as necessary to Kubrick's and Clarke's *Odyssey* as it was to Homer's."[23] And like the myth of Odysseus, this hero's return home symbolizes a kind of liberation or freedom. Humanity faces the threats of its own design—nuclear weapons, artificial intelligence, the eradication of emotion—symbolized in the cold, deadly calculations of the film's cyclopean monster, HAL. In defeating the cyclops, and communing with the divine, Bowman—whose name references the bow of Apollo that Odysseus uses to reclaim his home—completes the mythic arc that began millions of years earlier, when the first ape-man accepted the mysterious call of the monolith. According to Benson, Kubrick and Clarke believed that "*2001*'s conscious deployment of a mythological structure," was one of the foundational reasons "for the film's enduring power and relevance."[24]

In 1969, a year after *2001: A Space Odyssey* was released, science fiction author Brian Aldiss published a short story titled, "Super-Toys Last All Summer Long." The ten-page vignette explores a time in the near future when Earth suffers from overpopulation, and families—legally prevented from having babies—own robot children instead. The story focuses on one such robot, David, who constantly wonders if he is real. In addition to the theoretical exploration of sentient androids, the story also strikes the very human chords of loneliness and isolation.

While Kubrick was certainly drawn to the technological conceit of the story, given his long-standing interest in artificial intelligence, it was the quaint childlike wonder of Aldiss's story that seemed to spark his imagination. When Kubrick first met with Aldiss in July 1976 to discuss a potential film adaptation, he gave the author a copy of Carlo Collodi's *Pinocchio*, already sensing the opportunity to synthesize the two stories into a futuristic fairy tale. To Kubrick, the parallels were obvious, with the android child sharing the puppet's dream of becoming a real boy. However, Aldiss found the comparison troublesome. "I tried to persuade Stanley that he should create a great modern myth to rival *Dr. Strangelove* and *2001*," he recalled, arguing that Kubrick should "avoid fairy tale."[25] Although the pair worked closely for almost a decade, trying to crack the film version of the story, it proved impossible for Aldiss to come around to Kubrick's vision. By 1990, the two had parted ways, with Kubrick retaining the film rights to the short story and other writers lined up to replace Aldiss.

For six weeks, Kubrick worked with Bob Shaw, who quickly found the collaboration too demanding. Then, in May 1990, science fiction writer Ian Watson was brought in to take his shot at expanding Aldiss's brief scenario into a feature-length film story. Watson would prove to be much more in tune with Kubrick, and although the fruit of their labor would not be seen for more than a decade, much of Watson's completed story treatment led directly to Spielberg's eventual screenplay and the finished film. In her comprehensive recounting of the development process, Jane M. Struthers explains, "Over an intensive nine months, Watson generated endless ideas with Kubrick, venturing down many paths, not all of which made it through development. Early story treatments for David's quest showed influence from religion and Arthurian legend, as well as fairy tale."[26]

Watson embraced the fairy tale influence of *Pinocchio* and helped build David's story toward the climactic encounter with the Blue Fairy, following Kubrick's charge to "create something magical and enchanting."[27] The other essential reference point Kubrick provided was Bruno Bettelheim's landmark analytical work, *The Uses of Enchantment: The Meaning and Importance of Fairy Tales*. Like Campbell's *The Hero with a Thousand Faces*, Bettelheim's ideas would provide foundational principles the writers would use to craft the film's story. Picking up on the central theme of loneliness in Aldiss's original short story, Kubrick and Watson looked to Bettelheim's analysis of this kind of fairy tale: "There is no greater threat in life than that we will be deserted, left alone. Psychoanalysis has named this—man's greatest fear—separation anxiety; and the younger we are, the more excruciating is our anxiety when we feel deserted."[28]

Tying into Campbell's mythic rites of passage, this created the necessary template for *A.I.*'s first act to fulfill the initial narrative stage of *Separation*. In the film, David (Haley Joel Osment) and the audience grow accustomed to the ordinary world of Monica (Frances O'Connor) and Henry Swinton (Sam Robards)—an idyllic home, family meals, and bedtime stories—until the Swintons' biological son, Martin (Jake Thomas) enters the picture. Cured of a terrible illness, the once cryogenically frozen boy returns home to a surprise brother. While Monica has bonded with David in something resembling a mother-son relationship, Martin and Henry have trouble seeing him as anything other than a machine. After multiple mishaps in which David accidentally puts the family in danger, Henry convinces Monica to return the robot to the factory where it would be destroyed. Unable to commit to this, but also unable to risk keeping him, Monica abandons David in the forest, setting in motion the archetypal quest of Campbell's myths and Bettelheim's fairy tales. Internalizing one of Monica's bedtime stories, the tale of *Pinocchio*, David comes to believe that if he can find the Blue Fairy, she will make him a real boy, transforming him into something that a mother can truly love.

Separation undergirds the entire first act, not just in the culminating scene of abandonment, but from the start we are introduced to parents separated from their children. Professor Hobby (William Hurt), builds David as a replacement for his own dead son, while the first scene of Monica and Henry is of them visiting their own dying son, frozen in a cryochamber that evokes Snow White's glass coffin.[29] The poignant sorrow evoked throughout the film's early scenes keeps the human characters just out of reach for the audience, emotionally distant and somewhat cold—not unlike the humans of *2001* (although here, there is a more understandable narrative justification). David is also difficult to connect with, a forced smile and mechanical movements placing him firmly in the unsettling "uncanny valley" of artificial creations. This emotional vacuum makes David's abandonment all the more heart-wrenching, as that scene proves to be the first cathartic release of intense feelings in the film—an orchestrated flourish born out of the earlier scenes' deliberate restraint.

While *A.I.*'s first act feels like a natural expansion of the small domestic tale Brian Aldiss had written, the story enters uncharted territory once David is left in the woods to fend for himself. For the harsh, picaresque journey that encompasses the film's middle act, Kubrick and Watson drew extensive inspiration from *Pinocchio*, as well as the second stage of Campbell's monomyth, *Initiation*. In this arduous road of trials, Campbell's prototypical hero encounters allies who aid in the quest (like Jude Law's Gigolo Joe), overcome physical obstacles (such as the deadly Flesh Fair), and journey to the underworld (represented by both the salacious Rouge City and a flooded New York City). Amidst these challenges, David sets his eyes on his new objective—the Blue Fairy—and will stop at nothing to reach her. Spielberg's production designer for the film, Rick Carter, explains, "The only safe way through this carnal realm is to have a strong vision or goal for what you are actually there for."[30] In Campbell's analysis, the hero's trials are necessary for his maturation or for "moments of illumination."[31] David begins the film as an innocent, infantile child, but his perilous journey forces him to grow up. Without external signs of aging, Haley Joel Osment impressively portrays the android's internal evolution, shaped by the innumerable external obstacles he faces in his quest.

In Campbell's monomyth, this path to Initiation builds toward an *Atonement with the Father*—a sequence that Kubrick literally crafted into *A.I.*'s story when David's journey brings him face to face with his creator, Professor Hobby. Campbell suggests "the world of specialized adult action"[32] is the domain of the father and it is in this sequence where David comes of age—Hobby acknowledges that he has developed "self-motivated reasoning . . . something no machine has ever done before you."[33] Although David's physical form will always be childlike, his mind has matured beyond all others of his kind. This *apotheosis*—the psychological culmination of the second phase of the monomyth—drew the narrative back into the orbit of *2001: A Space Odyssey* and the mythic transformations that Kubrick and Clarke had crafted.

In fact, as Kubrick was struggling to solidify *A.I.*'s third act, Clarke returned to take a brief stab at his own version of the story in 1992. Unfortunately, Kubrick was not enchanted by Clarke's direction and soon moved on to another collaborator. In 1994, novelist Sara Maitland was brought in to refine the treatment that Watson had developed a few years earlier. Watson had already established the structural framework of the final scenes, set two thousand years later, following the extinction of humanity and a global ice age. Maitland was tasked with revising this sequence, in which advanced robots called SuperMechas now populate the Earth and discover David buried deep within the ice. He is a miracle to them—a link back to their long-deceased creators.

Working from the third and final phase of the monomyth, these concluding scenes embody the *Return* stage for David's character. Plumbing the depths of his memories, the SuperMechas re-create the Swintons' home for David, and then more miraculously, eventually bring back Monica as well; although it remains unclear whether she or the home exist in any tangible form or are simply virtual projections fabricated by the SuperMechas from David's memory files. The distinction is, to some degree, irrelevant given that biological materiality bears little significance to these artificial lifeforms. Regardless, the film concludes with a particularly ironic twist—instead of David becoming real in order to achieve the love of his mother, his mother is made artificial in order to be loved by David.

When crafting a story about artificial intelligence for Stanley Kubrick, it was easy for Watson and Maitland to draw connections back to *2001*, but at times Kubrick struggled to express the essential differences between the projects. Most significantly, *2001* was focused outwardly on grand concepts of cosmic immortality, while *A.I.* looked inward at a single character caught in a domestic struggle for love. This shift in focus was part of why Kubrick felt so committed to the fairy tale structure, following Campbell's distinction:

> Typically, the hero of the fairy tale achieves a domestic, microcosmic triumph, and the hero of myth a world-historical macrocosmic triumph. Whereas the former—the youngest or despised child who becomes the master of extraordinary powers—prevails over his personal oppressors, the latter brings back from his adventure the means for the regeneration of his society as a whole.[34]

Embedded within this fundamental difference, Kubrick saw it necessary to reframe how *A.I.* would answer the imminent threat of technology. Struthers explains, "It is no longer an extraterrestrial intelligence that will help mankind to transcend to the next stage in its evolution but, instead, man himself will create it."[35] This was a striking shift from *2001*, whereas before it had been a cosmic force that empowered humanity to survive extinction and overcome its machine creations, now Kubrick was suggesting that the next stage of "humanity" would simply *be* those machine creations. In her collaboration on the later drafts of the story, Maitland recalls Kubrick referring to the robots as his "grandchildren"[36]—that is, instead of humanity defeating HAL and transforming into the Star Child, this new story prophesied humanity's extinction, leaving HAL as its only surviving legacy.

This rather pessimistic reading of the conclusion aligns with many of Kubrick's statements about the threat of technology and it certainly would not be uncharacteristic for his films to end bleakly. Campbell even describes this kind of story, explaining, "Modern literature is devoted, in great measure, to a courageous, open-eyed observation of the sickeningly broken figurations that abound before us, around us, and within.... And there is no make-believe about heaven, future bliss, and compensation, to alleviate the bitter majesty, but only utter darkness, the void of unfulfillment."[37] It is an apt description of other Kubrick stories, from *Paths of Glory* (1957) to *Full Metal Jacket* (1987). However, in this context it also ignores his steadfast commitment to structuring *A.I.* as a fairy tale.

From the quaint use of devices like narration to the deeper motifs of rebirth, transcendence, and immortality, the overall thrust of *A.I.* is the optimistic arc of fantasy. That it ends somberly, should not be confused with it ending tragically. Bettelheim explains that, "the fairy story is optimistic, no matter how terrifyingly serious some features of the story may be."[38] It is no surprise that many viewers have been left confused by *A.I.*'s ending, given the nature of the genre; "The answers given by myths are definite, while the fairy tale is suggestive," Bettelheim argues. "The fairy tale never confronts us so directly, or tells us outright how we must choose."[39] In fact, the way many critics and viewers respond to *A.I.*'s ending would not surprise Bettelheim: "From an adult point of view and in terms of modern science, the answers which fairy stories offer are fantastic rather than true."[40] But it is through the fantastic that the fairy tale speaks in a childlike language. The fairy tale is reductive, simplifying the nature of the world so that it can be comprehended by a child. Adults tend to see this as a falsification, but it is instead, Bettelheim suggests, an abstraction or a projection. Campbell describes it as an essential shift in perspective: "The happy ending of the fairy tale . . . is to be read, not as a contradiction, but as a transcendence of the universal tragedy of man. The objective world remains what it was, but, because of a shift in emphasis within the subject, is beheld as though transformed."[41]

In this light, the final sequence in David's re-created home can be perceived not as artificial or hollow, but rather as a necessary progression further upward and further inward. Struthers reminds us that, "Kubrick had always seen film as the perfect medium in which to explore the subconscious, and several of his seminal films merge the 'real' with the 'imaginary.'"[42] In working with Maitland, his final collaborator on the film, Kubrick pushed her to craft a more "ethereal, magical, dream-like ending."[43] The language of dreams mirrors the inward focus of the fairy tale, as Campbell explains: "Dream is the personalized myth, myth the depersonalized dream; both myth and dream are symbolic in the same general way of the dynamics of the psyche. But in the dream the forms are quirked by the peculiar troubles of the dreamer, whereas in myth the problems and solutions shown are directly valid for all mankind."[44]

Viewers have often approached the ending of *A.I.* from this mythic perspective, seeking an answer that is definitive and universal. But the fairy tale asks us to submerge ourselves into the dream, accepting the abstractions and projections with the faith of a child. The adult viewer asks if Monica is really resurrected from her DNA, or whether she can really only be brought back to life for a single day, or whether the love expressed in the final moments of the film is genuine. But the film shows no such preoccupations, for these are not the kind of questions that David, the dreamer, would ever think to ask. Bettelheim calls it animistic thinking, in which "there is no clear line separating objects from living things; and whatever has life has life very much like our own."[45]

When David encounters the revivified Monica, he does not trouble himself with the "how," but rather accepts what he sees, hears, and touches. This is where Kubrick and Spielberg capitalize on the power of cinema to draw us into the dream, for to the viewer Monica is very much alive, just as she had been two thousand years prior (or was it just an hour ago since we last saw her?—time is hazy in cinema, as in a dream). David says optimistically of her temporary resuscitation, "Maybe the one day will be like the one day in the amphibicopter. Maybe it will last forever." And he is right, for what meaning does time have in this strange apparition? It is in these final moments that David embraces paradox, the mythical stage that Campbell calls the *Master of Two Worlds*, in which the hero "no longer resists the self-annihilation that is prerequisite to rebirth."[46] That is, in order to become truly alive, David must accept the curse of life: *human mortality*. In his story notes, Ian Watson wrote:

> Robots were the lost species. Robots were the cursed race, doomed to live forever yet to leave no enduring memory of themselves as a Shakespeare had done, or a Michelangelo, or an Einstein. What was their immortality worth, when the spark, the genius was absent? That spark existed in human beings because human beings were mortal. . . . Human beings also spoke of another world, a world of spirit and dream—source of all inspiration—which men and women entered into when they died. That other world was barred to robots. Robots could not enter it, for they were not mortal.[47]

And yet, David, in his unwavering dedication—one might even call it love—toward Monica, finds a way to reconcile these two opposing realities: his immortal artificiality and her mortal human spirit. Campbell draws examples from many myths, such as the *Bhagavad-Gita*, in which Krishna says "By devotion alone can I, as I really am, be known and seen and entered into,"[48] or Jesus, who promises, "whosoever will lose his life for my sake shall find it."[49]

David sacrifices everything to be reunited with his mother—to restore that which was separated at the start of the story. In this selfless perseverance, he accomplishes the impossible, finding his way through trials and initiations to a time and a place in which she could finally be returned to him. When, with her final breath, she at last tells him that she loves him, David's quest is completed. He has accomplished that for which he was created. As the narrator says, "That was the everlasting moment he had been waiting for. And the moment had passed, for Monica was sound asleep. More than merely asleep. Should he shake her she would never rouse." And yet, David lies down beside her, closing his eyes to join his mother in an endless rest, "And for the first time in his life, he went to that place where dreams are born."[50]

David's re-created home, the perfect day with Monica, and his everlasting moment are all observed by the SuperMechas, watching through a portal, just as we—the film's viewers—watch through the window of the cinema screen. More importantly, the whole story is told by the future robots, the lead mecha (voiced by Ben Kingsley) serving as the film's narrator. Just as Kubrick intended, the film is a futuristic fairy tale—that is, a fairy tale from the future; from a time when humanity has died. And yet through David's memories, humanity lives on, imparting its gift—in Watson's words, "spirit and dream"—to a new generation in need of that divine elixir. It is perhaps fitting then, that *A.I. Artificial Intelligence* is the one Kubrick film brought to life after he passed away. It is a story he loved dearly and labored over tirelessly, but in his mortality, was unable to see it realized. And yet out of devotion to his friend and selfless dedication to Kubrick's memory, Steven Spielberg resurrected this haunting fairy tale, and with the embalming power of cinema, has preserved it for the ages.

At one time, when Kubrick was pondering humanity's extinction, he wondered if this story might prove more relevant to our technological progeny—a fairy tale for robots. Musing about the end of our species, he was often prompted to consider what things of worth humanity had to offer the sentient life that followed us. In contemplating the external—that is, the mythic end of humankind, he found himself turned inward, focused on the personal, the intimate, the ordinary. When faced with the inevitability of death, Stanley Kubrick offered a fairy tale—a dream about sacrifice, love, and transformation. A story, he thought, that might save humanity, if only we believed it.

NOTES

1. Alexander Walker, Sybil Taylor, and Ulrich Ruchti, *Stanley Kubrick, Director* (New York: Norton, 2000), 13.
2. Ibid., 13.
3. Ibid., 43.
4. Jan Harlan, Jane M. Struthers, and Chris Baker, *A.I. Artificial Intelligence from Stanley Kubrick to Steven Spielberg: The Vision behind the Film* (London: Thames & Hudson, 2009), 8.
5. Michael Benson, *Space Odyssey: Stanley Kubrick, Arthur C. Clarke, and the Making of a Masterpiece* (New York: Simon & Schuster Paperbacks, 2019), 5.
6. Ibid., 36–37.
7. Ibid., 4.
8. Neil McAleer, *Arthur C. Clarke: Odyssey of a Visionary* (London: Ashgrove Publishing, 2017), 179.
9. Benson, *Space Odyssey*, 5.
10. Joseph Campbell, *The Hero with a Thousand Faces* (Princeton, NJ: Princeton University Press, 1968), 30.
11. Ibid.
12. Benson, *Space Odyssey*, 3.
13. Campbell, *The Hero with a Thousand Faces*, 87.

14. There is some debate about whether the spacecraft in the final film is a weapons satellite or not. At the script stage, Kubrick intended to include a voiceover establishing that the object in space is an orbiting nuclear weapons platform, which is also referenced in Clarke's novelization; however Kubrick abandoned the voiceover and nothing in the final film explicitly establishes the purpose of the spacecraft, leaving the impact of the cut somewhat open to interpretation—either positively noting the technological progress from primitive bone-tool to futuristic spacecraft, or pessimistically showing that man has simply built more and more complex killing machines.

15. Campbell, *The Hero with a Thousand Faces*, 120.
16. Ibid., 97.
17. Ibid., 109.
18. William Kloman, "In 2001, Will Love Be a Seven-Letter Word?" (*The New York Times*, April 14, 1968), https://nytimes.com/library/film/041468kubrick-2001.html (accessed September 30, 2019).
19. Ibid.
20. Eric Norden, "Playboy Interview: Stanley Kubrick," in *Stanley Kubrick Interviews*, 47–74 (Jackson, MS: University Press of Mississippi, 2013), 49.
21. C. G. Jung, *The Structure and Dynamics of the Psyche*, trans. R. F. C. Hull, 2nd ed. (Princeton, NJ: Princeton University Press, 1969), 55. Jung writes, "Although the God-concept is a spiritual principle *par excellence*, the collective metaphysical need nevertheless insists that it is at the same time a conception of the First Cause, from which proceed all those instinctual forces that are opposed to the spiritual principle. God would thus be not only the essence of spiritual light, appearing as the latest flower on the tree of evolution, not only the spiritual goal of salvation in which all creation culminates, not only the end and aim, but also the darkest, nethermost cause of Nature's blackest deeps."
22. Campbell, *The Hero with a Thousand Faces*, 234.
23. Benson, *Space Odyssey*, 3.
24. Ibid., 12.
25. Brian W. Aldiss, *Supertoys Last All Summer Long: and Other Stories of Future Time* (London: Orbit, 2001), xvi.
26. Harlan, *A.I. Artificial Intelligence from Stanley Kubrick to Steven Spielberg*, 13.
27. Ibid., 14.
28. Bruno Bettelheim, *The Uses of Enchantment: the Meaning and Importance of Fairy Tales* (New York: Vintage Books, 2010), 145.
29. When Martin is cured, it is a fairy tale-esque resurrection from his frozen coffin. This sequence is mirrored in the film's final act, when David finds himself frozen underwater in the amphibicopter, his own glass tomb. Like Martin, he is miraculously reawakened to a new world and then returned to a familiar home.
30. Harlan, *A.I. Artificial Intelligence from Stanley Kubrick to Steven Spielberg*, 64.
31. Campbell, *The Hero with a Thousand Faces*, 109.
32. Ibid., 136.
33. *A.I. Artificial Intelligence* (Directed by Steven Spielberg. USA: Amblin Entertainment Stanley Kubrick Productions, 2001).
34. Campbell, *The Hero with a Thousand Faces*, 37–38.
35. Harlan, *A.I. Artificial Intelligence from Stanley Kubrick to Steven Spielberg*, 17.
36. Ibid., 19.
37. Campbell, *The Hero with a Thousand Faces*, 27.
38. Bettelheim, *The Uses of Enchantment*, 37.
39. Ibid., 34, 45.
40. Ibid., 47.
41. Campbell, *The Hero with a Thousand Faces*, 28.
42. Harlan, *A.I. Artificial Intelligence from Stanley Kubrick to Steven Spielberg*, 22.
43. Ibid., 22.
44. Campbell, *The Hero with a Thousand Faces*, 19.
45. Bettelheim, *The Uses of Enchantment*, 46.
46. Campbell, *The Hero with a Thousand Faces*, 236–37.

47. Harlan, *A.I. Artificial Intelligence from Stanley Kubrick to Steven Spielberg*, 21.
48. Barbara Stoler Miller, tran., *The Bhagavad-Gita: Krishna's Counsel in Time of War* (New York: Bantam Dell, 1986), 11:54.
49. Matthew 16:25 (King James Version).
50. *A.I. Artificial Intelligence*.

REFERENCES

A.I. Artificial Intelligence. Directed by Steven Spielberg. USA: Amblin Entertainment, Stanley Kubrick Productions, 2001.

Aldiss, Brian W. *Supertoys Last All Summer Long: and Other Stories of Future Time*. London: Orbit, 2001.

Benson, Michael. *Space Odyssey: Stanley Kubrick, Arthur C. Clarke, and the Making of a Masterpiece*. New York: Simon & Schuster Paperbacks, 2019.

Bettelheim, Bruno. *The Uses of Enchantment: the Meaning and Importance of Fairy Tales*. New York: Vintage Books, 2010.

Campbell, Joseph. *The Hero with a Thousand Faces*. Princeton, NJ: Princeton University Press, 1968.

Harlan, Jan, Jane M. Struthers, and Chris Baker. *A.I. Artificial Intelligence from Stanley Kubrick to Steven Spielberg: The Vision behind the Film*. London: Thames & Hudson, 2009.

Jung, C. G. *The Structure and Dynamics of the Psyche*. Translated by R. F. C. Hull. 2nd ed. Princeton, NJ: Princeton University Press, 1969.

Kloman, William. "In 2001, Will Love Be a Seven-Letter Word?" *The New York Times*, April 14, 1968.

McAleer, Neil. *Arthur C. Clarke: Odyssey of a Visionary*. London: Ashgrove Publishing, 2017.

Miller, Barbara Stoler, trans. *The Bhagavad-Gita: Krishna's Counsel in Time of War*. New York: Bantam Dell, 1986.

Norden, Eric. "Playboy Interview: Stanley Kubrick." In *Stanley Kubrick Interviews*, 47–74. Jackson, MS: University Press of Mississippi, 2013.

2001: A Space Odyssey. Directed by Stanley Kubrick. USA: Metro-Goldwyn-Mayer, 1968.

Walker, Alexander, Sybil Taylor, and Ulrich Ruchti. *Stanley Kubrick, Director*. New York: Norton, 2000.

Index

adaptation, 2, 3, 5–6, 12, 16n10, 43, 46, 86, 98, 161, 197, 200–201, 202, 204, 208, 209–211, 214–217, 217n7, 217n33, 218n56, 268
A.I. Artificial Intelligence, 12–13, 62n12, 263–274
Alcott, John, 42, 44, 86
Aldiss, Brian, 12, 62n12, 268, 269
alienation, 48, 151–161
allegory, 84, 249–258
Ant Hill, 123, 125–127, 133, 199
Arbus, Diane, 38, 39
Aryan Papers, 13
auteur, 81, 207–217, 238

Bakhtin, Mikhail, 31, 139, 140–141, 145, 146, 148
Ballard, Lucien, 6, 53–54
Barry Lyndon, 10–11, 80–81, 84–88, 90n35, 179–181, 183–185, 186, 190, 215, 242, 244
Bazin, André, 47–48, 57–58, 242
Beethoven, Ludwig van, 158, 159, 168
Benjamin, Walter, 102, 245–246, 258
Bettelheim, Bruno, 17n41, 268–269, 272–273
Brecht, Bertolt, 151–156, 158, 160, 161
Brown, Garrett, 11, 45, 239
Bryna Productions, 6, 81, 195–198, 199–203, 204

Burgess, Anthony, 10, 159, 161, 162n31, 168, 173, 215, 218n44
burlesque, 66–69, 73, 74, 77

Campbell, Joseph, 265–273
Carlos, Wendy, 37, 156–158, 241
Cartier, Walter, 4, 25
censorship, 6, 8, 67, 77, 102, 165–175, 209, 210; BBFC (British Board of Censors), 10, 170–171, 173; FCB (Australian Film Censorship Board), 167, 173; MPAA (Motion Picture Association of America), 167, 172
Chaplin, Charles, 56, 116–118
chess, 4, 6, 25, 51, 53, 56, 58–59, 61, 62n7, 65, 115, 124–127, 129, 132, 251
Citizen Kane. See Welles, Orson
Clarke, Arthur C., 9, 214–215, 216, 218n44, 257, 265–268, 270, 275n14
classification, 10, 165–168, 170, 172–175, 175n2
A Clockwork Orange, 10, 17n35, 23, 26, 38, 57, 84, 85, 151–161, 165–175, 215, 235–236, 244–245, 264, 266–267
Cold War, 8, 93, 101, 111–112, 113, 115–116, 119, 127, 149n7, 172, 252, 253, 256
controversy, 10, 11, 79, 81, 83, 155, 167, 170, 171, 173, 204, 209, 212
Cruise, Tom, 7, 12–13, 27, 179, 188, 221

Day of the Fight, 5
Deleuze, Gilles, 24, 103, 257
desensitiz(ing), 152, 153, 167, 169, 172, 175
Doctor Sleep, 2, 48–49, 218n56
double, 5, 11, 25, 30, 33, 47, 52, 53, 58, 59, 60, 70, 71
Double Indemnity, 69, 70, 71, 72
Douglas, Kirk, 6, 7, 81–84, 86, 95, 126, 195–205, 217n14, 239
dream, 5, 66, 70, 76, 148, 152, 187, 189, 191n39, 214, 221, 230, 255, 266, 268, 272–273, 274
droogs, 10, 155–158, 160, 168–169, 245
Dr. Strangelove, 8–10, 39, 80, 89n13, 93, 94–97, 99–101, 103, 111–120, 122n32–122n33, 123, 127–129, 130, 132, 133, 138–139, 149n7, 152, 204, 216, 253, 267, 268
Dürer, Albrecht, 250, 252–254, 257, 258
Duvall, Shelley, 11, 179, 184
dystopia, 10, 154, 168, 236, 253, 255

entrapment, 30–33, 41, 59, 183, 189. *See also* prison
epic, 1, 7, 9, 80–81, 82, 84, 200, 202, 208, 235, 264, 265; theater, performance, 151–152, 153, 155–156, 158, 161
erotic, 8, 66, 77, 80, 221; homoerotic, 81, 139, 187
Eyes Wide Shut, 1, 2, 7, 12–13, 23, 24, 27, 38, 162n17, 179–186, 188–190, 221–231

fairy tale, 5, 39, 65, 66, 67, 184–185, 190, 222, 224, 225, 263, 264, 268–269, 271, 272, 274, 275n29
fantasy, 8, 13, 68, 70, 76, 79, 87, 142, 148, 158, 159–160, 180, 182, 184–185, 186, 189, 190, 221, 224, 226, 230, 250, 255–256, 272
fascism, 83, 97, 116, 117, 167, 171, 172, 174, 180
Fear and Desire, 1, 2, 5, 23, 38, 65, 80, 93–99, 103
femme fatale, 29–30, 57, 66, 68, 71, 77
film noir, 5, 29–30, 56–57, 65–73, 77
Foucault, Michel, 221–231, 232n38
fourth wall, breaking the, 27, 151, 154, 240

Freud, Sigmund, 17n41, 35n16, 96, 105n14, 251, 254
Friction of War, 126, 127, 130, 133
Full Metal Jacket, 1–2, 12, 80, 93–104, 105n17, 105n25, 106n31, 120, 123, 129–133, 137–148, 217n33, 271

gothic, 17n41, 66, 67, 70
The Great Dictator. *See* Chaplin, Charles
grotesque, 3, 24, 31, 32–33, 38, 39–40, 59–60, 61, 63n25, 67, 73, 77–78, 157, 159, 185

Harris, James B., 5–8, 16n10, 52–53, 196–201, 203–204, 209
Harris-Kubrick Pictures, 5–6, 7, 53, 62n9, 195–204
Hasford, Gustav, 12, 95, 97, 102, 105n13, 105n25, 131, 217n33
Hayden, Sterling, 6, 51, 53, 94, 237
Heraclitus, 111–120
heroism, 93–95, 98–99, 104n2, 151, 266
Herr, Michael, 12, 131–132, 133
heterotopic space, 221–231
historiophoty, 79–88
horror, 1, 37, 38, 39, 41, 43, 45, 46, 48, 59, 65, 70, 80, 120n2, 152–155, 159, 161, 166, 172, 208
hybridity, 45, 51–61, 65–78, 166, 176n8

insanity, 68, 71, 73, 99, 142, 149n7. *See also* madness
irony, 26, 33, 41, 42, 47, 48, 54, 66, 69, 73–74, 77, 82, 88, 94–95, 102, 103, 117, 127, 137–148, 148n1, 160, 181, 183, 253, 271
I Stole $16,000,000, 201–202

Johnson, Diane, 11, 17n41, 37, 43, 48, 185, 215, 216
Jung, Carl, 144, 256, 267, 275n21

Kael, Pauline, 9, 152–153, 172, 173, 242
Kidman, Nicole, 2, 12–13, 180
The Killers, 67, 69, 70, 72
Killer's Kiss, 5, 7, 23–34, 65, 68, 69, 264
The Killing, 2, 5, 7, 24, 27, 51–61, 65, 69, 123, 152, 196, 204, 212, 213, 236–237, 244

Index

King, Stephen, 2, 11, 37–38, 39, 43–44, 46, 184, 215, 216

labyrinth, 11, 42, 43, 46, 71, 249. *See also* maze
Lolita, 7–8, 31, 65–78, 179, 197, 200, 202–205, 209–214, 216, 264
Look magazine, 4, 24–25, 198, 245
Ludovico treatment, 156–157, 158, 160, 162n18, 169, 172

machine, 24, 99, 118, 129, 196, 250–251, 257, 263, 265, 269, 270, 271; Doomsday Machine, 112–113, 119, 122n33, 127, 129; killing machines, 139, 140, 143, 145, 147–148, 275n14
madness, 13, 41, 44, 73, 94–95, 103, 115, 180, 253, 256
male gaze, 72, 180, 189, 190, 241
Mann, Anthony, 7, 81, 202
marriage, 13, 179, 183–184, 186, 188, 189
masculinity, 10, 12, 97, 137–148, 148n2, 149n5, 169, 188, 221, 226, 230
maze, 38, 41–46, 48, 76, 239
melodrama, 56, 65–66, 69, 73–75, 77
metalepsis, 165–175
Metty, Russell, 7, 82
MGM (Metro-Goldwyn-Mayer), 6, 9–10, 16n10, 78n6, 197, 204
Mildred Pierce, 67, 70, 73
mirror, 5, 24, 30, 32–33, 42, 45, 67, 71, 72, 182, 185, 188, 210, 223, 228, 251, 266, 272, 275n29
myth, 39, 42, 61, 62n14, 76, 105n15, 106n31, 138, 149n5, 190, 195, 203, 252, 253, 254, 256, 259n9, 263–274

Nabokov, Vladimir, 7, 65–66, 69, 70, 71, 73–76, 78, 197, 209–216
naked, 77, 159, 181–182, 184–186, 189, 191n39, 241, 246
Napoleon, 10, 11, 16n10, 84
narrator, 5, 10, 23, 25–30, 32, 33, 34, 55, 69, 78, 87, 154, 159, 167, 168, 169, 180, 181, 183, 237–238, 273–274
NASA (National Aeronautics and Space Administration), 11, 86, 116, 253, 254, 256–257

Nazi, 8–9, 94, 97, 101, 103, 112, 113, 116–119, 200
Nicholson, Jack, 11, 37, 39, 40, 44, 240
nightmare, 25, 142–143, 154, 182, 187, 189, 210, 240
nuclear, 8–9, 103, 111–112, 113, 115, 117, 118–119, 121n24, 122n33, 123, 127, 129, 139, 179, 256, 257, 266, 267, 275n14

Overlook Hotel, 2, 11, 37, 39–45, 49, 182–183, 184, 187–188, 190, 239

painting, 11, 47, 67–68, 82, 86, 87, 88, 125, 181, 185, 242, 244, 253
parody, 66, 73, 77, 143
Parris Island, 12, 97, 131, 137–138, 141, 142–143, 147, 148
Paths of Glory, 1–2, 6–7, 8, 53, 65, 80, 82, 93, 94–95, 96, 98, 99–100, 103, 123, 124–127, 130, 132, 133, 152, 195, 196, 198–201, 203–204, 213, 239, 245, 271
patzer, 51, 52, 56, 60, 124–133
photography, 4, 11, 24–25, 29, 31, 38, 39, 46–48, 82, 117, 119, 154, 198, 207, 242, 245
prison, 30, 31–32, 41, 52, 56, 59, 68, 69, 71, 159, 160, 162n36, 169, 183

Rambo, 129–130
rape. *See* Sex/ual/ity, abuse, assault, violence
realism, 10, 24–25, 27, 34, 40, 43, 45–46, 56–58, 60, 71, 87, 100, 152, 160, 172, 175, 230, 249, 251; neoralism, 25, 26, 27, 56
room 237, 42, 45–46, 185–186, 187, 240–241

satire, 8, 10, 66, 74–78, 111, 116, 138, 149n6–149n7, 167, 177n49, 178, 179
Schnitzler, Arthur, 13, 221, 224
science fiction, 1, 2, 9, 62n12, 65, 208, 244, 249–250, 252–256, 258, 259n10, 259n14, 263, 265, 268
score, 12, 60, 66, 69, 89n10, 89n13, 156, 157–158, 162n26, 241, 250, 252
Sellers, Peter, 8, 67, 96, 112, 113, 116, 117, 122n32, 127, 216

Seven Arts, 7–8, 200
sex/ual/ity, 8, 10, 13, 55, 65, 76, 77, 96, 105n14, 140, 154, 157, 166, 173, 174, 186, 187–188, 221, 222, 226, 227, 228, 231, 241, 254, 265; abuse, assault, violence, 28, 75, 95–96, 155, 157, 159–160, 165, 168, 169, 171, 180; and death, 33, 35n18, 185; emancipation, freedom, 180, 189; female, 29, 143, 179, 182, 184–185, 188; male, 5, 30, 31, 32, 95, 96, 139, 146, 179–180, 182, 188, 202, 221, 225, 227
The Shining, 1–2, 4, 11–12, 13, 23, 37–49, 57, 85, 179–180, 182–190, 215, 216, 235, 236, 239–241, 245
Singin' in the Rain, 155, 159, 168
Somerton House, 185, 186, 188, 189, 223, 224, 228–230, 231
Southern, Terry, 8, 170
Spartacus, 1, 3, 7–8, 24, 65, 68, 80–86, 89n10, 89n18, 89n22, 151, 195, 202–204, 205, 207, 235, 238
spectacle, 9, 60, 61, 72, 87, 153, 173, 204, 235–246
Spielberg, Steven, 2, 12–13, 62n12, 264, 268, 270, 273, 274
Star Child, 9, 250, 251, 253, 254, 255, 257, 260n26, 267, 271
Star Gate, 9, 242, 244, 245, 251, 252, 255, 256
Steadicam, 11, 42–43, 47, 239–240, 241, 245
stillness, 181, 189, 239
Strauss, Johann, 9–10, 243
Strauss, Richard, 9
subjective, 23–34, 46, 52, 54, 56, 58, 60, 65, 70, 72, 73, 159, 244
sublime, 17n41, 236, 244

tableaux. *See* painting
technology, 12, 79, 94, 139, 169, 236, 243, 250, 251, 256, 263, 264, 266–267, 268, 271, 274
Thackeray, William Makepeace, 10, 84, 87, 88, 215
Thompson, Jim, 6, 53, 54, 212, 213, 214

tracking shot, 6, 43, 58, 63n23, 67, 69, 75–76, 82, 126, 236, 239, 240–244
transhumanism, 250, 255, 256, 257, 258n4
Trumbo, Dalton, 7, 81–84
2001: A Space Odyssey, 1, 2, 9–10, 27, 57, 80–81, 85, 86, 89n13, 90n35, 94, 105n18, 123, 152, 169, 204, 214, 218n52, 235–236, 242–244, 245, 249–258, 263–274

uncanny, 31, 33, 35n16, 38–39, 47, 66–67, 78, 224, 251, 253, 255, 257, 258, 269
United Artists (UA), 5–6, 53, 196, 197, 199, 204
Universal, 81, 89n16, 177n49, 202

Vietnam War, 12, 93, 95, 97, 101, 105n7, 105n17, 120, 129–133, 137–138, 142–148, 149n5
violence, 1, 10, 28, 37, 67–68, 97, 100, 113, 117, 139, 142, 144, 146, 151–161, 165–175, 177n49, 180, 184, 187–188, 190, 258
voiceover, 10, 25–27, 29, 30, 32, 54, 55, 56, 58, 60, 68, 69, 74, 106n26, 147, 148, 182, 275n14
voyeur, 5, 29, 40, 78, 90n35, 154, 160, 188

Warner Bros., 10, 11, 13, 85, 166, 177n49
Wayne, John, 97, 102, 138, 140, 149n5
Weegee, 4, 24, 39
Welles, Orson, 53, 57, 67
Western (films), 28, 34n13, 66, 68, 204
Willingham, Calder, 6, 213, 214
women/female characters, 26, 31, 66, 67, 70, 71, 73, 75, 96, 97, 113, 143, 147, 154, 157, 159, 168, 179–190, 221, 226, 227, 228, 232n45, 241, 253–254, 255, 259n10
World War I, 6, 82, 93, 124, 127
World War II, 93–104, 112, 115–118, 121n24, 200
Wunderkammern, 250–251, 253, 255, 258

zoom, 10, 41, 47, 48, 69, 129, 181, 242

About the Contributors

Jerold J. Abrams (PhD) is an associate professor of philosophy at Creighton University in Omaha, Nebraska. He teaches and writes in aesthetics, American philosophy, and philosophy of film. He is the editor of *The Philosophy of Stanley Kubrick* (2007).

James R. Britton (PhD) teaches writing at the University of Miami, where he is assistant director of composition. He has published or presented on topics such as nineteenth-century social reform, Nathaniel Hawthorne, Harriet Beecher Stowe, Edgar Allan Poe, and pedagogy in the writing classroom.

Rachel Cole (PhD) is a research affiliate of the Department of Gender and Cultural Studies at the University of Sydney, where she completed her PhD thesis on a history of media censorship and classification in Australia in 2019.

Elsa Colombani (PhD, University of Paris Nanterre) is an independent scholar. Her thesis focused on the influence of Gothic literature and cinema in Tim Burton's films. A frequent collaborator of the *Critical Companions to Popular Directors* series (Tim Burton, James Cameron, Steven Spielberg), she has recently published a chapter in *Tim Burton, a Cinema of Transformations* (ed. Gilles Menegaldo, 2018), as well as a study of Netflix films in the French periodical *Commentaire* (June 2019).

Carol Donelan (PhD, University of Massachusetts, Amherst) is professor of cinema and media studies at Carleton College. Her research interests include Hollywood film genres and archival research in American film history. Among her publications are essays in *The Routledge Companion to Philoso-*

phy and Film, The Oxford Handbook of Sound and Image in Digital Media, Quarterly Review of Film and Video, Film History: An International Journal, The Moving Image, and *Film Criticism*. She contributed a chapter to a previous volume in the *Critical Companion to Popular Directors* series on James Cameron.

James Fenwick is senior lecturer and course leader in media at Sheffield Hallam University. He has published widely on the life and work of Stanley Kubrick and Kirk Douglas. He is the author of *Stanley Kubrick Produces* (2020), editor of *Understanding Kubrick's 2001: A Space Odyssey: Representation and Interpretation* (2018), and coeditor of special issues of the *Historical Journal of Film, Radio and Television* and *Cinergie*. He is also researching the concept of "shadow cinema"—unmade or unreleased films from across the history of the American film industry—and is coediting a volume on the subject, *Shadow Cinema: Historical and Production Contexts* (2020).

William Gombash is a professor of communications at Valencia College, where he teaches courses in film and mass media studies. His most recent publications include "The Education of a Tenderfoot: Three Films Starring Jeff Bridges" in *Magazine Americana* (February 2019 online journal); and "Robert Altman, the Blackguard of American Elections" in *PopMatters* (December 6, 2016 online journal). His chapter "Death Wish: A Vigilante's Journey, an Urban Tragedy" in *Shockers!: The '70s Cinema of Trash, Terror, and Sexploitation*, edited by Xavier Mendik and Julian Petley will be published in 2021.

Vincent Jaunas recently defended his PhD at Bordeaux Montaigne University, with a doctoral dissertation entitled "Subjectivity through the Prism of Reflexivity in the Work of Stanley Kubrick, from *2001: A Space Odyssey* to *Eyes Wide Shut*." Jaunas has published various articles on the films of Stanley Kubrick. He also co-organized the international conference "Stanley Kubrick: Nouveaux Horizons" at Bordeaux-Montaigne University. He then coedited a special issue of the journal *Essais* also entitled *Stanley Kubrick: Nouveaux Horizons*, published in 2018.

Paul Johnson is an independent researcher engaging in the investigation of film, television, and media forms, with particular emphasis on modern cinema and the position of digital technology therein, most especially the use of digital visual effects. He also continues to explore the wider position of cinema in cultural history, examining Hollywood and other cinematic production bases from early cinema to the present.

About the Contributors   283

Gilles Menegaldo is an emeritus professor of film studies at the University of Poitiers. He has published many articles on filmic adaptation and film genre and has (co)edited thirty collections of essays among which are *Le western et les mythes de l'ouest* (with L. Guillaud, 2015); *Sherlock Holmes, un limier pour le XXIème siècle* (with H. Machinal and J-P Naugrette, 2016); *Lovecraft au prisme de l'image* (with C. Gelly, 2017); *Tim Burton, a Cinema of Transformations* (2018). Forthcoming: *Spectres of Poe* (with Jocelyn Dupont).

Guillaume Mouleux has a PhD in language and cultures of the Anglophone world from Université Sorbonne-Paris-Cité. A specialist of image in the society, history, and arts of the United States, his past contributions include a chapter in *L'Amérique des images, histoire et culture visuelles des États-Unis* edited by François Brunet (2013). Currently a freelance translator and part-time substitute teacher at university, his teaching experience at university includes Paris-Diderot, Paris X-Nanterre, and currently Paris-Est Marne-la-Vallée and Cergy-Pontoise.

Maurizia Natali (PhD) studied film history in Florence, Italy, and in Paris/Sorbonne Nouvelle (PhD in film aesthetics). Now an independent scholar, she has taught film at RISD, given courses at RI College and Brown University, and lectured at New York University, University of Montreal, Cerisy La Salle, London University, University of Rome III, and Lisbon University. Her interests concern science fiction cinema and the anthopocene, iconology, feminist aesthetics, and the environmental reinterpretations of science fiction and Italian cinema. She has published on landscape in American cinema, science fiction, and women in Italian films.

Annie Nissen (PhD) is a research associate and an associate lecturer in film studies at Lancaster University. She completed her doctorate at Lancaster University, where she also gained a BA (Hons) in film studies and literature and an MA in literary and cultural studies. Her main area of interest lies in adaptation studies with a focus on the role of writers and writing within adaptation practices and in particular early film history.

Sean O'Reilly is a graduate of Harvard University's history and East Asian languages doctoral program with a secondary field in film and visual studies. His research, which began with a Fulbright Scholarship to Japan in 2012, concerns the ways Japanese history is reinvented in film and popular culture. Publications include *Re-viewing the Past: The Uses of History in the Cinema of Imperial Japan* (2018). As associate professor of Japan studies at Akita International University, he teaches courses on the history, popular culture, and cinema of Japan.

Anne-Marie Paquet-Deyris is professor of film and TV series studies and (African) American literature at University Paris Nanterre. She published *Combining Aesthetic and Psychological Approaches to TV Series Addiction* with N. Camart, S. Lefait and L. Romo in 2018. One of her most recent volumes tackles the history of the American West in the Western film genre, *Histoire, légende, imaginaire: Nouvelles études sur le Western*, coedited with J.-L. Bourget and F. Zamour in 2018. In 2019, she participated in the special issue of *Post Script* "Islands and Film" edited by Ian Conrich (et alii) and contributed to the special issue of *Black Camera, The Birth of a Nation: The Cinematic Past in the Present* (Michael T. Martin, ed.).

Joshua Sikora (MFA) is the founder and director of the Cinema and New Media Arts program at Houston Baptist University, where he teaches cinematic theory, multimedia production, and developing technologies. An award-winning filmmaker and new media entrepreneur, Sikora is also the founder of New Renaissance Pictures, an independent production company through which he has produced a variety of feature films, TV series, and documentaries.

Carl Sweeney is a PhD candidate at the University of Wolverhampton, researching television stardom. His other research interests include star images in film and Foucauldian spatialities in narrative cinema. He completed an MA in Film Studies at Wolverhampton in 2018, with his final thesis representing a reevaluation of Robert De Niro's star persona. His publications include a chapter in *A Critical Companion to Steven Spielberg* (Lexington Books, 2019), focusing on heterotopic spaces in *Jurassic Park, The Terminal*, and *Ready Player One*.

Madison Mae Williams is a director, multidisciplinary artist, and scholar based in San Diego. She received a BA concentrating in musical theater, poetry, and Africana studies from Hampshire College. Her research areas include musical theater, sound studies, horror and the uncanny, counterculture studies, and use of the Brechtian alienation effect in media and performance. Madison is currently a PhD student in theater and dance at UC San Diego.

www.ingramcontent.com/pod-product-compliance
Lightning Source LLC
Chambersburg PA
CBHW050859300426
44111CB00010B/1303